BIG IDEAS MATH®
Modeling Real Life

Grade 7
Common Core Edition

Ron Larson
Laurie Boswell

Big Ideas Learning™

Erie, Pennsylvania
BigIdeasLearning.com

Big Ideas Learning, LLC
1762 Norcross Road
Erie, PA 16510-3838
USA

For product information and customer support, contact Big Ideas Learning
at **1-877-552-7766** or visit us at ***BigIdeasLearning.com***.

One Voice from Kindergarten Through Algebra 2

Written by renowned authors, Dr. Ron Larson and Dr. Laurie Boswell, *Big Ideas Math* offers a seamless math pedagogy from elementary through high school. Together, Ron and Laurie provide a consistent voice that encourages students to make connections through cohesive progressions and clear instruction. Since 1992, Ron and Laurie have authored over 50 mathematics programs.

Each time Laurie and I start working on a new program, we spend time putting ourselves in the position of the reader. How old is the reader? What is the reader's experience with mathematics? The answers to these questions become our writing guides. Our goal is to make the learning targets understandable and to develop these targets in a clear path that leads to student success.

Ron Larson

Ron Larson, Ph.D., is well known as lead author of a comprehensive and widely used mathematics program that ranges from elementary school through college. He holds the distinction of Professor Emeritus from Penn State Erie, The Behrend College, where he taught for nearly 40 years. He received his Ph.D. in mathematics from the University of Colorado. Dr. Larson engages in the latest research and advancements in mathematics education and consistently incorporates key pedagogical elements to ensure focus, coherence, rigor, and student self-reflection.

My passion and goal in writing is to provide an essential resource for exploring and making sense of mathematics. Our program is guided by research around the learning and teaching of mathematics in the hopes of improving the achievement of all students. May this be a successful year for you!

Laurie Boswell

Laurie Boswell, Ed.D., is the former Head of School at Riverside School in Lyndonville, Vermont. In addition to authoring textbooks, she provides mathematics consulting and embedded coaching sessions. Dr. Boswell received her Ed.D. from the University of Vermont in 2010. She is a recipient of the Presidential Award for Excellence in Mathematics Teaching and later served as president of CPAM. Laurie has taught math to students at all levels, elementary through college. In addition, Laurie has served on the NCTM Board of Directors and as a Regional Director for NCSM. Along with Ron, Laurie has co-authored numerous math programs and has become a popular national speaker.

Big Ideas Learning would like to express our gratitude to the mathematics education and instruction experts who served as our advisory panel, contributing specialists, and reviewers during the writing of *Big Ideas Math: Modeling Real Life*. Their input was an invaluable asset during the development of this program.

Contributing Specialists and Reviewers

- **Sophie Murphy**, Ph.D. Candidate, Melbourne School of Education, Melbourne, Australia
  Learning Targets and Success Criteria Specialist and Visible Learning Reviewer

- **Linda Hall**, Mathematics Educational Consultant, Edmond, OK
  Advisory Panel and Teaching Edition Contributor

- **Michael McDowell**, Ed.D., Superintendent, Ross, CA
  Project-Based Learning Specialist

- **Kelly Byrne**, Math Supervisor and Coordinator of Data Analysis, Downingtown, PA
  Advisory Panel and Content Reviewer

- **Jean Carwin**, Math Specialist/TOSA, Snohomish, WA
  Advisory Panel and Content Reviewer

- **Nancy Siddens**, Independent Language Teaching Consultant, Las Cruces, NM
  English Language Learner Specialist

- **Nancy Thiele**, Mathematics Consultant, Mesa, AZ
  Teaching Edition Contributor

- **Kristen Karbon**, Curriculum and Assessment Coordinator, Troy, MI
  Advisory Panel and Content Reviewer

- **Kery Obradovich**, K–8 Math/Science Coordinator, Northbrook, IL
  Advisory Panel and Content Reviewer

- **Jennifer Rollins**, Math Curriculum Content Specialist, Golden, CO
  Advisory Panel

- **Becky Walker**, Ph.D., School Improvement Services Director, Green Bay, WI
  Advisory Panel

- **Anthony Smith**, Ph.D., Associate Professor, Associate Dean, University of Washington Bothell, Seattle, WA
  Reading/Writing Reviewer

- **Nicole Dimich Vagle**, Educator, Author, and Consultant, Hopkins, MN
  Assessment Reviewer

- **Jill Kalb**, Secondary Math Content Specialist, Arvada, CO
  Content Reviewer

- **Janet Graham**, District Math Specialist, Manassas, VA
  Response to Intervention and Differentiated Instruction Reviewer

- **Sharon Huber**, Director of Elementary Mathematics, Chesapeake, VA
  Universal Design for Learning Reviewer

Student Reviewers

- Jackson Currier
- Mason Currier
- Taylor DeLuca
- Ajalae Evans
- Malik Goodwine
- Majesty Hamilton
- Reilly Koch

- Kyla Kramer
- Matthew Lindemuth
- Greer Lippert
- Zane Lippert
- Jeffrey Lobaugh
- Riley Moran
- Zoe Morin

- Deke Patton
- Brooke Smith
- Dylan Throop
- Jenna Urso
- Madison Whitford
- Jenna Wigham

Research

Ron Larson and Laurie Boswell used the latest in educational research, along with the body of knowledge collected from expert mathematics instructors, to develop the *Modeling Real Life* series. The pedagogical approach used in this program follows the best practices outlined in the most prominent and widely accepted educational research, including:

- *Visible Learning*
  John Hattie © 2009

- *Visible Learning for Teachers*
  John Hattie © 2012

- *Visible Learning for Mathematics*
  John Hattie © 2017

- *Principles to Actions: Ensuring Mathematical Success for All*
  NCTM © 2014

- *Adding It Up: Helping Children Learn Mathematics*
  National Research Council © 2001

- *Mathematical Mindsets: Unleashing Students' Potential through Creative Math, Inspiring Messages and Innovative Teaching*
  Jo Boaler © 2015

- *What Works in Schools: Translating Research into Action*
  Robert Marzano © 2003

- *Classroom Instruction That Works: Research-Based Strategies for Increasing Student Achievement*
  Marzano, Pickering, and Pollock © 2001

- *Principles and Standards for School Mathematics*
  NCTM © 2000

- *Rigorous PBL by Design: Three Shifts for Developing Confident and Competent Learners*
  Michael McDowell © 2017

- Common Core State Standards for Mathematics National Governors Association Center for Best Practices and Council of Chief State School Officers © 2010

- *Universal Design for Learning Guidelines*
  CAST © 2011

- Rigor/Relevance Framework® International Center for Leadership in Education

- *Understanding by Design*
  Grant Wiggins and Jay McTighe © 2005

- Achieve, ACT, and The College Board

- *Elementary and Middle School Mathematics: Teaching Developmentally*
  John A. Van de Walle and Karen S. Karp © 2015

- *Evaluating the Quality of Learning: The SOLO Taxonomy*
  John B. Biggs & Kevin F. Collis © 1982

- *Unlocking Formative Assessment: Practical Strategies for Enhancing Students' Learning in the Primary and Intermediate Classroom*
  Shirley Clarke, Helen Timperley, and John Hattie © 2004

- *Formative Assessment in the Secondary Classroom*
  Shirley Clarke © 2005

- *Improving Student Achievement: A Practical Guide to Assessment for Learning*
  Toni Glasson © 2009

Instructional Design

A single authorship team from Kindergarten through Algebra 2 results in a logical progression of focused topics with meaningful coherence from course to course.

FOCUS

A focused program reflects the balance in grade-level standards while simultaneously supporting and engaging you to develop conceptual understanding of the major work of the grade.

The **Learning Target** and **Success Criteria** for each section focus the learning into manageable chunks, using clear teaching text and Key Ideas.

2.1 Multiplying Integers

Learning Target: Find products of integers.

Success Criteria:
- I can explain the rules for multiplying integers.
- I can find products of integers with the same sign.
- I can find products of integers with different signs.

Key Idea

Ratios

Words A **ratio** is a comparison of two quantities. The **value of the ratio** a to b is the number $\frac{a}{b}$, which describes the multiplicative relationship between the quantities in the ratio.

Examples 2 snails *to* 6 fish

$\frac{1}{2}$ cup of milk *for every* $\frac{1}{4}$ cup of cream

Algebra The ratio of a to b can be written as $a : b$.

Laurie's Notes

Laurie's Notes, located in the Teaching Edition, prepare your teacher for the math concepts in each chapter and section and make connections to the threads of major topics for the course.

Chapter 5 Overview

The study of ratios and proportions in this chapter builds upon and connects to prior work with rates and ratios in the previous course. Students should have an understanding of how ratios are represented and how ratio tables are used to find equivalent ratios. Tape diagrams and double number lines were also used to represent and solve problems involving equivalent ratios.

a Single Authorship Team

COHERENCE

A single authorship team built a coherent program that has intentional progression of content within each grade and between grade levels. You will build new understanding on foundations from prior grades and connect concepts throughout the course.

The authors developed content that progresses from prior chapters and grades to future ones. In addition to charts like this one, Laurie's Notes give your teacher insights about where you have come from and where you are going in your learning progression.

Through the Grades

Grade 7	Grade 8	High School
• Use samples to draw inferences about populations. • Compare two populations from random samples using measures of center and variability. • Approximate the probability of a chance event and predict the approximate relative frequency given the probability.	• Construct and interpret scatter plots. • Find and assess lines of fit for scatter plots. • Use equations of lines to solve problems and interpret the slope and the y-intercept. • Construct and interpret a two-way table summarizing data. Use relative frequencies to describe possible association between the two variables.	• Classify data as quantitative or qualitative, choose and create appropriate data displays, and analyze misleading graphs. • Make and use two-way tables to recognize associations in data by finding marginal, relative, and conditional relative frequencies. • Interpret scatter plots, determine how well lines of fit model data, and distinguish between correlation and causation.

One author team thoughtfully wrote each course, creating a seamless progression of content from Kindergarten to Algebra 2.

Grade 1	Grade 2	Grade 3	Grade 4	Grade 5	Grade 6	Grade 7	Grade 8
			Operations and Algebraic Thinking		**Expressions and Equations**		
oblems involving n and subtraction 0. roperties of ns. ith addition and ion equations. s 1–5, 10, 11	Solve problems involving addition and subtraction within 20. Work with equal groups of objects. *Chapters 1–6, 15*	Solve problems involving multiplication and division within 100. Apply properties of multiplication. Solve problems involving the four operations, and identify and explain patterns in arithmetic. *Chapters 1–5, 8, 9, and 14*	Use the four operations with whole numbers to solve problems. Understand factors and multiples. Generate and analyze patterns. *Chapters 2–6, 12*	Write and interpret numerical expressions. Analyze patterns and relationships. *Chapters 2, 12*	Perform arithmetic with algebraic expressions. *Chapter 5* Solve one-variable equations and inequalities. *Chapters 6, 8* Analyze relationships between dependent and independent variables. *Chapter 6*	Write equivalent expressions. *Chapter 3* Use numerical and algebraic expressions, equations, and inequalities to solve problems. *Chapters 3, 4, 6*	Understand the connections between proportional relationships, lines, and linear equations. *Chapter 4* Solve linear equations and systems of linear equations. *Chapters 1, 5* Work with radicals and integer exponents. *Chapters 8, 9*
						Functions	
							Define, evaluate, and compare functions, and use functions to model relationships between quantities.

You have used number lines to find sums of positive numbers, which involve movement to the right. Now you will find sums with negative numbers, which involve movement to the left.

Throughout each course, lessons build on prior learning as new concepts are introduced. Here you are reminded that you have used number lines with positive numbers.

Using Number Lines to Find Sums

a. Find $4 + (-4)$.

Draw an arrow from 0 to 4 to represent 4. Then draw an arrow 4 units to the left to represent adding -4.

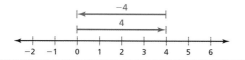

Rigor in Math: A Balanced Approach

Instructional Design

The authors wrote every chapter and every section to give you a meaningful balance of rigorous instruction.

RIGOR

A rigorous program provides a balance of three important building blocks.

- **Conceptual Understanding**
  Discovering why
- **Procedural Fluency**
  Learning how
- **Application**
  Knowing when to apply

Conceptual Understanding

You have the opportunity to develop foundational concepts central to the *Learning Target* in each *Exploration* by experimenting with new concepts, talking with peers, and asking questions.

EXPLORATION 1 **Understanding Quotients Involving N**

Work with a partner.

a. Discuss the relationship between multiplication your partner.

b. **INDUCTIVE REASONING** Complete the table. The for dividing (i) two integers with the same sign an different signs.

Expression	Type of Quotient	Quoti
$-15 \div 3$	Integers	
$12 \div (-6)$		
$10 \div (-2)$		

Conceptual Thinking

Conceptual questions ask you to think deeply.

29. **MP** **NUMBER SENSE** Without solving, determine whether $\dfrac{x}{4} = \dfrac{15}{3}$ and $\dfrac{x}{15} = \dfrac{4}{3}$ have the same solution. Explain your reasoning.

EXAMPLE 1 **Graphing a Linear Equation in Standard Form**

Graph $-2x + 3y = -6$.

Step 1: Write the equation in slope-intercept form.

$$-2x + 3y = -6 \qquad \text{Write the equation.}$$
$$3y = 2x - 6 \qquad \text{Add } 2x \text{ to each side.}$$
$$y = \frac{2}{3}x - 2 \qquad \text{Divide each side by 3.}$$

Step 2: Use the slope and the y-intercept to graph the equation.

$$y = \frac{2}{3}x + (-2)$$

slope y-intercept

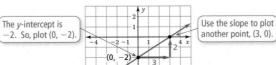

The y-intercept is -2. So, plot $(0, -2)$.

Use the slope to plot another point, $(3, 0)$.

$(0, -2)$

Procedural Fluency

Solidify learning with clear, stepped-out teaching and examples.

Then shift conceptual understanding into procedural fluency with *Try Its*, *Self-Assessments*, *Practice*, and *Review & Refresh*.

STEAM Video: "Trophic Status"

Name_____ Date_____

Chapter 3 — Performance Task

Chlorophyll in Plants

What is needed for photosynthesis? How can you use the amount of chlorophyll in a lake to determine the level of biological productivity?

Photosynthesis is the process by which plants acquire energy from the sun. Sunlight, carbon dioxide, and water are used by a plant to produce glucose and dioxygen.

Before: After:
6 Carbon Dioxide + 6 Water → Glucose + 6 Dioxygen

1. You want to make models of the molecules involved in photosynthesis for a science fair project. The table shows the number of each element used for each molecule. Let x, y, and z represent the costs of a model carbon atom, model hydrogen atom, and

	Number of Atoms		
Molecule	Carbon	Hydrogen	Oxygen
Carbon Dioxide	1	0	2
Water	0	2	1

36. **DIG DEEPER!** The *girth* of a package is the distance around the perimeter of a face that does not include the length as a side. A postal service says that a rectangular package can have a maximum combined length and girth of 108 inches.

   a. Write an inequality that represents the allowable dimensions for the package.

   b. Find three different sets of allowable dimensions that are reasonable for the package. Find the volume of each package.

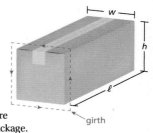

girth

THE PROBLEM-SOLVING PLAN

1. **Understand the Problem**
   Think about what the problem is asking, what information you know, and how you might begin to solve.

2. **Make a Plan**
   Plan your solution pathway before jumping in to solve. Identify any relationships and decide on a problem-solving strategy.

3. **Solve and Check**
   As you solve the problem, be sure to evaluate your progress and check your answers. Throughout the problem-solving process, you must continually ask, "Does this make sense?" and be willing to change course if necessary.

Embedded Mathematical Practices

Encouraging Mathematical Mindsets

Developing proficiency in the **Mathematical Practices** is about becoming a mathematical thinker. Learn to ask why, and to reason and communicate with others as you learn. Use this guide to develop proficiency with the mathematical practices.

1 One way to **Make Sense of Problems and Persevere in Solving Them** is to use the Problem-Solving Plan. Take time to analyze the given information and what the problem is asking to help you plan a solution pathway.

Look for labels such as:
- Explain the Meaning
- Find Entry Points
- Analyze Givens
- Make a Plan
- Interpret a Solution
- Consider Similar Problems
- Consider Simpler Forms
- Check Progress
- Problem Solving

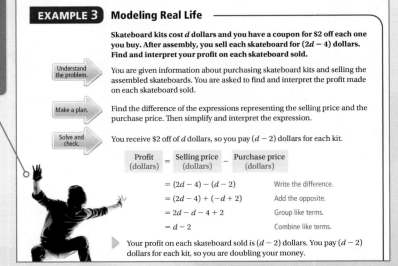

EXAMPLE 3 **Modeling Real Life**

Skateboard kits cost d dollars and you have a coupon for $2 off each one you buy. After assembly, you sell each skateboard for $(2d - 4)$ dollars. Find and interpret your profit on each skateboard sold.

Understand the problem. You are given information about purchasing skateboard kits and selling the assembled skateboards. You are asked to find and interpret the profit made on each skateboard sold.

Make a plan. Find the difference of the expressions representing the selling price and the purchase price. Then simplify and interpret the expression.

Solve and check. You receive $2 off of d dollars, so you pay $(d - 2)$ dollars for each kit.

$$\text{Profit (dollars)} = \text{Selling price (dollars)} - \text{Purchase price (dollars)}$$

$= (2d - 4) - (d - 2)$	Write the difference.
$= (2d - 4) + (-d + 2)$	Add the opposite.
$= 2d - d - 4 + 2$	Group like terms.
$= d - 2$	Combine like terms.

Your profit on each skateboard sold is $(d - 2)$ dollars. You pay $(d - 2)$ dollars for each kit, so you are doubling your money.

2 **Reason Abstractly** when you explore a concrete example and represent it symbolically. Other times, **Reason Quantitatively** when you see relationships in numbers or symbols and draw conclusions about a concrete example.

a. Represent each table in the same coordinate plane. Which graph represents a proportional relationship? How do you know?

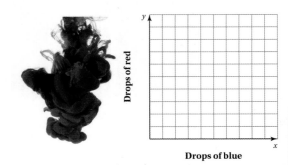

Drops of red

Drops of blue

Look for labels such as:
- Make Sense of Quantities
- Use Equations
- Use Expressions
- Understand Quantities
- Use Operations
- Number Sense
- Reasoning

Math Practice

Reasoning

How is the graph of the proportional relationship different from the other graph?

b. Which property can you use to solve each of the equations modeled by the algebra tiles? Solve each equation and explain your method.

46. ⓂⓅ LOGIC When you multiply or divide each side of an inequality by the same negative number, you must reverse the direction of the inequality symbol. Explain why.

Math Practice

Make Conjectures
Can you use algebra tiles to solve any equation? Explain your reasoning.

3 When you **Construct Viable Arguments and Critique the Reasoning of Others**, you make and justify conclusions and decide whether others' arguments are correct or flawed.

Look for labels such as:
- Use Assumptions
- Use Definitions
- Use Prior Results
- Make Conjectures
- Build Arguments
- Analyze Conjectures
- Use Counterexamples

- Justify Conclusions
- Compare Arguments
- Construct Arguments
- Listen and Ask Questions
- You Be the Teacher
- Logic

36. ⓂⓅ APPLY MATHEMATICS You decide to make and sell bracelets. The cost of your materials is $84.00. You charge $3.50 for each bracelet.

a. Write a function that represents the profit P for selling b bracelets.

b. Which variable is independent? dependent? Explain.

c. You will *break even* when the cost of your materials equals your income. How many bracelets must you sell to break even?

Look for labels such as:
- Apply Mathematics
- Simplify a Solution
- Use a Diagram
- Use a Table
- Use a Graph

- Use a Formula
- Analyze Relationships
- Interpret Results
- Modeling Real Life

4 To **Model with Mathematics**, apply the math you have learned to a real-life problem, and interpret mathematical results in the context of the situation.

BUILDING TO FULL UNDERSTANDING

Throughout each course, you have opportunities to demonstrate specific aspects of the mathematical practices. Labels throughout the book indicate gateways to those aspects. Collectively, these opportunities will lead to a full understanding of each mathematical practice. Developing these mindsets and habits will give meaning to the mathematics you learn.

Embedded Mathematical Practices (continue

5

To **Use Appropriate Tools Strategically**, you need to know what tools are available and think about how each tool might help you solve a mathematical problem. When you choose a tool to use, remember that it may have limitations.

Look for labels such as:
- Choose Tools
- Recognize Usefulness of Tools
- Use Other Resources
- Use Technology to Explore
- Using Tools

d. Enter the function $y = \left(\dfrac{1}{10}\right)^x$ into your graphing calculator. Use the *table* feature to evaluate the function for positive integer values of x until the calculator displays a y-value that is not in standard form. Do the results support your answer in part (c)? Explain.

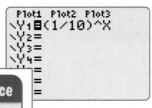 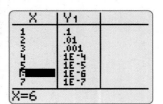

Math Practice

Use Technology to Explore

How can writing $\dfrac{1}{10}$ as a power of 10 help you understand the calculator display?

6

When you **Attend to Precision**, you are developing a habit of being careful in how you talk about concepts, label work, and write answers.

Look for labels such as:
- Communicate Precisely
- Use Clear Definitions
- State the Meaning of Symbols
- Specify Units
- Label Axes
- Calculate Accurately
- Precision

Add $1.459 + 23.7$.

$$\begin{array}{r} 1 \\ 1.459 \\ + \ 23.700 \\ \hline 25.159 \end{array}$$

Insert zeros so that both numbers have the same number of decimal places.

Math Practice

Calculate Accurately

Why is it important to line up the decimal points when adding or subtracting decimals?

49. **MP** **PRECISION** Consider the equation $c = ax - bx$, where a, b, and c are whole numbers. Which of the following result in values of a, b, and c so that the original equation has exactly one solution? Justify your answer.

| $a - b = 1, c = 0$ | $a = b, c \neq 0$ | $a = b, c = 0$ | $a \neq b, c = 0$ |

MP STRUCTURE Tell whether the triangles are similar. Explain.

14.

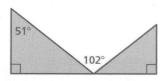

15.

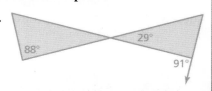

Look For and Make Use of Structure by looking closely to see structure within a mathematical statement, or stepping back for an overview to see how individual parts make one single object.

Find the sum of the areas of the faces.

Surface Area	=	Area of bottom	+	Area of a side	+	Area of a side	+	Area of a side	+	Area of a side	
S	=	49	+	35	+	35	+	35	+	35	= 189

Look for labels such as:
- Look for Structure
- Look for Patterns
- View as Components
- Structure
- Patterns

Math Practice

Look for Patterns
How can you find the surface area of a square pyramid by calculating the area of only two of the faces?

35. **MP REPEATED REASONING** You have been assigned a nine-digit identification number.

   a. Should you use the Fundamental Counting Principle or a tree diagram to find the total number of possible identification numbers? Explain.

   b. How many identification numbers are possible?

When you **Look For and Express Regularity in Repeated Reasoning**, you can notice patterns and make generalizations. Remember to keep in mind the goal of a problem, which will help you evaluate reasonableness of answers along the way.

Look for labels such as:
- Repeat Calculations
- Find General Methods
- Maintain Oversight
- Evaluate Results
- Repeated Reasoning

Visible Learning Through Learning Targets,

Making Learning Visible

Knowing the learning intention of a chapter or section helps you focus on the purpose of an activity, rather than simply completing it in isolation. This program supports visible learning through the consistent use of learning targets and success criteria to ensure positive outcomes for all students.

Every chapter and section shows a **Learning Target** and related **Success Criteria**. These are purposefully integrated into each carefully written lesson.

4.4 Writing and Graphing Inequalities

Learning Target: Write inequalities and represent solutions of inequalities on number lines.

Success Criteria:
- I can write word sentences as inequalities.
- I can determine whether a value is a solution of an inequality.
- I can graph the solutions of inequalities.

Chapter Learning Target:
Understand equations and inequalities.

Chapter Success Criteria:
- ☐ I can identify key words and phrases to write equations and inequalities.
- ☐ I can write word sentences as equations and inequalities.
- ■ I can solve equations and inequalities using properties.
- ■ I can use equations and inequalities to model and solve real-life problems.

The **Chapter Review** reminds you to rate your understanding of the learning targets.

▶ Chapter Self-Assessment

As you complete the exercises, use the scale below to rate your understanding of the success criteria in your journal.

1	**2**	**3**	**4**
I do not understand.	I can do it with help.	I can do it on my own.	I can teach someone else.

6.1 Writing Equations in One Variable (pp. 245–250)

Learning Target: Write equations in one variable and write equations that represent real-life problems.

Write the word sentence as an equation.

1. The product of a number m and 2 is 8.

Review each section with a reminder of that section's learning target.

QUESTIONS FOR LEARNING

As you progress through a section, you should be able to answer the following questions.

- What am I learning?
- Why am I learning this?
- Where am I in my learning?
- How will I know when I have learned it?
- Where am I going next?

Success Criteria, and Self-Assessment

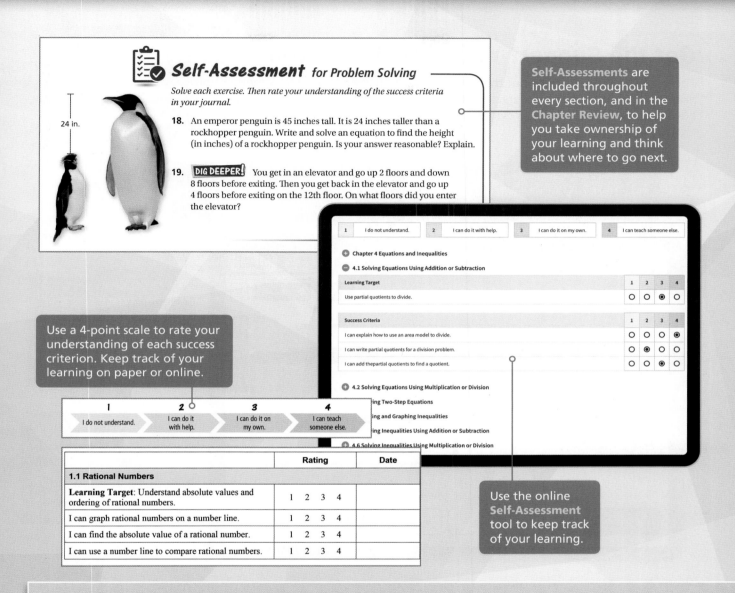

Self-Assessment for Problem Solving

Solve each exercise. Then rate your understanding of the success criteria in your journal.

24 in.

18. An emperor penguin is 45 inches tall. It is 24 inches taller than a rockhopper penguin. Write and solve an equation to find the height (in inches) of a rockhopper penguin. Is your answer reasonable? Explain.

19. **DIG DEEPER!** You get in an elevator and go up 2 floors and down 8 floors before exiting. Then you get back in the elevator and go up 4 floors before exiting on the 12th floor. On what floors did you enter the elevator?

Self-Assessments are included throughout every section, and in the **Chapter Review**, to help you take ownership of your learning and think about where to go next.

| 1 | I do not understand. | 2 | I can do it with help. | 3 | I can do it on my own. | 4 | I can teach someone else. |

Chapter 4 Equations and Inequalities

4.1 Solving Equations Using Addition or Subtraction

Learning Target	1	2	3	4
Use partial quotients to divide.	○	○	◉	○

Success Criteria	1	2	3	4
I can explain how to use an area model to divide.	○	○	○	◉
I can write partial quotients for a division problem.	○	◉	○	○
I can add the partial quotients to find a quotient.	○	○	◉	○

4.2 Solving Equations Using Multiplication or Division

...ing Two-Step Equations

...ing and Graphing Inequalities

...ing Inequalities Using Addition or Subtraction

4.6 Solving Inequalities Using Multiplication or Division

Use a 4-point scale to rate your understanding of each success criterion. Keep track of your learning on paper or online.

1	2	3	4
I do not understand.	I can do it with help.	I can do it on my own.	I can teach someone else.

	Rating	Date
1.1 Rational Numbers		
Learning Target: Understand absolute values and ordering of rational numbers.	1 2 3 4	
I can graph rational numbers on a number line.	1 2 3 4	
I can find the absolute value of a rational number.	1 2 3 4	
I can use a number line to compare rational numbers.	1 2 3 4	

Use the online **Self-Assessment** tool to keep track of your learning.

Ensuring Positive Outcomes

John Hattie's *Visible Learning* research consistently shows that using learning targets and success criteria can result in two years' growth in one year, ensuring positive outcomes for your learning and achievement.

Sophie Murphy, M.Ed., wrote the chapter-level learning targets and success criteria for this program. Sophie is currently completing her Ph.D. at the University of Melbourne in Australia with Professor John Hattie as her leading supervisor. Sophie completed her Master's thesis with Professor John Hattie in 2015. Sophie has over 20 years of experience as a teacher and school leader in private and public school settings in Australia.

Strategic Support for Online Learning

Get the Support You Need, When You Need It

There will be times throughout this course when you may need help. Whether you missed a section, did not understand the content, or just want to review, take advantage of the resources provided in the *Dynamic Student Edition*.

Use the **Self-Assessment** tool to keep track of your understanding of the section's success criteria.

Take notes throughout the lesson using the **My Notes** function. These notes will be organized by chapter and section.

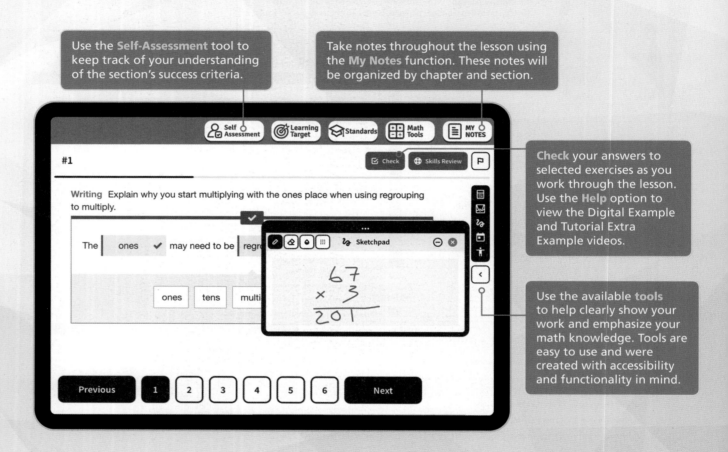

Check your answers to selected exercises as you work through the lesson. Use the **Help** option to view the Digital Example and Tutorial Extra Example videos.

Use the available **tools** to help clearly show your work and emphasize your math knowledge. Tools are easy to use and were created with accessibility and functionality in mind.

USE THESE QR CODES TO EXPLORE ADDITIONAL RESOURCES

Multi-Language Glossary

View definitions and examples of vocabulary words

Skills Trainer

Practice previously learned skills

Interactive Tools

Visualize mathematical concepts

Skills Review Handbook

A collection of review topics

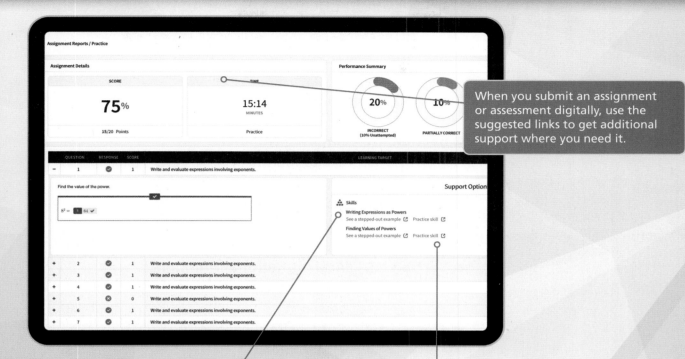

Assignment Reports / Practice

Assignment Details

SCORE	TIME
75%	**15:14**
	MINUTES
15/20 Points	Practice

Performance Summary

20% **10%**

INCORRECT
(10% Unattempted)

PARTIALLY CORRECT

QUESTION	RESPONSE	SCORE	LEARNING TARGET
− 1	✓	1	Write and evaluate expressions involving exponents.

Find the value of the power.

Support Option

$8^2 =$ 1 64 ✓

⛓ Skills

Writing Expressions as Powers
See a stepped-out example ↗ Practice skill ↗

Finding Values of Powers
See a stepped-out example ↗ Practice skill ↗

+	2	✓	1	Write and evaluate expressions involving exponents.
+	3	✓	1	Write and evaluate expressions involving exponents.
+	4	✓	1	Write and evaluate expressions involving exponents.
+	5	✗	0	Write and evaluate expressions involving exponents.
+	6	✓	1	Write and evaluate expressions involving exponents.
+	7	✓	1	Write and evaluate expressions involving exponents.

When you submit an assignment or assessment digitally, use the suggested links to get additional support where you need it.

Choose a skill to review and watch a video to see a stepped-out example of that skill. Whether you get a question incorrect, or want a second explanation, these videos can provide additional help with homework.

Choose a skill and launch the **Skills Trainer** for additional practice on that skill. Practicing repeated problems with instant feedback can help build confidence when solving problems.

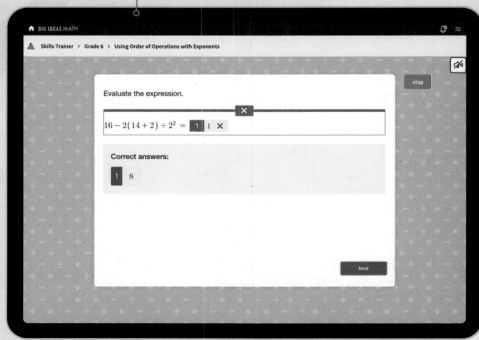

🏠 BIG IDEAS MATH

⛓ Skills Trainer > Grade 6 > Using Order of Operations with Exponents

stop

Evaluate the expression.

$16 - 2(14 + 2) \div 2^2 =$ 1 1 ✗

Correct answers:

1 8

Next

Adding and Subtracting Rational Numbers

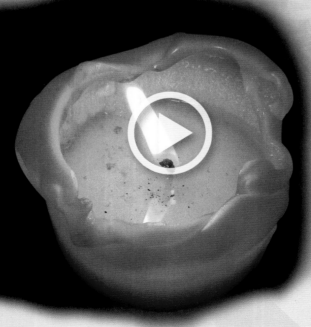

■ Major Topic
■ Supporting Topic
■ Additional Topic

Multiplying and Dividing Rational Numbers

Expressions

■ Major Topic
■ Supporting Topic
■ Additional Topic

Equations and Inequalities

5 Ratios and Proportions

■ Major Topic
■ Supporting Topic
■ Additional Topic

Percents

Probability

■ Major Topic
■ Supporting Topic
■ Additional Topic

Statistics

Geometric Shapes and Angles

■ Major Topic
■ Supporting Topic
■ Additional Topic

Surface Area and Volume

1 Adding and Subtracting Rational Numbers

Chapter Learning Target:
Understand adding and subtracting rational numbers.

Chapter Success Criteria:
- I can represent rational numbers on a number line.
- I can explain the rules for adding and subtracting integers using absolute value.
- I can apply addition and subtraction with rational numbers to model real-life problems.
- I can solve problems involving addition and subtraction of rational numbers.

STEAM Video: "Freezing Solids"

Freezing Solids

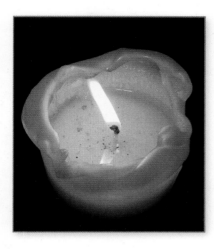

The Celsius temperature scale is defined using the freezing point, 0°C, and the boiling point, 100°C, of water. Why do you think the scale is defined using these two points?

Watch the STEAM Video "Freezing Solids." Then answer the following questions.

1. In the video, Tony says that the freezing point of wax is 53°C and the boiling point of wax is 343°C.

    a. Describe the temperature of wax that has just changed from liquid form to solid form. Explain your reasoning.

    b. After Tony blows out the candle, he demonstrates that there is still gas in the smoke. What do you know about the temperature of the gas that is in the smoke?

    c. In what form is wax when the temperature is at 100°C, the boiling point of water?

2. Consider wax in solid, liquid, and gaseous forms. Which is hottest? coldest?

Melting Matters

After completing this chapter, you will be able to use the concepts you learned to answer the questions in the *STEAM Video Performance Task*. You will answer questions using the melting points of the substances below.

Ice	**Tin**
Beeswax	**Ethanol**
Mercury	**Acetone**
Plastic	**Chocolate**

You will graph the melting points of the substances on a number line to make comparisons. How is the freezing point of a substance related to its melting point? What is meant when someone says it is below freezing outside? Explain.

Getting Ready for Chapter

Chapter Exploration

1. Work with a partner. Plot and connect the points to make a picture.

1(1, 11)	**2**(4, 10)	**3**(7, 10)	**4**(11, 9)	**5**(13, 8)
6(15, 5)	**7**(15, 3)	**8**(16, 1)	**9**(16, −1)	**10**(15, −1)
11(11, 1)	**12**(9, 2)	**13**(7, 1)	**14**(5, −1)	**15**(1, −1)
16(0, 0)	**17**(3, 1)	**18**(1, 1)	**19**(−2, 0)	**20**(−6, −2)
21(−9, −6)	**22**(−9, −7)	**23**(−7, −9)	**24**(−7, −11)	**25**(−8, −12)
26(−9, −11)	**27**(−11, −10)	**28**(−13, −11)	**29**(−15, −11)	**30**(−17, −12)
31(−17, −10)	**32**(−15, −7)	**33**(−12, −6)	**34**(−11, −6)	**35**(−10, −3)
36(−8, 2)	**37**(−5, 6)	**38**(−3, 9)	**39**(−4, 10)	**40**(−5, 10)
41(−2, 12)				

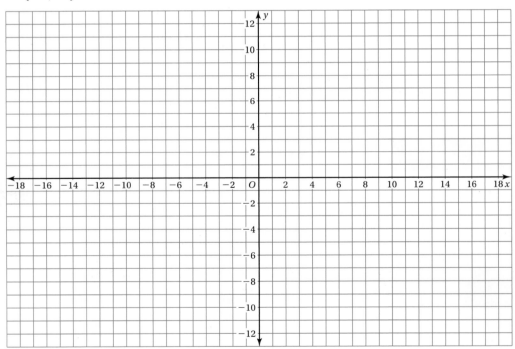

2. Create your own "dot-to-dot" picture. Use at least 20 points.

Vocabulary

The following vocabulary terms are defined in this chapter. Think about what each term might mean and record your thoughts.

integers   absolute value   rational number   additive inverse

1.1 Rational Numbers

Learning Target: Understand absolute values and ordering of rational numbers.

Success Criteria:
- I can graph rational numbers on a number line.
- I can find the absolute value of a rational number.
- I can use a number line to compare rational numbers.

Recall that **integers** are the set of whole numbers and their opposites. A **rational number** is a number that can be written as $\frac{a}{b}$, where a and b are integers and $b \neq 0$.

EXPLORATION 1

Using a Number Line

Work with a partner. Make a number line on the floor. Include both negative numbers and positive numbers.

a. Stand on an integer. Then have your partner stand on the opposite of the integer. How far are each of you from 0? What do you call the distance between a number and 0 on a number line?

b. Stand on a rational number that is not an integer. Then have your partner stand on any other number. Which number is greater? How do you know?

c. Stand on any number other than 0 on the number line. Can your partner stand on a number that is:

- greater than your number and farther from 0?

- greater than your number and closer to 0?

- less than your number and the same distance from 0?

- less than your number and farther from 0?

For each case in which it was not possible to stand on a number as directed, explain why it is not possible. In each of the other cases, how can you decide where your partner can stand?

Math Practice

Find Entry Points
What are some ways to determine which of two numbers is greater?

Key Vocabulary 🔊
integers, *p. 3*
rational number, *p. 3*
absolute value, *p. 4*

Math Practice

Use Clear Definitions
Explain to a classmate why $|4| \neq -4$.

🔑 Key Idea

Absolute Value

Words The **absolute value** of a number is the distance between the number and 0 on a number line. The absolute value of a number a is written as $|a|$.

(number line showing 4 units from −4 to 0 and 4 units from 0 to 4)

Numbers $\quad\quad |-4| = 4 \quad\quad\quad |4| = 4$

EXAMPLE 1 **Finding Absolute Values of Rational Numbers**

a. **Find the absolute value of −3.**

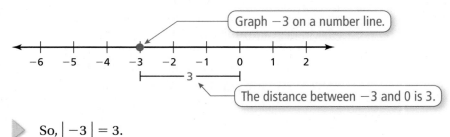

Graph −3 on a number line.

The distance between −3 and 0 is 3.

▷ So, $|-3| = 3$.

b. **Find the absolute value of $1\frac{1}{4}$.**

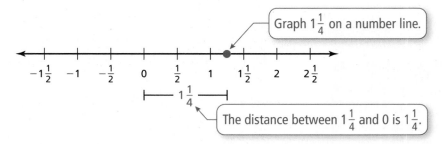

Graph $1\frac{1}{4}$ on a number line.

The distance between $1\frac{1}{4}$ and 0 is $1\frac{1}{4}$.

▷ So, $\left| 1\frac{1}{4} \right| = 1\frac{1}{4}$.

Try It **Find the absolute value.**

1. $|7|$ 　　　　　　　**2.** $\left| -\dfrac{5}{3} \right|$ 　　　　　　　**3.** $|-2.6|$

EXAMPLE 2 **Comparing Rational Numbers**

Compare $\left| -2.5 \right|$ and $\dfrac{3}{2}$.

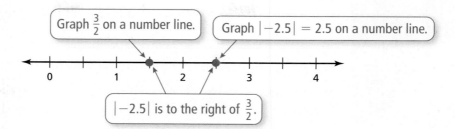

Graph $\dfrac{3}{2}$ on a number line.

Graph $\left| -2.5 \right| = 2.5$ on a number line.

$\left| -2.5 \right|$ is to the right of $\dfrac{3}{2}$.

Remember

Two numbers that are the same distance from 0 on a number line, but on opposite sides of 0, are called *opposites*. The opposite of a number a is $-a$.

So, $\left| -2.5 \right| > \dfrac{3}{2}$.

Try It Copy and complete the statement using <, >, or =.

4. $\left| 9 \right|$ ___ $\left| -9 \right|$

5. $-\left| \dfrac{1}{2} \right|$ ___ $-\dfrac{1}{4}$

6. 7 ___ $-\left| -4.5 \right|$

Self-Assessment *for Concepts & Skills*

Solve each exercise. Then rate your understanding of the success criteria in your journal.

7. **VOCABULARY** Which of the following numbers are integers?
$$9, \, 3.2, \, -1, \dfrac{1}{2}, \, -0.25, \, 15$$

8. **VOCABULARY** What is the absolute value of a number?

COMPARING RATIONAL NUMBERS Copy and complete the statement using <, >, or =. Use a number line to justify your answer.

9. 3.5 ___ $\left| -\dfrac{7}{2} \right|$

10. $\left| \dfrac{11}{4} \right|$ ___ $\left| -2.8 \right|$

11. **WRITING** You compare two numbers, a and b. Explain how $a > b$ and $\left| a \right| < \left| b \right|$ can both be true statements.

12. **WHICH ONE DOESN'T BELONG?** Which expression does *not* belong with the other three? Explain your reasoning.

$$\left| 6 \right| \qquad 6 \qquad -6 \qquad \left| -6 \right|$$

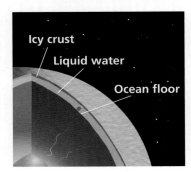

EXAMPLE 3   Modeling Real Life

A moon has an ocean underneath its icy surface. Scientists run tests above and below the surface. The table shows the elevations of each test. Which test is deepest? Which test is closest to the surface?

Test	Temperature	Salinity	Atmosphere	Organics	Ice
Elevation (miles)	−3.8	−5.15	0.3	−4.5	−0.25

To determine which test is deepest, find the least elevation. Graph the elevations on a vertical number line.

The number line shows that the salinity test is deepest. The number line also shows that the atmosphere test and the ice test are closest to the surface. To determine which is closer to the surface, identify which elevation has a lesser absolute value.

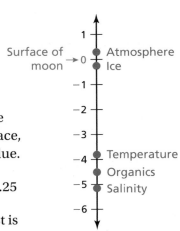

Atmosphere: $|0.3| = 0.3$ **Ice:** $|-0.25| = 0.25$

> So, the salinity test is deepest and the ice test is closest to the surface.

Self-Assessment for Problem Solving

Solve each exercise. Then rate your understanding of the success criteria in your journal.

13. An airplane is at an elevation of 5.5 miles. A submarine is at an elevation of −10.9 kilometers. Which is closer to sea level? Explain.

14. The image shows the corrective powers (in *diopters*) of contact lenses for eight people. The farther the number of diopters is from 0, the greater the power of the lens. Positive diopters correct *farsightedness* and negative diopters correct *nearsightedness*. Who is the most nearsighted? the most farsighted? Who has the best eyesight?

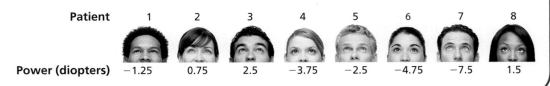

Patient	1	2	3	4	5	6	7	8
Power (diopters)	−1.25	0.75	2.5	−3.75	−2.5	−4.75	−7.5	1.5

1.1 Practice

Go to *BigIdeasMath.com* to get HELP with solving the exercises.

▶ Review & Refresh

Write the ratio.

1. deer to bears
2. bears to deer
3. bears to animals
4. animals to deer

Find the GCF of the numbers.

5. 8, 20   6. 12, 30   7. 7, 28   8. 48, 72

▶ Concepts, Skills, & Problem Solving

MP NUMBER SENSE Determine which number is greater and which number is farther from 0. Explain your reasoning. (See Exploration 1, p. 3.)

9. $4, -6$ 10. $-3.25, \dfrac{7}{2}$ 11. $-\dfrac{4}{5}, -1.3$

FINDING ABSOLUTE VALUES Find the absolute value.

12. $\left| 8 \right|$ 13. $\left| -2 \right|$ 14. $\left| -10 \right|$ 15. $\left| 10 \right|$

16. $\left| 0 \right|$ 17. $\left| \dfrac{1}{3} \right|$ 18. $\left| \dfrac{7}{8} \right|$ 19. $\left| -\dfrac{5}{9} \right|$

20. $\left| \dfrac{11}{8} \right|$ 21. $\left| 3.8 \right|$ 22. $\left| -5.3 \right|$ 23. $\left| -\dfrac{15}{4} \right|$

24. $\left| 7.64 \right|$ 25. $\left| -18.26 \right|$ 26. $\left| 4\dfrac{2}{5} \right|$ 27. $\left| -5\dfrac{1}{6} \right|$

COMPARING RATIONAL NUMBERS Copy and complete the statement using <, >, or =.

28. $2 \; \boxed{} \; \left| -5 \right|$ 29. $\left| -1 \right| \; \boxed{} \; \left| -8 \right|$ 30. $\left| 5 \right| \; \boxed{} \; \left| -5 \right|$

31. $\left| -2 \right| \; \boxed{} \; 0$ 32. $0.4 \; \boxed{} \; \left| -\dfrac{7}{8} \right|$ 33. $\left| 4.9 \right| \; \boxed{} \; \left| -5.3 \right|$

34. $-\left| 4.7 \right| \; \boxed{} \; \dfrac{1}{2}$ 35. $\left| -\dfrac{3}{4} \right| \; \boxed{} \; -\left| \dfrac{3}{4} \right|$ 36. $-\left| 1\dfrac{1}{4} \right| \; \boxed{} \; -\left| 1\dfrac{3}{8} \right|$

MP YOU BE THE TEACHER Your friend compares two rational numbers. Is your friend correct? Explain your reasoning.

37.

$$\left| -10 \right| = -10$$

38.

$$-\dfrac{4}{5} > -\dfrac{1}{2}$$

39. OPEN-ENDED Write a negative number whose absolute value is greater than 3.

40. **MP** **MODELING REAL LIFE** The *summit elevation* of a volcano is the elevation of the top of the volcano relative to sea level. The summit elevation of Kilauea, a volcano in Hawaii, is 1277 meters. The summit elevation of Loihi, an underwater volcano in Hawaii, is −969 meters. Which summit is higher? Which summit is closer to sea level?

41. **MP** **MODELING REAL LIFE** The *freezing point* of a liquid is the temperature at which the liquid becomes a solid.

Liquid	Freezing Point (°C)
Butter	35
Airplane fuel	−53
Honey	−3
Mercury	−39
Candle wax	53

    a. Which liquid in the table has the lowest freezing point?

    b. Is the freezing point of mercury or butter closer to the freezing point of water, 0°C?

ORDERING RATIONAL NUMBERS **Order the values from least to greatest.**

42. $8, |3|, -5, |-2|, -2$

43. $|-6.3|, -7.2, 8, |5|, -6.3$

44. $|3.5|, |-1.8|, 4.6, 3\frac{2}{5}, |2.7|$

45. $\left|-\frac{3}{4}\right|, \frac{5}{8}, \left|\frac{1}{4}\right|, -\frac{1}{2}, \left|-\frac{7}{8}\right|$

46. **MP** **PROBLEM SOLVING** The table shows golf scores, relative to *par*.

Player	Score
1	+5
2	0
3	−4
4	−1
5	+2

    a. The player with the lowest score wins. Which player wins?

    b. Which player is closest to par?

    c. Which player is farthest from par?

47. **DIG DEEPER!** You use the table below to record the temperature at the same location each hour for several hours. At what time is the temperature coldest? At what time is the temperature closest to the freezing point of water, 0°C?

Time	10:00 A.M.	11:00 A.M.	12:00 P.M.	1:00 P.M.	2:00 P.M.	3:00 P.M.
Temperature (°C)	−2.6	−2.7	−0.15	1.6	−1.25	−3.4

MP **REASONING** Determine whether $n \geq 0$ or $n \leq 0$.

48. $n + |-n| = 2n$

49. $n + |-n| = 0$

TRUE OR FALSE? **Determine whether the statement is *true* or *false*. Explain your reasoning.**

50. If $x < 0$, then $|x| = -x$.

51. The absolute value of every rational number is positive.

1.2 Adding Integers

Learning Target: Find sums of integers.

Success Criteria:
- I can explain how to model addition of integers on a number line.
- I can find sums of integers by reasoning about absolute values.
- I can explain why the sum of a number and its opposite is 0.

EXPLORATION 1

Using Integer Counters to Find Sums

$\boxed{+} = +1$
$\boxed{-} = -1$

Work with a partner. You can use the integer counters shown at the left to find sums of integers.

a. How can you use integer counters to model a sum? a sum that equals 0?

b. What expression is being modeled below? What is the value of the sum?

c. **INDUCTIVE REASONING** Use integer counters to complete the table.

Expression	Type of Sum	Sum	Sum: Positive, Negative, or Zero
$-3 + 2$	Integers with different signs		
$-4 + (-3)$			
$5 + (-3)$			
$7 + (-7)$			
$2 + 4$			
$-6 + (-2)$			
$-5 + 9$			
$15 + (-9)$			
$-10 + 10$			
$-6 + (-6)$			
$13 + (-13)$			

Math Practice

Make Conjectures
How can absolute values be used to write a rule about the sum of two integers?

d. How can you tell whether the sum of two integers is *positive*, *negative*, or *zero*?

e. Write rules for adding (i) two integers with the same sign, (ii) two integers with different signs, and (iii) two opposite integers.

Key Vocabulary 🔊
additive inverse, *p. 11*

You have used number lines to find sums of positive numbers, which involve movement to the right. Now you will find sums with negative numbers, which involve movement to the left.

EXAMPLE 1 **Using Number Lines to Find Sums**

a. **Find 4 + (−4).**

Draw an arrow from 0 to 4 to represent 4. Then draw an arrow 4 units to the left to represent adding −4.

> *The length of each arrow is the absolute value of the number it represents.*

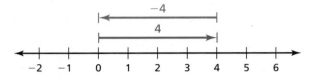

▷ So, $4 + (−4) = 0$.

b. **Find −1 + (−3).**

Draw an arrow from 0 to −1 to represent −1. Then draw an arrow 3 units to the left to represent adding −3.

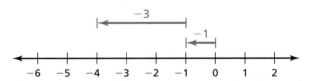

▷ So, $−1 + (−3) = −4$.

c. **Find −2 + 6.**

Draw an arrow from 0 to −2 to represent −2. Then draw an arrow 6 units to the right to represent adding 6.

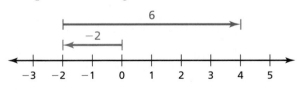

▷ So, $−2 + 6 = 4$.

Try It **Use a number line to find the sum.**

1. $−2 + 2$ **2.** $4 + (−5)$ **3.** $−3 + (−3)$

Using integer counters and number lines leads to the following rules for adding integers.

 Key Ideas

Math Practice

Justify Conclusions

Use a number line to justify the rule for adding integers with the same sign.

Notice that Example 1(a) shows the Additive Inverse Property.

Adding Integers with the Same Sign

Words   Add the absolute values of the integers. Then use the common sign.

Numbers $2 + 5 = 7$ $-2 + (-5) = -7$

Adding Integers with Different Signs

Words   Subtract the lesser absolute value from the greater absolute value. Then use the sign of the integer with the greater absolute value.

Numbers $8 + (-10) = -2$ $-13 + 17 = 4$

Additive Inverse Property

Words   The sum of a number and its **additive inverse,** or opposite, is 0.

Numbers $6 + (-6) = 0$ $-25 + 25 = 0$

Algebra $a + (-a) = 0$

EXAMPLE 2   **Adding Integers with the Same Sign**

Find $-4 + (-2)$.

$$-4 + (-2) = -6 \qquad \text{Add } \left| -4 \right| \text{ and } \left| -2 \right|.$$

Use the common sign.

▷   The sum is -6.

Check Use integer counters.

$$-4 \qquad + \qquad -2 \qquad = \qquad -6 \qquad \checkmark$$

Try It **Find the sum.**

4. $7 + 13$ **5.** $-8 + (-5)$ **6.** $-2 + (-15)$

EXAMPLE 3 **Adding Integers with Different Signs**

a. **Find 5 + (−10).**

$$5 + (-10) = -5$$

$|-10| > |5|$. So, subtract $|5|$ from $|-10|$.

Use the sign of −10.

▷ The sum is −5.

b. **Find −3 + 7.**

$$-3 + 7 = 4$$

$|7| > |-3|$. So, subtract $|-3|$ from $|7|$.

Use the sign of 7.

▷ The sum is 4.

c. **Find −12 + 12.**

$$-12 + 12 = 0$$

The sum is 0 by the Additive Inverse Property.

−12 and 12 are opposites.

▷ The sum is 0.

Try It **Find the sum.**

7. $-2 + 11$ **8.** $9 + (-10)$ **9.** $-31 + 31$

Self-Assessment *for Concepts & Skills*

Solve each exercise. Then rate your understanding of the success criteria in your journal.

10. **WRITING** Explain how to use a number line to find the sum of two integers.

ADDING INTEGERS **Find the sum. Use a number line to justify your answer.**

11. $-8 + 20$ **12.** $30 + (-30)$ **13.** $-10 + (-18)$

14. **MP NUMBER SENSE** Is $3 + (-4)$ the same as $-4 + 3$? Explain.

MP LOGIC **Tell whether the statement is *true* or *false*. Explain your reasoning.**

15. The sum of two negative integers is always negative.

16. The sum of an integer and its absolute value is always 0.

You can use the Commutative and Associative Properties of Addition to find sums of integers.

EXAMPLE 4 **Modeling Real Life**

Understand the problem.

The list shows four account transactions. Find the change in the account balance.

You are given amounts of two withdrawals and two deposits. You are asked to find how much the balance in the account changed.

JULY TRANSACTIONS	
Withdrawal	-$40
Deposit	$50
Deposit	$75
Withdrawal	-$50

Make a plan.

Find the sum of the transactions. Notice that 50 and −50 are opposites and combine to make 0. So, use properties of addition to first group those terms.

Solve and check.

$$-40 + 50 + 75 + (-50) = -40 + 75 + 50 + (-50) \qquad \text{Comm. Prop. of Add.}$$
$$= -40 + 75 + [50 + (-50)] \qquad \text{Assoc. Prop. of Add.}$$
$$= -40 + 75 + 0 \qquad \text{Add. Inv. Prop.}$$
$$= 35 + 0 \qquad \text{Add} -40 \text{ and } 75.$$
$$= 35 \qquad \text{Add. Prop. of Zero}$$

So, the account balance increased $35.

> **Another Method** Find the sum by grouping the first two terms and the last two terms.
>
> $$-40 + 50 + 75 + (-50) = (-40 + 50) + [75 + (-50)]$$
> $$= 10 + 25 = 35 \checkmark$$

Self-Assessment *for Problem Solving*

Solve each exercise. Then rate your understanding of the success criteria in your journal.

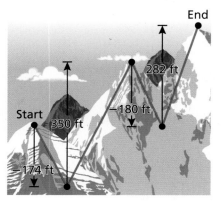

17. At 12:00 P.M., the water pressure on a submarine is 435 pounds per square inch. From 12:00 P.M. to 12:30 P.M., the water pressure increases 58 pounds per square inch. From 12:30 P.M. to 1:00 P.M., the water pressure decreases 116 pounds per square inch. What is the water pressure at 1:00 P.M.?

18. The diagram shows the elevation changes between checkpoints on a trail. The trail begins at an elevation of 8136 feet. What is the elevation at the end of the trail?

Go to *BigIdeasMath.com* to get
HELP with solving the exercises.

▶ Review & Refresh

Copy and complete the statement using <, >, or =.

1. 5 ⬜ $\left|-7\right|$ **2.** $\left|-2.6\right|$ ⬜ $\left|-2.06\right|$ **3.** $\left|-\dfrac{3}{5}\right|$ ⬜ $-\left|\dfrac{5}{8}\right|$

Add.

4. $8.43 + 5.21$

5. $2.316 + 4.09$

6. $\dfrac{5}{9} + \dfrac{3}{9}$

7. $\dfrac{1}{2} + \dfrac{1}{8}$

8. The regular price of a photograph printed on a canvas is \$18. You have a coupon for 15% off. How much is the discount?

   A. \$2.70   **B.** \$3   **C.** \$15   **D.** \$15.30

9. Represent the ratio relationship using a graph.

Time (hours)	1	2	3
Distance (miles)	55	110	165

▶▶ Concepts, Skills, & Problem Solving

USING INTEGER COUNTERS Use integer counters to complete the table.
(See Exploration 1, p. 9.)

	Expression	Type of Sum	Sum	Sum: Positive, Negative, or Zero
10.	$-5 + 8$			
11.	$-3 + (-7)$			

USING NUMBER LINES Write an addition expression represented by the number line. Then find the sum.

12.
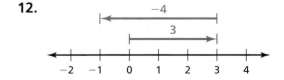

13.
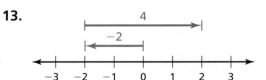

14.
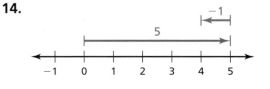

15.
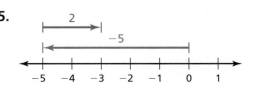

ADDING INTEGERS Find the sum. Use integer counters or a number line to verify your answer.

16. $6 + 4$ **17.** $-4 + (-6)$ **18.** $-2 + (-3)$ **19.** $-5 + 12$

20. $5 + (-7)$ **21.** $8 + (-8)$ **22.** $9 + (-11)$ **23.** $-3 + 13$

24. $-4 + (-16)$ **25.** $-3 + (-1)$ **26.** $14 + (-5)$ **27.** $0 + (-11)$

28. $-10 + (-15)$ **29.** $-13 + 9$ **30.** $18 + (-18)$ **31.** $-25 + (-9)$

(MP) YOU BE THE TEACHER Your friend finds the sum. Is your friend correct? Explain your reasoning.

32.

> $9 + (-6) = 3$

33.

> $-10 + (-10) = 0$

34. **(MP) MODELING REAL LIFE** The temperature is $-3°F$ at 7:00 A.M. During the next 4 hours, the temperature increases $21°F$. What is the temperature at 11:00 A.M.?

35. **(MP) MODELING REAL LIFE** Your bank account has a balance of $-\$12$. You deposit $\$60$. What is your new balance?

Lithium Atom

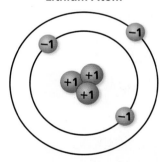

36. **(MP) PROBLEM SOLVING** A lithium atom has positively charged protons and negatively charged electrons. The sum of the charges represents the charge of the lithium atom. Find the charge of the atom.

37. **OPEN-ENDED** Write two integers with different signs that have a sum of -25. Write two integers with the same sign that have a sum of -25.

USING PROPERTIES Tell how the Commutative and Associative Properties of Addition can help you find the sum using mental math. Then find the sum.

38. $9 + 6 + (-6)$ **39.** $-8 + 13 + (-13)$ **40.** $9 + (-17) + (-9)$

41. $7 + (-12) + (-7)$ **42.** $-12 + 25 + (-15)$ **43.** $6 + (-9) + 14$

ADDING INTEGERS Find the sum.

44. $13 + (-21) + 16$ **45.** $22 + (-14) + (-12)$ **46.** $-13 + 27 + (-18)$

47. $-19 + 26 + 14$ **48.** $-32 + (-17) + 42$ **49.** $-41 + (-15) + (-29)$

DESCRIBING A SUM Describe the location of the sum, relative to p, on a number line.

50. $p + 3$ **51.** $p + (-7)$ **52.** $p + 0$ **53.** $p + q$

ALGEBRA Evaluate the expression when $a = 4$, $b = -5$, and $c = -8$.

54. $a + b$ **55.** $-b + c$ **56.** $|a + b + c|$

57. **MP MODELING REAL LIFE** The table shows the income and expenses for a school carnival. The school's goal was to raise $1100. Did the school reach its goal? Explain.

Games	Concessions	Donations	Flyers	Decorations
$650	$530	$52	−$28	−$75

OPEN-ENDED **Write a real-life story using the given topic that involves the sum of an integer and its additive inverse.**

58. income and expenses

59. the amount of water in a bottle

60. the elevation of a blimp

MENTAL MATH **Use mental math to solve the equation.**

61. $d + 12 = 2$

62. $b + (-2) = 0$

63. $-8 + m = -15$

64. **DIG DEEPER!** Starting at point A, the path of a dolphin jumping out of the water is shown.

   a. Is the dolphin deeper at point C or point E? Explain your reasoning.

   b. Is the dolphin higher at point B or point D? Explain your reasoning.

   c. What is the change in elevation of the dolphin from point A to point E?

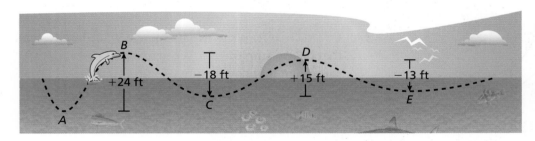

65. **MP NUMBER SENSE** Consider the integers p and q. Describe all of the possible values of p and q for each circumstance. Justify your answers.

   a. $p + q = 0$

   b. $p + q < 0$

   c. $p + q > 0$

66. **PUZZLE** According to a legend, the Chinese Emperor Yu-Huang saw a magic square on the back of a turtle. In a *magic square*, the numbers in each row and in each column have the same sum. This sum is called the *magic sum*.

Copy and complete the magic square so that each row and each column has a magic sum of 0. Use each integer from −4 to 4 exactly once.

1.3 Adding Rational Numbers

Learning Target: Find sums of rational numbers.

Success Criteria:
- I can explain how to model addition of rational numbers on a number line.
- I can find sums of rational numbers by reasoning about absolute values.
- I can use properties of addition to efficiently add rational numbers.

EXPLORATION 1

Adding Rational Numbers

Work with a partner.

a. Choose a unit fraction to represent the space between the tick marks on each number line. What addition expressions are being modeled? What are the sums?

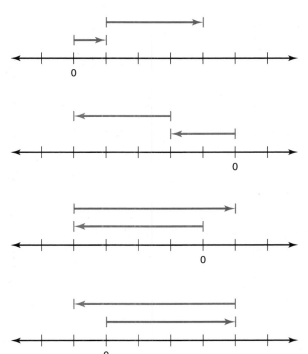

Math Practice

Look for Structure
How do the lengths and directions of the arrows determine the sign of the sum?

b. Do the rules for adding integers apply to all rational numbers? Explain your reasoning.

c. You have used the following properties to add integers. Do these properties apply to all rational numbers? Explain your reasoning.

- Commutative Property of Addition
- Associative Property of Addition
- Additive Inverse Property

1.3   Lesson

 **Key Idea**

Adding Rational Numbers

Words   To add rational numbers, use the same rules as you used for adding integers.

Numbers $\dfrac{3}{5} + \left(-\dfrac{1}{5}\right) = \left|\dfrac{3}{5}\right| - \left|-\dfrac{1}{5}\right|$

$\qquad\qquad = \dfrac{3}{5} - \dfrac{1}{5}$

$\qquad\qquad = \dfrac{2}{5}$

Model

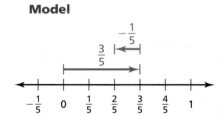

EXAMPLE 1   **Adding Rational Numbers**

Find $-\dfrac{8}{3} + \dfrac{5}{6}$.   **Estimate** $-3 + 1 = -2$

Because the signs are different and $\left|-\dfrac{8}{3}\right| > \left|\dfrac{5}{6}\right|$, subtract $\left|\dfrac{5}{6}\right|$ from $\left|-\dfrac{8}{3}\right|$.

$\left|-\dfrac{8}{3}\right| - \left|\dfrac{5}{6}\right| = \dfrac{8}{3} - \dfrac{5}{6}$ Find the absolute values.

$\qquad\qquad = \dfrac{16}{6} - \dfrac{5}{6}$ Rewrite $\dfrac{8}{3}$ as $\dfrac{16}{6}$.

$\qquad\qquad = \dfrac{16 - 5}{6}$ Write the difference of the numerators over the common denominator.

$\qquad\qquad = \dfrac{11}{6}$, or $1\dfrac{5}{6}$ Simplify.

Because $\left|-\dfrac{8}{3}\right| > \left|\dfrac{5}{6}\right|$, use the sign of $-\dfrac{8}{3}$.

▷ So, $-\dfrac{8}{3} + \dfrac{5}{6} = -1\dfrac{5}{6}$.   **Reasonable?** $-1\dfrac{5}{6} \approx -2$ ✓

Try It   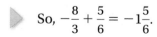 Find the sum. Write your answer in simplest form.

1. $-\dfrac{1}{2} + \left(-\dfrac{3}{2}\right)$ **2.** $-1\dfrac{3}{8} + \dfrac{3}{4}$ **3.** $4 + \left(-\dfrac{7}{2}\right)$

EXAMPLE 2 **Adding Rational Numbers**

Find $-0.75 + (-1.5)$. **Estimate** $-1 + (-1.5) = -2.5$

Because the signs are the same, add $\left| -0.75 \right|$ and $\left| -1.5 \right|$.

$$\left| -0.75 \right| + \left| -1.5 \right| = 0.75 + 1.5 \qquad \text{Find the absolute values.}$$

$$= 2.25 \qquad \text{Add.}$$

Because -0.75 and -1.5 are both negative, use a negative sign in the sum.

 So, $-0.75 + (-1.5) = -2.25$. **Reasonable?** $-2.25 \approx -2.5$

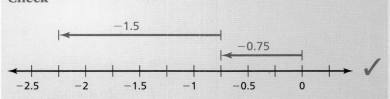

Check

Try It **Find the sum.**

4. $-3.3 + (-2.7)$ **5.** $-5.35 + 4$ **6.** $1.65 + (-0.9)$

 Self-Assessment *for Concepts & Skills*

Solve each exercise. Then rate your understanding of the success criteria in your journal.

7. WRITING Explain how to use a number line to find the sum of two rational numbers.

ADDING RATIONAL NUMBERS **Find the sum.**

8. $-\dfrac{7}{10} + \dfrac{1}{5}$ **9.** $-\dfrac{3}{4} + \left(-\dfrac{1}{3} \right)$ **10.** $-2.6 + 4.3$

11. DIFFERENT WORDS, SAME QUESTION Which is different? Find "both" answers.

Add -4.5 and 3.5.

What is the distance between -4.5 and 3.5?

What is -4.5 increased by 3.5?

Find the sum of -4.5 and 3.5.

EXAMPLE 3 Modeling Real Life

The table shows the annual profits (in millions of dollars) of an online gaming company from 2013 to 2017. Positive numbers represent *gains*, and negative numbers represent *losses*. Which statement describes the profit over the five-year period?

Year	Profit (millions of dollars)
2013	−1.7
2014	−4.75
2015	1.7
2016	0.8
2017	3.2

A. gain of $0.75 million

B. gain of $75,000

C. loss of $75,000

D. loss of $750,000

To determine the amount of the gain or loss, find the sum of the profits.

The Commutative and Associative Properties of Addition are true for all rational numbers.

five-year profit = $-1.7 + (-4.75) + 1.7 + 0.8 + 3.2$	Write the sum.
$= -1.7 + 1.7 + (-4.75) + 0.8 + 3.2$	Comm. Prop. of Add.
$= 0 + (-4.75) + 0.8 + 3.2$	Additive Inv. Prop.
$= -4.75 + 0.8 + 3.2$	Add. Prop. of Zero
$= -4.75 + (0.8 + 3.2)$	Assoc. Prop. of Add.
$= -4.75 + 4$	Add 0.8 and 3.2.
$= -0.75$	Add −4.75 and 4.

The five-year profit is −$0.75 million. So, the company has a five-year loss of $0.75 million, or $750,000.

▷ The correct answer is **D**.

Self-Assessment for Problem Solving

Solve each exercise. Then rate your understanding of the success criteria in your journal.

12. A bottle contains 10.5 cups of orange juice. You drink 1.2 cups of the juice each morning and 0.9 cup of the juice each afternoon. How much total juice do you drink each day? When will you run out of juice?

13. **DIG DEEPER!** The table shows the changes in elevation of a hiker each day for three days. How many miles of elevation must the hiker gain on the fourth day to gain $\frac{1}{4}$ mile of elevation over the four days?

Day	Change in elevation (miles)
1	$-\frac{1}{4}$
2	$\frac{1}{2}$
3	$-\frac{1}{5}$
4	?

1.3 Practice

? Go to *BigIdeasMath.com* to get HELP with solving the exercises.

▶ Review & Refresh

Find the sum. Use a number line to verify your answer.

1. $3 + 12$ **2.** $5 + (-7)$ **3.** $-4 + (-1)$ **4.** $-6 + 6$

Subtract.

5. $69 - 38$ **6.** $82 - 74$ **7.** $177 - 63$ **8.** $451 - 268$

9. What is the range of the numbers below?

$$12, 8, 17, 12, 15, 18, 30$$

A. 12 **B.** 15 **C.** 18 **D.** 22

▶ Concepts, Skills, & Problem Solving

MP USING TOOLS Choose a unit fraction to represent the space between the tick marks on the number line. Write the addition expression being modeled. Then find the sum. *(See Exploration 1, p. 17.)*

10. 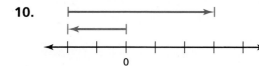 **11.**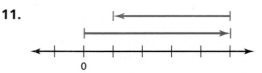

ADDING RATIONAL NUMBERS Find the sum. Write fractions in simplest form.

12. $\frac{11}{12} + \left(-\frac{7}{12}\right)$ **13.** $-1\frac{1}{5} + \left(-\frac{3}{5}\right)$ **14.** $-4.2 + 3.3$

15. $-\frac{9}{14} + \frac{2}{7}$ **16.** $12.48 + (-10.636)$ **17.** $-2\frac{1}{6} + \left(-\frac{2}{3}\right)$

18. $-20.25 + 15.711$ **19.** $-32.306 + (-24.884)$ **20.** $\frac{15}{4} + \left(-4\frac{1}{3}\right)$

21. **MP YOU BE THE TEACHER** Your friend finds the sum. Is your friend correct? Explain your reasoning.

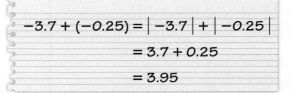

OPEN-ENDED Describe a real-life situation that can be represented by the addition expression modeled on the number line.

22.  **23.**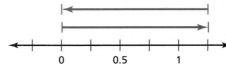

24. **MP** **MODELING REAL LIFE** You eat $\frac{3}{10}$ of a coconut. Your friend eats $\frac{1}{5}$ of the coconut. What fraction of the coconut do you and your friend eat?

25. **MP** **MODELING REAL LIFE** Your bank account balance is −$20.85. You deposit $15.50. What is your new balance?

26. **MP** **NUMBER SENSE** When is the sum of two negative mixed numbers an integer?

June	July	August
$-2\frac{1}{8}$	$1\frac{1}{4}$	$-\frac{7}{8}$

27. **WRITING** You are adding two rational numbers with different signs. How can you tell if the sum will be *positive*, *negative*, or *zero*?

28. **DIG DEEPER!** The table at the left shows the water level (in inches) of a reservoir for three months compared to the yearly average. When you include May and September, the water level for the five-month period is greater than the yearly average. Given that the level in September is below the yearly average, what can you determine about the level in May compared to the other four months? Justify your answer.

USING PROPERTIES Tell how the Commutative and Associative Properties of Addition can help you find the sum using mental math. Then find the sum.

29. $4.5 + (-6.21) + (-4.5)$ 30. $\frac{1}{3} + \left(\frac{2}{3} + \frac{5}{8}\right)$ 31. $8\frac{1}{2} + \left[4\frac{1}{10} + \left(-8\frac{1}{2}\right)\right]$

ADDING RATIONAL NUMBERS Find the sum. Explain each step.

32. $6 + 4\frac{3}{4} + (-2.5)$ 33. $-4.3 + \frac{4}{5} + 12$ 34. $5\frac{1}{3} + 7.5 + \left(-3\frac{1}{6}\right)$

35. **MP** **PROBLEM SOLVING** The table at the right shows the annual profits (in thousands of dollars) of a county fair from 2013 to 2016. What must the 2017 profit be (in hundreds of dollars) to break even over the five-year period?

Year	Profit (thousands of dollars)
2013	2.5
2014	1.4
2015	−3.3
2016	−1.4
2017	?

36. **MP** **REASONING** Is $|a + b| = |a| + |b|$ true for all rational numbers a and b? Explain.

37. **MP** **REPEATED REASONING** Evaluate the expression.

$$\frac{19}{20} + \left(-\frac{18}{20}\right) + \frac{17}{20} + \left(-\frac{16}{20}\right) + \cdots + \left(-\frac{4}{20}\right) + \frac{3}{20} + \left(-\frac{2}{20}\right) + \frac{1}{20}$$

1.4 Subtracting Integers

Learning Target: Find differences of integers.

Success Criteria:
- I can explain how subtracting integers is related to adding integers.
- I can explain how to model subtraction of integers on a number line.
- I can find differences of integers by reasoning about absolute values.

EXPLORATION 1

Using Integer Counters to Find Differences

Work with a partner.

a. Use integer counters to find the following sum and difference. What do you notice?

$$4 + (-2) \qquad 4 - 2$$

b. In part (a), you *removed* zero pairs to find the sums. How can you use integer counters and zero pairs to find $-3 - 1$?

c. INDUCTIVE REASONING Use integer counters to complete the table.

Expression	Operation: Add or Subtract	Answer
$4 - 2$	Subtract 2.	
$4 + (-2)$		
$-3 - 1$		
$-3 + (-1)$		
$3 - 8$		
$3 + (-8)$		
$9 - 13$		
$9 + (-13)$		
$-6 - (-3)$		
$-6 + 3$		
$-5 - (-12)$		
$-5 + 12$		

Math Practice

Interpret Results

What do the results tell you about the relationship between subtracting integers and adding integers?

d. Write a general rule for subtracting integers.

 **Key Idea**

Subtracting Integers

Words To subtract an integer, add its opposite.

Numbers $3 - 4 = 3 + (-4) = -1$

Models

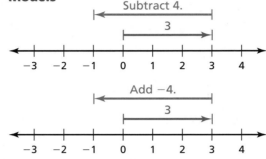

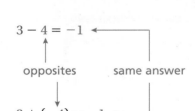

EXAMPLE 1 **Using Number Lines to Find Differences**

a. **Find $-2 - 4$.**

Draw an arrow from 0 to -2 to represent -2. Then draw an arrow 4 units to the left to represent subtracting 4, or adding -4.

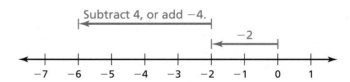

▶ So, $-2 - 4 = -6$.

b. **Find $-3 - (-7)$.**

Draw an arrow from 0 to -3 to represent -3. Then draw an arrow 7 units to the right to represent subtracting -7, or adding 7.

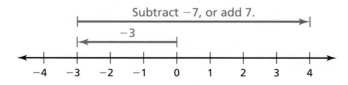

▶ So, $-3 - (-7) = 4$.

Try It **Use a number line to find the difference.**

1. $1 - 4$ **2.** $-5 - 2$ **3.** $6 - (-5)$

EXAMPLE 2 **Subtracting Integers**

a. **Find 3 − 12.**

$$3 - 12 = 3 + (-12)$$ Add the opposite of 12.

$$= -9$$ Add.

▷ The difference is −9.

b. **Find −8 − (−13).**

$$-8 - (-13) = -8 + 13$$ Add the opposite of −13.

$$= 5$$ Add.

▷ The difference is 5.

Math Practice

Construct Arguments

Let p and q be integers. How can you write $p + q$ as a subtraction expression? Explain your reasoning.

c. **Find 5 − (−4).**

$$5 - (-4) = 5 + 4$$ Add the opposite of −4.

$$= 9$$ Add.

▷ The difference is 9.

Try It **Find the difference.**

4. $8 - 3$ **5.** $9 - 17$ **6.** $-3 - 3$

7. $-14 - 9$ **8.** $10 - (-8)$ **9.** $-12 - (-12)$

 Self-Assessment for Concepts & Skills

Solve each exercise. Then rate your understanding of the success criteria in your journal.

10. **WRITING** Explain how to use a number line to find the difference of two integers.

MATCHING **Match the subtraction expression with the corresponding addition expression. Explain your reasoning.**

11. $9 - (-5)$ **12.** $-9 - 5$ **13.** $-9 - (-5)$ **14.** $9 - 5$

A. $-9 + 5$ **B.** $9 + (-5)$ **C.** $-9 + (-5)$ **D.** $9 + 5$

SUBTRACTING INTEGERS **Find the difference. Use a number line to justify your answer.**

15. $10 - 12$ **16.** $6 - (-8)$ **17.** $-7 - (-4)$

EXAMPLE 3 **Modeling Real Life**

Which continent has the greater range of elevations?

	North America	Africa
Highest Elevation	6198 m	5895 m
Lowest Elevation	−86 m	−155 m

Understand the problem.
You are given the highest and lowest elevations in North America and Africa. You are asked to find the continent with the greater difference between its highest and lowest elevations.

Make a plan.
Find the range of elevations for each continent by subtracting the lowest elevation from the highest elevation. Then compare the ranges.

Solve and check.

North America

range = 6198 − (−86)
= 6198 + 86
= 6284 m

Africa

range = 5895 − (−155)
= 5895 + 155
= 6050 m

Because 6284 meters is greater than 6050 meters, North America has the greater range of elevations.

Another Method North America's highest elevation is 6198 − 5895 = 303 meters higher than Africa's highest elevation. Africa's lowest elevation is $|-155| - |-86| = 69$ meters lower than North America's lowest elevation. Because 303 > 69, North America has the greater range of elevations. ✓

Self-Assessment *for Problem Solving*

Solve each exercise. Then rate your understanding of the success criteria in your journal.

18. A polar vortex causes the temperature to decrease from 3°C at 3:00 P.M. to −2°C at 4:00 P.M. The temperature continues to change by the same amount each hour until 8:00 P.M. Find the total change in temperature from 3:00 P.M. to 8:00 P.M.

19. **DIG DEEPER!** The table shows record high and low temperatures for three countries. Sweden has the greatest range of temperatures of the three countries. Describe the possible record low temperatures for Sweden.

	Norway	Sweden	Finland
High	96.1°F	100.4°F	99.0°F
Low	−60.5°F		−60.7°F

? Go to **BigIdeasMath.com** to get HELP with solving the exercises.

▶ Review & Refresh

Find the sum. Write fractions in simplest form.

1. $\dfrac{5}{9} + \left(-\dfrac{2}{9}\right)$

2. $-8.75 + 2.43$

3. $-3\dfrac{1}{8} + \left(-2\dfrac{3}{8}\right)$

Add.

4. $2.48 + 6.711$

5. $12.807 + 7.116$

6. $18.7126 + 14.033$

Write an addition expression represented by the number line. Then find the sum.

7.
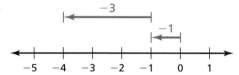

8.
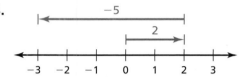

▶▶ Concepts, Skills, & Problem Solving

USING INTEGER COUNTERS Use integer counters to find the difference. (See Exploration 1, p. 23.)

9. $5 - 3$

10. $1 - 4$

11. $-2 - (-6)$

USING NUMBER LINES Write an addition expression and write a subtraction expression represented by the number line. Then evaluate the expressions.

12.

13.
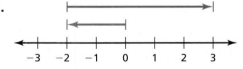

SUBTRACTING INTEGERS Find the difference. Use a number line to verify your answer.

14. $4 - 7$ **15.** $8 - (-5)$ **16.** $-6 - (-7)$ **17.** $-2 - 3$

18. $5 - 8$ **19.** $-4 - 6$ **20.** $-8 - (-3)$ **21.** $10 - 7$

22. $-8 - 13$ **23.** $15 - (-2)$ **24.** $-9 - (-13)$ **25.** $-7 - (-8)$

26. $-6 - (-6)$ **27.** $-10 - 12$ **28.** $32 - (-6)$ **29.** $0 - (-20)$

30. **MP YOU BE THE TEACHER** Your friend finds the difference. Is your friend correct? Explain your reasoning.

$$7 - (-12) = 7 + 12 = 19$$

31. **MP STRUCTURE** A scientist records the water temperature and the air temperature in Antarctica. The water temperature is −2°C. The air is 9°C colder than the water. Which expression can be used to find the air temperature? Explain your reasoning.

$$-2 + 9 \qquad -2 - 9 \qquad 9 - 2$$

32. **MP MODELING REAL LIFE** A shark is 80 feet below the surface of the water. It swims up and jumps out of the water to a height of 15 feet above the surface. Find the vertical distance the shark travels. Justify your answer.

33. **MP MODELING REAL LIFE** The figure shows a diver diving from a platform. The diver reaches a depth of 4 meters. What is the change in elevation of the diver?

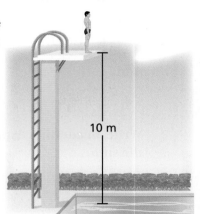

10 m

34. **OPEN-ENDED** Write two different pairs of negative integers, x and y, that make the statement $x - y = -1$ true.

USING PROPERTIES Tell how the Commutative and Associative Properties of Addition can help you evaluate the expression using mental math. Then evaluate the expression.

35. $2 - 7 + (-2)$ 36. $-6 - 8 + 6$ 37. $8 + (-8 - 5)$

38. $-39 + 46 - (-39)$ 39. $[13 + (-28)] - 13$ 40. $-2 + (-47 - 8)$

ALGEBRA Evaluate the expression when $k = -3$, $m = -6$, and $n = 9$.

41. $4 - n$ 42. $m - (-8)$ 43. $-5 + k - n$ 44. $|m - k|$

45. **MP MODELING REAL LIFE** The table shows the record monthly high and low temperatures for a city in Alaska.

	Jan	Feb	Mar	Apr	May	Jun	Jul	Aug	Sep	Oct	Nov	Dec
High (°F)	56	57	56	72	82	92	84	85	73	64	62	53
Low (°F)	−35	−38	−24	−15	1	29	34	31	19	−6	−21	−36

     a. Which month has the greatest range of temperatures?

     b. What is the range of temperatures for the year?

MP REASONING Tell whether the difference of the two integers is *always*, *sometimes*, or *never* positive. Explain your reasoning.

46. two positive integers   47. a positive integer and a negative integer

48. two negative integers   49. a negative integer and a positive integer

MP NUMBER SENSE For what values of a and b is the statement true?

50. $|a - b| = |b - a|$ 51. $|a - b| = |a| - |b|$

1.5 Subtracting Rational Numbers

Learning Target: Find differences of rational numbers and find distances between numbers on a number line.

Success Criteria:
- I can explain how to model subtraction of rational numbers on a number line.
- I can find differences of rational numbers by reasoning about absolute values.
- I can find distances between numbers on a number line.

EXPLORATION 1

Subtracting Rational Numbers

Work with a partner.

a. Choose a unit fraction to represent the space between the tick marks on each number line. What expressions involving subtraction are being modeled? What are the differences?

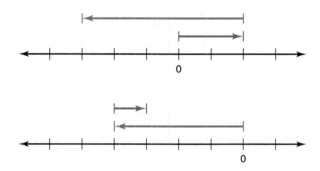

b. Do the rules for subtracting integers apply to all rational numbers? Explain your reasoning.

c. You have used the commutative and associative properties to add integers. Do these properties apply in expressions involving subtraction? Explain your reasoning.

EXPLORATION 2

Finding Distances on a Number Line

Work with a partner.

Math Practice

Find General Methods

How can you find the distance between any two rational numbers on a number line?

a. Find the distance between 3 and -2 on a number line.

b. The distance between 3 and 0 is the absolute value of 3, because $|3 - 0| = |3| = 3$. How can you use absolute values to find the distance between 3 and -2? Justify your answer.

c. Choose any two rational numbers. Use your method in part (b) to find the distance between the numbers. Use a number line to check your answer.

1.5 Lesson

 **Key Idea**

Subtracting Rational Numbers

Words To subtract rational numbers, use the same rules as you used for subtracting integers.

Numbers $\dfrac{1}{5} - \left(-\dfrac{4}{5}\right) = \dfrac{1}{5} + \dfrac{4}{5}$

$$= \dfrac{5}{5}$$

$$= 1$$

Model

Subtract $-\dfrac{4}{5}$, or add $\dfrac{4}{5}$.

$$-\dfrac{1}{5} \quad 0 \quad \dfrac{1}{5} \quad \dfrac{2}{5} \quad \dfrac{3}{5} \quad \dfrac{4}{5} \quad 1$$

EXAMPLE 1 **Subtracting Rational Numbers**

Find $-4\dfrac{1}{7} - \dfrac{5}{7}$.   **Estimate** $-4 - 1 = -5$

Rewrite the difference as a sum by adding the opposite.

$$-4\dfrac{1}{7} - \dfrac{5}{7} = -4\dfrac{1}{7} + \left(-\dfrac{5}{7}\right)$$

Because the signs are the same, add $\left| -4\dfrac{1}{7} \right|$ and $\left| -\dfrac{5}{7} \right|$.

$$\left| -4\dfrac{1}{7} \right| + \left| -\dfrac{5}{7} \right| = 4\dfrac{1}{7} + \dfrac{5}{7} \qquad \text{Find the absolute values.}$$

$$= 4 + \dfrac{1}{7} + \dfrac{5}{7} \qquad \text{Write } 4\dfrac{1}{7} \text{ as } 4 + \dfrac{1}{7}.$$

$$= 4 + \dfrac{6}{7}, \text{ or } 4\dfrac{6}{7} \qquad \text{Add fractions and simplify.}$$

Because $-4\dfrac{1}{7}$ and $-\dfrac{5}{7}$ are both negative, use a negative sign in the difference.

▶ So, $-4\dfrac{1}{7} - \dfrac{5}{7} = -4\dfrac{6}{7}$.   **Reasonable?** $-4\dfrac{6}{7} \approx -5$ ✔

Try It **Find the difference. Write your answer in simplest form.**

1. $\dfrac{1}{3} - \left(-\dfrac{1}{3}\right)$ **2.** $-3\dfrac{1}{3} - \dfrac{2}{3}$ **3.** $4 - 5\dfrac{1}{2}$

EXAMPLE 2 **Subtracting Rational Numbers**

Find 2.4 − 5.6.

Rewrite the difference as a sum by adding the opposite.

$$2.4 - 5.6 = 2.4 + (-5.6)$$

Because the signs are different and $|-5.6| > |2.4|$, subtract $|2.4|$ from $|-5.6|$.

$$|-5.6| - |2.4| = 5.6 - 2.4 \qquad \text{Find the absolute values.}$$
$$= 3.2 \qquad \text{Subtract.}$$

Because $|-5.6| > |2.4|$, use the sign of -5.6.

▷ So, $2.4 - 5.6 = -3.2$.

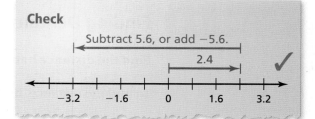

Check

Subtract 5.6, or add −5.6.

2.4

✓

−3.2   −1.6   0   1.6   3.2

Try It **Find the difference.**

4. $-2.1 - 3.9$ **5.** $-8.8 - (-8.8)$ **6.** $0.45 - (-0.05)$

EXAMPLE 3 **Using Properties of Addition**

Evaluate $-1\frac{3}{8} - 8\frac{1}{2} - \left(-6\frac{7}{8}\right)$.

Use properties of addition to group the mixed numbers that include fractions with the same denominator.

$$-1\frac{3}{8} - 8\frac{1}{2} - \left(-6\frac{7}{8}\right) = -1\frac{3}{8} + \left(-8\frac{1}{2}\right) + 6\frac{7}{8} \qquad \text{Rewrite as a sum of terms.}$$

$$= -1\frac{3}{8} + 6\frac{7}{8} + \left(-8\frac{1}{2}\right) \qquad \text{Comm. Prop. of Add.}$$

$$= 5\frac{1}{2} + \left(-8\frac{1}{2}\right) \qquad \text{Add } -1\frac{3}{8} \text{ and } 6\frac{7}{8}.$$

$$= -3 \qquad \text{Add } 5\frac{1}{2} \text{ and } -8\frac{1}{2}.$$

▷ So, $-1\frac{3}{8} - 8\frac{1}{2} - \left(-6\frac{7}{8}\right) = -3$.

Try It **Evaluate the expression. Write fractions in simplest form.**

7. $-2 - \frac{2}{5} + 1\frac{3}{5}$ **8.** $7.8 - 3.3 - (-1.2) + 4.3$

 **Key Idea**

Distance between Numbers on a Number Line

Words The distance between any two numbers on a number line is the absolute value of the difference of the numbers.

Model

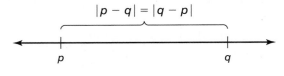

$$|p - q| = |q - p|$$

EXAMPLE 4 **Finding Distance on a Number Line**

Find the distance between $-\frac{1}{3}$ and -2 on a number line.

To find the distance, find the absolute value of the difference of the numbers.

$$\left| -2 - \left(-\frac{1}{3} \right) \right| = \left| -2 + \frac{1}{3} \right| \qquad \text{Add the opposite of } -\frac{1}{3}.$$

$$= \left| -1\frac{2}{3} \right| \qquad \text{Add } -2 \text{ and } \frac{1}{3}.$$

$$= 1\frac{2}{3} \qquad \text{Find the absolute value.}$$

▶ So, the distance between $-\frac{1}{3}$ and -2 is $1\frac{2}{3}$.

Try It Find the distance between the two numbers on a number line.

9. -3 and 9 **10.** -7.5 and -15.3 **11.** $1\frac{1}{2}$ and $-\frac{2}{3}$

 Self-Assessment for Concepts & Skills

Solve each exercise. Then rate your understanding of the success criteria in your journal.

12. WRITING Explain how to use a number line to find the difference of two rational numbers.

SUBTRACTING RATIONAL NUMBERS Find the difference. Use a number line to justify your answer.

13. $4.9 - 1.6$ **14.** $\frac{7}{8} - \left(-\frac{3}{4} \right)$ **15.** $\frac{1}{3} - 2\frac{1}{6}$

Connecting Concepts

1

Problem-Solving Strategies

Using an appropriate strategy will help you make sense of problems as you study the mathematics in this course. You can use the following strategies to solve problems that you encounter.

- Use a verbal model.
- Draw a diagram.
- Write an equation.

- Solve a simpler problem.
- Sketch a graph or number line.

- Make a table.
- Make a list.
- Break the problem into parts.

▶ Using the Problem-Solving Plan

1. A land surveyor uses a coordinate plane to draw a map of a park, where each unit represents 1 mile. The park is in the shape of a parallelogram with vertices $(-2.5, 1.5)$, $(-1.5, -2.25)$, $(2.75, -2.25)$, and $(1.75, 1.5)$. Find the area of the park.

 Understand the problem. You know the vertices of the parallelogram-shaped park and that each unit represents 1 mile. You are asked to find the area of the park.

 Make a plan. Use a coordinate plane to draw a map of the park. Then find the height and base length of the park. Find the area by using the formula for the area of a parallelogram.

 Solve and check. Use the plan to solve the problem. Then check your solution.

2. The diagram shows the height requirement for driving a go-cart. You are $5\frac{1}{4}$ feet tall. Write and solve an inequality to represent how much taller you must be to drive a go-cart.

Performance Task

Melting Matters

At the beginning of this chapter, you watched a STEAM Video called "Freezing Solids." You are now ready to complete the performance task related to this video, available at *BigIdeasMath.com*. Be sure to use the problem-solving plan as you work through the performance task.

▶ Review Vocabulary

Write the definition and give an example of each vocabulary term.

integers, *p. 3*

absolute value, *p. 4*

rational number, *p. 3*

additive inverse, *p. 11*

▶ Graphic Organizers

You can use a **Definition and Example Chart** to organize information about a concept. Here is an example of a Definition and Example Chart for the vocabulary term *absolute value*.

> Absolute value: the distance between a number and 0 on a number line
>
> Example
> $$|3| = 3$$
>
> Example
> $$|-5| = 5$$
>
> Example
> $$|0| = 0$$

Choose and complete a graphic organizer to help you study the concept.

1. integers

2. rational numbers

3. adding integers

4. Additive Inverse Property

5. adding rational numbers

6. subtracting integers

7. subtracting rational numbers

"I made a **Definition and Example Chart** to give my owner ideas for my birthday next week."

Chapter Self-Assessment

As you complete the exercises, use the scale below to rate your understanding of the success criteria in your journal.

1	2	3	4
I do not understand.	I can do it with help.	I can do it on my own.	I can teach someone else.

1.1 Rational Numbers *(pp. 3–8)*

Learning Target: Understand absolute values and ordering of rational numbers.

Find the absolute value.

1. $|3|$

2. $|-9|$

3. $\left|\dfrac{3}{4}\right|$

4. $|-5.2|$

5. $\left|-\dfrac{6}{7}\right|$

6. $|4.15|$

Copy and complete the statement using <, >, or =.

7. $|-2|$ ▨ -2

8. $\left|-\dfrac{1}{3}\right|$ ▨ $\left|-\dfrac{5}{6}\right|$

9. $-|1.7|$ ▨ -1.7

10. Order $|2.25|, |-1.5|, 1\dfrac{1}{4}, \left|2\dfrac{1}{2}\right|$, and -2 from least to greatest.

11. Your friend is in Death Valley, California, at an elevation of -282 feet. You are near the Mississippi River in Illinois at an elevation of 279 feet. Who is closer to sea level?

12. Give values for a and b so that $a < b$ and $|a| > |b|$.

13. The map shows the longitudes (in degrees) for Salvador, Brazil, and Nairobi, Kenya. Which city is closer to the Prime Meridian?

Salvador −38.5108°

Nairobi 36.8167°

Prime Meridian: 0°

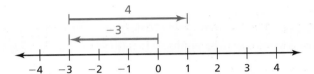

1.2 Adding Integers *(pp. 9–16)*

Learning Target: Find sums of integers.

14. Write an addition expression represented by the number line. Then find the sum.

Find the sum. Use a number line to verify your answer.

15. $-16 + (-11)$

16. $-15 + 5$

17. $100 + (-75)$

18. $-32 + (-2)$

19. $-2 + (-7) + 15$

20. $9 + (-14) + 3$

21. During the first play of a football game, you lose 3 yards. You gain 7 yards during the second play. What is your total gain of yards for these two plays?

22. Write an addition expression using integers that equals -2. Use a number line to justify your answer.

23. Describe a real-life situation that uses the sum of the integers -8 and 12.

1.3 Adding Rational Numbers *(pp. 17–22)*

Learning Target: Find sums of rational numbers.

Find the sum. Write fractions in simplest form.

24. $\dfrac{9}{10} + \left(-\dfrac{4}{5}\right)$

25. $-4\dfrac{5}{9} + \dfrac{8}{9}$

26. $-1.6 + (-2.4)$

27. Find the sum of $-4 + 6\dfrac{2}{5} + (-2.7)$. Explain each step.

28. You open a new bank account. The table shows the activity of your account for the first month. Positive numbers represent deposits and negative numbers represent withdrawals. What is your balance (in dollars) in the account at the end of the first month?

Date	Amount (dollars)
3/5	100
3/12	-12.25
3/16	25.82
3/21	14.95
3/29	-18.56

1.4 Subtracting Integers *(pp. 23–28)*

Learning Target: Find differences of integers.

Find the difference. Use a number line to verify your answer.

29. $8 - 18$ **30.** $-16 - (-5)$ **31.** $-18 - 7$ **32.** $-12 - (-27)$

33. Your score on a game show is -300. You answer the final question incorrectly, so you lose 400 points. What is your final score?

34. Oxygen has a boiling point of $-183°C$ and a melting point of $-219°C$. What is the temperature difference of the melting point and the boiling point?

35. In one month, you earn \$16 for mowing the lawn, \$15 for babysitting, and \$20 for allowance. You spend \$12 at the movie theater. How much more money do you need to buy a \$45 video game?

36. Write a subtraction expression using integers that equals -6.

37. Write two negative integers whose difference is positive.

1.5 Subtracting Rational Numbers *(pp. 29–36)*

Learning Target: Find differences of rational numbers and find distances between numbers on a number line.

Find the difference. Write fractions in simplest form.

38. $-\dfrac{5}{12} - \dfrac{3}{10}$ **39.** $3\dfrac{3}{4} - \dfrac{7}{8}$ **40.** $3.8 - (-7.45)$

41. Find the distance between -3.71 and -2.59 on a number line.

42. A turtle is $20\dfrac{5}{6}$ inches below the surface of a pond. It dives to a depth of $32\dfrac{1}{4}$ inches. What is the change in the turtle's position?

43. The lowest temperature ever recorded on Earth was $-89.2°C$ at Soviet Vostok Station in Antarctica. The highest temperature ever recorded was $56.7°C$ at Greenland Ranch in California. What is the difference between the highest and lowest recorded temperatures?

Find the absolute value.

1. $\left| -\dfrac{4}{5} \right|$

2. $\left| 6.43 \right|$

3. $\left| -22 \right|$

Copy and complete the statement using <, >, or =.

4. $4 \quad\boxed{}\quad \left| -8 \right|$

5. $\left| -7 \right| \quad\boxed{}\quad -12$

6. $-7 \quad\boxed{}\quad \left| 3 \right|$

Add or subtract. Write fractions in simplest form.

7. $-6 + (-11)$

8. $2 - (-9)$

9. $-\dfrac{4}{9} + \left(-\dfrac{23}{18} \right)$

10. $\dfrac{17}{12} - \left(-\dfrac{1}{8} \right)$

11. $9.2 + (-2.8)$

12. $2.86 - 12.1$

13. Write an addition expression and write a subtraction expression represented by the number line. Then evaluate the expressions.

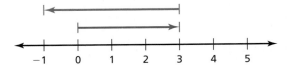

14. The table shows your scores, relative to *par*, for nine holes of golf. What is your total score for the nine holes?

Hole	1	2	3	4	5	6	7	8	9
Score	+1	−2	−1	0	−1	+3	−1	−3	+1

15. The elevation of a fish is −27 feet. The fish descends 32 feet, and then rises 14 feet. What is its new elevation?

16. The table shows the rainfall (in inches) for three months compared to the yearly average. Is the total rainfall for the three-month period greater than or less than the yearly average? Explain.

October	November	December
−0.86	2.56	−1.24

17. Bank Account A has $750.92, and Bank Account B has $675.44. Account A changes by –$216.38, and Account B changes by −$168.49. Which account has the greater balance? Explain.

18. On January 1, you recorded the lowest temperature as 23°F and the highest temperature as 6°C. A formula for converting from degrees Fahrenheit F to degrees Celsius C is $C = \dfrac{5}{9}F - \dfrac{160}{9}$. What is the temperature range (in degrees Celsius) for January 1?

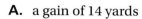

1. A football team gains 2 yards on the first play, loses 5 yards on the second play, loses 3 yards on the third play, and gains 4 yards on the fourth play. What is the team's total gain or loss?

   A. a gain of 14 yards   B. a gain of 2 yards

   C. a loss of 2 yards   D. a loss of 14 yards

2. Which expression is *not* equal to 0?

   F. $5 - 5$ G. $-7 + 7$

   H. $6 - (-6)$ I. $-8 - (-8)$

3. What is the value of the expression?

   $$\left| -2 - (-2.5) \right|$$

   A. -4.5 B. -0.5

   C. 0.5 D. 4.5

4. What is the value of the expression?

   $$17 - (-8)$$

5. What is the distance between the two numbers on the number line?

   F. $-2\frac{1}{8}$ G. $-1\frac{3}{8}$

   H. $1\frac{3}{8}$ I. $2\frac{1}{8}$

6. What is the value of the expression when $a = 8$, $b = 3$, and $c = 6$?

$$\left| a^2 - 2ac + 5b \right|$$

A. -65 **B.** -17

C. 17 **D.** 65

7. What is the value of the expression?

$$-9.74 + (-2.23)$$

8. Four friends are playing a game using the spinner shown. Each friend starts with a score of 0 and then spins four times. When you spin blue, you add the number to your score. When you spin red, you subtract the number from your score. The highest score after four spins wins. Each friend's spins are shown. Which spins belong to the winner?

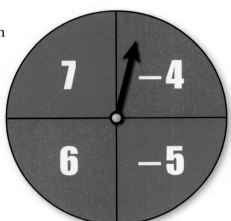

F. $6, 7, 7, 6$

G. $-4, -4, 7, -5$

H. $6, -5, -4, 7$

I. $-5, 6, -5, 6$

9. What number belongs in the box to make the equation true?

$$3\frac{1}{2} \div 5\frac{2}{3} = \frac{7}{2} \times \boxed{}$$

A. $\dfrac{3}{17}$ **B.** $\dfrac{3}{2}$

C. $\dfrac{17}{3}$ **D.** $\dfrac{13}{2}$

10. What is the value of the expression?

$$\frac{5.2 - 2.25}{0.05}$$

F. -346 **G.** 0.59

H. 5.9 **I.** 59

11. You leave school and walk 1.237 miles west. Your friend leaves school and walks 0.56 mile east. How far apart are you and your friend?

    A. 0.677 mile   **B.** 0.69272 mile

    C. 1.293 miles   **D.** 1.797 miles

12. Which property does the equation represent?

$$-80 + 30 + (-30) = -80 + [30 + (-30)]$$

    F. Commutative Property of Addition

    G. Associative Property of Addition

    H. Additive Inverse Property

    I. Addition Property of Zero

13. The values of which two points have the greatest sum?

    A. R and S **B.** R and U

    C. S and T **D.** T and U

14. Consider the number line shown.

    Part A   Use the number line to explain how to add -2 and -3.

    Part B   Use the number line to explain how to subtract 5 from 2.

15. Which expression represents a *negative* value?

    F. $2 - \left| -7 + 3 \right|$ **G.** $\left| -12 + 9 \right|$

    H. $\left| 5 \right| + \left| 11 \right|$ **I.** $\left| 8 - 14 \right|$

2 Multiplying and Dividing Rational Numbers

Chapter Learning Target:
Understand multiplying and dividing rational numbers.

Chapter Success Criteria:
- ▨ I can explain the rules for multiplying integers.
- ▨ I can explain the rules for dividing integers.
- ▪ I can evaluate expressions involving rational numbers.
- ▪ I can solve real-life problems involving multiplication and division of rational numbers.

STEAM Video: "Carpenter or Joiner"

Carpenter or Joiner

Carpenters and joiners must be precise with their measurements when building structures. In what other real-life situations must measurements be precise?

Watch the STEAM Video "Carpenter or Joiner." Then answer the following questions.

1. Robert says that changes in water content cause wood to shrink or expand *across* the grain more than *along* the grain. What does this mean?

2. Describe how you can cut a log so that the pieces shrink in different ways as they dry out.

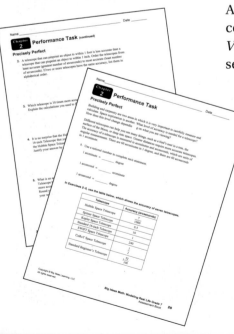

Precisely Perfect

After completing this chapter, you will be able to use the concepts you learned to answer the questions in the *STEAM Video Performance Task*. You will be given the accuracies of seven telescopes. For example:

Accuracy (arcseconds)

Hubble Space Telescope: $\dfrac{7}{1000}$

Kepler Space Telescope: 10

Standard Beginner's Telescope: $1\dfrac{52}{100}$

You will be asked to compare the accuracies of the telescopes. Why do different telescopes have different accuracies?

Getting Ready for Chapter

Chapter Exploration

1. Work with a partner. Use integer counters to find each product.

   a. $(+3) \times (-2)$

   $(+3) \times (-2)$
   Add 3 groups of -2.

   $(+3) \times (-2) = $ ____

   b. $(-2) \times (-2)$

   $(-2) \times (-2)$
   Remove 2 groups of -2.

   $(-2) \times (-2) = $ ____

   Start with enough zero pairs so
   you can remove 2 groups of -2.

   c. $(-2) \times (+3)$

   $(-2) \times (+3)$
   Remove 2 groups of 3.

   $(-2) \times (+3) = $ ____

   Start with enough zero pairs so
   you can remove 2 groups of 3.

Work with a partner. Use integer counters to find the product.

   2. $(+3) \times (+2)$ **3.** $(+3) \times (-1)$ **4.** $(+2) \times (-4)$

   5. $(-3) \times (+2)$ **6.** $(-2) \times (-3)$ **7.** $(-1) \times (-4)$

   8. $(-1) \times (-2)$ **9.** $(+3) \times (+1)$ **10.** $(-3) \times (-2)$

   11. $(-2) \times (+2)$ **12.** $(-2) \times (+4)$ **13.** $(-4) \times (-2)$

14. **MP MAKE CONJECTURES** Use your results in Exercises 1–13 to determine the
    sign of each product.

    a. negative integer and a positive integer

    b. two negative integers

    c. two positive integers

Vocabulary

**The following vocabulary terms are defined in this chapter. Think about what each
term might mean and record your thoughts.**

terminating decimal   repeating decimal   complex fraction

2.1 Multiplying Integers

Learning Target: Find products of integers.

Success Criteria:
- I can explain the rules for multiplying integers.
- I can find products of integers with the same sign.
- I can find products of integers with different signs.

EXPLORATION 1

Understanding Products Involving Negative Integers

Work with a partner.

a. The number line and integer counters model the product $3 \cdot 2$. How can you find $3 \cdot (-2)$? Explain.

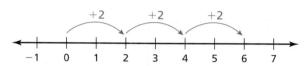

b. Use the tables to find $-3 \cdot 2$ and $-3 \cdot (-2)$. Explain your reasoning.

2	•	2	=	4
1	•	2	=	2
0	•	2	=	0
−1	•	2	=	
−2	•	2	=	
−3	•	2	=	

−3	•	3	=	−9
−3	•	2	=	−6
−3	•	1	=	−3
−3	•	0	=	
−3	•	−1	=	
−3	•	−2	=	

c. **INDUCTIVE REASONING** Complete the table. Then write general rules for multiplying (i) two integers with the same sign and (ii) two integers with different signs.

Expression	Type of Product	Product	Product: Positive or Negative
$3 \cdot 2$	Integers with the same sign		
$3 \cdot (-2)$			
$-3 \cdot 2$			
$-3 \cdot (-2)$			
$6 \cdot 3$			
$2 \cdot (-5)$			
$-6 \cdot 5$			
$-5 \cdot (-3)$			

Math Practice

Construct Arguments

Construct an argument that you can use to convince a friend of the rules you wrote in Exploration 1(c).

Consider the following methods for evaluating $3(-2 + 4)$.

Evaluate in parentheses:

$$3(-2 + 4) = 3(2)$$
$$= 6$$

Use the Distributive Property:

$$3(-2 + 4) = 3(-2) + 3(4)$$
$$= ? + 12$$

For the Distributive Property to be true, $3(-2)$ must equal -6. This leads to the following rules for multiplying integers.

 Key Ideas

Multiplying Integers with the Same Sign

Words   The product of two integers with the same sign is positive.

Numbers $2 \cdot 3 = 6$ $-2 \cdot (-3) = 6$

Multiplying Integers with Different Signs

Words   The product of two integers with different signs is negative.

Numbers $2 \cdot (-3) = -6$ $-2 \cdot 3 = -6$

EXAMPLE 1   **Multiplying Integers**

Find each product.

a. $-5 \cdot (-6)$

The integers have the same sign.

$$-5 \cdot (-6) = 30$$

The product is positive.

▷   The product is 30.

b. $3(-4)$

The integers have different signs.

$$3(-4) = -12$$

The product is negative.

▷   The product is -12.

Try It   **Find the product.**

1. $5 \cdot 5$ **2.** $-1(-9)$ **3.** $-7 \cdot (-8)$

4. $12 \cdot (-2)$ **5.** $4(-6)$ **6.** $-25(0)$

 **EXAMPLE 2** **Evaluating Expressions**

The expression $(-2)^2$ indicates to multiply the number in parentheses, -2, by itself.

The expression -2^2, however, indicates to find the opposite of 2^2.

a. Find $(-2)^2$.

$$(-2)^2 = (-2) \cdot (-2) \qquad \text{Write } (-2)^2 \text{ as repeated multiplication.}$$
$$= 4 \qquad \text{Multiply.}$$

b. Find -2^2.

$$-2^2 = -(2 \cdot 2) \qquad \text{Write } 2^2 \text{ as repeated multiplication.}$$
$$= -4 \qquad \text{Multiply 2 and 2.}$$

c. Find $-2 \cdot 17 \cdot (-5)$.

$$-2 \cdot 17 \cdot (-5) = -2 \cdot (-5) \cdot 17 \qquad \text{Commutative Property of Multiplication}$$
$$= 10 \cdot 17 \qquad \text{Multiply } -2 \text{ and } -5.$$
$$= 170 \qquad \text{Multiply 10 and 17.}$$

Remember

Use order of operations when evaluating an expression.

d. Find $-6(-3 + 4) + 6$.

$$-6(-3 + 4) + 6 = -6(1) + 6 \qquad \text{Perform operation in parentheses.}$$
$$= -6 + 6 \qquad \text{Multiplication Property of 1}$$
$$= 0 \qquad \text{Additive Inverse Property}$$

Try It **Evaluate the expression.**

7. $8 \cdot (-15) \cdot 0$ **8.** $24 - 3^3$ **9.** $10 - 7(3 - 5)$

Self-Assessment for Concepts & Skills

Solve each exercise. Then rate your understanding of the success criteria in your journal.

10. WRITING What can you conclude about two integers whose product is (a) positive and (b) negative?

EVALUATING AN EXPRESSION **Evaluate the expression.**

11. $4(-8)$ **12.** $-5(-7)$ **13.** $12 - 3^2 \cdot (-2)$

MP REASONING **Tell whether the statement is *true* or *false*. Explain your reasoning.**

14. The product of three positive integers is positive.

15. The product of three negative integers is positive.

 **EXAMPLE 3** **Modeling Real Life**

You solve a number puzzle on your phone. You start with 250 points. You finish the puzzle in 8 minutes 45 seconds and make 3 mistakes. What is your score?

Each mistake = -50 points

Each second under 10 min = 1 bonus point

 **Understand the problem.** You are given ways to gain points and lose points when completing a puzzle. You are asked to find your score after finishing the puzzle.

Make a plan. Use a verbal model to solve the problem. Find the sum of the starting points, mistake penalties, and time bonus.

Solve and check.

| Score | = | Starting points | + | Number of mistakes | · | Penalty per mistake | + | Time bonus |

$$= 250 + 3(-50) + 75$$

10 min − 8 min 45 sec = 1 min 15 sec
= 75 sec

$$= 250 + (-150) + 75$$

Another Method

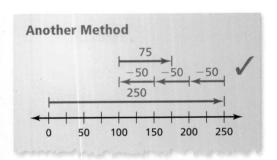

$$= 100 + 75$$

$$= 175$$

> So, your score is 175 points.

 Self-Assessment for Problem Solving

Solve each exercise. Then rate your understanding of the success criteria in your journal.

16. On a mountain, the temperature decreases by 18°F for each 5000-foot increase in elevation. At 7000 feet, the temperature is 41°F. What is the temperature at 22,000 feet? Justify your answer.

Player	Coins	Time
A	31	0:02:03
B	18	0:01:55
C	24	0:01:58
D	27	0:02:01
E		

17. **DIG DEEPER!** Players in a racing game earn 3 points for each coin and lose 5 points for each second later than the fastest time. The table shows results of a race. Can Player E finish with the third-best time and have the second-most points? Justify your answer.

? Go to *BigIdeasMath.com* to get HELP with solving the exercises.

▶ Review & Refresh

Find the distance between the two numbers on a number line.

1. -4.3 and 0.8
2. -7.7 and -6.4
3. $-2\frac{3}{5}$ and -1

Divide.

4. $27 \div 9$
5. $48 \div 6$
6. $56 \div 4$
7. $153 \div 8$

8. What is the prime factorization of 84?

   A. $2^2 \times 3^2$ **B.** $2^3 \times 7$ **C.** $3^3 \times 7$ **D.** $2^2 \times 3 \times 7$

▶▶ Concepts, Skills, & Problem Solving

MP CHOOSE TOOLS Use a number line or integer counters to find the product. (See Exploration 1, p. 49.)

9. $2(-4)$
10. $-6(3)$
11. $4(-5)$

MULTIPLYING INTEGERS Find the product.

12. $6 \cdot 4$
13. $7(-3)$
14. $-2(8)$
15. $-3(-4)$

16. $-6 \cdot 7$
17. $3 \cdot 9$
18. $8 \cdot (-5)$
19. $-1 \cdot (-12)$

20. $-5(10)$
21. $-13(0)$
22. $-9 \cdot 9$
23. $15(-2)$

24. $-10 \cdot 11$
25. $-6 \cdot (-13)$
26. $7(-14)$
27. $-11 \cdot (-11)$

28. **MP MODELING REAL LIFE** You burn 10 calories each minute you jog. What integer represents the change in your calories after you jog for 20 minutes?

29. **MP MODELING REAL LIFE** In a four-year period, about 80,000 acres of coastal wetlands in the United States are lost each year. What integer represents the total change in coastal wetlands?

EVALUATING EXPRESSIONS Evaluate the expression.

30. $(-4)^2$
31. -6^2
32. $-5 \cdot 3 \cdot (-2)$

33. $3 \cdot (-12) \cdot 0$
34. $-5(-7)(-20)$
35. $5 - 8^2$

36. $-5^2 \cdot 4$
37. $-2 \cdot (-3)^3$
38. $2 + 1 \cdot (-7 + 5)$

39. $4 - (-2)^3$
40. $4 \cdot (25 \cdot 3^2)$
41. $-4(3^2 - 8) + 1$

MP YOU BE THE TEACHER Your friend evaluates the expression. Is your friend correct? Explain your reasoning.

42.

$$-2(-7) = -14$$

43.

$$-10^2 = -100$$

MP PATTERNS Find the next two numbers in the pattern.

44. $-12, 60, -300, 1500, \ldots$

45. $7, -28, 112, -448, \ldots$

46. **MP PROBLEM SOLVING** In a scavenger hunt, each team earns 25 points for each item that they find. Each team loses 15 points for every minute after 4:00 P.M. that they report to the city park. The table shows the number of items found by each team and the time that each team reported to the park. Which team wins the scavenger hunt? Justify your answer.

Team	Items	Time
A	13	4:03 P.M.
B	15	4:07 P.M.
C	11	3:56 P.M.
D	12	4:01 P.M.

47. **MP REASONING** The height of an airplane during a landing is given by $22,000 + (-480t)$, where t is the time in minutes. Estimate how many minutes it takes the plane to land. Explain your reasoning.

48. **MP PROBLEM SOLVING** The table shows the price of a bluetooth speaker each month for 4 months.

Month	Price (dollars)
June	165
July	$165 + (-12)$
August	$165 + 2(-12)$
September	$165 + 3(-12)$

a. Describe the change in the price of the speaker.

b. The table at the right shows the amount of money you save each month. When do you have enough money saved to buy the speaker? Explain your reasoning.

Amount Saved	
June	$35
July	$55
August	$45
September	$18

49. **DIG DEEPER!** Two integers, a and b, have a product of 24. What is the least possible sum of a and b?

50. **MP NUMBER SENSE** Consider two integers p and q. Explain why $p \times (-q) = (-p) \times q = -pq$.

2.2 Dividing Integers

Learning Target: Find quotients of integers.

Success Criteria:
- I can explain the rules for dividing integers.
- I can find quotients of integers with the same sign.
- I can find quotients of integers with different signs.

EXPLORATION 1

Understanding Quotients Involving Negative Integers

Work with a partner.

a. Discuss the relationship between multiplication and division with your partner.

b. **INDUCTIVE REASONING** Complete the table. Then write general rules for dividing (i) two integers with the same sign and (ii) two integers with different signs.

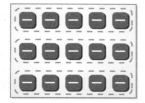

Math Practice

Recognize Usefulness of Tools

Can you use number lines or integer counters to reach the same conclusions as in part (b)? Explain why or why not.

Expression	Type of Quotient	Quotient	Quotient: Positive, Negative, or Zero
$-15 \div 3$	Integers with different signs		
$12 \div (-6)$			
$10 \div (-2)$			
$-6 \div 2$			
$-12 \div (-12)$			
$-21 \div (-7)$			
$0 \div (-15)$			
$0 \div 4$			
$-5 \div 4$			
$5 \div (-4)$			

c. Find the values of $-\dfrac{8}{4}$, $\dfrac{-8}{4}$, and $\dfrac{8}{-4}$. What do you notice? Is this true for $-\dfrac{a}{b}$, $\dfrac{-a}{b}$, and $\dfrac{a}{-b}$ when a and b are integers? Explain.

d. Is every quotient of integers a rational number? Explain your reasoning.

2.2 Lesson

 Key Ideas

Remember

Division by 0 is undefined.

Dividing Integers with the Same Sign

Words The quotient of two integers with the same sign is positive.

Numbers $8 \div 2 = 4$ $\qquad$ $-8 \div (-2) = 4$

Dividing Integers with Different Signs

Words The quotient of two integers with different signs is negative.

Numbers $8 \div (-2) = -4$ $\qquad$ $-8 \div 2 = -4$

EXAMPLE 1 **Dividing Integers with the Same Sign**

Find $-18 \div (-6)$.

> The integers have the same sign.

$$-18 \div (-6) = 3$$

> The quotient is positive.

▶ The quotient is 3.

Try It Find the quotient.

1. $14 \div 2$ $\qquad$ **2.** $-32 \div (-4)$ $\qquad$ **3.** $-40 \div (-8)$

EXAMPLE 2 **Dividing Integers with Different Signs**

Find each quotient.

   a. $75 \div (-25)$ $\qquad\qquad\qquad$ **b.** $\dfrac{-54}{6}$

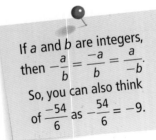

If a and b are integers, then $-\dfrac{a}{b} = \dfrac{-a}{b} = \dfrac{a}{-b}$. So, you can also think of $\dfrac{-54}{6}$ as $-\dfrac{54}{6} = -9$.

> The integers have different signs.

$$75 \div (-25) = -3 \qquad\qquad \frac{-54}{6} = -9$$

> The quotient is negative.

▶ The quotient is -3. $\qquad\qquad$ ▶ The quotient is -9.

Try It Find the quotient.

4. $0 \div (-6)$ $\qquad$ **5.** $\dfrac{-49}{7}$ $\qquad$ **6.** $\dfrac{21}{-3}$

56 **Chapter 2** Multiplying and Dividing Rational Numbers

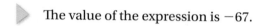

EXAMPLE 3 **Evaluating Expressions**

Find the value of each expression when $x = 8$ and $y = -4$.

a. $\dfrac{x}{2y}$

$$\dfrac{x}{2y} = \dfrac{8}{2(-4)}$$ Substitute 8 for x and -4 for y.

$$= \dfrac{8}{-8}$$ Multiply 2 and -4.

$$= -1$$ Divide 8 by -8.

▷ The value of the expression is -1.

b. $-x^2 + 12 \div y$

$$-x^2 + 12 \div y = -8^2 + 12 \div (-4)$$ Substitute 8 for x and -4 for y.

$$= -(8 \cdot 8) + 12 \div (-4)$$ Write 8^2 as repeated multiplication.

$$= -64 + 12 \div (-4)$$ Multiply 8 and 8.

$$= -64 + (-3)$$ Divide 12 by -4.

$$= -67$$ Add.

▷ The value of the expression is -67.

Try It Evaluate the expression when $a = -18$ and $b = -6$.

7. $a \div b$ **8.** $\dfrac{a + 6}{3}$ **9.** $\dfrac{b^2}{a} + 4$

 Self-Assessment for Concepts & Skills

Solve each exercise. Then rate your understanding of the success criteria in your journal.

10. WRITING What can you conclude about two integers whose quotient is (a) positive, (b) negative, or (c) zero?

DIVIDING INTEGERS Find the quotient.

11. $-12 \div 4$ **12.** $\dfrac{-6}{-2}$ **13.** $15 \div (-3)$

14. WHICH ONE DOESN'T BELONG? Which expression does *not* belong with the other three? Explain your reasoning.

$$\dfrac{10}{-5} \qquad \dfrac{-10}{5} \qquad \dfrac{-10}{-5} \qquad -\dfrac{10}{5}$$

EXAMPLE 4 **Modeling Real Life**

You measure the height of the tide using the support beams of a pier. What is the mean hourly change in the height?

To find the mean hourly change in the height of the tide, divide the change in the height by the elapsed time.

59 inches at 2 P.M. →
8 inches at 8 P.M. →

$$\text{mean hourly change} = \frac{\text{final height} - \text{initial height}}{\text{elapsed time}}$$

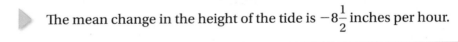

Math Practice

Communicate Precisely

Explain to a classmate why the change in height is represented by $8 - 59$ rather than $59 - 8$.

> The elapsed time from 2 P.M. to 8 P.M. is 6 hours.

$= \dfrac{8 - 59}{6}$ Substitute.

$= \dfrac{-51}{6}$ Subtract.

$= -8\dfrac{1}{2}$ Divide.

▷ The mean change in the height of the tide is $-8\dfrac{1}{2}$ inches per hour.

 Self-Assessment *for Problem Solving*

Solve each exercise. Then rate your understanding of the success criteria in your journal.

15. A female grizzly bear weighs 500 pounds. After hibernating for 6 months, she weighs only 350 pounds. What is the mean monthly change in weight?

16. The table shows the change in the number of crimes committed in a city each year for 4 years. What is the mean yearly change in the number of crimes?

Year	2014	2015	2016	2017
Change in Crimes	215	−321	−185	95

17. **DIG DEEPER!** At a restaurant, when a customer buys 4 pretzels, the fifth pretzel is free. Soft pretzels cost $3.90 each. You order 12 soft pretzels. What is your mean cost per pretzel?

2.2 Practice

? Go to *BigIdeasMath.com* to get HELP with solving the exercises.

▶ Review & Refresh

Find the product.

1. $8 \cdot 10$
2. $-6(9)$
3. $4(7)$
4. $-9(-8)$

Order the numbers from least to greatest.

5. $28\%, \frac{1}{4}, 0.24$
6. $42\%, 0.45, \frac{2}{5}$
7. $\frac{7}{10}, 0.69, 71\%, \frac{9}{10}, 0.84$

Write an addition expression and write a subtraction expression represented by the number line. Then evaluate the expressions.

8.

9.
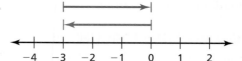

▶▶ Concepts, Skills, & Problem Solving

MP CHOOSE TOOLS Complete the table. (See Exploration 1, p. 55.)

	Expression	Type of Quotient	Quotient	Quotient: Positive, Negative, or Zero
10.	$14 \div (-2)$			
11.	$-24 \div 12$			
12.	$-55 \div (-5)$			

DIVIDING INTEGERS Find the quotient, if possible.

13. $4 \div (-2)$
14. $21 \div (-7)$
15. $-20 \div 4$
16. $-18 \div (-3)$

17. $\frac{-14}{2}$
18. $\frac{0}{6}$
19. $\frac{-15}{-5}$
20. $\frac{54}{-9}$

21. $-\frac{33}{11}$
22. $-49 \div (-7)$
23. $0 \div (-2)$
24. $\frac{60}{-6}$

25. $\frac{-56}{14}$
26. $\frac{18}{0}$
27. $-\frac{65}{5}$
28. $\frac{-84}{-7}$

MP YOU BE THE TEACHER Your friend finds the quotient. Is your friend correct? Explain your reasoning.

29.
$$\frac{-63}{-9} = -7$$

30.
$$0 \div (-5) = -5$$

31. **MP** **MODELING REAL LIFE** You read 105 pages of a novel over 7 days. What is the mean number of pages you read each day?

USING ORDER OF OPERATIONS **Evaluate the expression.**

32. $-8 - 14 \div 2 + 5$

33. $24 \div (-4) + (-2) \cdot (-5)$

EVALUATING EXPRESSIONS **Evaluate the expression when** $x = 10$, $y = -2$, **and** $z = -5$.

34. $x \div y$

35. $12 \div (3y)$

36. $\dfrac{2z}{y}$

37. $\dfrac{-x + y}{6}$

38. $100 \div (-z^2)$

39. $\dfrac{10y^2}{z}$

40. $\left| \dfrac{xz}{-y} \right|$

41. $\dfrac{-x^2 + 6z}{y}$

42. **MP** **PATTERNS** Find the next two numbers in the pattern $-128, 64, -32, 16, \dots$. Explain your reasoning.

43. **MP** **MODELING REAL LIFE** The Detroit-Windsor Tunnel is an underwater highway that connects the cities of Detroit, Michigan, and Windsor, Ontario. How many times deeper is the roadway than the bottom of the ship?

0 ft
−15 ft
Detroit-Windsor Tunnel
−75 ft
Not drawn to scale

44. **MP** **MODELING REAL LIFE** A snowboarder descends from an elevation of 2253 feet to an elevation of 1011 feet in 3 minutes. What is the mean change in elevation per minute?

45. **MP** **REASONING** The table shows a golfer's scores relative to *par* for three out of four rounds of a tournament.

   a. What was the golfer's mean score per round for the first 3 rounds?

   b. The golfer's goal for the tournament is to have a mean score no greater than -3. Describe how the golfer can achieve this goal.

Scorecard	
Round 1	+1
Round 2	−4
Round 3	−3
Round 4	?

46. **MP** **PROBLEM SOLVING** The regular admission price for an amusement park is $72. For a group of 15 or more, the admission price is reduced by $25 per person. How many people need to be in a group to save $500?

47. **DIG DEEPER!** Write a set of five different integers that has a mean of -10. Explain how you found your answer.

2.3 Converting Between Fractions and Decimals

Learning Target: Convert between different forms of rational numbers.

Success Criteria:
- I can explain the difference between terminating and repeating decimals.
- I can write fractions and mixed numbers as decimals.
- I can write decimals as fractions and mixed numbers.

EXPLORATION 1

Analyzing Denominators of Decimal Fractions

Work with a partner.

a. Write each decimal as a fraction or mixed number.

   0.7   1.29   12.831   0.0041

b. What do the factors of the denominators of the fractions you wrote have in common? Is this always true for decimal fractions?

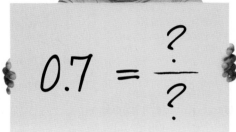

EXPLORATION 2

Exploring Decimal Representations

Work with a partner.

a. A fraction $\dfrac{a}{b}$ can be interpreted as $a \div b$. Use a calculator to convert each unit fraction to a decimal. Do some of the decimals look different than the others? Explain.

$$\frac{1}{2} \qquad \frac{1}{3} \qquad \frac{1}{4} \qquad \frac{1}{5}$$

$$\frac{1}{6} \qquad \frac{1}{7} \qquad \frac{1}{8}$$

$$\frac{1}{9} \qquad \frac{1}{10} \qquad \frac{1}{11} \qquad \frac{1}{12}$$

Math Practice

Use Technology to Explore

How do calculators help you learn about different types of decimals? How can you find decimal forms of fractions without using a calculator?

b. Compare and contrast the fractions in part (a) with the fractions you wrote in Exploration 1. What conclusions can you make?

c. Does every fraction have a decimal form that either *terminates* or *repeats*? Explain your reasoning.

Key Vocabulary 🔊

terminating decimal,
  p. 62
repeating decimal,
  p. 62

Because you can divide any integer by any nonzero integer, you can use long division to write fractions and mixed numbers as decimals. These decimals are rational numbers and will either *terminate* or *repeat*.

A **terminating decimal** is a decimal that ends.

$$1.5, -0.25, 10.824$$

A **repeating decimal** is a decimal that has a pattern that repeats.

$$-1.333\ldots = -1.\overline{3}$$
$$0.151515\ldots = 0.\overline{15}$$

Use *bar notation* to show which of the digits repeat.

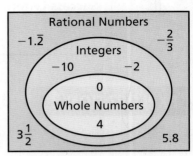

Rational Numbers

$-1.\overline{2}$ Integers $-\dfrac{2}{3}$

-10 -2

0

Whole Numbers

$3\dfrac{1}{2}$ 4

5.8

EXAMPLE 1 **Writing Fractions and Mixed Numbers as Decimals**

a. **Write $-2\dfrac{1}{4}$ as a decimal.**

Notice that $-2\dfrac{1}{4} = -\dfrac{9}{4}$.

Use long division to divide 9 by 4.

Divide 9 by 4.

$$\begin{array}{r} 2.25 \\ 4\overline{)9.00} \\ -8 \\ \hline 1\,0 \\ -8 \\ \hline 20 \\ -20 \\ \hline 0 \end{array}$$

The remainder is 0. So, it is a terminating decimal.

▷ So, $-2\dfrac{1}{4} = -2.25.$

Another Method
Use equivalent fractions.

$$\dfrac{1}{4} = \dfrac{1 \times 25}{4 \times 25} = \dfrac{25}{100}$$

$$\text{So, } -2\dfrac{1}{4} = -2\dfrac{25}{100}$$

$$= -2.25. \checkmark$$

b. **Write $\dfrac{5}{11}$ as a decimal.**

Use long division to divide 5 by 11.

Divide 5 by 11.

$$\begin{array}{r} 0.4545 \\ 11\overline{)5.0000} \\ -4\,4 \\ \hline 60 \\ -55 \\ \hline 50 \\ -44 \\ \hline 60 \\ -55 \\ \hline 5 \end{array}$$

The remainder repeats. So, it is a repeating decimal.

▷ So, $\dfrac{5}{11} = 0.\overline{45}.$

Try It **Write the fraction or mixed number as a decimal.**

1. $-\dfrac{6}{5}$ 2. $-7\dfrac{3}{8}$ 3. $-\dfrac{3}{11}$ 4. $1\dfrac{5}{27}$

Any terminating decimal can be written as a fraction whose denominator is a power of 10. You can often simplify the resulting fraction by *dividing out* any common factors, which is the same as removing the common factor from the numerator and denominator.

$$0.48 = \frac{48}{100} = \frac{48 \div 4}{100 \div 4} = \frac{12}{25} \quad \text{or} \quad 0.48 = \frac{48}{100} = \frac{12 \cdot \cancel{4}}{25 \cdot \cancel{4}} = \frac{12}{25}$$

EXAMPLE 2 ## Writing a Terminating Decimal as a Fraction

Write -0.26 as a fraction in simplest form.

$$-0.26 = -\frac{26}{100}$$

> Write the digits after the decimal point in the numerator.

> The last digit is in the hundredths place. So, use 100 in the denominator.

$$= -\frac{13 \cdot \cancel{2}}{50 \cdot \cancel{2}}$$ Divide out the common factor, 2.

$$= -\frac{13}{50}$$ Simplify.

> So, $-0.26 = -\dfrac{13}{50}$.

Reading
-0.26 is read as "negative twenty-six hundredths."

Try It Write the decimal as a fraction or mixed number in simplest form.

5. -0.3 **6.** 0.125 **7.** -3.1 **8.** -10.25

Self-Assessment *for Concepts & Skills*

Solve each exercise. Then rate your understanding of the success criteria in your journal.

9. WRITING Compare and contrast terminating decimals and repeating decimals.

WRITING A FRACTION OR MIXED NUMBER AS A DECIMAL Write the fraction or mixed number as a decimal.

10. $\dfrac{3}{16}$ **11.** $-\dfrac{7}{15}$ **12.** $6\dfrac{17}{20}$

WRITING A DECIMAL AS A FRACTION OR MIXED NUMBER Write the decimal as a fraction or mixed number in simplest form.

13. 0.6 **14.** -12.48 **15.** 0.408

EXAMPLE 3 **Modeling Real Life**

Creature	Elevation (kilometers)
Anglerfish	$-\dfrac{13}{10}$
Shark	$-\dfrac{2}{11}$
Squid	$-2\dfrac{1}{5}$
Whale	-0.8

The table shows the elevations of four sea creatures relative to sea level. Which of the sea creatures are deeper than the whale? Explain.

One way to compare the depths of the creatures is to use a number line. First, write each fraction or mixed number as a decimal.

$$-\frac{13}{10} = -1.3$$

$$-\frac{2}{11} = -0.\overline{18}$$

Divide 2 by 11.

$$-2\frac{1}{5} = -2\frac{2}{10} = -2.2$$

$$\begin{array}{r} 0.1818 \\ 11\overline{)2.0000} \\ -\,1\,1 \\ \hline 90 \\ -\,88 \\ \hline 20 \\ -\,11 \\ \hline 90 \\ -\,88 \\ \hline 2 \end{array}$$

The remainder repeats. So, it is a repeating decimal.

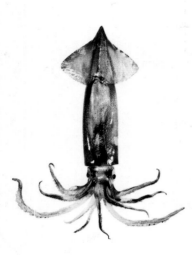

Then graph each decimal on a number line.

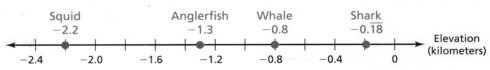

▶ Both -2.2 and -1.3 are less than -0.8. So, the squid and the anglerfish are deeper than the whale.

 Self-Assessment *for Problem Solving*

Solve each exercise. Then rate your understanding of the success criteria in your journal.

16. A box turtle hibernates in sand at an elevation of -1.625 feet. A spotted turtle hibernates at an elevation of $-1\dfrac{7}{12}$ feet. Which turtle hibernates deeper in the sand? How much deeper?

Elevation (miles)	
50.6	$50\dfrac{13}{25}$
$50\dfrac{8}{15}$	$\dfrac{155}{3}$

17. A *red sprite* is an electrical flash that occurs in Earth's upper atmosphere. The table shows the elevations of four red sprites. What is the range of the elevations?

2.3 Practice

▶ Review & Refresh

Find the quotient.

1. $12 \div (-6)$ **2.** $-48 \div 8$ **3.** $-42 \div (-7)$ **4.** $-33 \div (-3)$

Find the product.

5. $\begin{array}{r} 5.88 \\ \times\ \ 6 \end{array}$ **6.** $2.0035 \cdot 4$ **7.** 5.49×13.509 **8.** $\begin{array}{r} 1.0006 \\ \times\ 0.003 \end{array}$

9. Find the missing values in the ratio table. Then write the equivalent ratios.

Hours	2		$\frac{4}{3}$
Dollars Earned	18	72	

▶▶ Concepts, Skills, & Problem Solving

MP STRUCTURE Without dividing, determine whether the decimal form of the fraction *terminates* or *repeats*. **Explain.** (See Explorations 1 & 2, p. 61.)

10. $\frac{3}{8}$ **11.** $\frac{5}{7}$ **12.** $\frac{11}{40}$ **13.** $\frac{5}{24}$

WRITING A FRACTION OR MIXED NUMBER AS A DECIMAL Write the fraction or mixed number as a decimal.

14. $\frac{7}{8}$ **15.** $\frac{1}{11}$ **16.** $-3\frac{1}{2}$ **17.** $-\frac{7}{9}$

18. $-\frac{17}{40}$ **19.** $1\frac{5}{6}$ **20.** $4\frac{2}{15}$ **21.** $\frac{25}{24}$

22. $-\frac{13}{11}$ **23.** $-2\frac{17}{18}$ **24.** $-5\frac{7}{12}$ **25.** $8\frac{15}{22}$

26. **MP YOU BE THE TEACHER** Your friend writes $-\frac{7}{11}$ as a decimal. Is your friend correct? Explain your reasoning.

$$-\frac{7}{11} = -0.6\overline{3}$$

WRITING A DECIMAL AS A FRACTION OR MIXED NUMBER Write the decimal as a fraction or mixed number in simplest form.

27. -0.9 **28.** 0.45 **29.** -0.258 **30.** -0.312

31. -2.32 **32.** -1.64 **33.** 6.012 **34.** -12.405

35. **MP MODELING REAL LIFE** You find one quarter, two dimes, and two nickels.

    a. Write the dollar amount as a decimal.

    b. Write the dollar amount as a fraction or mixed number in simplest form.

COMPARING RATIONAL NUMBERS Copy and complete the statement using < or >.

36. $-4\frac{6}{10}$ ▢ -4.65

37. $-5\frac{3}{11}$ ▢ $-5.\overline{2}$

38. $-2\frac{13}{16}$ ▢ $-2\frac{11}{14}$

39. **MP MODELING REAL LIFE** Is the half pipe deeper than the skating bowl? Explain.

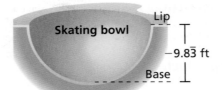

Half pipe — Lip, Base, $-9\frac{5}{6}$ ft

Skating bowl — Lip, Base, $-9.8\overline{3}$ ft

Player	Hits	At Bats
1	42	90
2	38	80

40. **MP MODELING REAL LIFE** In softball, a batting average is the number of hits divided by the number of times at bat. Does Player 1 or Player 2 have the greater batting average?

ORDERING RATIONAL NUMBERS Order the numbers from least to greatest.

41. $-\frac{3}{4}, 0.5, \frac{2}{3}, -\frac{7}{3}, 1.2$

42. $\frac{9}{5}, -2.5, -1.1, -\frac{4}{5}, 0.8$

43. $-1.4, -\frac{8}{5}, 0.6, -0.9, \frac{1}{4}$

44. $2.1, -\frac{6}{10}, -\frac{9}{4}, -0.75, \frac{5}{3}$

45. $-\frac{7}{2}, -2.8, -\frac{5}{4}, \frac{4}{3}, 1.3$

46. $-\frac{11}{5}, -2.4, 1.6, \frac{15}{10}, -2.25$

47. **MP MODELING REAL LIFE** The table shows the changes in the water level of a pond over several weeks. Order the numbers from least to greatest.

Week	1	2	3	4
Change (inches)	$-\frac{7}{5}$	$-1\frac{5}{11}$	-1.45	$-1\frac{91}{200}$

48. **OPEN-ENDED** Find one terminating decimal and one repeating decimal between $-\frac{1}{2}$ and $-\frac{1}{3}$.

49. **MP PROBLEM SOLVING** You miss 3 out of 10 questions on a science quiz and 4 out of 15 questions on a math quiz. On which quiz did you have a greater percentage of correct answers?

50. **CRITICAL THINKING** A hackberry tree has roots that reach a depth of $6\frac{5}{12}$ meters. The top of the tree is $18.2\overline{8}$ meters above the ground. Find the total height from the bottom of the roots to the top of the tree.

51. **DIG DEEPER!** Let a and b be integers.

a. When can $-\frac{1}{a}$ be written as a positive, repeating decimal?

b. When can $\frac{1}{ab}$ be written as a positive, terminating decimal?

2.4 Multiplying Rational Numbers

Learning Target: Find products of rational numbers.

Success Criteria:
- I can explain the rules for multiplying rational numbers.
- I can find products of rational numbers with the same sign.
- I can find products of rational numbers with different signs.

EXPLORATION 1

Finding Products of Rational Numbers

Work with a partner.

a. Write a multiplication expression represented by each area model. Then find the product.

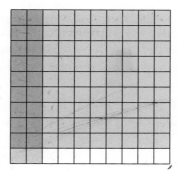 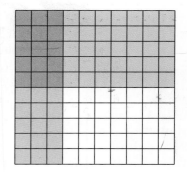

b. Complete the table.

	Expression	Product	Expression	Product
i.	0.2×0.9		-0.2×0.9	
ii.	$0.3(0.5)$		$0.3(-0.5)$	
iii.	$\dfrac{1}{4} \cdot \dfrac{1}{2}$		$\dfrac{1}{4} \cdot \left(-\dfrac{1}{2}\right)$	
iv.	$1.2(0.4)$		$-1.2(-0.4)$	
v.	$\dfrac{3}{10}\left(\dfrac{2}{5}\right)$		$-\dfrac{3}{10}\left(-\dfrac{2}{5}\right)$	
vi.	0.6×1.8		-0.6×1.8	
vii.	$1\dfrac{1}{4} \cdot 2\dfrac{1}{2}$		$-1\dfrac{1}{4} \cdot \left(-2\dfrac{1}{2}\right)$	

c. Do the rules for multiplying integers apply to all rational numbers? Explain your reasoning.

Math Practice

Consider Similar Problems

How is multiplying integers similar to multiplying other rational numbers? How is it different?

2.4 Lesson

 Key Idea

> When the signs of two numbers are different, their product is negative. When the signs of two numbers are the same, their product is positive.

Multiplying Rational Numbers

Words   To multiply rational numbers, use the same rules for signs as you used for multiplying integers.

Numbers $-\dfrac{2}{7} \cdot \dfrac{1}{3} = -\dfrac{2}{21}$ $-\dfrac{2}{7} \cdot \left(-\dfrac{1}{3}\right) = \dfrac{2}{21}$

EXAMPLE 1   **Multiplying Rational Numbers**

a.   **Find -2.5×3.6.**   **Estimate** $-2.5 \cdot 4 = -10$

Because the decimals have different signs, the product is negative. So, find the opposite of the product of 2.5 and 3.6.

Math Practice

Justify Conclusions
Explain each step in multiplying 2.5 and 3.6.

$$
\begin{array}{r}
2.5 \\
\times\, 3.6 \\
\hline
1\,5\,0 \\
7\,5\,0 \\
\hline
9.0\,0
\end{array}
$$

2.5 ←——— 1 decimal place
× 3.6 ←——— + 1 decimal place

9.0 0 ←——— 2 decimal places

▸ So, $-2.5 \times 3.6 = -9$.   **Reasonable?** $-9 \approx -10$ ✓

b.   **Find $-\dfrac{1}{3}\left(-2\dfrac{3}{4}\right)$.**   **Estimate** $-\dfrac{1}{3} \cdot (-3) = 1$

Because the numbers have the same sign, the product is positive. So, find the product of $\dfrac{1}{3}$ and $2\dfrac{3}{4}$.

$\dfrac{1}{3}\left(2\dfrac{3}{4}\right) = \dfrac{1}{3}\left(\dfrac{11}{4}\right)$ Write the mixed number as an improper fraction.

$= \dfrac{11}{12}$ Multiply the numerators and the denominators.

▸ So, $-\dfrac{1}{3}\left(-2\dfrac{3}{4}\right) = \dfrac{11}{12}$.   **Reasonable?** $\dfrac{11}{12} \approx 1$ ✓

Try It   Find the product. Write fractions in simplest form.

1. -5.1×1.8 **2.** $-6.3(-0.6)$ **3.** $-\dfrac{4}{5}\left(-\dfrac{2}{3}\right)$ **4.** $4\dfrac{1}{2} \cdot \left(-2\dfrac{1}{3}\right)$

The properties of multiplication you have used apply to all rational numbers. You can also write $-\dfrac{a}{b}$ as $\dfrac{-a}{b}$ or $\dfrac{a}{-b}$ when performing operations with rational numbers.

EXAMPLE 2 **Using Properties to Multiply Rational Numbers**

Find $\left(-\dfrac{1}{7}\cdot\dfrac{4}{5}\right)\cdot(-7)\cdot\left(-\dfrac{1}{2}\right)$.

You can use properties of multiplication to find the product.

$$\left(-\dfrac{1}{7}\cdot\dfrac{4}{5}\right)\cdot(-7)\cdot\left(-\dfrac{1}{2}\right) = -7\cdot\left(-\dfrac{1}{7}\cdot\dfrac{4}{5}\right)\cdot\left(-\dfrac{1}{2}\right) \qquad \text{Commutative Property of Multiplication}$$

$$= \left[-7\cdot\left(-\dfrac{1}{7}\right)\right]\cdot\dfrac{4}{5}\cdot\left(-\dfrac{1}{2}\right) \qquad \text{Associative Property of Multiplication}$$

$$= 1\cdot\dfrac{4}{5}\cdot\left(-\dfrac{1}{2}\right) \qquad \text{Multiplicative Inverse Property}$$

$$= \dfrac{4}{5}\cdot\left(\dfrac{-1}{2}\right) \qquad \text{Multiplication Property of One}$$

$$= \dfrac{\overset{2}{4}\cdot(-1)}{5\cdot\underset{1}{2}} \qquad \text{Multiply. Divide out the common factor, 2.}$$

$$= \dfrac{-2}{5}, \text{ or } -\dfrac{2}{5} \qquad \text{Simplify.}$$

Notice that Example 2 uses different notation to demonstrate the following.

$$\dfrac{4\cdot(-1)}{5\cdot2} = \dfrac{2\cdot\overset{1}{2}\cdot(-1)}{5\cdot\underset{1}{2}}$$

Try It Find the product. Write fractions in simplest form.

5. $-\dfrac{2}{3}\cdot 7\dfrac{7}{8}\cdot\dfrac{3}{2}$

6. $-7.02(0.1)(100)(-10)$

 Self-Assessment for Concepts & Skills

Solve each exercise. Then rate your understanding of the success criteria in your journal.

7. **WRITING** Explain how to determine whether a product of two rational numbers is *positive* or *negative*.

MULTIPLYING RATIONAL NUMBERS Find the product. Write fractions in simplest form.

8. $-\dfrac{3}{10}\times\left(-\dfrac{8}{15}\right)$

9. $-\dfrac{2}{3}\cdot 1\dfrac{1}{3}$

10. $-2.8(-1.7)$

11. $1\dfrac{3}{5}\cdot\left(-3\dfrac{3}{4}\right)$

EXAMPLE 3 **Modeling Real Life**

A school record for the 40-meter dash is 15.24 seconds. Predict the school record after 15 years when the school record decreases by about 0.06 second per year.

Use a verbal model to solve the problem. Because the school record *decreases* by about 0.06 second per year, the change in the school record each year is −0.06 second.

School record after 15 years	=	Current school record	+	Number of years	•	Average yearly change

$$= 15.24 + 15(-0.06) \qquad \text{Substitute.}$$

$$= 15.24 + (-0.9) \qquad \text{Multiply 15 and } -0.06.$$

$$= 14.34 \qquad \text{Add 15.24 and } -0.9.$$

▷ You can predict that the school record will be about 14.34 seconds after 15 years.

Check Reasonableness

Because 0.06 < 0.1, the school record decreases by less than 0.1 • 15 = 1.5 seconds. So, the school record is greater than 15.24 − 1.5 = 13.74 seconds.

Because 14.34 > 13.74, the answer is reasonable. ✔

Self-Assessment for *Problem Solving*

Solve each exercise. Then rate your understanding of the success criteria in your journal.

12. A swimmer's best time in an event is 53.87 seconds. On average, his best time decreases by 0.28 second each of the next five times he swims the event. Does he accomplish his goal of swimming the event in less than 52.5 seconds?

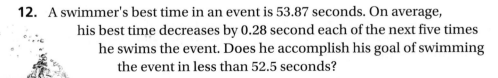

13. **DIG DEEPER!** *Terminal velocity* is the fastest speed that an object can fall through the air. A skydiver reaches a terminal velocity of 120 miles per hour. What is the change in elevation of the skydiver after falling at terminal velocity for 15 seconds? Justify your answer.

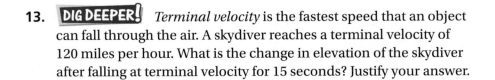

2.4 Practice

? Go to *BigIdeasMath.com* to get HELP with solving the exercises.

▶ Review & Refresh

Write the fraction or mixed number as a decimal.

1. $\frac{5}{16}$

2. $-\frac{9}{22}$

3. $6\frac{8}{11}$

4. $-\frac{26}{24}$

Find the area of the figure.

5.
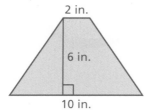
2 in.
6 in.
10 in.

6.
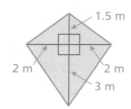
1.5 m
2 m
2 m
3 m

7.
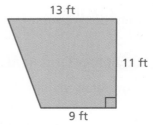
13 ft
11 ft
9 ft

▶▶ Concepts, Skills, & Problem Solving

FINDING PRODUCTS OF RATIONAL NUMBERS Write a multiplication expression represented by the area model. Then find the product. (See Exploration 1, p. 67.)

8.
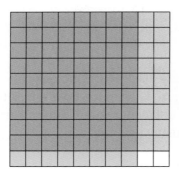

9.
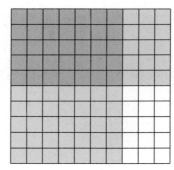

MP REASONING Without multiplying, tell whether the value of the expression is positive or negative. Explain your reasoning.

10. $-1\left(\frac{4}{5}\right)$

11. $\frac{4}{7} \cdot \left(-3\frac{1}{2}\right)$

12. $-0.25(-3.659)$

MULTIPLYING RATIONAL NUMBERS Find the product. Write fractions in simplest form.

13. $-\frac{1}{4} \times \left(-\frac{4}{3}\right)$

14. $\frac{5}{6}\left(-\frac{8}{15}\right)$

15. $-2\left(-1\frac{1}{4}\right)$

16. $-3\frac{1}{3} \cdot \left(-2\frac{7}{10}\right)$

17. $0.4 \times (-0.03)$

18. $-0.05 \times (-0.5)$

19. $-8(0.09)(-0.5)$

20. $\frac{5}{6} \cdot \left(-4\frac{1}{2}\right) \cdot \left(-2\frac{1}{5}\right)$

21. $\left(-1\frac{2}{3}\right)^3$

MP YOU BE THE TEACHER Your friend evaluates the expression. Is your friend correct? Explain your reasoning.

22.
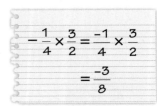

$$-\frac{1}{4} \times \frac{3}{2} = \frac{-1}{4} \times \frac{3}{2}$$
$$= \frac{-3}{8}$$

23.

$$-2.2 \times (-3.7) = -8.14$$

24. **MP** MODELING REAL LIFE The hour hand of a clock moves $-30°$ every hour. How many degrees does it move in $2\frac{1}{5}$ hours?

25. **MP** MODELING REAL LIFE A 14.5-gallon gasoline tank is $\frac{3}{4}$ full. How many gallons will it take to fill the tank?

26. **OPEN-ENDED** Write two fractions whose product is $-\frac{3}{5}$.

USING PROPERTIES Find the product. Write fractions in simplest form.

27. $\frac{1}{5} \cdot \frac{3}{8} \cdot (-5)$

28. $0.01(4.6)(-200)$

29. $(-17.2 \times 2.5) \times 4$

30. $\left(-\frac{5}{9} \times \frac{2}{7}\right) \times \left(-\frac{7}{2}\right)$

31. $\left[-\frac{2}{3} \cdot \left(-\frac{5}{7}\right)\right] \cdot \left(-\frac{9}{4}\right)$

32. $(-4.5 \cdot 8.61) \cdot \left(-\frac{2}{9}\right)$

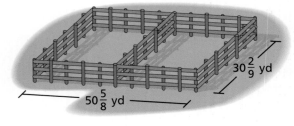

$30\frac{2}{9}$ yd

$50\frac{5}{8}$ yd

33. **MP** PROBLEM SOLVING Fencing costs $25.80 per yard. How much does it cost to enclose two adjacent rectangular pastures as shown? Justify your answer.

ALGEBRA Evaluate the expression when $x = -2$, $y = 3$, and $z = -\frac{1}{5}$.

34. $x \cdot z$

35. xyz

36. $\frac{1}{3} + x \cdot z$

37. $\frac{1}{2}z - \frac{2}{3}y$

EVALUATING AN EXPRESSION Evaluate the expression. Write fractions in simplest form.

38. $-4.2 + 8.1 \times (-1.9)$

39. $-3\frac{3}{4} \times \frac{5}{6} - 2\frac{1}{3}$

40. $\left(-\frac{2}{3}\right)^2 - \frac{3}{4}\left(2\frac{1}{3}\right)$

41. **DIG DEEPER!** Use positive or negative integers to fill in the blanks so that the product is $\frac{1}{4}$. Justify your answer.

$$\frac{\boxed{}}{2} \times \left(-\frac{5}{\boxed{}}\right) \times \frac{\boxed{}}{\boxed{}}$$

2.5 Dividing Rational Numbers

Learning Target: Find quotients of rational numbers.

Success Criteria:
- I can explain the rules for dividing rational numbers.
- I can find quotients of rational numbers with the same sign.
- I can find quotients of rational numbers with different signs.

EXPLORATION 1

Finding Quotients of Rational Numbers

Work with a partner.

a. Write two division expressions represented by the area model. Then find the quotients.

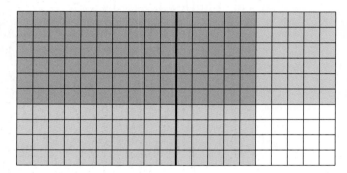

b. Complete the table.

	Expression	Quotient	Expression	Quotient
i.	$0.9 \div 1.5$		$-0.9 \div 1.5$	
ii.	$1 \div \dfrac{1}{2}$		$-1 \div \dfrac{1}{2}$	
iii.	$2 \div 0.25$		$2 \div (-0.25)$	
iv.	$0 \div \dfrac{4}{5}$		$0 \div \left(-\dfrac{4}{5}\right)$	
v.	$1\dfrac{1}{2} \div 3$		$-1\dfrac{1}{2} \div (-3)$	
vi.	$0.8 \div 0.1$		$-0.8 \div (-0.1)$	

Math Practice

Apply Mathematics

How does interpreting a division expression in a real-life story help you make sense of the quotient?

c. Do the rules for dividing integers apply to all rational numbers? Explain your reasoning.

d. Write a real-life story involving the quotient $-0.75 \div 3$. Interpret the quotient in the context of the story.

2.5 Lesson

Key Idea

Dividing Rational Numbers

Words To divide rational numbers, use the same rules for signs as you used for dividing integers.

Numbers $-\dfrac{1}{2} \div \dfrac{4}{9} = -\dfrac{1}{2} \cdot \dfrac{9}{4} = -\dfrac{9}{8}$ $-\dfrac{1}{2} \div \left(-\dfrac{4}{9}\right) = -\dfrac{1}{2} \cdot \left(-\dfrac{9}{4}\right) = \dfrac{9}{8}$

EXAMPLE 1 **Dividing Rational Numbers**

a. **Find $-8.4 \div (-3.6)$.**

Because the decimals have the same sign, the quotient is positive. Use long division to divide 8.4 by 3.6.

$$3.6\overline{)8.4} \longrightarrow \begin{array}{r} 2.33 \\ 36\overline{)84.00} \\ -72 \\ \hline 12\,0 \\ -10\,8 \\ \hline 1\,20 \\ -1\,08 \\ \hline 12 \end{array}$$

> The remainder repeats. So, it is a repeating decimal.

Another Method Write the division expression as a fraction.

$$\dfrac{-8.4}{-3.6} = \dfrac{84}{36}$$
$$= \dfrac{7}{3}$$
$$= 2\dfrac{1}{3}, \text{ or } 2.\overline{3} \checkmark$$

▷ So, $-8.4 \div (-3.6) = 2.\overline{3}$.

b. **Find $\dfrac{6}{5} \div \left(-\dfrac{4}{3}\right)$.**

$\dfrac{6}{5} \div \left(-\dfrac{4}{3}\right) = \dfrac{6}{5} \cdot \left(-\dfrac{3}{4}\right)$ Multiply by the reciprocal of $-\dfrac{4}{3}$.

$= \dfrac{\overset{3}{6} \cdot (-3)}{5 \cdot \underset{2}{4}}$ Multiply the numerators and the denominators. Divide out the common factor, 2.

$= \dfrac{-9}{10}, \text{ or } -\dfrac{9}{10}$ Simplify.

▷ So, $\dfrac{6}{5} \div \left(-\dfrac{4}{3}\right) = -\dfrac{9}{10}$.

Try It **Find the quotient. Write fractions in simplest form.**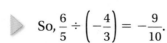

1. $-2.4 \div 3.2$ **2.** $-6 \div (-1.1)$ **3.** $-\dfrac{6}{5} \div \left(-\dfrac{1}{2}\right)$ **4.** $-\dfrac{1}{3} \div 2\dfrac{2}{3}$

You can represent division involving fractions using *complex fractions*. A **complex fraction** has at least one fraction in the numerator, denominator, or both.

EXAMPLE 2 **Evaluating a Complex Fraction**

Evaluate $\dfrac{-\dfrac{10}{9}}{-\dfrac{1}{6}+1}$.

Rewrite the complex fraction as a division expression.

$-\dfrac{10}{9} \div \left(-\dfrac{1}{6}+1\right) = -\dfrac{10}{9} \div \left(\dfrac{-1}{6}+\dfrac{6}{6}\right)$ Rewrite $-\dfrac{1}{6}$ as $\dfrac{-1}{6}$ and 1 as $\dfrac{6}{6}$.

$= -\dfrac{10}{9} \div \dfrac{5}{6}$ Add fractions.

$= -\dfrac{10}{9} \cdot \dfrac{6}{5}$ Multiply by the reciprocal of $\dfrac{5}{6}$.

$= -\dfrac{\overset{2}{10} \cdot \overset{2}{6}}{\underset{3}{9} \cdot \underset{1}{5}}$ Multiply. Divide out common factors.

$= -\dfrac{4}{3}$ Simplify.

Math Practice

Maintain Oversight

Why can you write $-\dfrac{1}{6}$ as $\dfrac{-1}{6}$? Why is it helpful when evaluating the expression?

Try It **Evaluate the expression. Write fractions in simplest form.**

5. $\dfrac{-\dfrac{1}{2}}{6}$

6. $\dfrac{-2\dfrac{1}{2}}{-\dfrac{3}{4}}$

7. $\dfrac{-1\dfrac{2}{3} \cdot \left(-\dfrac{3}{5}\right)}{\left(\dfrac{1}{3}\right)^2}$

 Self-Assessment for Concepts & Skills

Solve each exercise. Then rate your understanding of the success criteria in your journal.

8. **WRITING** Explain how to determine whether a quotient of two rational numbers is *positive* or *negative*.

EVALUATING AN EXPRESSION **Evaluate the expression. Write fractions in simplest form.**

9. $\dfrac{3}{8} \div \left(-\dfrac{9}{5}\right)$

10. $-6.8 \div (-3.6)$

11. $\dfrac{-\dfrac{2}{9}}{2\dfrac{2}{5}}$

EXAMPLE 3 Modeling Real Life

A restaurant launches a mobile app that allows customers to rate their food on a scale from −5 to 5. So far, customers have given the lasagna scores of 2.25, −3.5, 0, −4.5, 1.75, −1, 3.5, and −2.5. Should the restaurant consider changing the recipe? Explain.

 Understand the problem.

You are given eight scores for lasagna. You are asked to determine whether the restaurant should make changes to the lasagna recipe.

 Make a plan.

Use the mean score to determine whether people generally like the lasagna. Then decide whether the recipe should change.

 Solve and check.

Divide the sum of the scores by the number of scores. Group together scores that are convenient to add.

Look Back
Only 3 of the 8 scores were better than "mediocre." So, it makes sense to conclude that the restaurant should change the recipe. ✓

$$\text{mean} = \frac{0 + (-3.5 + 3.5) + (2.25 + 1.75) + [(-4.5) + (-2.5) + (-1)]}{8}$$

$$= \frac{0 + 0 + 4 + (-8)}{8}$$

$$= \frac{-4}{8}, \text{ or } -0.5$$

The mean score is below the "mediocre" score of 0.

▷ So, the restaurant should consider changing the recipe.

 Self-Assessment *for Problem Solving*

Solve each exercise. Then rate your understanding of the success criteria in your journal.

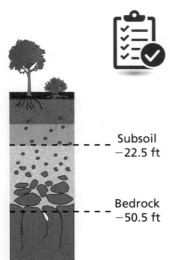

Subsoil
−22.5 ft

Bedrock
−50.5 ft

12. **DIG DEEPER!** Soil is composed of several layers. A geologist measures the depths of the *subsoil* and the *bedrock*, as shown. Find and interpret two quotients involving the depths of the subsoil and the bedrock.

13. The restaurant in Example 3 receives additional scores of −0.75, −1.5, −1.25, 4.75, −0.25, −0.5, 5, and −0.5 for the lasagna. Given the additional data, should the restaurant consider changing the recipe? Explain.

Go to **BigIdeasMath.com** to get HELP with solving the exercises.

▶ Review & Refresh

Find the product. Write fractions in simplest form.

1. $-0.5(1.31)$

2. $\dfrac{9}{10}\left(-1\dfrac{1}{4}\right)$

3. $-\dfrac{7}{12}\left(-\dfrac{3}{14}\right)$

Identify the terms, coefficients, and constants in the expression.

4. $3b + 12$

5. $14 + z + 6f$

6. $8g + 14 + 5c + 7$

7. $42m + 18 + 12c^2$

▶▶ Concepts, Skills, & Problem Solving

 USING TOOLS Write two division expressions represented by the area model. **Then find the quotients.** (See Exploration 1, p. 73.)

8.
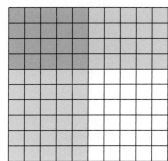

9.
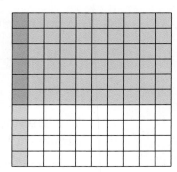

DIVIDING RATIONAL NUMBERS **Find the quotient. Write fractions in simplest form.**

10. $-\dfrac{7}{10} \div \dfrac{2}{5}$

11. $-0.18 \div 0.03$

12. $-3.45 \div (-15)$

13. $-8 \div (-2.2)$

14. $\dfrac{1}{4} \div \left(-\dfrac{3}{8}\right)$

15. $8.722 \div (-3.56)$

16. $12.42 \div (-4.8)$

17. $-2\dfrac{4}{5} \div (-7)$

18. $-10\dfrac{2}{7} \div \left(-4\dfrac{4}{11}\right)$

MP YOU BE THE TEACHER Your friend evaluates the expression. Is your friend correct? Explain your reasoning.

19.
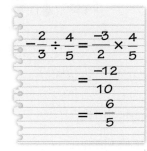

$$-\frac{2}{3} \div \frac{4}{5} = \frac{-3}{2} \times \frac{4}{5}$$
$$= \frac{-12}{10}$$
$$= -\frac{6}{5}$$

20.

$$-4.25 \div 1.7 = 2.5$$

21. **(MP) MODELING REAL LIFE** How many 0.75-pound packages can you make with 4.5 pounds of sunflower seeds?

EVALUATING AN EXPRESSION Evaluate the expression. Write fractions in simplest form.

22. $\dfrac{\frac{14}{9}}{-\frac{1}{3}-\frac{1}{6}}$

23. $\dfrac{-\frac{12}{5}+\frac{3}{10}}{\frac{11}{14}-\left(-\frac{9}{14}\right)}$

24. $-0.42 \div 0.8 + 0.2$

25. $2.85 - 6.2 \div 2^2$

26. $\dfrac{3}{4} + \dfrac{7}{10} - \dfrac{1}{8} \div \left(-\dfrac{1}{2}\right)$

27. $\dfrac{\frac{7}{6}}{\left(-\frac{11}{5}\right)\left(10\frac{1}{2}\right)\left(-\frac{5}{11}\right)}$

28. **(MP) PROBLEM SOLVING** The section of the boardwalk shown is made using boards that are each $9\frac{1}{4}$ inches wide. The spacing between each board is equal. What is the width of the spacing between each board?

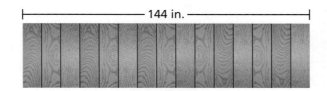

— 144 in. —

Day	Change in pressure
Monday	−0.05
Tuesday	0.09
Wednesday	−0.04
Thursday	−0.08

29. **(MP) REASONING** The table shows the daily changes in the barometric pressure (in inches of mercury) for four days.
   a. What is the mean change?
   b. The mean change for Monday through Friday is −0.01 inch. What is the change in the barometric pressure on Friday? Explain.

30. **(MP) LOGIC** In an online survey, gym members react to the statement shown by adjusting the position of the needle. The responses have values of −4.2, 1.6, 0.4, 0, 2.1, −5.0, −4.7, 0.6, 1.1, 0.8, 0.4, and 2.1. Explain how two people can use the results of the survey to reach different conclusions about whether the gym should adjust its membership prices.

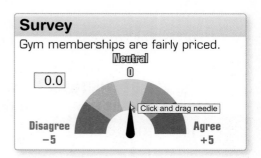

31. **CRITICAL THINKING** Determine whether the statement is *sometimes*, *always*, or *never* true. Explain your reasoning.

   a. The product of two terminating decimals is a terminating decimal.

   b. The quotient of two terminating decimals is a terminating decimal.

2 Connecting Concepts

▶ Using the Problem-Solving Plan

1. You feed several adult hamsters equal amounts of a new food recipe over a period of 1 month. You record the changes in the weights of the hamsters in the table. Use the data to answer the question "What is the typical weight change of a hamster that is fed the new recipe?"

Weight Change (ounces)				
−0.07	−0.03	−0.11	−0.04	−0.08
0.02	−0.08	−0.08	−0.06	−0.05
−0.11	−0.1	0	−0.07	−0.08

 Understand the problem. You know the weight changes of 15 hamsters. You want to use this information to find the typical weight change.

Make a plan. Display the data in a dot plot to see the distribution of the data. Then use the distribution to determine the most appropriate measure of center.

Solve and check. Use the plan to solve the problem. Then check your solution.

2. Evaluate the expression shown at the right. Write your answer in simplest form.

$$\dfrac{-\dfrac{1}{2} + \dfrac{2}{3}}{\dfrac{3}{5}\left(\dfrac{3}{4} - \dfrac{11}{8}\right)}$$

3. You drop a racquetball from a height of 60 inches. On each bounce, the racquetball bounces to a height that is 70% of its previous height. What is the change in the height of the racquetball after 3 bounces?

Performance Task

Precisely Perfect

At the beginning of this chapter, you watched a STEAM Video called "Carpenter or Joiner." You are now ready to complete the performance task related to this video, available at *BigIdeasMath.com*. Be sure to use the problem-solving plan as you work through the performance task.

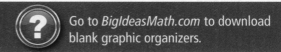

▶ Review Vocabulary

Write the definition and give an example of each vocabulary term.

terminating decimal, *p. 62*   repeating decimal, *p. 62*   complex fraction, *p. 75*

▶ Graphic Organizers

You can use an **Information Frame** to help organize and remember a concept. Here is an example of an Information Frame for *multiplying integers*.

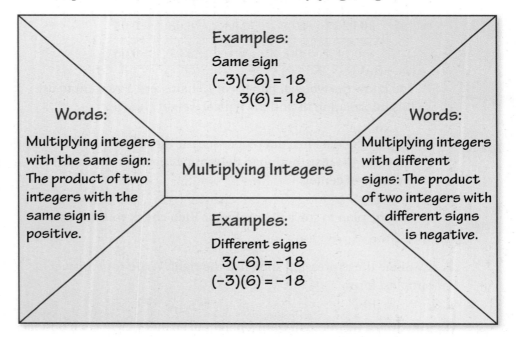

Choose and complete a graphic organizer to help you study the concept.

1. dividing integers

2. writing fractions or mixed numbers as decimals

3. writing decimals as fractions or mixed numbers

4. multiplying rational numbers

5. dividing rational numbers

"I finished my Information Frame about rainforests. It makes me want to visit Costa Rica. How about you?"

Chapter Self-Assessment

As you complete the exercises, use the scale below to rate your understanding of the success criteria in your journal.

1	2	3	4
I do not understand.	I can do it with help.	I can do it on my own.	I can teach someone else.

2.1 Multiplying Integers (pp. 49–54)

Learning Target: Find products of integers.

Find the product.

1. $-8 \cdot 6$
2. $10(-7)$
3. $-3 \cdot (-6)$

4. You and a group of friends participate in a game where you must use clues to escape from a room. You have a limited amount of time to escape and are allowed 3 free clues. Additional clues may be requested, but each removes 5 minutes from your remaining time. What integer represents the total change in the time when you use 5 clues?

Evaluate the expression.

5. $(-3)^3$
6. $(-3)(-4)(10)$
7. $24 - 3(2 - 4^2)$

8. Write three integers whose product is negative.

9. You are playing laser tag. The table shows how many points you gain or lose when you tag or are tagged by another player in different locations. You are tagged three times on the back, twice on the shoulder, and twice on the laser. You tag two players on the front, four players on the back, and one player on the laser. What is your score?

Tag Locations	Points Gained	Points Lost
Front	200	50
Back	100	25
Shoulder	50	12
Laser	50	12

10. The product of three integers is positive. How many of the integers can be negative? Explain.

11. Two integers, c and d, have a product of -6. What is the *greatest* possible sum of c and d?

2.2 Dividing Integers *(pp. 55–60)*

Learning Target: Find quotients of integers.

Find the quotient.

12. $-18 \div 9$ **13.** $\dfrac{-42}{-6}$ **14.** $\dfrac{-30}{6}$ **15.** $84 \div (-7)$

Evaluate the expression when $x = 3$, $y = -4$, and $z = -6$.

16. $z \div x$ **17.** $\dfrac{xy}{z}$ **18.** $\dfrac{z - 2x}{y}$

Find the mean of the integers.

19. $-3, -8, 12, -15, 9$ **20.** $-54, -32, -70, -25, -65, -42$

21. The table shows the weekly profits of a fruit vendor. What is the mean profit for these weeks?

Week	1	2	3	4
Profit	−$125	−$86	$54	−$35

2.3 Converting Between Fractions and Decimals *(pp. 61–66)*

Learning Target: Convert between different forms of rational numbers.

Write the fraction or mixed number as a decimal.

22. $-\dfrac{8}{15}$ **23.** $\dfrac{5}{8}$ **24.** $-\dfrac{13}{6}$ **25.** $1\dfrac{7}{16}$

Write the decimal as a fraction or mixed number in simplest form.

26. -0.6 **27.** -0.35 **28.** -5.8 **29.** 24.23

30. The table shows the changes in the average yearly precipitation (in inches) in a city for several months. Order the numbers from least to greatest.

February	March	April	May
-1.75	$\dfrac{3}{11}$	0.3	$-1\dfrac{7}{9}$

2.4 Multiplying Rational Numbers (pp. 67–72)

Learning Target: Find products of rational numbers.

Find the product. Write fractions in simplest form.

31. $-\dfrac{4}{9}\left(-\dfrac{7}{9}\right)$

32. $\dfrac{8}{15}\left(-\dfrac{2}{3}\right)$

33. $-5.9(-9.7)$

34. $4.5(-5.26)$

35. $-\dfrac{2}{3}\left(2\dfrac{1}{2}\right)(-3)$

36. $-1.6(0.5)(-20)$

37. The elevation of a sunken ship is -120 feet. You are in a submarine at an elevation that is $\dfrac{5}{8}$ of the ship's elevation. What is your elevation?

38. Write two fractions whose product is between $\dfrac{1}{5}$ and $\dfrac{1}{2}$, and whose sum is negative.

2.5 Dividing Rational Numbers (pp. 73–78)

Learning Target: Find quotients of rational numbers.

Find the quotient. Write fractions in simplest form.

39. $\dfrac{9}{10} \div \left(-\dfrac{6}{5}\right)$

40. $-\dfrac{4}{11} \div \dfrac{2}{7}$

41. $-\dfrac{7}{8} \div \left(-\dfrac{5}{12}\right)$

42. $6.4 \div (-3.2)$

43. $-15.4 \div (-2.5)$

44. $-23.8 \div 5.6$

45. You use a debit card to purchase several shirts. Your account balance after buying the shirts changes by $-\$30.60$. For each shirt you purchased, the change in your account balance was $-\$6.12$. How many shirts did you buy?

46. Evaluate $\dfrac{z}{y - \dfrac{3}{4} + x}$ when $x = 4$, $y = -3$, and $z = -\dfrac{1}{8}$.

Evaluate the expression. Write fractions in simplest form.

1. $-9 \cdot 2$

2. $-72 \div (-3)$

3. $3\frac{9}{10} \times \left(-\frac{8}{3}\right)$

4. $-1\frac{5}{6} \div 4\frac{1}{6}$

5. $-4.4 \times (-6.02)$

6. $-5 \div 1.5$

Write the fraction or mixed number as a decimal.

7. $\frac{7}{40}$

8. $-\frac{1}{9}$

9. $-1\frac{5}{16}$

Write the decimal as a fraction or mixed number in simplest form.

10. -0.122

11. 0.33

12. -7.09

Evaluate the expression when $x = 5$, $y = -3$, and $z = -2$.

13. $\dfrac{y + z}{x}$

14. $\dfrac{x - 5z}{y}$

15. $\dfrac{\frac{1}{3}x}{\frac{y}{z}}$

16. Find the mean of 11, -7, -14, 10, and -5.

17. A driver receives -25 points for each rule violation. What integer represents the change in points after 4 rule violations?

18. How many 2.25-pound containers can you fill with 24.75 pounds of almonds?

19. In a recent 10-year period, the change in the number of visitors to U.S. national parks was about $-11{,}150{,}000$ visitors.

   a. What was the mean yearly change in the number of visitors?

   b. During the seventh year, the change in the number of visitors was about 10,800,000. Explain how the change for the 10-year period can be negative.

20. You have a $50 gift card to go shopping for school supplies. You buy 2 packs of pencils, 5 notebooks, 6 folders, 1 pack of pens, 3 packs of paper, 1 pack of highlighters, and 2 binders.

   a. What number represents the change in the value of the gift card after buying your school supplies?

   b. What percentage of the value remains on your gift card?

1. When José and Sean were each 5 years old, José was $1\frac{1}{2}$ inches taller than Sean. Then José grew at an average rate of $2\frac{3}{4}$ inches per year until he was 13 years old. José was 63 inches tall when he was 13 years old. How tall was Sean when he was 5 years old?

   A. $39\frac{1}{2}$ in.   **B.** $42\frac{1}{2}$ in.

   C. $44\frac{3}{4}$ in.   **D.** $47\frac{3}{4}$ in.

2. What is the value of $-5 + (-7)$?

   F. -12 **G.** -2

   H. 2 **I.** 12

3. What is the value of the expression?

   $$-\frac{9}{16} + \frac{9}{8}$$

4. What is the value of $\left| a^2 - 2ac + 5b \right|$ when $a = -2$, $b = 3$, and $c = -5$?

   A. -9 **B.** -1

   C. 1 **D.** 9

5. Your friend evaluated the expression.

   $$2 - 3 - (-5) = -5 - (-5)$$
   $$= -5 + 5$$
   $$= 0$$

   What should your friend do to correct the error that he made?

   F. Subtract 5 from -5 instead of adding.

   G. Rewrite $2 - 3$ as -1.

   H. Subtract -5 from 3 before subtracting 3 from 2.

   I. Rewrite $-5 + 5$ as -10.

6. What is the value of $-1\frac{1}{2} - \left(-1\frac{3}{4}\right)$?

    A. $-3\frac{1}{4}$ **B.** $\frac{1}{4}$

    C. $\frac{6}{7}$ **D.** $2\frac{5}{8}$

7. What is the value of the expression when $q = -2$, $r = -12$, and $s = 8$?

$$\frac{-q^2 - r}{s}$$

    F. -2 **G.** -1

    H. 1 **I.** 2

8. You are stacking wooden blocks with the dimensions shown. How many blocks do you need to stack vertically to build a block tower that is $7\frac{1}{2}$ inches tall?

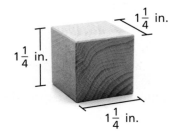

$1\frac{1}{4}$ in.

$1\frac{1}{4}$ in.

$1\frac{1}{4}$ in.

9. Your friend evaluated an expression.

$$-4\frac{3}{4} + 2\frac{1}{5} = -\frac{19}{4} + \frac{11}{5}$$
$$= -\frac{95}{20} + \frac{44}{20}$$
$$= \frac{-95 + 44}{20}$$
$$= \frac{-139}{20}$$
$$= -6\frac{19}{20}$$

What should your friend do to correct the error that she made?

    A. Rewrite $-\frac{19}{4} + \frac{11}{5}$ as $\frac{-19 + 11}{4 + 5}$.

    B. Rewrite $-95 + 44$ as -51.

    C. Rewrite $\frac{-95 + 44}{20}$ as $\frac{51}{20}$.

    D. Rewrite $-4\frac{3}{4}$ as $-\frac{13}{4}$.

10. Which expression has the greatest value when $x = -2$ and $y = -3$?

   F. $-xy$ **G.** xy

   H. $x - y$ **I.** $-x - y$

11. Four points are graphed on the number line.

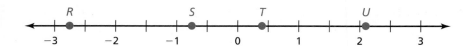

   Part A   Choose the two points whose values have the greatest sum. Approximate this sum. Explain your reasoning.

   Part B   Choose the two points whose values have the greatest difference. Approximate this difference. Explain your reasoning.

   Part C   Choose the two points whose values have the greatest product. Approximate this product. Explain your reasoning.

   Part D   Choose the two points whose values have the greatest quotient. Approximate this quotient. Explain your reasoning.

12. What number belongs in the box to make the equation true?

$$\frac{-0.4}{\boxed{}} + 0.8 = -1.2$$

   A. -1 **B.** -0.2

   C. 0.2 **D.** 1

13. Which expression has a negative value when $x = -4$ and $y = 2$?

   F. $-x + y$ **G.** $y - x$

   H. $x - y$ **I.** $-x - y$

14. What is the area of a triangle with a base of $2\frac{1}{2}$ inches and a height of 2 inches?

   A. $2\frac{1}{4}$ in.^{2} **B.** $2\frac{1}{2}$ in.^{2}

   C. $4\frac{1}{2}$ in.^{2} **D.** 5 in.^{2}

15. Which decimal is equivalent to $\frac{2}{9}$?

   F. 0.2 **G.** $0.\overline{2}$

   H. 0.29 **I.** 4.5

3 Expressions

Chapter Learning Target:
Understand algebraic expressions.

Chapter Success Criteria:
- I can identify parts of an algebraic expression.
- I can write algebraic expressions.
- I can solve problems using algebraic expressions.
- I can interpret algebraic expressions in real-life problems.

STEAM Video: "Trophic Status"

Trophic Status

In an ecosystem, energy and nutrients flow between *biotic* and *abiotic* components. Biotic components are the living parts of an ecosystem. Abiotic components are the non-living parts of an ecosystem. What is an example of an ecosystem?

Watch the STEAM video "Trophic Status." Then answer the following questions.

1. Give examples of both biotic and abiotic components in an ecosystem. Explain.

2. When an organism is eaten, its energy flows into the organism that consumes it. Explain how to use an expression to represent the total energy that a person gains from eating each of the items shown.

Chlorophyll in Plants

After completing this chapter, you will be able to use the concepts you learned to answer the questions in the *STEAM Video Performance Task*. You will be given the numbers of atoms found in molecules involved in photosynthesis.

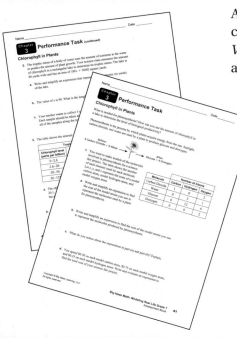

Glucose Molecule

6 carbon atoms

12 hydrogen atoms

6 oxygen atoms

You will be asked to determine the total cost for a model of a molecule given the costs of different types of atom models. How can you find the total cost of purchasing several identical objects?

Getting Ready for Chapter 3

Chapter Exploration

Work with a partner. Rewrite the algebraic expression so that it has fewer symbols but still has the same value when evaluated for any value of *x*.

Original Expression	Simplified Expression		Original Expression	Simplified Expression
1. $2x + 4 + x$		**2.**	$3(x + 1) - 4$	
3. $x - (3 - x)$		**4.**	$5 + 2x - 3$	
5. $x + 3 + 2x - 4$		**6.**	$2x + 2 - x + 3$	

7. WRITING GUIDELINES Work with a partner. Use your answers in Exercises 1–6 to write guidelines for simplifying an expression.

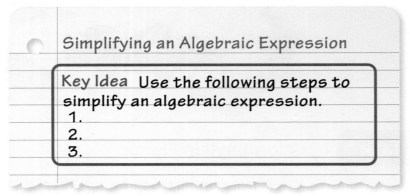

Simplifying an Algebraic Expression

Key Idea Use the following steps to simplify an algebraic expression.
1.
2.
3.

APPLYING A DEFINITION Work with a partner. Two expressions are equivalent if they have the same value when evaluated for any value of *x*. Decide which two expressions are equivalent. Explain your reasoning.

	Expression A	Expression B	Expression C
8.	$x - (2x + 1)$	$-x + 1$	$-x - 1$
9.	$2x + 3 - x + 4$	$x + 7$	$x - 1$
10.	$3 + x - 2(x + 1)$	$-x + 1$	$-x + 5$
11.	$2 - 2x - (x + 2)$	$-3x$	$-3x + 4$

Vocabulary

The following vocabulary terms are defined in this chapter. Think about what each term might mean and record your thoughts.

like terms   linear expression   factoring an expression

3.1 Algebraic Expressions

Learning Target: Simplify algebraic expressions.

Success Criteria:
- I can identify terms and like terms of algebraic expressions.
- I can combine like terms to simplify algebraic expressions.
- I can write and simplify algebraic expressions to solve real-life problems.

EXPLORATION 1

Simplifying Algebraic Expressions

Work with a partner.

a. Choose a value of x other than 0 or 1 for the last column in the table. Complete the table by evaluating each algebraic expression for each value of x. What do you notice?

Expression		Value When		
		$x = 0$	$x = 1$	$x = ?$
A.	$-\dfrac{1}{3} + x + \dfrac{7}{3}$			
B.	$0.5x + 3 - 1.5x - 1$			
C.	$2x + 6$			
D.	$x + 4$			
E.	$-2x + 2$			
F.	$\dfrac{1}{2}x - x + \dfrac{3}{2}x + 4$			
G.	$-4.8x + 2 - x + 3.8x$			
H.	$x + 2$			
I.	$-x + 2$			
J.	$3x + 2 - x + 4$			

Math Practice

Analyze Conjectures

A student says that x and x^3 are equivalent because they have the same value when $x = -1$, $x = 0$, and $x = 1$. Explain why the student is or is not correct.

b. How can you use properties of operations to justify your answers in part (a)? Explain your reasoning.

c. To subtract a number, you can add its opposite. Does a similar rule apply to the terms of an algebraic expression? Explain your reasoning.

3.1 Lesson

Key Vocabulary
like terms, *p. 92*
simplest form, *p. 92*

In an algebraic expression, **like terms** are terms that have the same variables raised to the same exponents. Constant terms are also like terms. To identify terms and like terms in an expression, first write the expression as a sum of its terms.

EXAMPLE 1   Identifying Terms and Like Terms

Identify the terms and like terms in each expression.

a. $9x - 2 + 7 - x$

Rewrite as a sum of terms.

$$9x + (-2) + 7 + (-x)$$

Terms: $9x,\quad -2,\quad 7,\quad -x$

Like terms: $9x$ and $-x$, -2 and 7

b. $z^2 + 5z - 3z^2 + z$

Rewrite as a sum of terms.

$$z^2 + 5z + (-3z^2) + z$$

Terms: $z^2,\quad 5z,\quad -3z^2,\quad z$

Like terms: z^2 and $-3z^2$, $5z$ and z

Try It   Identify the terms and like terms in the expression.

1. $y + 10 - \dfrac{3}{2}y$ **2.** $2r^2 + 7r - r^2 - 9$ **3.** $7 + 4p - 5 + p + 2q$

An algebraic expression is in **simplest form** when it has no like terms and no parentheses. To *combine* like terms that have variables, use the Distributive Property to add or subtract the coefficients.

EXAMPLE 2   Simplifying Algebraic Expressions

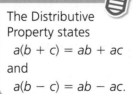

Remember
The Distributive Property states
$a(b + c) = ab + ac$
and
$a(b - c) = ab - ac$.

a. Simplify $6n - 10n$.

$$6n - 10n = (6 - 10)n \qquad \text{Distributive Property}$$
$$= -4n \qquad \text{Subtract.}$$

b. Simplify $-8.5w + 5.2w + w$.

$$-8.5w + 5.2w + w = -8.5w + 5.2w + 1w \qquad \text{Multiplication Property of 1}$$
$$= (-8.5 + 5.2 + 1)w \qquad \text{Distributive Property}$$
$$= -2.3w \qquad \text{Add.}$$

Try It   Simplify the expression.

4. $-10y + 15y$ **5.** $\dfrac{3}{8}b - \dfrac{3}{4}b$ **6.** $2.4g - 2.4g - 9.8g$

EXAMPLE 3 **Simplifying Algebraic Expressions**

a. Simplify $\frac{3}{4}y + 12 - \frac{1}{2}y - 6$.

$$\frac{3}{4}y + 12 - \frac{1}{2}y - 6 = \frac{3}{4}y + 12 + \left(-\frac{1}{2}y\right) + (-6)$$ Rewrite as a sum.

$$= \frac{3}{4}y + \left(-\frac{1}{2}y\right) + 12 + (-6)$$ Commutative Property of Addition

$$= \left[\frac{3}{4} + \left(-\frac{1}{2}\right)\right]y + 12 + (-6)$$ Distributive Property

$$= \frac{1}{4}y + 6$$ Combine like terms.

b. Simplify $-3y - 5y + 4z + 9z$.

$$-3y - 5y + 4z + 9z = (-3 - 5)y + (4 + 9)z$$ Distributive Property

$$= -8y + 13z$$ Simplify.

Try It Simplify the expression.

7. $14 - 3z + 8 + z$ 8. $2.5x + 4.3x - 5$ 9. $2s - 9s + 8t - t$

Self-Assessment for Concepts & Skills

Solve each exercise. Then rate your understanding of the success criteria in your journal.

10. **WRITING** Explain how to identify the terms and like terms of $3y - 4 - 5y$.

SIMPLIFYING ALGEBRAIC EXPRESSIONS Simplify the expression.

11. $7p + 6p$ 12. $\frac{4}{5}n - 3 + \frac{7}{10}n$ 13. $2w - g - 7w + 3g$

14. **VOCABULARY** Is the expression $3x + 2x - 4$ in simplest form? Explain.

15. **WHICH ONE DOESN'T BELONG?** Which expression does *not* belong with the other three? Explain your reasoning.

$-4 + 6 + 3x$	$3x + 9 - 7$
$5x - 10 - 2x$	$5x - 4 + 6 - 2x$

EXAMPLE 4 Modeling Real Life

Each person in a group buys an evening ticket, a medium drink, and a large popcorn. How much does the group pay when there are 5 people in the group?

Write an expression that represents the sum of the costs of the items purchased. Use a verbal model.

Daytime Tickets	$5.00
Evening Tickets	$7.50
REFRESHMENTS	
Drinks	
Small	$1.75
Medium	$2.75
Large	$3.50
Popcorn	
Small	$3.00
Large	$4.00

Verbal Model

Number of tickets	·	Cost per ticket	+	Number of medium drinks	·	Cost per medium drink	+	Number of large popcorns	·	Cost per large popcorn

Variable The same number of each item is purchased. So, x can represent the number of tickets, the number of medium drinks, and the number of large popcorns.

Expression $7.50x$ + $2.75x$ + $4x$

$7.50x + 2.75x + 4x = (7.50 + 2.75 + 4)x$ Distributive Property

$= 14.25x$ Add coefficients.

The expression $14.25x$ indicates that the cost per person is $14.25. To find the cost for a group of 5 people, evaluate the expression when $x = 5$.

$$14.25(5) = 71.25$$

▷ The total cost for a group of 5 people is $71.25.

Remember

Variables can be lowercase or uppercase. Make sure you consistently use the same case for a variable when solving a problem.

 Self-Assessment for Problem Solving

Solve each exercise. Then rate your understanding of the success criteria in your journal.

16. **MP MODELING REAL LIFE** An exercise mat is 3.3 times as long as it is wide. Write expressions in simplest form that represent the perimeter and the area of the exercise mat.

17. **DIG DEEPER!** A group of friends visits the movie theater in Example 4. Each person buys a daytime ticket and a small drink. The group buys 1 large popcorn for every 2 people in the group. What is the average cost per person when there are 4 people in the group?

Go to *BigIdeasMath.com* to get HELP with solving the exercises.

▶ Review & Refresh

Find the product or quotient. Write fractions in simplest form.

1. $-\dfrac{2}{7} \times \dfrac{7}{4}$

2. $-\dfrac{2}{3}\left(-\dfrac{9}{10}\right)$

3. $1\dfrac{4}{9} \div \left(-\dfrac{2}{9}\right)$

Order the numbers from least to greatest.

4. $\dfrac{7}{8}$, 0.85, 87%, $\dfrac{3}{4}$, 78%

5. 15%, 14.8, $15\dfrac{4}{5}$, 1450%

6. A bird's nest is 12 feet above the ground. A mole's den is 12 inches below the ground. What is the difference in height of these two positions?

    A. 24 in.   **B.** 11 ft   **C.** 13 ft   **D.** 24 ft

▶▶ Concepts, Skills, & Problem Solving

MP REASONING **Determine whether the expressions are equivalent. Explain your reasoning.** (See Exploration 1, p. 91.)

7.

Expression 1	$3 - 5x$
Expression 2	$4.25 - 5x - 4.25$

8.

Expression 1	$1.25x + 4 + 0.75x - 3$
Expression 2	$2x + 1$

IDENTIFYING TERMS AND LIKE TERMS **Identify the terms and like terms in the expression.**

9. $t + 8 + 3t$

10. $3z + 4 + 2 + 4z$

11. $2n - n - 4 + 7n$

12. $-x - 9x^2 + 12x^2 + 7$

13. $1.4y + 5 - 4.2 - 5y^2 + z$

14. $\dfrac{1}{2}s - 4 + \dfrac{3}{4}s + \dfrac{1}{8} - s^3$

15. **MP YOU BE THE TEACHER** Your friend identifies the terms and like terms in the expression $3x - 5 - 2x + 9x$. Is your friend correct? Explain your reasoning.

> $3x - 5 - 2x + 9x$
> Terms: $3x$, 5, $2x$, and $9x$
> Like Terms: $3x$, $2x$, and $9x$

SIMPLIFYING ALGEBRAIC EXPRESSIONS **Simplify the expression.**

16. $12g + 9g$

17. $11x + 9 - 7$

18. $8s - 11s + 6s$

19. $4b - 24 + 19$

20. $4p - 5p - 30p$

21. $4.2v - 5 - 6.5v$

22. $8 + 4a + 6.2 - 9a$

23. $\dfrac{2}{5}y - 4 + 7 - \dfrac{9}{10}y$

24. $-\dfrac{2}{3}c - \dfrac{9}{5} + 14c + \dfrac{3}{10}$

25. **MP** **MODELING REAL LIFE** On a hike, each hiker carries the items shown. Write and interpret an expression in simplest form that represents the weight carried by x hikers. How much total weight is carried when there are 4 hikers?

4.6 lb

3.4 lb

2.2 lb

26. **MP** **STRUCTURE** Evaluate the expression $-8x + 5 - 2x - 4 + 5x$ when $x = 2$ before and after simplifying. Which method do you prefer? Explain.

27. **OPEN-ENDED** Write an expression with five different terms that is equivalent to $8x^2 + 3x^2 + 3y$. Justify your answer.

28. **MP** **STRUCTURE** Which of the following shows a correct way of simplifying $6 + (3 - 5x)$? Explain the errors made in the other choices.

A. $6 + (3 - 5x) = (6 + 3 - 5)x = 4x$

B. $6 + (3 - 5x) = 6 + (3 - 5)x = 6 + (-2)x = 6 - 2x$

C. $6 + (3 - 5x) = (6 + 3) - 5x = 9 - 5x$

D. $6 + (3 - 5x) = (6 + 3 + 5) - x = 14 - x$

29. **MP** **PRECISION** Two comets orbit the Sun. One comet travels 30,000 miles per hour and the other comet travels 28,500 miles per hour. What is the most efficient way to calculate the difference of the distances traveled by the comets for any given number of minutes? Justify your answer.

	Car	Truck
Wash	$8	$10
Wax	$12	$15

30. **MP** **MODELING REAL LIFE** Find the earnings for washing and waxing 12 cars and 8 trucks. Justify your answer.

31. **CRITICAL THINKING** You apply gold foil to a piece of red poster board to make the design shown.

   a. Find the area of the gold foil when $x = 3$. Justify your answer.

   b. The pattern at the right is called "St. George's Cross." Find a country that uses this pattern as its flag.

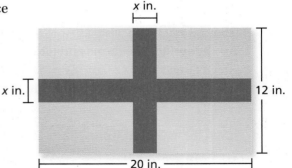

x in.

x in.

12 in.

20 in.

32. **GEOMETRY** Two rectangles have different dimensions. Each rectangle has a perimeter of $(7x + 5)$ inches. Draw and label diagrams that represent possible dimensions of the rectangles.

3.2 Adding and Subtracting Linear Expressions

Learning Target: Find sums and differences of linear expressions.

Success Criteria:
- I can explain the difference between linear and nonlinear expressions.
- I can find opposites of terms that include variables.
- I can apply properties of operations to add and subtract linear expressions.

EXPLORATION 1

Using Algebra Tiles

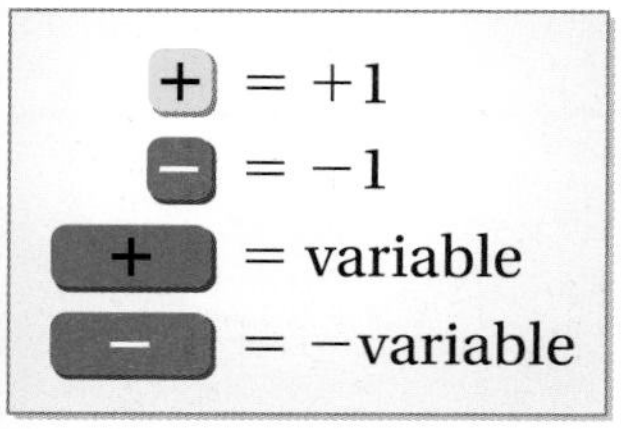

$\boxed{+} = +1$

$\boxed{-} = -1$

$\boxed{+\ } = $ variable

$\boxed{-\ } = -$variable

Work with a partner. You can use the algebra tiles shown at the left to find sums and differences of algebraic expressions.

a. How can you use algebra tiles to model a sum of terms that equals 0? Explain your reasoning.

b. Write each sum or difference modeled below. Then use the algebra tiles to simplify the expression.

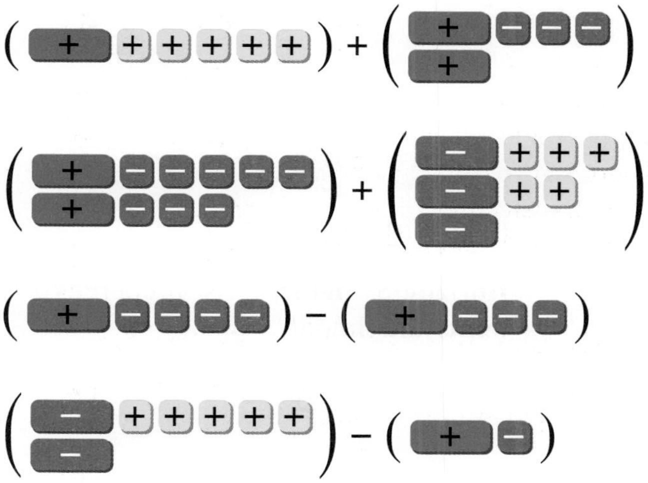

Math Practice

Consider Similar Problems

How is using integer counters to find sums and differences of integers similar to using algebra tiles to find sums and differences of algebraic expressions?

c. Write two algebraic expressions of the form $ax + b$, where a and b are rational numbers. Find the sum and difference of the expressions.

EXPLORATION 2

Using Properties of Operations

Work with a partner.

a. Do algebraic expressions, such as $2x$, $-3y$, and $3z + 1$ have additive inverses? How do you know?

b. How can you find the sums and differences modeled in Exploration 1 without using algebra tiles? Explain your reasoning.

A **linear expression** is an algebraic expression in which the exponent of each variable is 1.

Linear Expressions	$-4x$	$3x + 5y$	$5 - \dfrac{1}{6}x$
Nonlinear Expressions	$\dfrac{1}{2}x^2$	$-7x^3 + x$	$x^5 + 1$

You can use either a vertical or a horizontal method to add linear expressions.

EXAMPLE 1   **Adding Linear Expressions**

Find each sum.

a. $(x - 2) + (3x + 8)$

Vertical method: Align like terms vertically and add.

$$
\begin{array}{r}
x - 2 \\
+\ 3x + 8 \\
\hline
4x + 6
\end{array}
$$

 The sum is $4x + 6$.

 Linear expressions are usually written with the variable term first.

b. $(-4y + 3) + (11y - 5)$

Horizontal method: Use properties of operations to group like terms and simplify.

$(-4y + 3) + (11y - 5) = -4y + 3 + 11y - 5$	Rewrite the sum.
$= -4y + 11y + 3 - 5$	Commutative Property of Addition
$= (-4y + 11y) + (3 - 5)$	Group like terms.
$= 7y - 2$	Combine like terms.

The sum is $7y - 2$.

Try It   **Find the sum.**

1. $(x + 3) + (2x - 1)$ **2.** $(-8z + 4) + (8z - 7)$

3. $(4.5 - n) + (-10n + 6.5)$ **4.** $\left(\dfrac{1}{2}w - 3\right) + \left(\dfrac{1}{4}w + 3\right)$

 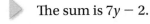

To subtract one linear expression from another, add the opposite of each term in the expression. You can use a vertical or a horizontal method.

EXAMPLE 2 **Subtracting Linear Expressions**

Find each difference.

   a. $(5x + 6) - (-x + 6)$

      Vertical method: Align like terms vertically and subtract.

$$
\begin{array}{r}
(5x + 6) \\
- (-x + 6) \\
\hline
\end{array}
\quad \boxed{\text{Add the opposite.}} \longrightarrow \quad
\begin{array}{r}
5x + 6 \\
+ \quad x - 6 \\
\hline
6x
\end{array}
$$

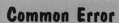 The difference is $6x$.

> **Common Error**
>
> When subtracting an expression, make sure you add the opposite of each term in the expression, not just the first term.

   b. $(7y + 5) - (8y - 6)$

      Horizontal method: Use properties of operations to group like terms and simplify.

$$
\begin{aligned}
(7y + 5) - (8y - 6) &= (7y + 5) + (-8y + 6) &&\text{Add the opposite.} \\
&= 7y + (-8y) + 5 + 6 &&\text{Commutative Property of Addition} \\
&= [7y + (-8y)] + (5 + 6) &&\text{Group like terms.} \\
&= -y + 11 &&\text{Combine like terms.}
\end{aligned}
$$

    The difference is $-y + 11$.

Try It **Find the difference.**

   5. $(m - 3) - (-m + 12)$ **6.** $(-2c + 5) - (6.3c + 20)$

 Self-Assessment *for Concepts & Skills*

Solve each exercise. Then rate your understanding of the success criteria in your journal.

   7. WRITING Describe how to distinguish a linear expression from a nonlinear expression. Give an example of each.

   8. DIFFERENT WORDS, SAME QUESTION Which is different? Find "both" answers.

> What is x more than $3x - 1$?

> Find $3x - 1$ decreased by x.

> What is the difference of $3x - 1$ and x?

> Subtract $(x + 1)$ from $3x$.

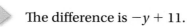

EXAMPLE 3 **Modeling Real Life**

Skateboard kits cost d dollars and you have a coupon for $2 off each one you buy. After assembly, you sell each skateboard for $(2d - 4)$ dollars. Find and interpret your profit on each skateboard sold.

 Understand the problem.

You are given information about purchasing skateboard kits and selling the assembled skateboards. You are asked to find and interpret the profit made on each skateboard sold.

 Make a plan.

Find the difference of the expressions representing the selling price and the purchase price. Then simplify and interpret the expression.

 Solve and check.

You receive $2 off of d dollars, so you pay $(d - 2)$ dollars for each kit.

$$\underset{\text{(dollars)}}{\text{Profit}} = \underset{\text{(dollars)}}{\text{Selling price}} - \underset{\text{(dollars)}}{\text{Purchase price}}$$

$= (2d - 4) - (d - 2)$ Write the difference.

$= (2d - 4) + (-d + 2)$ Add the opposite.

$= 2d - d - 4 + 2$ Group like terms.

$= d - 2$ Combine like terms.

▶ Your profit on each skateboard sold is $(d - 2)$ dollars. You pay $(d - 2)$ dollars for each kit, so you are doubling your money.

Look Back Assume each kit is $40. Verify that you double your money.

When $d = 40$:   You pay $d - 2 = 40 - 2 = \$38$.
You sell it for $2d - 4 = 2(40) - 4 = 80 - 4 = \$76$.
Because $\$38 \cdot 2 = \$76$, you double your money. ✓

 Self-Assessment for Problem Solving

Solve each exercise. Then rate your understanding of the success criteria in your journal.

9. **DIG DEEPER!** In a basketball game, the home team scores $(2m + 39)$ points and the away team scores $(3m + 40)$ points, where m is the number of minutes since halftime. Who wins the game? What is the difference in the scores m minutes after halftime? Explain.

10. Electric guitar kits originally cost d dollars online. You buy the kits on sale for 50% of the original price, plus a shipping fee of $4.50 per kit. After painting and assembly, you sell each guitar online for $(1.5d + 4.5)$ dollars. Find and interpret your profit on each guitar sold.

3.2 Practice

 Go to *BigIdeasMath.com* to get HELP with solving the exercises.

▶ Review & Refresh

Simplify the expression.

1. $4f + 11f$

2. $b + 4b - 9b$

3. $-4z - 6 - 7z + 3$

Evaluate the expression when $x = -\dfrac{4}{5}$ and $y = \dfrac{1}{3}$.

4. $x + y$

5. $2x + 6y$

6. $-x + 4y$

7. What is the surface area of a cube that has a side length of 5 feet?

   A. $25\ \text{ft}^2$ **B.** $75\ \text{ft}^2$ **C.** $125\ \text{ft}^2$ **D.** $150\ \text{ft}^2$

▶▶ Concepts, Skills, & Problem Solving

USING ALGEBRA TILES Write the sum or difference modeled by the algebra tiles. Then use the algebra tiles to simplify the expression. (See Exploration 1, p. 97.)

8.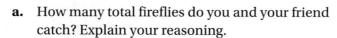

9.

ADDING LINEAR EXPRESSIONS Find the sum.

10. $(n + 8) + (n - 12)$

11. $(7 - b) + (3b + 2)$

12. $(2w - 9) + (-4w - 5)$

13. $(2x - 6) + (4x - 12)$

14. $(-3.4k - 7) + (3k + 21)$

15. $\left(-\dfrac{7}{2}z + 4\right) + \left(\dfrac{1}{5}z - 15\right)$

16. $(6 - 2.7h) + (-1.3j - 4)$

17. $\left(\dfrac{7}{4}x - 5\right) + (2y - 3.5) + \left(-\dfrac{1}{4}x + 5\right)$

18. **MP MODELING REAL LIFE** While catching fireflies, you and a friend decide to have a competition. After m minutes, you have $(3m + 13)$ fireflies and your friend has $(4m + 6)$ fireflies.

   a. How many total fireflies do you and your friend catch? Explain your reasoning.

   b. The competition lasts 3 minutes. Who has more fireflies? Justify your answer.

SUBTRACTING LINEAR EXPRESSIONS Find the difference.

19. $(-2g + 7) - (g + 11)$

20. $(6d + 5) - (2 - 3d)$

21. $(4 - 5y) - (2y - 16)$

22. $(2n - 9) - (-2.4n + 4)$

23. $\left(-\dfrac{1}{8}c + 16\right) - \left(\dfrac{3}{8} + 3c\right)$

24. $\left(\dfrac{9}{4}x + 6\right) - \left(-\dfrac{5}{4}x - 24\right)$

25. $\left(\dfrac{1}{3} - 6m\right) - \left(\dfrac{1}{4}n - 8\right)$

26. $(1 - 5q) - (2.5s + 8) - (0.5q + 6)$

27.  Your friend finds the difference $(4m + 9) - (2m - 5)$. Is your friend correct? Explain your reasoning.

$$(4m + 9) - (2m - 5) = 4m + 9 - 2m - 5$$
$$= 4m - 2m + 9 - 5$$
$$= 2m + 4$$

28. **GEOMETRY** The expression $17n + 11$ represents the perimeter of the triangle. What is the length of the third side? Explain your reasoning.

$5n + 6$ $\qquad$ $4n + 5$

29. **MP LOGIC** Your friend says the sum of two linear expressions is always a linear expression. Is your friend correct? Explain.

30. **MP MODELING REAL LIFE** You burn 265 calories running and then 7 calories per minute swimming. Your friend burns 273 calories running and then 11 calories per minute swimming. You each swim for the same number of minutes. Find and interpret the difference in the amounts of calories burned by you and your friend.

31. **DIG DEEPER!** You start a new job. After w weeks, you have $(10w + 120)$ dollars in your savings account and $(45w + 25)$ dollars in your checking account.

    a. What is the total amount of money in the accounts? Explain.

    b. How much money did you have before you started your new job? How much money do you save each week?

    c. You want to buy a new phone for $150, and still have $500 left in your accounts afterwards. Explain how to determine when you can buy the phone.

32. **MP REASONING** Write an expression in simplest form that represents the vertical distance between the two lines shown. What is the distance when $x = 3$? when $x = -3$?

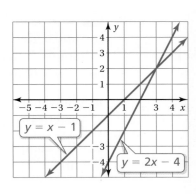

$y = x - 1$

$y = 2x - 4$

3.3 The Distributive Property

Learning Target: Apply the Distributive Property to generate equivalent expressions.

Success Criteria:
- I can explain how to apply the Distributive Property.
- I can use the Distributive Property to simplify algebraic expressions.

EXPLORATION 1

Using Models to Write Expressions

Work with a partner.

a. Write an expression that represents the area of the shaded region in each figure.

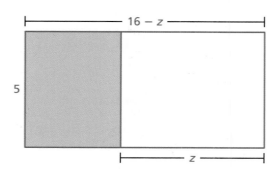

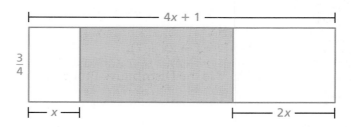

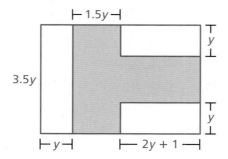

Math Practice

Find General Methods

Let a, b, and c be rational numbers. How can you write $a(bx + c)$ as a sum of two terms?

b. Compare your expressions in part (a) with other groups in your class. Did other groups write expressions that look different than yours? If so, determine whether the expressions are equivalent.

You can use the Distributive Property to simplify expressions involving variable terms and rational numbers.

EXAMPLE 1   **Using the Distributive Property**

Simplify each expression.

a. $-\dfrac{1}{3}(3n - 6)$

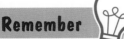

Remember

The Distributive Property states
$a(b + c) = ab + ac$
and
$a(b - c) = ab - ac.$

$$-\dfrac{1}{3}(3n - 6) = -\dfrac{1}{3}(3n) - \left(-\dfrac{1}{3}\right)(6)$$ Distributive Property

$$= -n - (-2)$$ Multiply.

$$= -n + 2$$ Add the opposite.

b. $5(-x + 3y)$

$$5(-x + 3y) = 5(-x) + 5(3y)$$ Distributive Property

$$= -5x + 15y$$ Multiply.

Try It   Simplify the expression.

1. $-1(x + 9)$ 2. $\dfrac{2}{3}(-3z - 6)$ 3. $-1.5(8m - n)$

EXAMPLE 2   **Simplifying Expressions**

Simplify $-3(-1 + 2x + 7)$.

Method 1: Use the Distributive Property before combining like terms.

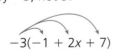

Common Error

Multiply each term in the sum by -3, not 3.

$-3(-1 + 2x + 7)$

$$-3(-1 + 2x + 7) = -3(-1) + (-3)(2x) + (-3)(7)$$ Distributive Property

$$= 3 + (-6x) + (-21)$$ Multiply.

$$= -6x - 18$$ Combine like terms.

Method 2: Combine like terms in parentheses before using the Distributive Property.

$$-3(-1 + 2x + 7) = -3(2x + 6)$$ Combine like terms.

$$= (-3)(2x) + (-3)(6)$$ Distributive Property

$$= -6x - 18$$ Multiply.

Try It   Simplify the expression.

4. $2(-3s + 1 - 5)$ 5. $-\dfrac{3}{2}(a - 4 - 2a)$

EXAMPLE 3 **Simplifying Expressions**

Simplify each expression.

Math Practice

Use Technology to Explore
Use technology to explore the equivalence of the original and simplified expressions in part (a).

a. $-\dfrac{1}{2}(6n + 4) + 2n$

$$-\dfrac{1}{2}(6n + 4) + 2n = -\dfrac{1}{2}(6n) + \left(-\dfrac{1}{2}\right)(4) + 2n \qquad \text{Distributive Property}$$

$$= -3n + (-2) + 2n \qquad \text{Multiply.}$$

$$= -n - 2 \qquad \text{Combine like terms.}$$

b. $(6d - 5) - 8\left(\dfrac{3}{4}d - 1\right)$

$$(6d - 5) - 8\left(\dfrac{3}{4}d - 1\right) = (6d - 5) - \left[8\left(\dfrac{3}{4}d\right) - 8(1)\right] \qquad \text{Distributive Property}$$

$$= (6d - 5) - (6d - 8) \qquad \text{Multiply.}$$

$$= (6d - 5) + (-6d + 8) \qquad \text{Add the opposite.}$$

$$= [6d + (-6d)] + (-5 + 8) \qquad \text{Group like terms.}$$

$$= 3 \qquad \text{Combine like terms.}$$

You can multiply an expression by −1 to find the opposite of the expression.

Try It Simplify the expression.

6. $3.5m - 1.5(m - 10)$

7. $\dfrac{4}{5}(10w - 5) - 2(w + 9)$

Self-Assessment for Concepts & Skills

Solve each exercise. Then rate your understanding of the success criteria in your journal.

8. **WRITING** Explain how to use the Distributive Property when simplifying an expression.

USING THE DISTRIBUTIVE PROPERTY Simplify the expression.

9. $\dfrac{5}{6}(-2y + 3)$

10. $6(3s - 2.5 - 5s)$

11. $\dfrac{3}{10}(4m - 8) + 9m$

12. $2.25 - 2(7.5 - 4h)$

8	3x
$\dfrac{3}{2}$	4x

13. **MP STRUCTURE** Use the terms at the left to complete the expression below so that it is equivalent to $9x - 12$. Justify your answer.

$$\blacksquare \left(\blacksquare - \blacksquare\right) + \blacksquare$$

EXAMPLE 4 **Modeling Real Life**

A square pool has a side length of *s* feet. How many 1-foot square tiles does it take to tile the border of the pool?

You are given information about a square pool and square tiles. You are asked to find the number of tiles it takes to tile the border of the pool.

Make a plan.

Draw a diagram that represents the situation. Use the diagram to write an expression for the number of tiles needed.

Solve and check.

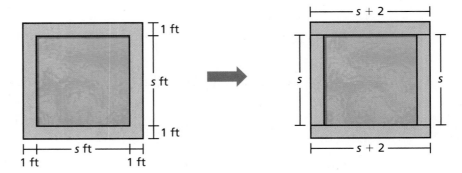

The diagram shows that the tiled border can be divided into two sections that each require *s* + 2 tiles and two sections that each require *s* tiles. So, the number of tiles can be represented by 2(*s* + 2) + 2*s*. Simplify the expression.

$$2(s + 2) + 2s = 2(s) + 2(2) + 2s \qquad \text{Distributive Property}$$
$$= 4s + 4 \qquad \text{Simplify.}$$

▷ The expression 4*s* + 4 represents the number of tiles that are needed.

Another Method
Draw a different diagram.

$$4(s + 1) = 4(s) + 4(1)$$
$$= 4s + 4 \checkmark$$

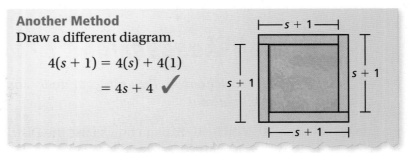

Self-Assessment for Problem Solving

Solve each exercise. Then rate your understanding of the success criteria in your journal.

14. How many 2-foot square tiles does it take to tile the border of the pool in Example 4? Explain.

15. **DIG DEEPER!** The length of a handwoven Peruvian rug is 1 foot greater than its width. The perimeter of the rug is 14 feet. What is the least number of these rugs needed to form a square without any rugs overlapping?

3.3 Practice

? Go to *BigIdeasMath.com* to get HELP with solving the exercises.

► Review & Refresh

Find the sum or difference.

1. $(5b - 9) + (b + 8)$

2. $(3m + 5) - (6 - 5m)$

3. $(1 - 9z) + 3(z - 2)$

4. $(7g - 6) - (-3n - 4)$

Evaluate the expression.

5. -6^2

6. $-9^2 \cdot 3$

7. $(-7) \cdot (-2) \cdot (-4)$

Copy and complete the statement using <, >, or =.

8. $11 \quad\boxed{}\quad |-11|$

9. $|3.5| \quad\boxed{}\quad |-5.8|$

10. $|-3.5| \quad\boxed{}\quad \left|\dfrac{17}{5}\right|$

►► Concepts, Skills, & Problem Solving

USING MODELS Write two different expressions that represent the area of the shaded region. Show that the expressions are equivalent. *(See Exploration 1, p. 103.)*

11.
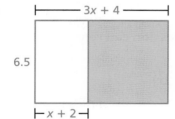

12.
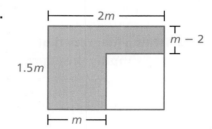

USING THE DISTRIBUTIVE PROPERTY Simplify the expression.

13. $3(a - 7)$

14. $-6(2 + x)$

15. $-5(3m - 4)$

16. $-9(-5 - 4c)$

17. $4.5(3s + 6)$

18. $-1.4(-5 + 7g)$

19. $\dfrac{2}{5}(6 - 5p)$

20. $-\dfrac{4}{3}(3q - 10)$

21. $2(3 + 4y + 5)$

22. $-9(8 + 6n - 4)$

23. $-6(-4d - 8.3 + 3d)$

24. $2.3h(6 - k)$

25. $-\dfrac{3}{8}(-4y + z)$

26. $2(-2w - 1.2 + 7x)$

27. $\dfrac{5}{3}\left(\dfrac{4}{3}a + 9b + \dfrac{2}{3}a\right)$

(MP) YOU BE THE TEACHER Your friend simplifies the expression. Is your friend correct? Explain your reasoning.

28.
$$-2(h + 8k) = -2(h) + 2(8k)$$
$$= -2h + 16k$$

29.
$$-3(4 - 5b + 7) = -3(11 - 5b)$$
$$= -3(11) + (-3)(5b)$$
$$= -33 - 15b$$

SIMPLIFYING EXPRESSIONS Simplify the expression.

30. $-3(5g + 1) + 8g$

31. $-6a + 7(-2a - 4)$

32. $9 - 3(5 - 4x)$

33. $-\frac{3}{4}(5p - 12) + 2\left(8 - \frac{1}{4}p\right)$

34. $c(4 + 3c) - 0.75(c + 3)$

35. $-1 - \frac{2}{3}\left(\frac{6}{7} - \frac{3}{7}n\right)$

36. **MP** **MODELING REAL LIFE** The cost (in dollars) of a custom-made sweatshirt is represented by $3.5n + 29.99$, where n is the number of different colors in the design. Write and interpret a simplified expression that represents the cost of 15 sweatshirts.

37. **MP** **MODELING REAL LIFE** A ski resort makes snow using a snow fan that costs \$1200. The fan has an average daily operation cost of \$9.50. Write and interpret a simplified expression that represents the cost to purchase and operate 6 snow fans.

38. **MP** **NUMBER SENSE** Predict whether the instructions below will produce equivalent expressions. Then show whether your prediction is correct.

- Subtract 3 from n, add 3 to the result, and then triple that expression.
- Subtract 3 from n, triple the result, and then add 3 to that expression.

USING A MODEL Draw a diagram that shows how the expression can represent the area of a figure. Then simplify the expression.

39. $5(2 + x + 3)$

40. $(4 + 1)(x + 2x)$

41. **DIG DEEPER!** A square fire pit with a side length of s feet is bordered by 1-foot square stones as shown.

a. How many stones does it take to border the fire pit with two rows of stones? Use a diagram to justify your answer.

b. You border the fire pit with n rows of stones. How many stones are in the nth row? Explain your reasoning.

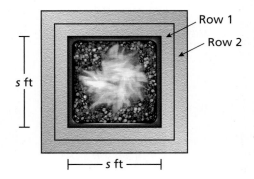

Row 1
Row 2
s ft
s ft

42. **PUZZLE** Your friend asks you to perform the following steps.

1) Pick any number except 0.
2) Add 2 to your number.
3) Multiply the result by 3.
4) Subtract 6 from the result.
5) Divide the result by your original number.

Your friend says, "The final result is 3!" Is your friend correct? If so, explain how your friend knew the final result. If not, explain why not.

3.4 Factoring Expressions

Learning Target: Factor algebraic expressions.

Success Criteria:
- I can identify the greatest common factor of terms, including variable terms.
- I can use the Distributive Property to factor algebraic expressions.
- I can write a term as a product involving a given factor.

EXPLORATION 1

Finding Dimensions

Work with a partner.

a. The models show the areas (in square units) of parts of rectangles. Use the models to find the missing values that complete the expressions. Explain your reasoning.

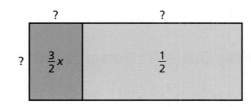

$$\frac{4}{5} + \frac{8}{5} = ?(? + ?)$$

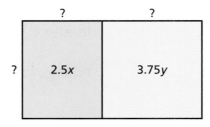

$$\frac{3}{2}x + \frac{1}{2} = ?(? + ?)$$

$$2.5x + 3.75y = ?(? + ?)$$

> **Math Practice**
>
> **View as Components**
>
> How does viewing each rectangle as two distinct parts help you complete the expressions?

b. Are the expressions you wrote in part (a) equivalent to the original expressions? Explain your reasoning.

c. Explain how you can use the Distributive Property to find rational number factors of an expression.

Key Vocabulary 🔊

factoring an
  expression, *p. 110*

When **factoring an expression**, you write the expression as a product of factors. You can use the Distributive Property to factor any rational number from an expression.

EXAMPLE 1 Factoring Out the GCF

Factor $24x - 18$ using the GCF.

Find the GCF of $24x$ and 18.

Math Practice

Communicate Precisely
Help a classmate recall how to find the GCF of two numbers.

$$24x = 2 \cdot 2 \cdot 2 \cdot 3 \cdot x$$
$$18 = 2 \cdot 3 \cdot 3$$

Circle the common prime factors.

So, the GCF of $24x$ and 18 is $2 \cdot 3 = 6$. Use the GCF to factor the expression.

$$24x - 18 = 6(4x) - 6(3) \qquad \text{Rewrite using GCF.}$$
$$= 6(4x - 3) \qquad \text{Distributive Property}$$

Try It **Factor the expression using the GCF.**

1. $15x + 25$ **2.** $4y - 20$ **3.** $36c + 24d$

EXAMPLE 2 Factoring Out a Rational Number

Factor $\dfrac{1}{2}$ out of $\dfrac{1}{2}x + \dfrac{3}{2}$.

Write each term as a product of $\dfrac{1}{2}$ and another factor.

$$\frac{1}{2}x = \frac{1}{2} \cdot x \qquad \text{Think: } \frac{1}{2}x \text{ is } \frac{1}{2} \text{ times what?}$$

$$\frac{3}{2} = \frac{1}{2} \cdot 3 \qquad \text{Think: } \frac{3}{2} \text{ is } \frac{1}{2} \text{ times what?}$$

Use the Distributive Property to factor out $\dfrac{1}{2}$.

$$\frac{1}{2}x + \frac{3}{2} = \frac{1}{2} \cdot x + \frac{1}{2} \cdot 3 \qquad \text{Rewrite the expression.}$$

$$= \frac{1}{2}(x + 3) \qquad \text{Distributive Property}$$

Try It **Factor out the coefficient of the variable term.**

4. $\dfrac{1}{2}n - \dfrac{1}{2}$ **5.** $\dfrac{3}{4}p - \dfrac{3}{2}$ **6.** $5 + 2.5q$

🔊 Multi-Language Glossary at *BigIdeasMath.com*

EXAMPLE 3 **Factoring Out a Negative Number**

Factor -2 out of $-4p + 10$.

Write each term as a product of -2 and another factor.

$-4p = -2 \cdot 2p$ Think: $-4p$ is -2 times what?

$10 = -2 \cdot (-5)$ Think: 10 is -2 times what?

Use the Distributive Property to factor out -2.

$-4p + 10 = -2 \cdot 2p + (-2) \cdot (-5)$ Rewrite the expression.

$= -2[2p + (-5)]$ Distributive Property

$= -2(2p - 5)$ Simplify.

▷ So, $-4p + 10 = -2(2p - 5)$.

Try It

7. Factor -5 out of $-5d + 30$.

8. Factor -4 out of $-8k - 12$.

 Self-Assessment for Concepts & Skills

Solve each exercise. Then rate your understanding of the success criteria in your journal.

FACTORING OUT THE GCF Factor the expression using the GCF.

9. $16n - 24$ **10.** $42a + 14b$

FACTORING OUT A RATIONAL NUMBER Factor out the coefficient of the variable term.

11. $\dfrac{1}{10}k - \dfrac{7}{10}$ **12.** $42 + 3.5h$

FACTORING OUT A NEGATIVE NUMBER Factor out the indicated number.

13. Factor -8 out of $-32d + 56$.

14. Factor -12 out of $-24k + 120$.

15. **WRITING** Describe the relationship between using the Distributive Property to simplify an expression and to factor an expression. Give an example to justify your answer.

EXAMPLE 4 **Modeling Real Life**

A rectangular landing platform for a rocket is 60 yards wide and has an area of (60x + 3600) square yards. Write an expression that represents the perimeter (in yards) of the platform.

Factor the width of 60 yards out of the given area expression to find an expression that represents the length (in yards) of the platform.

$60x + 3600 = 60 \cdot x + 60 \cdot 60$	Rewrite the expression.
$= 60(x + 60)$	Distributive Property

So, the length (in yards) of the platform can be represented by $x + 60$. Use the perimeter formula to write an expression that represents the perimeter of the platform.

$P = 2\ell + 2w$	Perimeter of a rectangle
$= 2(x + 60) + 2(60)$	Substitute for ℓ and w.
$= 2x + 120 + 120$	Multiply.
$= 2x + 240$	Add.

So, an expression that represents the perimeter (in yards) of the platform is $2x + 240$.

Self-Assessment for Problem Solving

Solve each exercise. Then rate your understanding of the success criteria in your journal.

16. An organization drills 3 wells to provide access to clean drinking water. The cost (in dollars) to drill and maintain the wells for n years is represented by $34,500 + 540n$. Write and interpret an expression that represents the cost to drill and maintain one well for n years.

17. A photograph is 16 inches long and has an area of $(16x + 96)$ square inches. A custom-made frame is 2 inches wide and costs $0.50 per square inch. Write an expression that represents the cost of the frame.

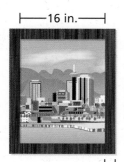

├──16 in.──┤

╟
2 in.

▶ Review & Refresh

Simplify the expression.

1. $8(k - 5)$

2. $-4.5(-6 + 2d)$

3. $-\dfrac{1}{4}(3g - 6 - 5g)$

Find the difference. Write fractions in simplest form.

4. $\dfrac{2}{3} - \left(-\dfrac{5}{3}\right)$

5. $-4.7 - 5.6$

6. $-4\dfrac{3}{8} - \left(-2\dfrac{1}{4}\right)$

Evaluate the expression when $x = 4$, $y = -6$, and $z = -3$.

7. $y \div z$

8. $\dfrac{4y}{2x}$

9. $\dfrac{3x - 2y}{z}$

▶▶ Concepts, Skills, & Problem Solving

FINDING DIMENSIONS The model shows the area (in square units) of each part of a rectangle. Use the model to find the missing values that complete the expression. Explain your reasoning. (See Exploration 1, p. 109.)

10. $2.25x + 3 = \boxed{}\left(\boxed{} + \boxed{}\right)$

11. $\dfrac{5}{6}m + \dfrac{2}{3}n = \boxed{}\left(\boxed{} + \boxed{}\right)$

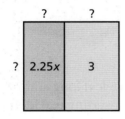

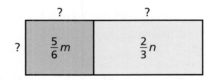

FACTORING OUT THE GCF Factor the expression using the GCF.

12. $9b + 21$

13. $32z - 48$

14. $8x + 2$

15. $3y - 24$

16. $14p - 28$

17. $6 + 16k$

18. $21 - 14d$

19. $20z - 8$

20. $15w + 65$

21. $36a + 16b$

22. $21m - 49n$

23. $12 + 9g - 30h$

FACTORING OUT A RATIONAL NUMBER Factor out the coefficient of the variable term.

24. $\dfrac{1}{7}a + \dfrac{1}{7}$

25. $\dfrac{1}{3}b - \dfrac{1}{3}$

26. $\dfrac{3}{8}d + \dfrac{3}{4}$

27. $2.2x + 4.4$

28. $1.5y - 6$

29. $0.8w + 3.6$

30. $\dfrac{15}{4} + \dfrac{3}{8}x$

31. $4h - 3$

32. $0.15c - 0.072$

33. $\dfrac{3}{8}z + 1$

34. $6s - \dfrac{3}{4}$

35. $\dfrac{5}{2}k - 2$

MP **YOU BE THE TEACHER** Your friend factors the expression. Is your friend correct? Explain your reasoning.

36.
> $16p - 28 = 4(4p - 28)$

37.
> $\frac{2}{3}y - \frac{14}{3} = \frac{2}{3} \cdot y - \frac{2}{3} \cdot 7$
>
> $\quad = \frac{2}{3}(y - 7)$

FACTORING OUT A NEGATIVE NUMBER Factor out the indicated number.

38. Factor -4 out of $-8d + 20$.

39. Factor -6 out of $18z - 15$.

40. Factor -0.25 out of $7g + 3.5$.

41. Factor $-\frac{1}{2}$ out of $-\frac{1}{2}x + 6$.

42. Factor -1.75 out of $-14m - 5.25n$.

43. Factor $-\frac{1}{4}$ out of $-\frac{1}{2}x - \frac{5}{4}y$.

44. **MP** **STRUCTURE** A rectangle has an area of $(4x + 12)$ square units. Write three multiplication expressions that can represent the product of the length and the width of the rectangle.

45. **MP** **MODELING REAL LIFE** A square wrestling mat has a perimeter of $(12x - 32)$ feet. Explain how to use the expression to find the length (in feet) of the mat. Justify your answer.

46. **MP** **MODELING REAL LIFE** A table is 6 feet long and 3 feet wide. You extend the length of the table by inserting two identical table *leaves*. The extended table is rectangular with an area of $(18 + 6x)$ square feet. Write and interpret an expression that represents the length (in feet) of the extended table.

47. **DIG DEEPER!** A three-dimensional printing pen uses heated plastic to create three-dimensional objects. A kit comes with one 3D-printing pen and p packages of plastic. An art club purchases 6 identical kits for $(180 + 58.5p)$ dollars. Write and interpret an expression that represents the cost of one kit.

48. **MP** **STRUCTURE** The area of the trapezoid is $\left(\frac{3}{4}x - \frac{1}{4}\right)$ square centimeters. Write two different pairs of expressions that represent the possible base lengths (in centimeters). Justify your answers.

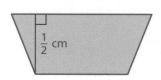

$\frac{1}{2}$ cm

Connecting Concepts

▶ *Using the Problem-Solving Plan*

1. The runway shown has an area of $(0.05x + 0.125)$ square miles. Write an expression that represents the perimeter (in feet) of the runway.

0.05 mi

Understand the problem.

You know the area of the rectangular runway in square miles and the width of the runway in miles. You want to know the perimeter of the runway in feet.

Make a plan.

Factor the width of 0.05 mile out of the expression that represents the area to find an expression that represents the length of the runway. Then write an expression that represents the perimeter (in miles) of the runway. Finally, use a measurement conversion to write the expression in terms of feet.

Solve and check.

Use the plan to solve the problem. Then check your solution.

2. The populations of two towns after t years can be modeled by $-300t + 7000$ and $-200t + 5500$. What is the combined population of the two towns after t years? The combined population of the towns in Year 10 is what percent of the combined population in Year 0?

FREEDOM

POP   7000

ELEV   5900

Performance Task

Chlorophyll in Plants

At the beginning of this chapter, you watched a STEAM Video called "Tropic Status." You are now ready to complete the performance task related to this video, available at *BigIdeasMath.com*. Be sure to use the problem-solving plan as you work through the performance task.

▶ Review Vocabulary

Write the definition and give an example of each vocabulary term.

like terms, *p. 92*
simplest form, *p. 92*

linear expression, *p. 98*

factoring an expression,
  p. 110

▶ Graphic Organizers

You can use an **Example and Non-Example Chart** to list examples and non-examples of a concept. Here is an Example and Non-Example Chart for *like terms*.

Like Terms

Examples	Non-Examples
2 and −3	y and 4
$3x$ and $-7x$	$3x$ and $3y$
x^2 and $6x^2$	$4x$ and $-2x^2$
y and $5y$	$2y$ and 5

Choose and complete a graphic organizer to help you study the concept.

1. simplest form

2. equivalent expressions

3. linear expression

4. Distributive Property

5. factoring an expression

"Here is my Example and Non-Example Chart about things that scare cats."

▶ Chapter Self-Assessment

As you complete the exercises, use the scale below to rate your understanding of the success criteria in your journal.

1	2	3	4
I do not understand.	I can do it with help.	I can do it on my own.	I can teach someone else.

3.1 Algebraic Expressions (pp. 91–96)

Learning Target: Simplify algebraic expressions.

Identify the terms and like terms in the expression.

1. $z + 8 - 4z$

2. $3n + 7 - n - 3$

3. $10x^2 - y + 12 - 3x^2$

Simplify the expression.

4. $4h - 8h$

5. $6.4r - 7 - 2.9r$

6. $2m - m - 7m$

7. $6y + 9 + 3y - 7$

8. $\frac{3}{5}x + 19 - \frac{3}{20}x - 7$

9. $\frac{2}{3}y + 14 - \frac{1}{6}y - 8$

10. Write an expression with 4 different terms that is equivalent to $5x^2 - 8$. Justify your answer.

11. Find the earnings for selling the same number of each type of sandwich. Justify your answer.

	Turkey	Ham
Pretzel Roll	2.25	1.55
Bagel	2.00	1.30

12. You buy the same number of brushes, rollers, and paint cans.

    a. Write and interpret an expression in simplest form that represents the total amount of money you spend on painting supplies.

    b. How much do you spend when you buy one set of supplies for each of 3 painters?

Paint
$21.79

Brush
$3.99

Paint roller
$6.89

3.2 Adding and Subtracting Linear Expressions (pp. 97–102)

Learning Target: Find sums and differences of linear expressions.

Find the sum.

13. $(c - 4) + (3c + 9)$

14. $(5z + 4) + (3z - 6)$

15. $(-2.1m - 5) + (3m - 7)$

16. $\left(\frac{5}{4}q + 1\right) + (q - 4) + \left(-\frac{1}{4}q + 2\right)$

Find the difference.

17. $(x - 1) - (3x + 2)$

18. $(4y + 3) - (2y - 9)$

19. $\left(\frac{1}{2}h + 7\right) - \left(\frac{3}{2}h + 9\right)$

20. $(4 - 3.7b) - (-5.4b - 4) - (1.2b + 1)$

21. A basket holds n apples. You pick $(2n - 3)$ apples, and your friend picks $(n + 4)$ apples. How many apples do you and your friend pick together? How many baskets do you need to carry all the apples? Justify your answer.

22. Greenland has a population of x people. Barbados has a population of about 4500 more than 5 times the population of Greenland. Find and interpret the difference in the populations of these two countries.

3.3 The Distributive Property (pp. 103–108)

Learning Target: Apply the Distributive Property to generate equivalent expressions.

Simplify the expression.

23. $2(a - 3)$

24. $-3(4x - 10)$

25. $-2.5(8 - b)$

26. $-7(1 - 3d - 5)$

27. $9(-3w - 6.2 + 2w)$

28. $\frac{3}{4}\left(8g - \frac{1}{4} - \frac{2}{3}g\right)$

29. Mars has m moons. The number of moons of Pluto is one more than twice the number of moons of Mars. The number of moons of Neptune is one less than 3 times the number of moons of Pluto. Write and interpret a simplified expression that represents the number of moons of Neptune.

Simplify the expression.

30. $3(2 + q) + 15$

31. $\frac{1}{8}(16m - 8) - 17$

32. $-1.5(4 - n) + 2.8$

33. $\frac{2}{5}(d - 10) - \frac{2}{3}(d + 6)$

34. The expression for degrees Fahrenheit is $\frac{9}{5}C + 32$, where C represents degrees Celsius. The temperature today is 5 degrees Celsius more than yesterday. Write and simplify an expression for the difference in degrees Fahrenheit for these two days.

3.4 Factoring Expressions (pp. 109–114)

Learning Target: Factor algebraic expressions.

Factor the expression using GCF.

35. $18a - 12$

36. $2b + 8$

37. $9 - 15x$

Factor out the coefficient of the variable term.

38. $\frac{1}{4}y + \frac{3}{8}$

39. $1.7j - 3.4$

40. $-5p + 20$

41. Factor $-\frac{3}{4}$ out of $\frac{3}{2}x - \frac{9}{4}y$.

42. You and 4 friends are buying tickets for a concert. The cost to buy one ticket is c dollars. If you buy all the tickets together, there is a discount and the cost is $(5c - 12.5)$ dollars. How much do you save per ticket when you buy the tickets together?

43. The rectangular pupil of an octopus is estimated to be 20 millimeters long with an area of $(20x - 200)$ square millimeters. Write an expression that represents the perimeter (in millimeters) of the octopus pupil.

44. A building block has a square base that has a perimeter of $(12x - 9)$ inches. Explain how to use the expression to find the length (in inches) of the wall shown.

1. Identify the terms and like terms in $4x + 9x^2 - 2x + 2$.

Simplify the expression.

2. $8x - 5 + 2x$

3. $2.5w - 3y + 4w$

4. $\frac{5}{7}x + 15 - \frac{9}{14}x - 9$

5. $(3j + 11) + (8j - 7)$

6. $(2r - 13) - (-6r + 4)$

7. $-2(4 - 3n)$

8. $3(5 - 2n) + 9n$

9. $\frac{1}{3}(6x + 9) - 2$

10. $\frac{3}{4}(8p + 12) + \frac{3}{8}(16p - 8)$

11. $-2.5(2s - 5) - 3(4.5s - 5.2)$

Factor out the coefficient of the variable term.

12. $6n - 24$

13. $\frac{1}{2}q + \frac{5}{2}$

14. $-4x + 36$

15. Find the earnings for giving a haircut and a shampoo to m men and w women. Justify your answer.

	Women	Men
Haircut	$45	$15
Shampoo	$12	$7

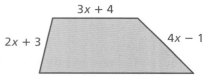
3x + 4
2x + 3
4x − 1

16. The expression $15x + 11$ represents the perimeter of the trapezoid. What is the length of the fourth side? Explain your reasoning.

17. The maximum number of charms that will fit on a bracelet is $3\left(d - \frac{2}{3}\right)$, where d is the diameter (in centimeters) of the bracelet.

    a. Write and interpret a simplified expression that represents the maximum number of charms on a bracelet.

    b. What is the maximum number of charms that fit on a bracelet that has a diameter of 6 centimeters?

18. You expand a rectangular garden so the perimeter is now twice the perimeter of the old garden. The expression $12w + 16$ represents the perimeter of the new garden, where w represents the width of the old garden.

    a. Write an expression that represents the perimeter of the old garden. Justify your answer.

    b. Write an expression that represents the area of the old garden.

1. What is the simplified form of the expression?

$$3.7x - 5 - 2.3x$$

A. $-3.6x$

B. $6x - 5$

C. $1.4x - 5$

D. $3.7x - 7.3$

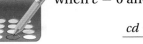

2. What is the value of the expression when $c = 0$ and $d = -6$?

$$\frac{cd - d^2}{4}$$

Test-Taking Strategy
Answer Easy Questions First

x mummies are added to (x + 2) mummies. How many mummies are there?
Ⓐ 2x + 2   Ⓑ 1 million
Ⓒ 11
Ⓓ 0

Tests about mummies get me all wound up.

"Scan the test and answer the easy questions first. Because x must be in the expression, A is correct."

3. What is the value of the expression?

$$-38 - (-14)$$

F. -52 **G.** -24

H. 24 **I.** 52

4. The daily low temperatures for a week are shown.

What is the mean low temperature of the week?

A. $-2°F$ **B.** $6°F$

C. $8°F$ **D.** $10°F$

5. You and a friend collect seashells on a beach. After h minutes, you have collected $(11 + 2h)$ seashells and your friend has collected $(5h - 2)$ seashells. How many total seashells have you and your friend collected?

    F. $7h + 9$ **G.** $3h - 13$

    H. $16h$ **I.** $7h + 13$

6. What is the value of the expression?

$$-0.28 \div (-0.07)$$

7. Which list is ordered from least to greatest?

    A. $-\left|\dfrac{3}{4}\right|, -\dfrac{1}{2}, \left|\dfrac{3}{8}\right|, -\dfrac{1}{4}, \left|-\dfrac{7}{8}\right|$ **B.** $-\dfrac{1}{2}, -\dfrac{1}{4}, \left|\dfrac{3}{8}\right|, -\left|\dfrac{3}{4}\right|, \left|-\dfrac{7}{8}\right|$

    C. $\left|-\dfrac{7}{8}\right|, \left|\dfrac{3}{8}\right|, -\dfrac{1}{4}, -\dfrac{1}{2}, -\left|\dfrac{3}{4}\right|$ **D.** $-\left|\dfrac{3}{4}\right|, -\dfrac{1}{2}, -\dfrac{1}{4}, \left|\dfrac{3}{8}\right|, \left|-\dfrac{7}{8}\right|$

8. Which number is equivalent to the expression shown?

$$-2\dfrac{1}{4} - \left(-8\dfrac{3}{8}\right)$$

    F. $-10\dfrac{5}{8}$ **G.** $-10\dfrac{1}{3}$

    H. $6\dfrac{1}{8}$ **I.** $6\dfrac{1}{2}$

9. What is the simplified form of the expression?

$$7x - 2(3x + 6)$$

    A. $15x + 30$ **B.** $x - 12$

    C. $13x + 12$ **D.** $-11x$

10. Which expression is *not* equivalent to the expression?

$$72m - 60$$

F. $6(12m - 10)$

G. $4(18m - 15)$

H. $12m$

I. $12(6m - 5)$

11. You want to buy a bicycle with your friend. You have $43.50 saved and plan to save an additional $7.25 every week. Your friend has $24.50 saved and plans to save an additional $8.75 every week.

Think
Solve
Explain

Part A Simplify and interpret an expression that represents the amount of money you and your friend save after *w* weeks.

Part B After 10 weeks, you and your friend use all of the money and buy the bike. How much does the bike cost? Who pays more towards the cost of the bike? Explain your reasoning.

12. Your friend evaluated $3 + x^2 \div y$ when $x = -2$ and $y = 4$.

$$3 + x^2 \div y = 3 + \left(-2^2\right) \div 4$$
$$= 3 - 4 \div 4$$
$$= 3 - 1$$
$$= 2$$

What should your friend do to correct his error?

A. Divide 3 by 4 before subtracting.

B. Square -2, then divide.

C. Divide -2 by 4, then square.

D. Subtract 4 from 3 before dividing.

4 Equations and Inequalities

4.1 Solving Equations Using Addition or Subtraction

4.2 Solving Equations Using Multiplication or Division

4.3 Solving Two-Step Equations

4.4 Writing and Graphing Inequalities

4.5 Solving Inequalities Using Addition or Subtraction

4.6 Solving Inequalities Using Multiplication or Division

4.7 Solving Two-Step Inequalities

Chapter Learning Target:
Understand equations and inequalities.

Chapter Success Criteria:
- ▪ I can identify key words and phrases to write equations and inequalities.
- ▪ I can write word sentences as equations and inequalities.
- ▪ I can solve equations and inequalities using properties.
- ▪ I can use equations and inequalities to model and solve real-life problems.

STEAM Video: "Space Cadets"

Space Cadets

Inequalities can be used to help determine whether someone is qualified to be an astronaut. Can you think of any other real-life situations where inequalities are useful?

Watch the STEAM Video "Space Cadets." Then answer the following questions. Tori and Robert use the inequalities below to represent requirements for applying to be an astronaut, where height is measured in inches and age is measured in years.

$h \geq 62$ $h \leq 72$ $Q \geq G + 3$ $Q \geq V + 1$
h: height Q: current age G: college graduation age
V: age when vision corrected

1. Can you use equations to correctly describe the requirements? Explain your reasoning.

2. The graph shows when a person who recently had vision correction surgery can apply to be an astronaut. Explain how you can determine when they had the surgery.

Months

Distance and Brightness of the Stars

After completing this chapter, you will be able to use the concepts you learned to answer the questions in the *STEAM Video Performance Task*. You will be given information about the celestial bodies below.

Sirius	Earth
Centauri	Sun

You will use inequalities to calculate the distances of stars from Earth and to calculate the brightnesses, or *apparent magnitudes*, of several stars. How do you think you can use one value to describe the brightnesses of all the stars that can be seen from Earth? Explain your reasoning.

Getting Ready for Chapter

Chapter Exploration

$\boxed{+} = +1$

$\boxed{-} = -1$

$\boxed{\ +\ } = x$

1. Work with a partner. Use algebra tiles to model and solve each equation.

   a. $x + 4 = -2$

   $\boxed{\ +\ }\ \boxed{+}\boxed{+}\boxed{+}\boxed{+} = \boxed{-}\boxed{-}$ Model the equation $x + 4 = -2$.

   $\boxed{\ +\ }\ \begin{matrix}\boxed{+}\boxed{+}\boxed{+}\boxed{+}\\\boxed{-}\boxed{-}\boxed{-}\boxed{-}\end{matrix} = \begin{matrix}\boxed{-}\boxed{-}\boxed{-}\\\boxed{-}\boxed{-}\boxed{-}\end{matrix}$ Add four -1 tiles to each side.

   $\boxed{\ +\ } = \begin{matrix}\boxed{-}\boxed{-}\boxed{-}\\\boxed{-}\boxed{-}\boxed{-}\end{matrix}$ Remove the zero pairs from the left side.

   $\boxed{\ +\ } = \quad\quad$ Write the solution of the equation.

   b. $-3 = x - 4$

   $\boxed{-}\boxed{-}\boxed{-} = \boxed{\ +\ }\ \boxed{-}\boxed{-}\boxed{-}\boxed{-}$ Model the equation $-3 = x - 4$.

   $\begin{matrix}\boxed{-}\boxed{-}\boxed{-}\\\boxed{+}\boxed{+}\boxed{+}\boxed{+}\end{matrix} = \boxed{\ +\ }\ \begin{matrix}\boxed{-}\boxed{-}\boxed{-}\boxed{-}\\\boxed{+}\boxed{+}\boxed{+}\boxed{+}\end{matrix}$ Add four $+1$ tiles to each side.

   $\boxed{+} = \boxed{\ +\ }$ Remove the zero pairs from each side.

   $\quad\quad = \boxed{\ +\ }$ Write the solution of the equation.

   c. $x - 6 = 2$ **d.** $x - 7 = -3$ **e.** $-15 = x - 5$

   f. $x + 3 = -5$ **g.** $7 + x = -1$ **h.** $-5 = x - 3$

2. **WRITE GUIDELINES** Work with a partner. Use your models in Exercise 1 to summarize the algebraic steps that you use to solve an equation.

Vocabulary

The following vocabulary terms are defined in this chapter. Think about what each term might mean and record your thoughts.

equivalent equations   inequality   solution set

4.1 Solving Equations Using Addition or Subtraction

Learning Target: Write and solve equations using addition or subtraction.

Success Criteria:
- I can apply the Addition and Subtraction Properties of Equality to produce equivalent equations.
- I can solve equations using addition or subtraction.
- I can apply equations involving addition or subtraction to solve real-life problems.

EXPLORATION 1

Using Algebra Tiles to Solve Equations

Work with a partner.

a. Use the examples to explain the meaning of each property.

Addition Property of Equality:
$$x + 2 = 1$$
$$x + 2 + 5 = 1 + 5$$

Subtraction Property of Equality:
$$x + 2 = 1$$
$$x + 2 - 1 = 1 - 1$$

Are these properties true for equations involving negative numbers? Explain your reasoning.

b. Write the four equations modeled by the algebra tiles. Explain how you can use algebra tiles to solve each equation. Then find the solutions.

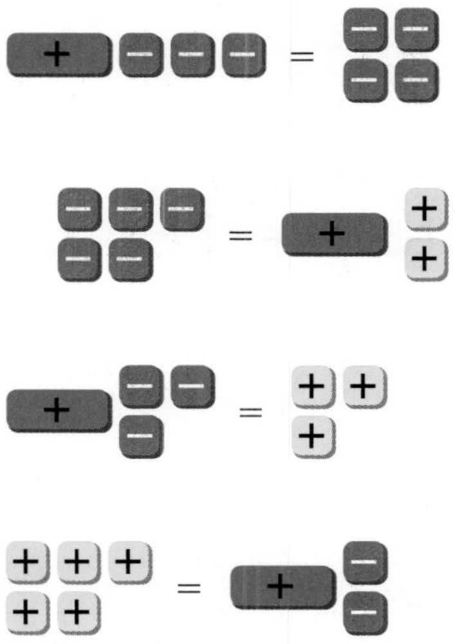

Math Practice

Analyze Relationships

How can you use the relationship between addition and subtraction to solve $x + 3 = -5$?

c. How can you solve each equation in part (b) without using algebra tiles?

Key Vocabulary
equivalent equations,
p. 128

Two equations are **equivalent equations** when they have the same solutions. The Addition and Subtraction Properties of Equality can be used to produce equivalent equations.

 Key Ideas

Addition Property of Equality

Words   Adding the same number to each side of an equation produces an equivalent equation.

Algebra   If $a = b$, then $a + c = b + c$.

Subtraction Property of Equality

Words   Subtracting the same number from each side of an equation produces an equivalent equation.

Algebra   If $a = b$, then $a - c = b - c$.

Remember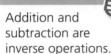

Addition and subtraction are inverse operations.

EXAMPLE 1   **Solving Equations**

a.   Solve $x - 5 = -1$.

$$x - 5 = -1$$ Write the equation.

Undo the subtraction. ⟶ $\underline{+\,5 \quad +\,5}$ Addition Property of Equality

$$x = 4$$ Simplify.

▶ The solution is $x = 4$.

Check

$x - 5 = -1$

$4 - 5 \overset{?}{=} -1$

$-1 = -1$ ✓

b.   Solve $z + \dfrac{3}{2} = \dfrac{1}{2}$.

$$z + \frac{3}{2} = \frac{1}{2}$$ Write the equation.

Undo the addition. ⟶ $\underline{-\dfrac{3}{2} \quad -\dfrac{3}{2}}$ Subtraction Property of Equality

$$z = -1$$ Simplify.

▶ The solution is $z = -1$.

Check

$z + \dfrac{3}{2} = \dfrac{1}{2}$

$-1 + \dfrac{3}{2} \overset{?}{=} \dfrac{1}{2}$

$\dfrac{1}{2} = \dfrac{1}{2}$ ✓

Try It   **Solve the equation. Check your solution.**

1. $p - 5 = -2$ **2.** $w + 13.2 = 10.4$ **3.** $x - \dfrac{5}{6} = -\dfrac{1}{6}$

EXAMPLE 2 **Writing an Equation**

A skydiving company has a profit of $750 this week. This profit is $900 more than the profit P last week. Which equation can be used to find P?

    A. $750 = 900 - P$

    B. $750 = P + 900$

    C. $900 = P - 750$

    D. $900 = P + 750$

Write an equation by rewriting the given information.

Words	The profit this week is $900 more than the profit last week.			
Equation	750	=	P	+	900

▷ The equation is $750 = P + 900$. The correct answer is **B**.

Math Practice

Recognize Usefulness of Tools

Would it be efficient to use algebra tiles to solve the equations in Example 2? What other tools could you use?

Try It

4. A bakery has a profit of $120.50 today. This profit is $145.25 less than the profit P yesterday. Write an equation that can be used to find P.

Self-Assessment for Concepts & Skills

Solve each exercise. Then rate your understanding of the success criteria in your journal.

SOLVING AN EQUATION Solve the equation. Check your solution.

    5. $c - 12 = -4$ **6.** $k + 8.4 = -6.3$ **7.** $-\dfrac{2}{3} = w - \dfrac{7}{3}$

    8. **WRITING** Are the equations $m + 3 = -5$ and $m - 4 = -12$ equivalent? Explain.

    9. **WHICH ONE DOESN'T BELONG?** Which equation does *not* belong with the other three? Explain your reasoning.

             | $x + 3 = -1$ | $x + 1 = -5$ |
             | $x - 2 = -6$ | $x - 9 = -13$ |

EXAMPLE 3 **Modeling Real Life**

You and your friend play a video game. The line graph shows both of your scores after each level. What is your score after Level 4?

Understand the problem.

You are given a line graph that shows that after Level 4, your friend's score of -8 is 33 points less than your score. You are asked to find your score after Level 4.

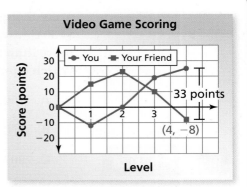

Video Game Scoring

Make a plan.

Use the information to write and solve an equation to find your score after Level 4.

Solve and check.

Words Your friend's score is 33 points less than your score.

Variable Let s be your score after Level 4.

Equation $-8 \quad = \quad s \quad - \quad 33$

$-8 = s - 33$	Write equation.
$\underline{+\ 33} \qquad \underline{+\ 33}$	Addition Property of Equality
$25 = s$	Simplify.

▷ Your score after Level 4 is 25 points.

> **Another Method** After Level 4, your score is 33 points greater than your friend's score. So, your score is $-8 + 33 = 25$. ✓

Self-Assessment for Problem Solving

Solve each exercise. Then rate your understanding of the success criteria in your journal.

10. You have \$512.50. You earn additional money by shoveling snow. Then you purchase a new cell phone for \$249.95 and have \$482.55 left. How much money do you earn shoveling snow?

11. **DIG DEEPER!** You swim 4 lengths of a pool and break a record by 0.72 second. The table shows your time for each length compared to the previous record holder. How much faster or slower is your third length than the previous record holder?

Length	Time (seconds)
1	-0.23
2	0.11
3	?
4	-0.42

Go to **BigIdeasMath.com** to get HELP with solving the exercises.

▶ Review & Refresh

Factor out the coefficient of the variable term.

1. $4x - 20$
2. $-6y - 18$
3. $-\dfrac{2}{5}w + \dfrac{4}{5}$
4. $0.75z - 6.75$

Multiply or divide.

5. -7×8
6. $6 \times (-12)$
7. $18 \div (-2)$
8. $-26 \div 4$

9. A class of 144 students voted for a class president. Three-fourths of the students voted for you. Of the students who voted for you, $\dfrac{5}{9}$ are female. How many female students voted for you?

   A. 50   **B.** 60   **C.** 80   **D.** 108

▶▶ Concepts, Skills, & Problem Solving

USING ALGEBRA TILES Solve the equation using algebra tiles. Explain your reasoning. (See Exploration 1, p. 127.)

10. $6 + x = 4$
11. $x - 3 = -5$
12. $-7 + x = -9$

SOLVING AN EQUATION Solve the equation. Check your solution.

13. $a - 6 = 13$
14. $-3 = z - 8$
15. $-14 = k + 6$
16. $x + 4 = -14$
17. $g - 9 = -19$
18. $c - 7.6 = -4$
19. $-10.1 = w + 5.3$
20. $\dfrac{1}{2} = q + \dfrac{2}{3}$
21. $p - 3\dfrac{1}{6} = -2\dfrac{1}{2}$
22. $-9.3 = d - 3.4$
23. $4.58 + y = 2.5$
24. $x - 5.2 = -18.73$
25. $q + \dfrac{5}{9} = \dfrac{5}{6}$
26. $-2\dfrac{1}{4} = r - \dfrac{4}{5}$
27. $w + 3\dfrac{3}{8} = 1\dfrac{5}{6}$

28. **MP** **YOU BE THE TEACHER** Your friend solves the equation $x + 8 = -10$. Is your friend correct? Explain your reasoning.

$$x + 8 = -10$$
$$\underline{-8 \quad -8}$$
$$x = -18$$

WRITING AND SOLVING AN EQUATION Write the word sentence as an equation. Then solve the equation.

29. 4 less than a number n is -15.
30. 10 more than a number c is 3.
31. The sum of a number y and -3 is -8.
32. The difference of a number p and 6 is -14.

33. **MP MODELING REAL LIFE** The temperature of dry ice is $-109.3°F$. This is 184.9°F less than the outside temperature. Write and solve an equation to find the outside temperature.

34. **MP MODELING REAL LIFE** A company makes a profit of $1.38 million. This is $2.54 million more than last year. What was the profit last year? Justify your answer.

35. **MP MODELING REAL LIFE** The difference in elevation of a helicopter and a submarine is $18\frac{1}{2}$ meters. The elevation of the submarine is $-7\frac{3}{4}$ meters. What is the elevation of the helicopter? Justify your answer.

GEOMETRY **What is the unknown side length?**

36. Perimeter = 12 cm

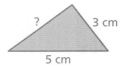

37. Perimeter = 24.2 in.

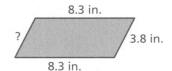

38. Perimeter = 34.6 ft

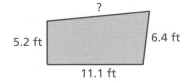

39. **MP MODELING REAL LIFE** The total height of the Statue of Liberty and its pedestal is 153 feet more than the height of the statue. What is the height of the statue? Justify your answer.

40. **MP PROBLEM SOLVING** When bungee jumping, you reach a positive elevation on your first jump that is $50\frac{1}{6}$ feet greater than the elevation you reach on your second jump. Your change in elevation on the first jump is $-200\frac{2}{3}$ feet. What is your change in elevation on the second jump?

305 ft

41. **MP MODELING REAL LIFE** Boatesville is a $65\frac{3}{5}$-kilometer drive from Stanton. A bus traveling from Stanton to Boatesville is $24\frac{1}{3}$ kilometers from Boatesville. How far has the bus traveled? Justify your answer.

42. **GEOMETRY** The sum of the measures of the angles of a triangle equals 180°. What is the missing angle measure?

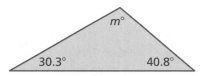

43. **DIG DEEPER!** The table shows your scores in a skateboarding competition. The first-place finisher scores 311.62 total points, which is 4.72 more points than you score. What is your score in the fourth round?

Round	1	2	3	4
Points	63.43	87.15	81.96	?

44. **CRITICAL THINKING** Find the value of $2x - 1$ when $x + 6 = -2$.

CRITICAL THINKING **Solve the equation.**

45. $|x| = 2$

46. $|x| - 2 = -2$

47. $|x| + 5 = 18$

4.2 Solving Equations Using Multiplication or Division

Learning Target: Write and solve equations using multiplication or division.

Success Criteria:
- I can apply the Multiplication and Division Properties of Equality to produce equivalent equations.
- I can solve equations using multiplication or division.
- I can apply equations involving multiplication or division to solve real-life problems.

EXPLORATION 1

Using Algebra Tiles to Solve Equations

Work with a partner.

a. Use the examples to explain the meaning of each property.

Multiplication Property of Equality:

$$3x = 1$$
$$2 \cdot 3x = 2 \cdot 1$$

Division Property of Equality:

$$3x = 1$$
$$\frac{3x}{4} = \frac{1}{4}$$

Are these properties true for equations involving negative numbers? Explain your reasoning.

b. Write the three equations modeled by the algebra tiles. Explain how you can use algebra tiles to solve each equation. Then find the solutions.

c. How can you solve each equation in part (b) without using algebra tiles?

Key Ideas

Multiplication Property of Equality

Words Multiplying each side of an equation by the same number produces an equivalent equation.

Algebra If $a = b$, then $a \cdot c = b \cdot c$.

Division Property of Equality

Words Dividing each side of an equation by the same number produces an equivalent equation.

Algebra If $a = b$, then $a \div c = b \div c, c \neq 0$.

> **Remember**
>
> Multiplication and division are inverse operations.

EXAMPLE 1 **Solving Equations**

a. Solve $\dfrac{x}{3} = -6$.

$$\dfrac{x}{3} = -6 \qquad \text{Write the equation.}$$

Undo the division. $\longrightarrow$ $3 \cdot \dfrac{x}{3} = 3 \cdot (-6) \qquad \begin{array}{l}\text{Multiplication Property}\\ \text{of Equality}\end{array}$

$$x = -18 \qquad \text{Simplify.}$$

▶ The solution is $x = -18$.

Check

$$\dfrac{x}{3} = -6$$

$$\dfrac{-18}{3} \overset{?}{=} -6$$

$$-6 = -6 \ \checkmark$$

b. Solve $18 = -4y$.

$$18 = -4y \qquad \text{Write the equation.}$$

Undo the multiplication. $\longrightarrow$ $\dfrac{18}{-4} = \dfrac{-4y}{-4} \qquad \text{Division Property of Equality}$

$$-4.5 = y \qquad \text{Simplify.}$$

▶ The solution is $y = -4.5$.

Check

$$18 = -4y$$

$$18 \overset{?}{=} -4(-4.5)$$

$$18 = 18 \ \checkmark$$

Try It **Solve the equation. Check your solution.**

1. $\dfrac{x}{5} = -2$ **2.** $-a = -24$ **3.** $3 = -1.5n$

EXAMPLE 2 **Solving Equations Using Reciprocals**

a. Solve $-\dfrac{4}{5}x = -8$.

$$-\dfrac{4}{5}x = -8 \qquad\qquad \text{Write the equation.}$$

Multiply each side by $-\dfrac{5}{4}$, the reciprocal of $-\dfrac{4}{5}$.

$$-\dfrac{5}{4}\cdot\left(-\dfrac{4}{5}x\right) = -\dfrac{5}{4}\cdot(-8) \qquad \text{Multiplication Property of Equality}$$

$$x = 10 \qquad\qquad \text{Simplify.}$$

▶ The solution is $x = 10$.

b. Solve $-6 = \dfrac{3}{2}z$.

$$-6 = \dfrac{3}{2}z \qquad\qquad \text{Write the equation.}$$

Multiply each side by $\dfrac{2}{3}$, the reciprocal of $\dfrac{3}{2}$.

$$\dfrac{2}{3}\cdot(-6) = \dfrac{2}{3}\cdot\dfrac{3}{2}z \qquad \text{Multiplication Property of Equality}$$

$$-4 = z \qquad\qquad \text{Simplify.}$$

▶ The solution is $z = -4$.

Try It Solve the equation. Check your solution.

4. $-\dfrac{8}{5}b = 5$

5. $\dfrac{3}{8}h = -9$

6. $-14 = \dfrac{2}{3}x$

 Self-Assessment for Concepts & Skills

Solve each exercise. Then rate your understanding of the success criteria in your journal.

SOLVING AN EQUATION Solve the equation. Check your solution.

7. $6d = 24$

8. $\dfrac{t}{3} = -4$

9. $-\dfrac{2}{5}p = -6$

10. **WRITING** Explain why you can use multiplication to solve equations involving division.

11. **MP STRUCTURE** Are the equations $\dfrac{2}{3}m = -4$ and $-4m = 24$ equivalent? Explain.

MP REASONING Describe the inverse operation that will undo the given operation.

12. subtracting 12

13. multiplying by $-\dfrac{1}{8}$

14. adding -6

EXAMPLE 3 **Modeling Real Life**

The temperature at midnight is shown at the left. The temperature decreases 4.5°F each hour. When will the temperature be 32°F?

The temperature at midnight is 56°F. To determine when the temperature will reach 32°F, find how long it will take the temperature to decrease 56°F − 32°F = 24°F. Write and solve an equation to find the time.

Verbal Model

Change in temperature (°F)	=	Hourly change in temperature (°F per hour)	·	Time (hours)

Variable   Let t be the time for the temperature to decrease 24°F.

> The changes in temperature are negative because they are decreasing.

Equation -24 $=$ -4.5 · t

$$-24 = -4.5t \qquad \text{Write equation.}$$

$$\frac{-24}{-4.5} = \frac{-4.5t}{-4.5} \qquad \text{Division Property of Equality}$$

$$5.\overline{3} = t \qquad \text{Simplify.}$$

Math Practice

Understand Quantities
Describe a procedure you can use to find the number of minutes in $\frac{1}{3}$ hour.

The temperature will be 32°F at $5\frac{1}{3}$ hours after midnight, or 5 hours and 20 minutes after midnight.

▷   So, the temperature will be 32°F at 5:20 A.M.

 Self-Assessment for Problem Solving

Solve each exercise. Then rate your understanding of the success criteria in your journal.

15. The elevation of the surface of a lake is 315 feet. During a drought, the water level of the lake changes $-3\frac{1}{5}$ feet per week.
Find how long it takes for the surface of the lake to reach an elevation of 299 feet. Justify your answer.

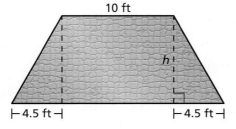

10 ft

h

⊦4.5 ft⊣   ⊦4.5 ft⊣

16. **DIG DEEPER!** The patio shown has an area of 116 square feet. What is the value of h? Justify your answer.

▶ Review & Refresh

Solve the equation. Check your solution.

1. $n - 9 = -12$

2. $-\dfrac{1}{2} = m - \dfrac{7}{4}$

3. $-6.4 = h + 8.7$

Find the difference.

4. $5 - 12$

5. $-7 - 2$

6. $4 - (-8)$

7. $-14 - (-5)$

8. Of the 120 apartments in a building, 75 have been scheduled to receive new carpet. What percent of the apartments have not been scheduled to receive new carpet?

    A. 25%   **B.** 37.5%   **C.** 62.5%   **D.** 75%

▶▶ Concepts, Skills, & Problem Solving

USING ALGEBRA TILES Solve the equation using algebra tiles. Explain your reasoning. (See Exploration 1, p. 133.)

9. $4x = -16$

10. $2x = -6$

11. $-5x = -20$

SOLVING AN EQUATION Solve the equation. Check your solution.

12. $3h = 15$

13. $-5t = -45$

14. $\dfrac{n}{2} = -7$

15. $\dfrac{k}{-3} = 9$

16. $5m = -10$

17. $8t = -32$

18. $-0.2x = 1.6$

19. $-10 = -\dfrac{b}{4}$

20. $-6p = 48$

21. $-72 = 8d$

22. $\dfrac{n}{1.6} = 5$

23. $-14.4 = -0.6p$

24. $\dfrac{3}{4}g = -12$

25. $8 = -\dfrac{2}{5}c$

26. $-\dfrac{4}{9}f = -3$

27. $26 = -\dfrac{8}{5}y$

28. **MP YOU BE THE TEACHER** Your friend solves the equation $-4.2x = 21$. Is your friend correct? Explain your reasoning.

$$-4.2x = 21$$
$$\frac{-4.2x}{4.2} = \frac{21}{4.2}$$
$$x = 5$$

WRITING AND SOLVING AN EQUATION Write the word sentence as an equation. Then solve the equation.

29. A number divided by -9 is -16.

30. A number multiplied by $\dfrac{2}{5}$ is $\dfrac{3}{20}$.

31. The product of 15 and a number is -75.

32. The quotient of a number and -1.5 is 21.

33. **MP** **MODELING REAL LIFE** You make a profit of $0.75 for every bracelet you sell. Write and solve an equation to determine how many bracelets you must sell to earn enough money to buy the soccer cleats shown.

Soccer Cleats $36

34. **MP** **MODELING REAL LIFE** A rock climber averages $12\frac{3}{5}$ feet climbed per minute. How many feet does the rock climber climb in 30 minutes? Justify your answer.

OPEN-ENDED Write (a) a multiplication equation and (b) a division equation that has the given solution.

35. -3 **36.** -2.2 **37.** $-\frac{1}{2}$ **38.** $-1\frac{1}{4}$

39. **MP** **REASONING** Which method(s) can you use to solve $-\frac{2}{3}c = 16$?

Multiply each side by $-\frac{2}{3}$.

Multiply each side by $-\frac{3}{2}$.

Divide each side by $-\frac{2}{3}$.

Multiply each side by 3, then divide each side by -2.

40. **MP** **MODELING REAL LIFE** A stock has a return of $-\$1.26$ per day. Find the number of days until the total return is $-\$10.08$. Justify your answer.

41. **MP** **PROBLEM SOLVING** In a school election, $\frac{3}{4}$ of the students vote. There are 1464 votes. Find the number of students. Justify your answer.

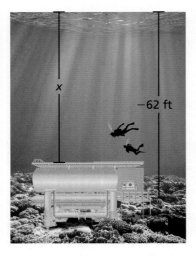

x

−62 ft

42. **DIG DEEPER!** The diagram shows Aquarius, an underwater ocean laboratory located in the Florida Keys National Marine Sanctuary. The equation $\frac{31}{25}x = -62$ can be used to calculate the depth of Aquarius. Interpret the equation. Then find the depth of Aquarius. Justify your answer.

43. **MP** **PROBLEM SOLVING** The price of a bike at Store A is $\frac{5}{6}$ the price at Store B. The price at Store A is $150.60. Find how much you save by buying the bike at Store A. Justify your answer.

44. **CRITICAL THINKING** Solve $-2|m| = -10$.

45. **MP** **NUMBER SENSE** In 4 days, your family drives $\frac{5}{7}$ of the total distance of a trip. The total distance is 1250 miles. At this rate, how many more days will it take to reach your destination? Justify your answer.

4.3 Solving Two-Step Equations

Learning Target: Write and solve two-step equations.

Success Criteria:
- I can apply properties of equality to produce equivalent equations.
- I can solve two-step equations using the basic operations.
- I can apply two-step equations to solve real-life problems.

EXPLORATION 1

Using Algebra Tiles to Solve Equations

Work with a partner.

a. What is being modeled by the algebra tiles below? What is the solution?

b. Use properties of equality to solve the original equation in part (a). How do your steps compare to the steps performed with algebra tiles?

c. Write the three equations modeled by the algebra tiles below. Then solve each equation using algebra tiles. Check your answers using properties of equality.

Math Practice

Use Operations
In part (c), what operations are you performing first? Why?

d. Explain how to solve an equation of the form $ax + b = c$ for x.

4.3 Lesson

EXAMPLE 1 **Solving a Two-Step Equation**

Solve $-3x + 5 = 2$.

$$-3x + 5 = 2 \qquad \text{Write the equation.}$$

Undo the addition. → $\underline{\quad -5 \qquad -5\quad}$ — Subtraction Property of Equality

$$-3x = -3 \qquad \text{Simplify.}$$

Undo the multiplication. → $\dfrac{-3x}{-3} = \dfrac{-3}{-3}$ — Division Property of Equality

$$x = 1 \qquad \text{Simplify.}$$

▷ The solution is $x = 1$.

Check

$$-3x + 5 = 2$$

$$-3(1) + 5 \overset{?}{=} 2$$

$$-3 + 5 \overset{?}{=} 2$$

$$2 = 2 \checkmark$$

Try It Solve the equation. Check your solution.

1. $2x + 12 = 4$ **2.** $-5c + 9 = -16$ **3.** $9 = 3x - 12$

EXAMPLE 2 **Solving a Two-Step Equation**

Solve $\dfrac{x}{8} - \dfrac{1}{2} = -\dfrac{7}{2}$.

Math Practice

Consider Simpler Forms
Can you solve the original equation by first multiplying each side by 8? Explain your reasoning.

$$\dfrac{x}{8} - \dfrac{1}{2} = -\dfrac{7}{2} \qquad \text{Write the equation.}$$

$$\underline{\quad +\dfrac{1}{2} \qquad +\dfrac{1}{2}\quad} \qquad \text{Addition Property of Equality}$$

$$\dfrac{x}{8} = -3 \qquad \text{Simplify.}$$

$$8 \cdot \dfrac{x}{8} = 8 \cdot (-3) \qquad \text{Multiplication Property of Equality}$$

$$x = -24 \qquad \text{Simplify.}$$

▷ The solution is $x = -24$.

Check

$$\dfrac{x}{8} - \dfrac{1}{2} = -\dfrac{7}{2}$$

$$\dfrac{-24}{8} - \dfrac{1}{2} \overset{?}{=} -\dfrac{7}{2}$$

$$-3 - \dfrac{1}{2} \overset{?}{=} -\dfrac{7}{2}$$

$$-\dfrac{7}{2} = -\dfrac{7}{2} \checkmark$$

Try It Solve the equation. Check your solution.

4. $\dfrac{m}{2} + 6 = 10$ **5.** $-\dfrac{z}{3} + 5 = 9$ **6.** $\dfrac{2}{5} + 4a = -\dfrac{6}{5}$

EXAMPLE 3 **Combining Like Terms Before Solving**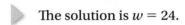

a. **Solve $3y - 8y = 25$.**

$3y - 8y = 25$	Write the equation.
$-5y = 25$	Combine like terms.
$y = -5$	Divide each side by -5.

▶ The solution is $y = -5$.

b. **Solve $-6 = \dfrac{1}{4}w - \dfrac{1}{2}w$.**

$-6 = \dfrac{1}{4}w - \dfrac{1}{2}w$	Write the equation.
$-6 = -\dfrac{1}{4}w$	Combine like terms.
$24 = w$	Multiply each side by -4.

▶ The solution is $w = 24$.

Try It **Solve the equation. Check your solution.**

7. $4 - 2y + 3 = -9$ **8.** $7x - 10x = 15$ **9.** $-8 = 1.3m - 2.1m$

 Self-Assessment *for Concepts & Skills*

Solve each exercise. Then rate your understanding of the success criteria in your journal.

MATCHING **Match the equation with the step(s) to solve it.**

10. $4 + 4n = 12$ **11.** $4n = 12$ **12.** $\dfrac{n}{4} = 12$ **13.** $\dfrac{n}{4} - 4 = 12$

A. Add 4 to each side. Then multiply each side by 4.

B. Subtract 4 from each side. Then divide each side by 4.

C. Multiply each side by 4.

D. Divide each side by 4.

SOLVING AN EQUATION **Solve the equation. Check your solution.**

14. $4p + 5 = 3$ **15.** $-\dfrac{d}{5} - 1 = -6$ **16.** $3.6g = 21.6$

17. **WRITING** Are the equations $3x + 12 = 6$ and $-2 = 4 - 3x$ equivalent? Explain.

EXAMPLE 4 **Modeling Real Life**

You install 500 feet of invisible fencing along the perimeter of a rectangular yard. The width of the yard is 100 feet. What is the length of the yard?

Understand the problem.

You are given that the perimeter of a rectangular yard is 500 feet and the width is 100 feet. You are asked to find the length of the yard.

Make a plan.

Draw a diagram of the yard. Then use the formula for the perimeter of a rectangle to write and solve an equation to find the length of the yard.

100 ft

ℓ $P = 500$ ft ℓ

100 ft

Solve and check.

$P = 2\ell + 2w$	Perimeter of a rectangle
$500 = 2\ell + 2(100)$	Substitute for P and w.
$500 = 2\ell + 200$	Multiply.
$300 = 2\ell$	Subtract 200 from each side.
$150 = \ell$	Divide each side by 2.

So, the length of the yard is 150 feet.

Another Method Use a different form of the formula for the perimeter of a rectangle, $P = 2(\ell + w)$.

$500 = 2(\ell + 100)$	Substitute for P and w.
$250 = \ell + 100$	Divide each side by 2.
$150 = \ell$	Subtract 100 from each side.

So, the length of the yard is 150 feet. ✓

Self-Assessment *for Problem Solving*

Solve each exercise. Then rate your understanding of the success criteria in your journal.

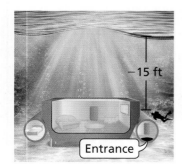

−15 ft

Entrance

18. You must scuba dive to the entrance of your room at Jules' Undersea Lodge in Key Largo, Florida. The diver is 1 foot deeper than $\frac{2}{3}$ of the elevation of the entrance. What is the elevation of the entrance?

19. **DIG DEEPER!** A car drives east along a road at a constant speed of 46 miles per hour. At 4:00 P.M., a truck is 264 miles away, driving west along the same road at a constant speed. The vehicles pass each other at 7:00 P.M. What is the speed of the truck?

Go to **BigIdeasMath.com** to get
HELP with solving the exercises.

▶ Review & Refresh

Solve the equation.

1. $3z = 18$ **2.** $-8p = 40$ **3.** $-\dfrac{m}{4} = 5$ **4.** $\dfrac{5}{6}k = -10$

Multiply or divide.

5. -6.2×5.6 **6.** $\dfrac{8}{3} \times \left(-2\dfrac{1}{2}\right)$ **7.** $\dfrac{5}{2} \div \left(-\dfrac{4}{5}\right)$ **8.** $-18.6 \div (-3)$

9. Which fraction is *not* equivalent to 0.75?

    A. $\dfrac{15}{20}$ **B.** $\dfrac{9}{12}$ **C.** $\dfrac{6}{9}$ **D.** $\dfrac{3}{4}$

▶▶ Concepts, Skills, & Problem Solving

USING ALGEBRA TILES **Write the equation modeled by the algebra tiles. Then solve the equation using algebra tiles. Check your answer using properties of equality.**
(See Exploration 1, p. 139.)

10.

11.

SOLVING AN EQUATION **Solve the equation. Check your solution.**

12. $2v + 7 = 3$ **13.** $4b + 3 = -9$ **14.** $17 = 5k - 2$

15. $-6t - 7 = 17$ **16.** $8n + 16.2 = 1.6$ **17.** $-5g + 2.3 = -18.8$

18. $2t + 8 = -10$ **19.** $-4p + 9 = -5$ **20.** $15 = -5x + 10$

21. $10.35 + 2.3h = -9.2$ **22.** $-4.8f + 6.4 = -8.48$ **23.** $7.3y - 5.18 = -51.9$

MP **YOU BE THE TEACHER** **Your friend solves the equation. Is your friend correct? Explain your reasoning.**

24.

$$-6 + 2x = -10$$
$$-6 + \frac{2x}{2} = -\frac{10}{2}$$
$$-6 + x = -5$$
$$x = 1$$

25.

$$-3(x + 6) = 12$$
$$-3x = 6$$
$$\frac{-3x}{-3} = \frac{6}{-3}$$
$$x = -2$$

SOLVING AN EQUATION **Solve the equation. Check your solution.**

26. $\dfrac{3}{5}g - \dfrac{1}{3} = -\dfrac{10}{3}$ **27.** $\dfrac{a}{4} - \dfrac{5}{6} = -\dfrac{1}{2}$ **28.** $-\dfrac{1}{3}(4 + z) = -\dfrac{5}{6}$

29. $2 - \dfrac{b}{3} = -\dfrac{5}{2}$ **30.** $-\dfrac{2}{3}\left(x + \dfrac{3}{5}\right) = \dfrac{1}{2}$ **31.** $-\dfrac{9}{4}v + \dfrac{4}{5} = \dfrac{7}{8}$

Temperature at 1:00 P.M.

←— 35°F

32. **MP** **PRECISION** Starting at 1:00 P.M., the temperature changes −4°F per hour. Write and solve an equation to determine how long it will take for the temperature to reach −1°F.

COMBINING LIKE TERMS Solve the equation. Check your solution.

33. $3v - 9v = 30$

34. $12t - 8t = -52$

35. $-8d - 5d + 7d = 72$

36. $-3.8g + 5 + 2.7g = 12.7$

37. **MP** **MODELING REAL LIFE** You have $9.25. How many games can you bowl if you rent bowling shoes? Justify your answer.

38. **MP** **MODELING REAL LIFE** A cell phone company charges a monthly fee plus $0.25 for each text message you send. The monthly fee is $30.00. You owe $59.50. How many text messages did you send? Justify your answer.

Shoe Rentals: $2.50

Bowling: $2.25 per game

39. **MP** **PROBLEM SOLVING** The height at the top of a roller coaster hill is 10 times the height h of the starting point. The height decreases 100 feet from the top to the bottom of the hill. The height at the bottom of the hill is −10 feet. Find h.

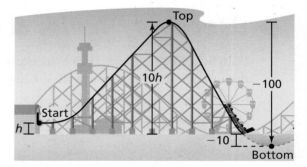

Top

10h

−100

Start

h

−10

Bottom

40. **MP** **MODELING REAL LIFE** On a given day, the coldest surface temperature on the Moon, −280°F, is 53.6°F colder than twice the coldest surface temperature on Earth. What is the coldest surface temperature on Earth that day? Justify your answer.

41. **DIG DEEPER!** On Saturday, you catch insects for your science class. Five of the insects escape. The remaining insects are divided into three groups to share in class. Each group has nine insects.

   a. Write and solve an equation to find the number of insects you catch on Saturday.

   b. Find the number of insects you catch on Saturday without using an equation. Compare the steps used to solve the equation in part (a) with the steps used to solve the problem in part (b).

   c. Describe a problem that is more convenient to solve using an equation. Then describe a problem that is more convenient to solve without using an equation.

42. **GEOMETRY** How can you change the dimensions of the rectangle so that the ratio of the length to the width stays the same, but the perimeter is 185 centimeters? Write an equation that shows how you found your answer.

12 cm

25 cm

4.4 Writing and Graphing Inequalities

Learning Target: Write inequalities and represent solutions of inequalities on number lines.

Success Criteria:
- I can write word sentences as inequalities.
- I can determine whether a value is a solution of an inequality.
- I can graph the solutions of inequalities.

EXPLORATION 1

Understanding Inequality Statements

Work with a partner. Create a number line on the floor with both positive and negative numbers.

a. For each statement, stand at a number on your number line that could represent the situation. On what other numbers can you stand?

- At least 3 students from our school are in a chess tournament.

- Your ring size is less than 7.5.

- The temperature is no more than −1 degree Fahrenheit.

- The elevation of a frogfish is greater than $-8\frac{1}{2}$ meters.

Math Practice

State the Meaning of Symbols

What do the symbols $<, >, \leq$, and $\geq$ mean?

b. How can you represent all of the solutions for each statement in part (a) on a number line?

Key Vocabulary
inequality, *p. 146*
solution of an
    inequality, *p. 146*
solution set, *p. 146*
graph of an
    inequality, *p. 148*

An **inequality** is a mathematical sentence that compares expressions. It contains the symbols $<$, $>$, $\leq$, or $\geq$. To write a word sentence as an inequality, look for the following phrases to determine where to place the inequality symbol.

Inequality Symbols				
Symbol	$<$	$>$	$\leq$	$\geq$
Key Phrases	• is less than • is fewer than	• is greater than • is more than	• is less than or equal to • is at most • is no more than	• is greater than or equal to • is at least • is no less than

EXAMPLE 1 ▶ **Writing an Inequality**

A number q plus 5 is less than or equal to -7.9. Write this word sentence as an inequality.

A <u>number q plus 5</u> <u>is less than or equal to</u> -7.9.

$$\underbrace{q + 5} \qquad \underbrace{\leq} \qquad -7.9$$

▶ An inequality is $q + 5 \leq -7.9$.

Try It **Write the word sentence as an inequality.**

1. A number x is at least -10.

2. Twice a number y is more than $-\dfrac{5}{2}$.

A **solution of an inequality** is a value that makes the inequality true. An inequality can have more than one solution. The set of all solutions of an inequality is called the **solution set**.

Value of x	$x + 2 \leq -1$	Is the inequality true?
-2	$-2 + 2 \overset{?}{\leq} -1$ $0 \not\leq -1$ ✗	no
-3	$-3 + 2 \overset{?}{\leq} -1$ $-1 \leq -1$ ✓	yes
-4	$-4 + 2 \overset{?}{\leq} -1$ $-2 \leq -1$ ✓	yes

Reading

The symbol $\not\leq$ means *is not less than or equal to.*

◀)) *Multi-Language Glossary at BigIdeasMath.com*

EXAMPLE 2 **Checking Solutions**

a. **Tell whether −2 is a solution of** $y - 5 \geq -6$.

$$y - 5 \geq -6 \qquad \text{Write the inequality.}$$

$$-2 - 5 \overset{?}{\geq} -6 \qquad \text{Substitute } -2 \text{ for } y.$$

$$-7 \not\geq -6 \quad \textbf{✗} \qquad \text{Simplify.}$$

▷ So, −2 is *not* a solution of the inequality.

b. **Tell whether −2 is a solution of** $-5.5y < 14$.

$$-5.5y < 14 \qquad \text{Write the inequality.}$$

$$-5.5(-2) \overset{?}{<} 14 \qquad \text{Substitute } -2 \text{ for } y.$$

$$11 < 14 \quad \textbf{✓} \qquad \text{Simplify.}$$

▷ So, −2 is a solution of the inequality.

Math Practice

Consider Similar Problems
Compare the solution of $y - 5 = -6$ to the solutions of $y - 5 \geq -6$.

Try It **Tell whether −5 is a solution of the inequality.**

3. $x + 12 > 7$ **4.** $1 - 2p \leq -9$ **5.** $n \div 2.5 \geq -3$

Self-Assessment *for Concepts & Skills*

Solve each exercise. Then rate your understanding of the success criteria in your journal.

6. (MP) **REASONING** Do $x < 5$ and $5 < x$ represent the same inequality? Explain.

7. **DIFFERENT WORDS, SAME QUESTION** Which is different? Write "both" inequalities.

A number k is less than or equal to −3.

A number k is at least −3.   A number k is at most −3.

A number k is no more than −3.

CHECKING SOLUTIONS **Tell whether −4 is a solution of the inequality.**

8. $c + 6 \leq 3$ **9.** $6 > p \div (-0.5)$ **10.** $-7 < 2g + 1$

The **graph of an inequality** shows all the solutions of the inequality on a number line. An open circle ○ is used when a number is *not* a solution. A closed circle ● is used when a number is a solution. An arrow to the left or right shows that the graph continues in that direction.

EXAMPLE 3   Modeling Real Life

A rock climber's sleeping bag is recommended for temperatures no less than −15°C. Write and graph an inequality that represents the recommended temperatures for the sleeping bag.

Words	temperatures	no less than	−15°C
Variable	Let t be the recommended temperatures.		
Inequality	t	$\geq$	-15

An inequality is $t \geq -15$. Graph the inequality.

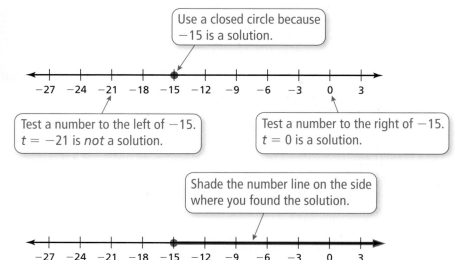

Use a closed circle because −15 is a solution.

Test a number to the left of −15. $t = -21$ is *not* a solution.

Test a number to the right of −15. $t = 0$ is a solution.

Shade the number line on the side where you found the solution.

The graph in Example 3 shows that the inequality has *infinitely many* solutions.

Self-Assessment *for Problem Solving*

Solve each exercise. Then rate your understanding of the success criteria in your journal.

11. The three requirements to pass a fitness test are shown. Write and graph three inequalities that represent the requirements. Then give a set of possible values for a person who passes the test.

Fitness Test
− Jog at least 2 kilometers

− Perform 25 or more push-ups

− Perform at least 10 pull-ups

12. To set a depth record, a submersible vehicle must reach a water depth less than −715 feet. A vehicle breaks the record by more than 10 feet. Write and graph an inequality that represents the possible depths reached by the vehicle.

4.4 Practice

? Go to **BigIdeasMath.com** to get HELP with solving the exercises.

▶ Review & Refresh

Solve the equation. Check your solution.

1. $p - 8 = 3$

2. $8.7 + w = 5.1$

3. $x - 2 = -9$

4. $8v + 5 = 1$

5. $\dfrac{7}{8} - \dfrac{1}{4}n = -\dfrac{3}{8}$

6. $1.8 = 2.1h - 5.7 - 4.6h$

7. Which expression has a value less than -5?

   A. $5 + 8$ **B.** $-9 + 5$ **C.** $1 + (-8)$ **D.** $7 + (-2)$

▶▶ Concepts, Skills, & Problem Solving

UNDERSTANDING INEQUALITY STATEMENTS Choose a number that could represent the situation. What other numbers could represent the situation? (See Exploration 1, p. 145.)

8. Visibility in an airplane is greater than 6.5 miles.

9. You must sell no fewer than 20 raffle tickets for a fundraiser.

10. You consume at most 1800 calories per day.

11. The elevation of the Dead Sea is less than -400 meters.

WRITING AN INEQUALITY Write the word sentence as an inequality.

12. A number y is no more than -8.

13. A number w added to 2.3 is more than 18.

14. A number t multiplied by -4 is at least $-\dfrac{2}{5}$.

15. A number b minus 4.2 is less than -7.5.

16. $-\dfrac{5}{9}$ is no less than 5 times a number k.

17. **MP YOU BE THE TEACHER** Your friend writes the word sentence as an inequality. Is your friend correct? Explain your reasoning.

> Twice a number x is at most -24.
>
> $2x \le -24$

CHECKING SOLUTIONS Tell whether the given value is a solution of the inequality.

18. $n + 8 \le 13; n = 4$

19. $-15 < 5h; h = -5$

20. $p + 1.4 \le 0.5; p = 0.1$

21. $\dfrac{a}{6} > -4; a = -18$

22. $6 \ge -\dfrac{2}{3}s; s = -9$

23. $\dfrac{7}{8} - 3k < -\dfrac{1}{2}; k = \dfrac{1}{4}$

GRAPHING AN INEQUALITY Graph the inequality on a number line.

24. $r \leq -9$

25. $g > 2.75$

26. $x \geq -3\frac{1}{2}$

27. $1\frac{1}{4} > z$

28. **MP MODELING REAL LIFE** Each day at lunchtime, at least 53 people buy food from a food truck. Write and graph an inequality that represents this situation.

CHECKING SOLUTIONS Tell whether the given value is a solution of the inequality.

29. $4k < k + 8; k = 3$

30. $\frac{w}{3} \geq w - 12; w = 15$

31. $7 - 2y > 3y + 13; y = -1$

32. $\frac{3}{4}b - 2 \leq 2b + 8; b = -4$

33. **MP PROBLEM SOLVING** A single subway ride for a student costs \$1.25. A monthly pass costs \$35.

    a. Write an inequality that represents the numbers of times you can ride the subway each month for the monthly pass to be a better deal.

    b. You ride the subway about 45 times per month. Should you buy the monthly pass? Explain.

34. **MP LOGIC** Consider the inequality $b > -2$.

    a. Describe the values of b that are solutions of the inequality.

    b. Describe the values of b that are *not* solutions of the inequality. Write an inequality that represents these values.

    c. What do all the values in parts (a) and (b) represent? Is this true for any similar pair of inequalities? Explain your reasoning.

Habitable Zone

35. **MP MODELING REAL LIFE** A planet orbiting a star at a distance such that its temperatures are right for liquid water is said to be in the star's *habitable zone*. The habitable zone of a particular star is at least 0.023 AU and at most 0.054 AU from the star (1 AU is equal to the distance between Earth and the Sun). Draw a graph that represents the habitable zone.

36. **DIG DEEPER!** The *girth* of a package is the distance around the perimeter of a face that does not include the length as a side. A postal service says that a rectangular package can have a maximum combined length and girth of 108 inches.

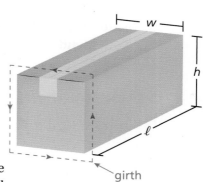

    a. Write an inequality that represents the allowable dimensions for the package.

    b. Find three different sets of allowable dimensions that are reasonable for the package. Find the volume of each package.

4.5 Solving Inequalities Using Addition or Subtraction

Learning Target: Write and solve inequalities using addition or subtraction.

Success Criteria:
- I can apply the Addition and Subtraction Properties of Inequality to produce equivalent inequalities.
- I can solve inequalities using addition or subtraction.
- I can apply inequalities involving addition or subtraction to solve real-life problems.

EXPLORATION 1

Writing Inequalities

Work with a partner. Use two number cubes on which the odd numbers are negative on one of the number cubes and the even numbers are negative on the other number cube.

- Roll the number cubes. Write an inequality that compares the numbers.

- Roll one of the number cubes. Add the number to each side of the inequality and record your result.

- Repeat the previous two steps five more times.

Math Practice

Analyze Conjectures

Use your conjecture to solve $x + 3 < 1$. Does the solution make sense?

a. When you add the same number to each side of an inequality, does the inequality remain true? Explain your reasoning.

b. When you subtract the same number from each side of an inequality, does the inequality remain true? Use inequalities generated by number cubes to justify your answer.

c. Use your results in parts (a) and (b) to make a conjecture about how to solve an inequality of the form $x + a < b$ for x.

🔑 Key Ideas

You can solve inequalities in the same way you solve equations. Use inverse operations to get the variable by itself.

Addition Property of Inequality

Words When you add the same number to each side of an inequality, the inequality remains true.

Numbers

$$-4 \;<\; 3$$
$$\underline{+\,2 \quad +\,2}$$
$$-2 \;<\; 5$$

Algebra If $a < b$, then $a + c < b + c$.

If $a > b$, then $a + c > b + c$.

Subtraction Property of Inequality

Words When you subtract the same number from each side of an inequality, the inequality remains true.

Numbers

$$-2 \;<\; 2$$
$$\underline{-\,3 \quad -\,3}$$
$$-5 \;<\; -1$$

Algebra If $a < b$, then $a - c < b - c$.

If $a > b$, then $a - c > b - c$.

These properties are also true for $\leq$ and $\geq$.

EXAMPLE 1   Solving an Inequality Using Addition

Solve $x - 5 < -3$. Graph the solution.

$x - 5 < -3$	Write the inequality.
Undo the subtraction. → $\underline{+\,5 \quad +\,5}$	Addition Property of Inequality
$x < 2$	Simplify.

Check:

$x = 0$: $0 - 5 \overset{?}{<} -3$

$\quad\quad\quad -5 < -3$ ✓

$x = 5$: $5 - 5 \overset{?}{<} -3$

$\quad\quad\quad 0 \not< -3$ ✗

The solution is $x < 2$.

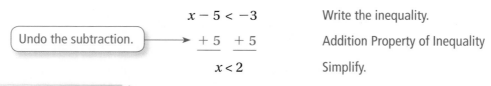

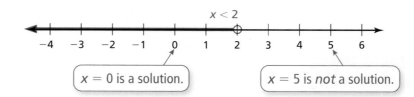

$x = 0$ is a solution.

$x = 5$ is *not* a solution.

Try It **Solve the inequality. Graph the solution.**

1. $y - 6 > -7$

2. $b - 3.8 \leq 1.7$

3. $-\dfrac{1}{2} > z - \dfrac{1}{4}$

 **EXAMPLE 2** **Solving an Inequality Using Subtraction**

Solve $13 \leq x + 14$. Graph the solution.

$$13 \leq x + 14 \qquad \text{Write the inequality.}$$

Undo the addition. $\longrightarrow$
$$\underline{-14 \qquad\quad -14} \qquad \text{Subtraction Property of Inequality}$$
$$-1 \leq x \qquad\qquad \text{Simplify.}$$

Reading
The inequality $-1 \leq x$ is the same as $x \geq -1$.

▶ The solution is $x \geq -1$.

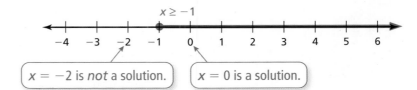

$x \geq -1$

$x = -2$ is *not* a solution. $x = 0$ is a solution.

Try It Solve the inequality. Graph the solution.

4. $w + 3 \leq -1$ **5.** $8.5 \geq d + 10$ **6.** $x + \dfrac{3}{4} > 1\dfrac{1}{2}$

 ## Self-Assessment for Concepts & Skills

Solve each exercise. Then rate your understanding of the success criteria in your journal.

7. WRITING Are the inequalities $c + 3 > 5$ and $c - 1 > 1$ equivalent? Explain.

8. WHICH ONE DOESN'T BELONG? Which inequality does *not* belong with the other three? Explain your reasoning.

$$w + \dfrac{7}{4} < \dfrac{3}{4} \qquad\qquad w - \dfrac{3}{4} > -\dfrac{7}{4}$$

$$w + \dfrac{7}{4} > \dfrac{3}{4} \qquad\qquad -\dfrac{7}{4} < w - \dfrac{3}{4}$$

SOLVING AN INEQUALITY Solve the inequality. Graph the solution.

9. $x - 4 > -6$ **10.** $z + 4.5 \leq 3.25$ **11.** $\dfrac{7}{10} > \dfrac{4}{5} + g$

12. OPEN-ENDED Write two different inequalities that can be represented using the graph. Justify your answers.

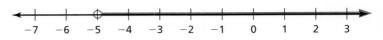

EXAMPLE 3 **Modeling Real Life**

To become an astronaut pilot for NASA, a person can be no taller than 6.25 feet. Your friend is 5 feet 9 inches tall. How much can your friend grow and still meet the requirement?

Because the height requirement is given in feet and your friend's height is given in feet and inches, rewrite your friend's height in feet.

$$9 \text{ in.} = 9 \text{ in.} \times \frac{1 \text{ ft}}{12 \text{ in.}} = \frac{9}{12} \text{ ft} = 0.75 \text{ ft}$$

$$5 \text{ ft } 9 \text{ in.} = 5 \text{ ft} + 0.75 \text{ ft} = 5.75 \text{ ft}$$

Use a verbal model to write an inequality that represents the situation.

Verbal Model	Current height (feet)	+	Amount your friend can grow (feet)	≤	Height limit (feet)

Variable   Let h be the possible amounts (in feet) your friend can grow.

Inequality   5.75   + h ≤   6.25

$5.75 + h \le$	6.25	Write the inequality.
-5.75	-5.75	Subtraction Property of Inequality
$h \le$	0.5	Simplify.

▷ So, your friend can grow no more than 0.5 foot, or 6 inches.

 Self-Assessment for Problem Solving

Solve each exercise. Then rate your understanding of the success criteria in your journal.

13. **DIG DEEPER!** A volcanologist rappels 1200 feet into a volcano. He wants to climb out of the volcano in less than 4 hours. He climbs the first 535 feet in 100 minutes. Graph an inequality that represents the average rates at which he can climb the remaining distance and meet his goal. Justify your answer.

14. You install a mailbox by burying a post as shown. According to postal service guidelines, the bottom of the box must be at least 41 inches, but no more than 45 inches, above the road. Write and interpret two inequalities that describe the possible lengths of the post.

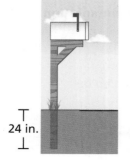

24 in.

4.5 Practice

Go to *BigIdeasMath.com* to get HELP with solving the exercises.

Review & Refresh

Write the word sentence as an inequality.

1. A number p is greater than 5.

2. A number z times 3 is at most -4.8.

3. The sum of a number n and $\frac{2}{3}$ is no less than $5\frac{1}{3}$.

Solve the equation. Check your solution.

4. $4x = 36$

5. $\frac{w}{3} = -9$

6. $-2b = 44$

7. $60 = \frac{3}{4}h$

8. Which fraction is equivalent to -2.4?

   A. $-\frac{12}{5}$

   B. $-\frac{51}{25}$

   C. $-\frac{8}{5}$

   D. $-\frac{6}{25}$

Concepts, Skills, & Problem Solving

WRITING AN INEQUALITY **Write an inequality that compares the given numbers. Does the inequality remain true when you add 2 to each side? Justify your answer.** (See Exploration 1, p. 151.)

9. $-1; 4$

10. $-3; -6$

11. $-4; -1$

SOLVING AN INEQUALITY **Solve the inequality. Graph the solution.**

12. $x + 7 \geq 18$

13. $a - 2 > 4$

14. $3 \leq 7 + g$

15. $8 + k \leq -3$

16. $-12 < y - 6$

17. $n - 4 < 5$

18. $t - 5 \leq -7$

19. $p + \frac{1}{4} \geq 2$

20. $\frac{2}{7} > b + \frac{5}{7}$

21. $z - 4.7 \geq -1.6$

22. $-9.1 < d - 6.3$

23. $\frac{8}{5} > s + \frac{12}{5}$

24. $-\frac{7}{8} \geq m - \frac{13}{8}$

25. $r + 0.2 < -0.7$

26. $h - 6 \leq -8.4$

MP **YOU BE THE TEACHER** **Your friend solves the inequality and graphs the solution. Is your friend correct? Explain your reasoning.**

27.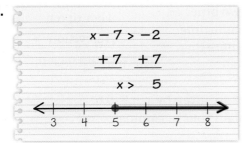

28.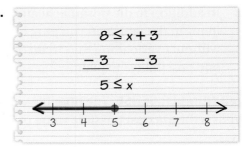

29. **MP MODELING REAL LIFE** A small airplane can hold 44 passengers. Fifteen passengers board the plane.

  a. Write and solve an inequality that represents the additional numbers of passengers that can board the plane.

  b. Can 30 more passengers board the plane? Explain.

GEOMETRY Find the possible values of *x*.

30. The perimeter is less than 28 feet.

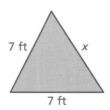

7 ft   x

7 ft

31. The base is greater than the height.

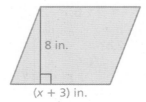

8 in.

(x + 3) in.

32. The perimeter is less than or equal to 51 meters.

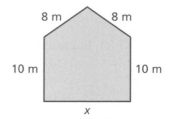

8 m   8 m

10 m   10 m

x

33. **MP REASONING** The inequality $d + s > -3$ is equivalent to $d > -7$. What is the value of *s*?

34. **MP LOGIC** You can spend up to $35 on a shopping trip.

  a. You want to buy a shirt that costs $14. Write and solve an inequality that represents the remaining amounts of money you can spend if you buy the shirt.

  b. You notice that the shirt is on sale for 30% off. How does this change your inequality in part (a)?

35. **DIG DEEPER!** If items plugged into a circuit use more than 2400 watts of electricity, the circuit overloads. A portable heater that uses 1050 watts of electricity is plugged into the circuit.

  a. Find the additional numbers of watts you can plug in without overloading the circuit.

  b. In addition to the portable heater, what two other items in the table can you plug in at the same time without overloading the circuit? Is there more than one possibility? Explain.

Item	Watts
Aquarium	200
Hair dryer	1200
Television	150
Vacuum cleaner	1100

36. **MP NUMBER SENSE** The possible values of *x* are given by $x + 8 \le 6$. What is the greatest possible value of $7x$? Explain your reasoning.

4.6 Solving Inequalities Using Multiplication or Division

Learning Target: Write and solve inequalities using multiplication or division.

Success Criteria:
- I can apply the Multiplication and Division Properties of Inequality to produce equivalent inequalities.
- I can solve inequalities using multiplication or division.
- I can apply inequalities involving multiplication or division to solve real-life problems.

EXPLORATION 1

Writing Inequalities

Work with a partner. Use two number cubes on which the odd numbers are negative on one of the number cubes and the even numbers are negative on the other number cube.

> - Roll the number cubes. Write an inequality that compares the numbers.
>
> - Roll one of the number cubes. Multiply each side of the inequality by the number and record your result.
>
> - Repeat the previous two steps nine more times.

a. When you multiply each side of an inequality by the same number, does the inequality remain true? Explain your reasoning.

b. When you divide each side of an inequality by the same number, does the inequality remain true? Use inequalities generated by number cubes to justify your answer.

c. Use your results in parts (a) and (b) to make a conjecture about how to solve an inequality of the form $ax < b$ for x when $a > 0$ and when $a < 0$.

Math Practice

Use Counterexamples
Use a counterexample to show that $2a \geq a$ is not true for every value of a.

4.6 Lesson

🔑 Key Idea

Multiplication and Division Properties of Inequality (Case 1)

Words When you multiply or divide each side of an inequality by the same *positive* number, the inequality remains true.

Numbers $-4 < 6$ $4 > -6$

$$2 \cdot (-4) < 2 \cdot 6 \qquad\qquad \frac{4}{2} > \frac{-6}{2}$$

$$-8 < 12 \qquad\qquad\qquad 2 > -3$$

Algebra If $a < b$ and c is positive, then

$$a \cdot c < b \cdot c \qquad \text{and} \qquad \frac{a}{c} < \frac{b}{c}.$$

If $a > b$ and c is positive, then

$$a \cdot c > b \cdot c \qquad \text{and} \qquad \frac{a}{c} > \frac{b}{c}.$$

These properties are also true for $\leq$ and $\geq$.

EXAMPLE 1 **Solving an Inequality Using Multiplication**

Solve $\dfrac{x}{5} \leq -3$. Graph the solution.

$$\frac{x}{5} \leq -3 \qquad\qquad \text{Write the inequality.}$$

Undo the division. → $\quad 5 \cdot \dfrac{x}{5} \leq 5 \cdot (-3) \qquad$ Multiplication Property of Inequality

$$x \leq -15 \qquad\qquad \text{Simplify.}$$

▶ The solution is $x \leq -15$.

$x \leq -15$

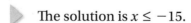

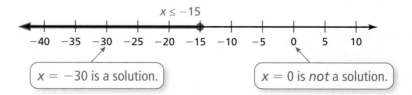

$x = -30$ is a solution. $x = 0$ is *not* a solution.

Try It Solve the inequality. Graph the solution.

1. $n \div 3 < 1$ **2.** $-0.5 \leq \dfrac{m}{10}$ **3.** $-3 > \dfrac{2}{3}p$

EXAMPLE 2 **Solving an Inequality Using Division**

Solve $6x > -18$. Graph the solution.

$$6x > -18 \qquad \text{Write the inequality.}$$

Undo the multiplication. ⟶ $\dfrac{6x}{6} > \dfrac{-18}{6} \qquad \text{Division Property of Inequality}$

$$x > -3 \qquad \text{Simplify.}$$

▷ The solution is $x > -3$.

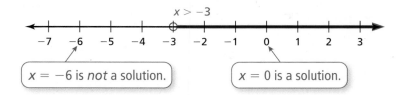

$x = -6$ is *not* a solution. $x = 0$ is a solution.

Try It **Solve the inequality. Graph the solution.**

4. $4b \geq 2$ **5.** $12k \leq -24$ **6.** $-15 < 2.5q$

 Key Idea

Multiplication and Division Properties of Inequality (Case 2)

Words When you multiply or divide each side of an inequality by the same *negative* number, the direction of the inequality symbol must be reversed for the inequality to remain true.

Numbers $-4 < 6$ $4 > -6$

$$-2 \cdot (-4) > -2 \cdot 6 \qquad \dfrac{4}{-2} < \dfrac{-6}{-2}$$

$$8 > -12 \qquad\qquad -2 < 3$$

Algebra If $a < b$ and c is negative, then

$$a \cdot c > b \cdot c \qquad \text{and} \qquad \dfrac{a}{c} > \dfrac{b}{c}.$$

If $a > b$ and c is negative, then

$$a \cdot c < b \cdot c \qquad \text{and} \qquad \dfrac{a}{c} < \dfrac{b}{c}.$$

These properties are also true for $\leq$ and $\geq$.

Common Error

A negative sign in an inequality does not necessarily mean you must reverse the inequality symbol.

Only reverse the inequality symbol when you multiply or divide each side by a negative number.

EXAMPLE 3 **Solving an Inequality Using Multiplication**

Solve $-\dfrac{3}{2}n \leq 6$. Graph the solution.

$-\dfrac{3}{2}n \leq 6$ Write the inequality.

$-\dfrac{2}{3} \cdot \left(-\dfrac{3}{2}n\right) \geq -\dfrac{2}{3} \cdot 6$ Use the Multiplication Property of Inequality. Reverse the inequality symbol.

$n \geq -4$ Simplify.

▶ The solution is $n \geq -4$.

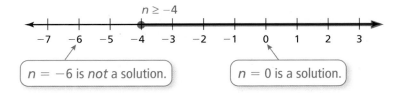

$n \geq -4$

$n = -6$ is *not* a solution.

$n = 0$ is a solution.

Math Practice

Look for Structure
Why do you reverse the inequality symbol when solving in Example 3, but not when solving in Examples 1 and 2?

Try It Solve the inequality. Graph the solution.

7. $\dfrac{x}{-3} > -4$

8. $0.5 \leq -\dfrac{y}{2}$

9. $-12 \geq \dfrac{6}{5}m$

10. $-\dfrac{2}{5}h \leq -8$

Self-Assessment for Concepts & Skills

Solve each exercise. Then rate your understanding of the success criteria in your journal.

11. **OPEN-ENDED** Write an inequality that you can solve using the Division Property of Inequality where the direction of the inequality symbol must be reversed.

12. **MP PRECISION** Explain how solving $4x < -16$ is different from solving $-4x < 16$.

SOLVING AN INEQUALITY Solve the inequality. Graph the solution.

13. $6n < -42$

14. $4 \geq -\dfrac{g}{8}$

15. **WRITING** Are the inequalities $12c > -15$ and $4c < -5$ equivalent? Explain.

160   **Chapter 4**   Equations and Inequalities

4.7 Solving Two-Step Inequalities

Learning Target: Write and solve two-step inequalities.

Success Criteria:
• I can apply properties of inequality to generate equivalent inequalities.
• I can solve two-step inequalities using the basic operations.
• I can apply two-step inequalities to solve real-life problems.

EXPLORATION 1

Using Algebra Tiles to Solve Inequalities

Work with a partner.

a. What is being modeled by the algebra tiles below? What is the solution?

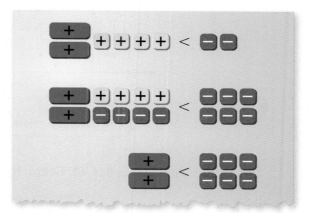

b. Use properties of inequality to solve the original inequality in part (a). How do your steps compare to the steps performed with algebra tiles?

c. Write the three inequalities modeled by the algebra tiles below. Then solve each inequality using algebra tiles. Check your answer using properties of inequality.

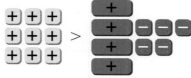

Math Practice

Consider Similar Problems

How is using algebra tiles to solve inequalities similar to using algebra tiles to solve equations?

d. Explain how solving a two-step inequality is similar to solving a two-step equation.

4.7 Lesson

You can solve two-step inequalities in the same way you solve two-step equations.

EXAMPLE 1 Solving Two-Step Inequalities

a. Solve $5x - 4 \geq 11$. Graph the solution.

$5x - 4 \geq \quad 11$	Write the inequality.
$\underline{+\,4 \qquad +\,4}$	Addition Property of Inequality
$5x \geq \quad 15$	Simplify.
$\dfrac{5x}{5} \geq \dfrac{15}{5}$	Division Property of Inequality
$x \geq 3$	Simplify.

Step 1: Undo the subtraction.

Step 2: Undo the multiplication.

▶ The solution is $x \geq 3$.

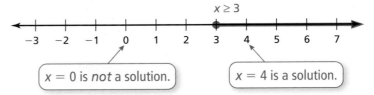

$x = 0$ is *not* a solution.

$x = 4$ is a solution.

b. Solve $\dfrac{b}{-3} + 4 < 13$. Graph the solution.

$\dfrac{b}{-3} + 4 < \quad 13$	Write the inequality.
$\underline{-\,4 \qquad -\,4}$	Subtraction Property of Inequality
$\dfrac{b}{-3} < \quad 9$	Simplify.
$-3 \cdot \dfrac{b}{-3} > -3 \cdot 9$	Use the Multiplication Property of Inequality. Reverse the inequality symbol.
$b > -27$	Simplify.

Step 1: Undo the addition.

Step 2: Undo the division.

▶ The solution is $b > -27$.

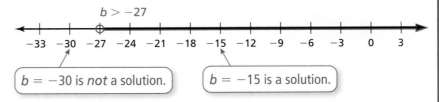

$b = -30$ is *not* a solution.

$b = -15$ is a solution.

Try It Solve the inequality. Graph the solution.

1. $6y - 7 > 5$ **2.** $4 - 3d \geq 19$ **3.** $\dfrac{w}{-4} + 8 > 9$

EXAMPLE 2 **Graphing an Inequality**

Which graph represents the solution of $-7(x + 3) \leq 28$?

A.
$$-10 \quad -9 \quad -8 \quad -7 \quad -6 \quad -5 \quad -4$$

B.
$$-10 \quad -9 \quad -8 \quad -7 \quad -6 \quad -5 \quad -4$$

C.
$$4 \quad 5 \quad 6 \quad 7 \quad 8 \quad 9 \quad 10$$

D.
$$4 \quad 5 \quad 6 \quad 7 \quad 8 \quad 9 \quad 10$$

$-7(x + 3) \leq 28$	Write the inequality.
$-7x - 21 \leq 28$	Distributive Property

Step 1: Undo the subtraction. $\quad \dfrac{+\,21 \quad +\,21}{-7x \leq 49}$

Addition Property of Inequality

Simplify.

Step 2: Undo the multiplication. $\quad \dfrac{-7x}{-7} \geq \dfrac{49}{-7}$

Use the Division Property of Inequality.
Reverse the inequality symbol.

$x \geq -7$ $\qquad$ Simplify.

 The correct answer is **B**.

Try It **Solve the inequality. Graph the solution.**

4. $2(k - 5) < 6$ $\qquad$ **5.** $-4(n - 10) < 32$ $\qquad$ **6.** $-3 \leq 0.5(8 + y)$

 ## Self-Assessment *for Concepts & Skills*

Solve each exercise. Then rate your understanding of the success criteria in your journal.

SOLVING AN INEQUALITY **Solve the inequality. Graph the solution.**

7. $3d - 7 \geq 8$ $\qquad$ **8.** $-6 > \dfrac{z}{-2} + 1$ $\qquad$ **9.** $-6(g + 4) \leq 12$

10. **(MP) STRUCTURE** Describe two different ways to solve the inequality $3(a + 5) < 9$.

11. **WRITING** Are the inequalities $-6x + 18 \leq 12$ and $2x - 4 \leq -2$ equivalent? Explain.

12. **OPEN-ENDED** Write a two-step inequality that can be represented by the graph. Justify your answer.

EXAMPLE 3 **Modeling Real Life**

A football team orders the sweatshirts shown. The price per sweatshirt decreases $0.05 for each sweatshirt that is ordered. How many sweatshirts should the team order for the price per sweatshirt to be no greater than $32.50?

Write and solve an inequality to determine how many sweatshirts the team should order for the price per sweatshirt to be no greater than $32.50.

Verbal Model	Base price (dollars)	−	Price decrease (dollars)	•	Number of sweatshirts ordered	≤	Desired price (dollars)

Variable Let n be the number of sweatshirts ordered.

Inequality	40	−	0.05	•	n	≤	32.50

$$40 - 0.05n \leq 32.50 \qquad \text{Write the inequality.}$$
$$\underline{-40} \qquad\qquad \underline{-40} \qquad \text{Subtraction Property of Inequality}$$
$$-0.05n \leq -7.50 \qquad \text{Simplify.}$$
$$\frac{-0.05n}{-0.05} \geq \frac{-7.50}{-0.05} \qquad \begin{array}{l}\text{Use the Division Property of Inequality.}\\ \text{Reverse the inequality symbol.}\end{array}$$
$$n \geq 150 \qquad \text{Simplify.}$$

▷ So, the team should order at least 150 sweatshirts for the price per sweatshirt to be no greater than $32.50.

Self-Assessment for Problem Solving

Solve each exercise. Then rate your understanding of the success criteria in your journal.

13. A fair rents a thrill ride for $3000. It costs $4 to purchase a token for the ride. Write and solve an inequality to determine the numbers of ride tokens that can be sold for the fair to make a profit of at least $750.

14. **DIG DEEPER!** A theater manager predicts that 1000 tickets to a play will be sold if each ticket costs $60. The manager predicts that 20 less tickets will be sold for every $1 increase in price. For what prices can the manager predict that at least 800 tickets will be sold? Use an inequality to justify your answer.

4.7 Practice

? Go to *BigIdeasMath.com* to get HELP with solving the exercises.

▶ Review & Refresh

Solve the inequality. Graph the solution.

1. $-3x \geq 18$

2. $\dfrac{2}{3}d > 8$

3. $2 \geq \dfrac{g}{-4}$

Find the missing values in the ratio table. Then write the equivalent ratios.

4.

Flutes	7		28
Clarinets	4	12	

5.

Boys	6	3	
Girls	10		50

6. What is the volume of the cube?

A. $8\ \text{ft}^3$

B. $16\ \text{ft}^3$

C. $24\ \text{ft}^3$

D. $32\ \text{ft}^3$

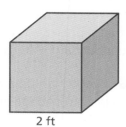

2 ft

▶▶ Concepts, Skills, & Problem Solving

USING ALGEBRA TILES Write the inequality modeled by the algebra tiles. Then solve the inequality using algebra tiles. Check your answer using properties of inequality. (See Exploration 1, p. 165.)

7.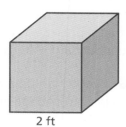

8.

SOLVING A TWO-STEP INEQUALITY Solve the inequality. Graph the solution.

9. $8y - 5 < 3$

10. $3p + 2 \geq -10$

11. $2 > 8 - \dfrac{4}{3}h$

12. $-2 > \dfrac{m}{6} - 7$

13. $-1.2b - 5.3 \geq 1.9$

14. $-1.3 \geq 2.9 - 0.6r$

15. $5(g + 4) > 15$

16. $4(w - 6) \leq -12$

17. $-8 \leq \dfrac{2}{5}(k - 2)$

18. $-\dfrac{1}{4}(d + 1) < 2$

19. $7.2 > 0.9(n + 8.6)$

20. $20 \geq -3.2(c - 4.3)$

MP YOU BE THE TEACHER Your friend solves the inequality. Is your friend correct? Explain your reasoning.

21.

$$\dfrac{x}{3} + 4 < 6$$
$$x + 4 < 18$$
$$x < 14$$

22.

$$3(w - 2) \geq 10$$
$$3w \geq 12$$
$$w \geq 4$$

23. **MP MODELING REAL LIFE** The first jump in a unicycle high-jump contest is shown. The bar is raised 2 centimeters after each jump. Solve the inequality $2n + 10 \geq 26$ to find the numbers of additional jumps needed to meet or exceed the goal of clearing a height of 26 centimeters.

10 cm

SOLVING AN INEQUALITY Solve the inequality. Graph the solution.

24. $9x - 4x + 4 \geq 36 - 12$

25. $3d - 7d + 2.8 < 5.8 - 27$

26. **MP MODELING REAL LIFE** A cave explorer is at an elevation of -38 feet. The explorer starts moving at a rate of -12 feet per minute. Write and solve an inequality that represents how long it will take the explorer to reach an elevation deeper than -200 feet.

27. **CRITICAL THINKING** A contestant in a weight-loss competition wants to lose an average of at least 8 pounds per month during a five-month period. Based on the progress report, how many pounds must the contestant lose in the fifth month to meet the goal?

Progress Report	
Month	Pounds Lost
1	12
2	9
3	5
4	8

28. **MP REASONING** A student theater charges $8.50 per ticket.

   a. The theater has already sold 70 tickets. How many more tickets does the theater need to sell to earn at least $750?

   b. The theater increases the ticket price by $1. Without solving an inequality, describe how this affects the total number of tickets needed to earn at least $750. Explain your reasoning.

29. **DIG DEEPER!** A zoo does not have room to add any more tigers to an enclosure. According to regulations, the area of the enclosure must increase by 150 square feet for each tiger that is added. The zoo is able to enlarge the 450 square foot enclosure for a total area no greater than 1000 square feet.

   a. Write and solve an inequality that represents this situation.

   b. Describe the possible numbers of tigers that can be added to the enclosure. Explain your reasoning.

30. **GEOMETRY** For what values of r will the area of the shaded region be greater than or equal to 12 square units?

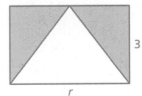

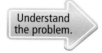

Connecting Concepts

▶ Using the Problem-Solving Plan

1. Fencing costs $7 per foot. You install x feet of the fencing along one side of a property, as shown. The property has an area of 15,750 square feet. What is the total cost of the fence?

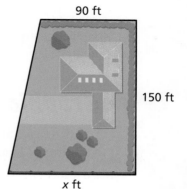

90 ft

150 ft

x ft

Understand the problem. You know the area, height, and one base length of the trapezoid-shaped property. You are asked to find the cost of x feet of fencing, given that the fencing costs $7 per foot.

Make a plan. Use the formula for the area of a trapezoid to find the length of fencing that you buy. Then multiply the length of fencing by $7 to find the total cost.

Solve and check. Use the plan to solve the problem. Then check your solution.

2. A pool is in the shape of a rectangular prism with a length of 15 feet, a width of 10 feet, and a depth of 4 feet. The pool is filled with water at a rate no faster than 3 cubic feet per minute. How long does it take to fill the pool?

3. The table shows your scores on 9 out of 10 quizzes that are each worth 20 points. What score do you need on the final quiz to have a mean score of at least 17 points?

Quiz Scores				
15	14	16	19	18
19	20	15	16	?

Performance Task

Distance and Brightness of the Stars

At the beginning of this chapter, you watched a STEAM Video called "Space Cadets." You are now ready to complete the performance task related to this video, available at **BigIdeasMath.com**. Be sure to use the problem-solving plan as you work through the performance task.

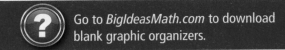 Go to *BigIdeasMath.com* to download blank graphic organizers.

▶ Review Vocabulary

Write the definition and give an example of each vocabulary term.

equivalent equations, *p. 128*
inequality, *p. 146*

solution of an inequality,
p. 146

solution set, *p. 146*
graph of an inequality, *p. 148*

▶ Graphic Organizers

You can use a **Summary Triangle** to explain a concept. Here is an example of a Summary Triangle for *Addition Property of Equality*.

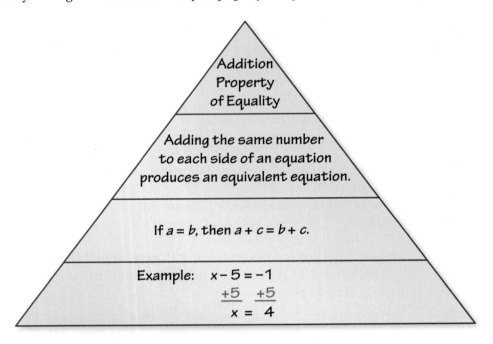

Addition Property of Equality

Adding the same number to each side of an equation produces an equivalent equation.

If $a = b$, then $a + c = b + c$.

Example: $x - 5 = -1$
$$\underline{+5 \quad +5}$$
$$x = 4$$

Choose and complete a graphic organizer to help you study the concept.

1. equivalent equations

2. Subtraction Property of Equality

3. Multiplication Property of Equality

4. Division Property of Equality

5. graphing inequalities

6. Addition and Subtraction Properties of Inequality

7. Multiplication and Division Properties of Inequality

"I finished my **Summary Triangle** about characteristics of hyenas."

▶ Chapter Self-Assessment

As you complete the exercises, use the scale below to rate your understanding of the success criteria in your journal.

1	2	3	4
I do not understand.	I can do it with help.	I can do it on my own.	I can teach someone else.

4.1 Solving Equations Using Addition or Subtraction *(pp. 127–132)*

Learning Target: Write and solve equations using addition or subtraction.

Solve the equation. Check your solution.

1. $p - 3 = -4$
2. $6 + q = 1$
3. $-2 + j = -22$
4. $b - 19 = -11$

5. $n + \dfrac{3}{4} = \dfrac{1}{4}$
6. $v - \dfrac{5}{6} = -\dfrac{7}{8}$
7. $t - 3.7 = 1.2$
8. $\ell + 15.2 = -4.5$

9. Write the word sentence as an equation. Then solve the equation.

$$\text{5 more than a number } x \text{ is } -4.$$

10. The perimeter of the trapezoid-shaped window frame is 23.59 feet. Write and solve an equation to find the unknown side length (in feet).

11. You are 5 years older than your cousin. How old is your cousin when you are 12 years old? Justify your answer.

4.2 Solving Equations Using Multiplication or Division *(pp. 133–138)*

Learning Target: Write and solve equations using multiplication or division.

Solve the equation. Check your solution.

12. $\dfrac{x}{3} = -8$
13. $-7 = \dfrac{y}{7}$
14. $-\dfrac{z}{4} = -\dfrac{3}{4}$
15. $-\dfrac{w}{20} = -2.5$

16. $4x = -8$
17. $-10 = 2y$
18. $-5.4z = -32.4$
19. $-6.8w = 3.4$

20. Write "3 times a number y is -42" as an equation. Then solve the equation.

21. The mean temperature change is $-3.2°F$ per day for 5 days. Write and solve an equation to find the total change over the 5-day period.

22. Describe a real-life situation that can be modeled by $7x = 1.75$.

4.3 Solving Two-Step Equations (pp. 139–144)

Learning Target: Write and solve two-step equations.

Solve the equation. Check your solution.

23. $-2c + 6 = -8$

24. $5 - 4t = 6$

25. $-3x - 4.6 = 5.9$

26. $\dfrac{w}{6} + \dfrac{5}{8} = -1\dfrac{3}{8}$

27. $3(3w - 4) = -20$

28. $-6y + 8y = -24$

29. The floor of a canyon has an elevation of -14.5 feet. Erosion causes the elevation to change by -1.5 feet per year. How many years will it take for the canyon floor to reach an elevation of -31 feet? Justify your solution.

4.4 Writing and Graphing Inequalities (pp. 145–150)

Learning Target: Write inequalities and represent solutions of inequalities on number lines.

Write the word sentence as an inequality.

30. A number w is greater than -3.

31. A number y minus $\dfrac{1}{2}$ is no more than $-\dfrac{3}{2}$.

Tell whether the given value is a solution of the inequality.

32. $5 + j > 8; j = 7$

33. $6 \div n \le -5; n = -3$

34. $7p \ge p - 12; p = -2$

Graph the inequality on a number line.

35. $q > -1.3$

36. $s < 1\dfrac{3}{4}$

37. The Enhanced Fujita scale rates the intensity of tornadoes based on wind speed and damage caused. An EF5 tornado is estimated to have wind speeds greater than 200 miles per hour. Write and graph an inequality that represents this situation.

4.5 Solving Inequalities Using Addition or Subtraction (pp. 151–156)

Learning Target: Write and solve inequalities using addition or subtraction.

Solve the inequality. Graph the solution.

38. $d + 12 < 19$

39. $t - 4 \le -14$

40. $-8 \le z + 6.4$

41. A small cruise ship can hold up to 500 people. There are 115 crew members on board the ship.

    a. Write and solve an inequality that represents the additional numbers of people that can board the ship.

    b. Can 385 more people board the ship? Explain.

42. Write an inequality that can be solved using the Subtraction Property of Inequality and has a solution of all numbers less than -3.

4.6   Solving Inequalities Using Multiplication or Division   *(pp. 157–164)*

Learning Target: Write and solve inequalities using multiplication or division.

Solve the inequality. Graph the solution.

43. $6q < -18$ **44.** $-\dfrac{r}{3} \le 6$ **45.** $-4 > -\dfrac{4}{3}s$

46. Write the word sentence as an inequality. Then solve the inequality.

    The product of -3 and a number p is greater than 21.

47. You are organizing books on a shelf. Each book has a width of $\dfrac{3}{4}$ inch. Write and solve an inequality for the numbers of books b that can fit on the shelf.

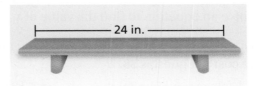

24 in.

4.7   Solving Two-Step Inequalities   *(pp. 165–170)*

Learning Target: Write and solve two-step inequalities.

Solve the inequality. Graph the solution.

48. $3x + 4 > 16$ **49.** $\dfrac{z}{-2} - 6 \le -2$ **50.** $-2t - 5 < 9$

51. $7(q + 2) < -77$ **52.** $-\dfrac{1}{3}(p + 9) \le 4$ **53.** $1.2(j + 3.5) \ge 4.8$

54. Your goal is to raise at least $50 in a charity fundraiser. You earn $3.50 for each candle sold. You also receive a $15 donation. Write and solve an inequality that represents the numbers of candles you must sell to reach your goal.

4 Practice Test

Solve the equation. Check your solution.

1. $7x = -3$

2. $2(x + 1) = -2$

3. $\frac{2}{9}g = -8$

4. $z + 14.5 = 5.4$

5. $-14 = c - 10$

6. $\frac{2}{7}k - \frac{3}{8} = -\frac{19}{8}$

Write the word sentence as an inequality.

7. A number k plus 19.5 is less than or equal to 40.

8. A number q multiplied by $\frac{1}{4}$ is greater than -16.

Tell whether the given value is a solution of the inequality.

9. $n - 3 \leq 4$; $n = 7$

10. $-\frac{3}{7}m < 1 + m$; $m = -7$

Solve the inequality. Graph the solution.

11. $x - 4 > -6$

12. $-\frac{2}{9} + y \leq \frac{5}{9}$

13. $-6z \geq 36$

14. $-5.2 \geq \frac{p}{4}$

15. $4k - 8 \geq 20$

16. $-0.6 > -0.3(d + 6)$

17. You lose 0.3 point for stepping out of bounds during a gymnastics floor routine. Your final score is 9.124. Write and solve an equation to find your score without the penalty.

18. Half the area of the rectangle shown is 24 square inches. Write and solve an equation to find the value of x.

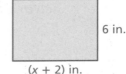

6 in.

$(x + 2)$ in.

19. You can spend no more than $100 on a party you are hosting. The cost per guest is $8.

    a. Write and solve an inequality that represents the numbers of guests you can invite to the party.

    b. What is the greatest number of guests that you can invite to the party? Explain your reasoning.

20. You have $30 to buy baseball cards. Each pack of cards costs $5. Write and solve an inequality that represents the numbers of packs of baseball cards you can buy and still have at least $10 left.

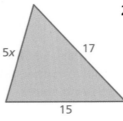

5x   17

15

21. The sum of the lengths of any two sides of a triangle is greater than the length of the third side.

    a. Write and solve three inequalities for the previous statement using the triangle shown.

    b. What values for x make sense?

4 Cumulative Practice

1. Which equation represents the word sentence?

> The quotient of a number b and 0.3 equals negative 10.

A. $0.3b = 10$

B. $\dfrac{b}{0.3} = -10$

C. $\dfrac{0.3}{b} = -10$

D. $\dfrac{b}{0.3} = 10$

Test-Taking Strategy
After Answering Easy Questions, Relax

You are being chased by x hyenas where $2x - 1 = 11$. How many is that?
Ⓐ 5 Ⓑ 6 Ⓒ 10 Ⓓ 11

I can't relax. I have to run faster.

"After answering the easy questions, relax and try the harder ones. For this, $2x = 12$, so $x = 6$ hyenas."

2. What is the value of the expression?

$$-\frac{3}{8} \cdot \frac{2}{5}$$

F. $-\dfrac{20}{3}$

G. $-\dfrac{16}{15}$

H. $-\dfrac{15}{16}$

I. $-\dfrac{3}{20}$

3. Which graph represents the inequality?

$$\frac{x}{-4} - 8 \geq -9$$

A. number line from −3 to 6, closed point at 4

B. number line from −6 to 3, closed point at −4

C. number line from −6 to 3, closed point at −4

D. number line from −3 to 6, closed point at 4

4. Which equation is equivalent to $-\dfrac{3}{4}x + \dfrac{1}{8} = -\dfrac{3}{8}$?

F. $-\dfrac{3}{4}x = -\dfrac{3}{8} - \dfrac{1}{8}$

G. $-\dfrac{3}{4}x = -\dfrac{3}{8} + \dfrac{1}{8}$

H. $x + \dfrac{1}{8} = -\dfrac{3}{8} \cdot \left(-\dfrac{4}{3}\right)$

I. $x + \dfrac{1}{8} = -\dfrac{3}{8} \cdot \left(-\dfrac{3}{4}\right)$

5. What is the decimal form of $2\dfrac{5}{8}$?

6. What is the value of the expression when $x = -5$, $y = 3$, and $z = -1$?

$$\frac{x^2 - 3y}{z}$$

A. -34

B. -16

C. 16

D. 34

7. Which expression is equivalent to $9h - 6 + 7h - 5$?

F. $3h + 2$

G. $16h + 1$

H. $2h - 1$

I. $16h - 11$

8. Your friend solved the equation $-96 = -6(x - 15)$.

$$-96 = -6(x - 15)$$
$$-96 = -6x - 90$$
$$-96 + 90 = -6x - 90 + 90$$
$$-6 = -6x$$
$$\frac{-6}{-6} = \frac{-6x}{-6}$$
$$1 = x$$

What should your friend do to correct her error?

A. First add 6 to both sides of the equation.

B. First subtract x from both sides of the equation.

C. Distribute the -6 to get $6x - 90$.

D. Distribute the -6 to get $-6x + 90$.

9. Which expression does *not* represent the perimeter of the rectangle?

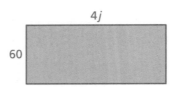

F. $4j(60)$

G. $8j + 120$

H. $2(4j + 60)$

I. $8(j + 15)$

10. What is the value of the expression?

$$\frac{5}{12} - \frac{7}{8}$$

11. You are selling T-shirts to raise money for a charity. You sell the T-shirts for $10 each.

Part A You have already sold 2 T-shirts. How many more T-shirts must you sell to raise at least $500? Explain.

Part B Your friend is raising money for the same charity and has not sold any T-shirts previously. He sells the T-shirts for $8 each. What are the total numbers of T-shirts he can sell to raise at least $500? Explain.

Part C Who has to sell more T-shirts in total? How many more? Explain.

12. Which expression has the same value as $-\frac{2}{3} - \left(-\frac{4}{9}\right)$?

A. $-\frac{1}{3} + \frac{1}{9}$

B. $-\frac{2}{3} \times \left(-\frac{1}{3}\right)$

C. $-\frac{1}{3} - \frac{7}{9}$

D. $\frac{3}{2} \div \left(-\frac{1}{3}\right)$

13. You recycle $(6c + 10)$ water bottles. Your friend recycles twice as many water bottles as you recycle. Which expression represents the amount of water bottles your friend recycles?

F. $3c + 5$

G. $12c + 10$

H. $12c + 20$

I. $6c + 12$

14. What is the value of the expression?

$$-\frac{4}{5} + \left(-\frac{2}{3}\right)$$

A. $-\frac{22}{15}$

B. $-\frac{2}{15}$

C. $\frac{2}{15}$

D. $\frac{8}{15}$

5 Ratios and Proportions

Chapter Learning Target:
Understand ratios and proportions.

Chapter Success Criteria:
- ☐ I can write and interpret ratios.
- ☐ I can describe ratio relationships and proportional relationships.
- ■ I can represent equivalent ratios.
- ■ I can model ratio relationships and proportional relationships to solve real-life problems.

STEAM Video: "Painting a Large Room"

Painting a Large Room

Shades of paint can be made by mixing other paints. What colors of paints can you mix to make green paint?

Watch the STEAM Video "Painting a Large Room." Then answer the following questions.

1. Enid estimates that they need 2 gallons of paint to apply two coats to the wall shown. How many square feet does she expect $\frac{1}{2}$ gallon of paint will cover?

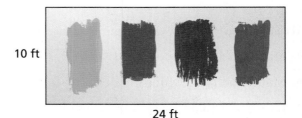

10 ft

24 ft

2. Describe a room that requires $5\frac{1}{2}$ gallons of paint to apply one coat of paint to each of the four walls.

Performance Task

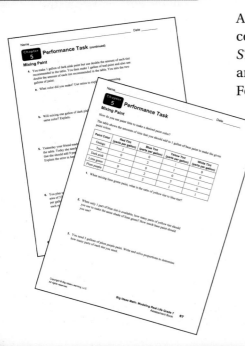

Mixing Paint

After completing this chapter, you will be able to use the concepts you learned to answer the questions in the *STEAM Video Performance Task.* You will be given the amounts of each tint used to make different colors of paint. For example:

Plum Purple Paint

3 parts red tint per gallon

2 parts blue tint per gallon

1 part yellow tint per gallon

1 part white tint per gallon

You will be asked to solve various ratio problems about mixing paint. Given any color of paint, how can you make the paint slightly lighter in color?

Getting Ready for Chapter 5

Chapter Exploration

The Meaning of a Word ▶ Rate

When you rent snorkel gear at the beach, you should pay attention to the rental **rate**. The rental rate is in dollars per hour.

Snorkel Rentals $8.75 per hour

Snorkel Rentals $7.50 per hour

1. **Work with a partner. Complete each step.**

   • Match each description with a rate.

   • Match each rate with a fraction.

   • Give a reasonable value for each fraction. Then give an unreasonable value.

Description	Rate	Fraction
Your speed in the 100-meter dash	Dollars per hour	$\dfrac{\boxed{}\text{ inches}}{\text{year}}$
The hourly wage of a worker at a fast-food restaurant	Inches per year	$\dfrac{\boxed{}\text{ pounds}}{\text{square foot}}$
The average annual rainfall in a rain forest	Pounds per square foot	$\dfrac{\$\boxed{}}{\text{hour}}$
The amount of fertilizer spread on a lawn	Meters per second	$\dfrac{\boxed{}\text{ meters}}{\text{second}}$

2. **Work with a partner.** Describe a situation to which the given fraction can apply. Show how to rewrite each expression as a division problem. Then simplify and interpret your result.

   a. $\dfrac{\frac{1}{2}\text{ cup}}{4\text{ fluid ounces}}$

   b. $\dfrac{2\text{ inches}}{\frac{3}{4}\text{ second}}$

   c. $\dfrac{\frac{3}{8}\text{ cup sugar}}{\frac{3}{4}\text{ cup flour}}$

   d. $\dfrac{\frac{5}{6}\text{ gallon}}{\frac{2}{3}\text{ second}}$

Vocabulary

The following vocabulary terms are defined in this chapter. Think about what each term might mean and record your thoughts.

proportional   constant of proportionality   scale drawing

5.1 Ratios and Ratio Tables

Learning Target: Understand ratios of rational numbers and use ratio tables to represent equivalent ratios.

Success Criteria:
- I can write and interpret ratios involving rational numbers.
- I can use various operations to create tables of equivalent ratios.
- I can use ratio tables to solve ratio problems.

EXPLORATION 1 Describing Ratio Relationships

Work with a partner. Use the recipe shown.

Chicken Soup

stewed tomatoes	9 ounces	chopped spinach	9 ounces
chicken broth	15 ounces	grated parmesan	5 tablespoons
chopped chicken	1 cup		

a. Identify several ratios in the recipe.

b. You halve the recipe. Describe your ratio relationships in part (a) using the new quantities. Is the relationship between the ingredients the same as in part (a)? Explain.

EXPLORATION 2 Completing Ratio Tables

Work with a partner. Use the ratio tables shown.

x	5			
y	1			

x	$\frac{1}{4}$			
y	$\frac{1}{2}$			

Math Practice

Communicate Precisely

How can you determine whether the ratios in each table are equivalent?

a. Complete the first ratio table using multiple operations. Use the same operations to complete the second ratio table.

b. Are the ratios in the first table equivalent? the second table? Explain.

c. Do the strategies for completing ratio tables of whole numbers work for completing ratio tables of fractions? Explain your reasoning.

Key Vocabulary
ratio, *p. 184*
value of a ratio, *p. 184*
equivalent ratios, *p. 185*
ratio table, *p. 185*

Key Idea

Reading

Recall that phrases indicating ratios include *for each*, *for every*, and *per*.

Ratios

Words A **ratio** is a comparison of two quantities. The **value of the ratio** *a* to *b* is the number $\frac{a}{b}$, which describes the multiplicative relationship between the quantities in the ratio.

Examples 2 snails *to* 6 fish

$\frac{1}{2}$ cup of milk *for every* $\frac{1}{4}$ cup of cream

Algebra The ratio of *a* to *b* can be written as $a : b$.

EXAMPLE 1 Writing and Interpreting Ratios

You make *flubber* using the ingredients shown.

Flubber Ingredients

cold water	3/2 cups
hot water	4/3 cups
glue	2 cups
borax	3 teaspoons

a. Write the ratio of cold water to glue.

The recipe uses $\frac{3}{2}$ cups of water per 2 cups of glue.

▶ So, the ratio of cold water to glue is $\frac{3}{2}$ to 2, or $\frac{3}{2} : 2$.

b. Find and interpret the value of the ratio in part (a).

The value of the ratio $\frac{3}{2} : 2$ is

$$\frac{\frac{3}{2}}{2} = \frac{3}{2} \div 2$$

$$= \frac{3}{2} \cdot \frac{1}{2}$$

$$= \frac{3}{4}.$$

So, the multiplicative relationship is $\frac{3}{4}$.

▶ The amount of cold water in the recipe is $\frac{3}{4}$ the amount of glue.

Try It

1. You mix $\frac{2}{3}$ teaspoon of baking soda with 3 teaspoons of salt. Find and interpret the value of the ratio of baking soda to salt.

 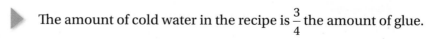

Two ratios that describe the same relationship are **equivalent ratios**. The values of equivalent ratios are equivalent. You can find and organize equivalent ratios in a **ratio table** by:

- adding or subtracting quantities in equivalent ratios.
- multiplying or dividing each quantity in a ratio by the same number.

EXAMPLE 2 **Completing A Ratio Table**

Find the missing values in the ratio table. Then write the equivalent ratios.

Cups	3	12	15	
Quarts	$\frac{3}{4}$			$\frac{5}{4}$

Notice that you obtain the third column by adding the values in the first column to the values in the second column.

$$3 + 12 = 15$$
$$\frac{3}{4} + 3 = \frac{15}{4}$$

You can use a combination of operations to find the missing values.

$$\times 4 \quad + 3 \quad \div 3$$

Cups	3	12	15	5
Quarts	$\frac{3}{4}$	3	$\frac{15}{4}$	$\frac{5}{4}$

$$\times 4 \quad + \frac{3}{4} \quad \div 3$$

▶ The equivalent ratios are $3 : \frac{3}{4}$, $12 : 3$, $15 : \frac{15}{4}$, and $5 : \frac{5}{4}$.

Try It **Find the missing values in the ratio table. Then write the equivalent ratios.**

2.

Kilometers	$\frac{5}{2}$		5
Hours	4	16	

3.

Gallons	0.4	1.2	1.6
Days	0.75		

Self-Assessment for Concepts & Skills

Solve each exercise. Then rate your understanding of the success criteria in your journal.

4. **WRITING AND INTERPRETING RATIOS** You include $\frac{1}{2}$ tablespoon of essential oils in a solution for every 12 tablespoons of jojoba oil. Find and interpret the value of the ratio of jojoba oil to essential oils.

5. **MP NUMBER SENSE** Find the missing values in the ratio table. Then write the equivalent ratios.

Pounds	$\frac{3}{2}$		$\frac{21}{2}$
Years	$\frac{1}{12}$	$\frac{2}{3}$	

EXAMPLE 3 **Modeling Real Life**

You mix $\frac{1}{2}$ cup of yellow paint for every $\frac{3}{4}$ cup of blue paint to make 15 cups of green paint. How much yellow paint do you use?

Math Practice

Maintain Oversight

What value are you trying to obtain in the ratio table to solve the problem? How can you find the solution using only one operation?

Method 1: The ratio of yellow paint to blue paint is $\frac{1}{2}$ to $\frac{3}{4}$. Use a ratio table to find an equivalent ratio in which the total amount of yellow paint and blue paint is 15 cups.

Yellow (cups)	Blue (cups)	Total (cups)
$\frac{1}{2}$	$\frac{3}{4}$	$\frac{1}{2} + \frac{3}{4} = \frac{5}{4}$
2	3	5
6	9	15

$\times 4$ and $\times 3$ applied to left side; $\times 4$ and $\times 3$ applied to right side.

▶ So, you use 6 cups of yellow paint.

Method 2: You can use the ratio of yellow paint to blue paint to find the fraction of the green paint that is made from yellow paint. You use $\frac{1}{2}$ cup of yellow paint for every $\frac{3}{4}$ cup of blue paint, so the fraction of the green paint that is made from yellow paint is

yellow $\rightarrow$
green $\rightarrow$
$$\frac{\frac{1}{2}}{\frac{1}{2} + \frac{3}{4}} = \frac{\frac{1}{2}}{\frac{5}{4}} = \frac{1}{2} \cdot \frac{4}{5} = \frac{2}{5}.$$

▶ So, you use $\frac{2}{5} \cdot 15 = 6$ cups of yellow paint.

 Self-Assessment for Problem Solving

Solve each exercise. Then rate your understanding of the success criteria in your journal.

6. **DIG DEEPER!** A satellite orbiting Earth travels $14\frac{1}{2}$ miles every 3 seconds. How far does the satellite travel in $\frac{3}{4}$ minute?

7. An engine runs on a mixture of 0.1 quart of oil for every 3.5 quarts of gasoline. You make 3 quarts of the mixture. How much oil and how much gasoline do you use?

5.1 Practice

 Go to *BigIdeasMath.com* to get HELP with solving the exercises.

▶ Review & Refresh

Solve the inequality. Graph the solution.

1. $4p + 7 \geq 19$

2. $14 < -6n - 10$

3. $-3(2 + d) \leq 15$

Find the quotient. Write fractions in simplest form.

4. $\dfrac{2}{9} \div \dfrac{4}{3}$

5. $10.08 \div 12$

6. $-\dfrac{5}{6} \div \dfrac{3}{10}$

7. Which ratio can be represented by the tape diagram?

   A. $3 : 4$ B. $4 : 5$

   C. $4 : 9$ D. $8 : 12$

Quantity 1

Quantity 2

▶▶ Concepts, Skills, & Problem Solving

OPEN-ENDED Complete the ratio table using multiple operations. Are the ratios in the table equivalent? Explain. (See Exploration 2, p. 183.)

8.

x	4			
y	10			

9.

x	$\frac{4}{5}$			
y	$\frac{1}{2}$			

Fruit Punch Ingredients

chopped watermelon	3 cups
sugar	3/4 cup
mint leaves	1/2 cup
white grape juice	2 cups
lime juice	3/4 cup
club soda	4 cups

WRITING AND INTERPRETING RATIOS Find the ratio. Then find and interpret the value of the ratio.

10. club soda : white grape juice

11. mint leaves : chopped watermelon

12. white grape juice to sugar

13. lime juice to mint leaves

14. **MP YOU BE THE TEACHER** You have blue ribbon and red ribbon in the ratio $\dfrac{1}{2} : \dfrac{1}{5}$. Your friend finds the value of the ratio. Is your friend correct? Explain your reasoning.

> The value of the ratio is
> $$\dfrac{\frac{1}{2}}{\frac{1}{5}} = \dfrac{1}{2} \div \dfrac{1}{5} = \dfrac{1}{10}.$$

COMPLETING A RATIO TABLE Find the missing values in the ratio table. Then write the equivalent ratios.

15.

Calories	20		10	90
Miles	$\frac{1}{6}$	$\frac{2}{3}$		

16.

Meters	8	4		
Minutes	$\frac{1}{3}$		$\frac{1}{4}$	$\frac{5}{12}$

17.

Feet	$\frac{1}{24}$		$\frac{1}{8}$	
Inches	$\frac{1}{2}$	1		$\frac{1}{4}$

18.

Tea (cups)	3.75			
Milk (cups)	1.5	1	3.5	2.5

19. CRITICAL THINKING Are the two statements equivalent? Explain your reasoning.

- The ratio of boys to girls is 2 to 3.
- The ratio of girls to boys is 3 to 2.

20. **MP** **MODELING REAL LIFE** A city dumps plastic *shade balls* into a reservoir to prevent water from evaporating during a drought. It costs $5760 for 16,000 shade balls. How much does it cost for 12,000 shade balls?

21. **MP** **MODELING REAL LIFE** An oil spill spreads 25 square meters every $\frac{1}{6}$ hour. What is the area of the oil spill after 2 hours?

22. **MP** **MODELING REAL LIFE** You mix 0.25 cup of juice concentrate for every 2 cups of water to make 18 cups of juice. How much juice concentrate do you use? How much water do you use?

23. **MP** **MODELING REAL LIFE** A store sells $2\frac{1}{4}$ pounds of mulch for every $1\frac{1}{2}$ pounds of gravel sold. The store sells 180 pounds of mulch and gravel combined. How many pounds of each item does the store sell?

24. **DIG DEEPER!** You mix $\frac{1}{4}$ cup of red paint for every $\frac{1}{2}$ cup of blue paint to make 3 gallons of purple paint.

a. How much red paint do you use? How much blue paint do you use?

b. You decide that you want to make a lighter purple paint. You make the new mixture by adding $\frac{1}{4}$ cup of white paint for every $\frac{1}{4}$ cup of red paint and $\frac{1}{2}$ cup of blue paint. How much red paint, blue paint, and white paint do you use to make $1\frac{1}{2}$ gallons of the lighter purple paint?

5.2 Rates and Unit Rates

Learning Target: Understand rates involving fractions and use unit rates to solve problems.

Success Criteria:
• I can find unit rates for rates involving fractions.
• I can use unit rates to solve rate problems.

EXPLORATION 1

Writing Rates

Work with a partner.

a. How many degrees does the minute hand on a clock move every 15 minutes? Write a rate that compares the number of degrees moved by the minute hand to the number of hours elapsed.

Math Practice

Recognize Usefulness of Tools

Can you use a protractor to find the number of degrees the minute hand moves in 15 minutes? in 1 hour?

b. Can you use the rate in part (a) to determine how many degrees the minute hand moves in $\frac{1}{2}$ hour? Explain your reasoning.

c. Write a rate that represents the number of degrees moved by the minute hand every hour. How can you use this rate to find the number of degrees moved by the minute hand in $2\frac{1}{2}$ hours?

d. Draw a clock with hour and minute hands. Draw another clock that shows the time after the minute hand moves 900°. How many degrees does the hour hand move in this time? in one hour? Explain your reasoning.

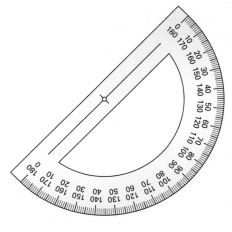

Key Vocabulary 🔊
rate, *p. 190*
unit rate, *p. 190*
equivalent rates, *p. 190*

 Key Idea

Rates and Unit Rates

Words A **rate** is a ratio of two quantities using different units. A **unit rate** compares a quantity to one unit of another quantity. **Equivalent rates** have the same unit rate.

Numbers You pay \$350 for every $\frac{1}{4}$ ounce of gold.

\$350	\$350	\$350	\$350

Rate: $\$350 : \frac{1}{4}$ oz

$\frac{1}{4}$ oz	$\frac{1}{4}$ oz	$\frac{1}{4}$ oz	$\frac{1}{4}$ oz

Unit Rate: $\$1400 : 1$ oz

Algebra Rate: a units : b units   Unit rate: $\frac{a}{b}$ units : 1 unit

---

EXAMPLE 1 **Finding Unit Rates**

A nutrition label shows that every $\frac{1}{4}$ cup of tuna has $\frac{1}{2}$ gram of fat.

a. How many grams of fat are there for every cup of tuna?

There is $\frac{1}{2}$ gram of fat for every $\frac{1}{4}$ cup of tuna. Find the unit rate.

▷ There are $\dfrac{\frac{1}{2}}{\frac{1}{4}} = 2$ grams of fat for every cup of tuna.

$\frac{1}{4}$ c	$\frac{1}{4}$ c	$\frac{1}{4}$ c	$\frac{1}{4}$ c

$\frac{1}{2}$ g	$\frac{1}{2}$ g	$\frac{1}{2}$ g	$\frac{1}{2}$ g

b. How many cups of tuna are there for every gram of fat?

There is $\frac{1}{4}$ cup of tuna for every $\frac{1}{2}$ gram of fat. Find the unit rate.

▷ There is $\dfrac{\frac{1}{4}}{\frac{1}{2}} = \frac{1}{2}$ cup of tuna per gram of fat.

Try It

1. There is $\frac{1}{4}$ gram of fat for every $\frac{1}{3}$ tablespoon of powdered peanut butter. How many grams of fat are there for every tablespoon of the powder?

EXAMPLE 2 **Using a Unit Rate to Solve a Rate Problem**

A scientist estimates that a jet of liquid iron in the Earth's core travels 9 feet every $\frac{1}{2}$ hour. How far does the liquid iron travel in 1 day?

The ratio of feet to hours is $9 : \frac{1}{2}$. Using a ratio table, divide the quantity by $\frac{1}{2}$ to find the unit rate in feet per hour. Then multiply each quantity by 24 to find the distance traveled in 24 hours, or 1 day.

$$\times 2 \quad \times 24$$

Distance (feet)	9	18	432
Time (hours)	$\frac{1}{2}$	1	24

$$\times 2 \quad \times 24$$

▷ So, the liquid iron travels about 432 feet in 1 day.

Try It

2. WHAT IF? The scientist later states that the iron travels 3 feet every 10 minutes. Does this change your answer in Example 2? Explain.

Self-Assessment *for Concepts & Skills*

Solve each exercise. Then rate your understanding of the success criteria in your journal.

3. VOCABULARY How can you tell when a rate is a unit rate?

4. WRITING Explain why rates are usually written as unit rates.

Find the unit rate.

5. $1.32 for 12 ounces

6. $\frac{1}{4}$ gallon for every $\frac{3}{10}$ mile

7. MP USING TOOLS Find the missing values in the ratio table. Then write the unit rate of grams per cup and the unit rate of cups per gram.

Grams	$\frac{5}{2}$		1	$\frac{15}{4}$	
Cups	$\frac{2}{3}$	$\frac{1}{6}$			4

EXAMPLE 3 **Modeling Real Life**

You hike up a mountain trail at a rate of $\frac{1}{4}$ **mile every 10 minutes. You hike 5 miles every 2 hours on the way down the trail. How much farther do you hike in 3 hours on the way down than in 3 hours on the way up?**

Because 10 minutes is $\frac{1}{6}$ of an hour, the ratio of miles to hours on the way up is $\frac{1}{4} : \frac{1}{6}$. On the way down, the ratio is 5 : 2. Use ratio tables to find how far you hike in 3 hours at each rate.

Hiking Up	
Distance (miles)	Time (hours)
$\frac{1}{4}$	$\frac{1}{6}$
$\frac{3}{2}$	1
$\frac{9}{2}$	3

Hiking Down	
Distance (miles)	Time (hours)
5	2
$\frac{5}{2}$	1
$\frac{15}{2}$	3

Find the unit rate for each part of the hike.

Find the distance you hike in 3 hours on each part of the hike.

▶ So, you hike $\frac{15}{2} - \frac{9}{2} = \frac{6}{2} = 3$ miles farther in 3 hours on the way down than you hike in 3 hours on the way up.

Check Your rate on the way down is $\frac{5}{2} - \frac{3}{2} = \frac{2}{2} = 1$ mile per hour faster than your rate on the way up. So, you hike 3 miles farther in 3 hours on the way down than you hike in 3 hours on the way up. ✓

 Self-Assessment for Problem Solving

Solve each exercise. Then rate your understanding of the success criteria in your journal.

8. Two people compete in a five-mile go-kart race. Person A travels $\frac{1}{10}$ mile every 15 seconds. Person B travels $\frac{3}{8}$ mile every 48 seconds. Who wins the race? What is the difference of the finish times of the competitors?

9. **DIG DEEPER!** A bus travels 0.8 mile east every 45 seconds. A second bus travels 0.55 mile west every 30 seconds. The buses start at the same location. Use two methods to determine how far apart the buses are after 15 minutes. Explain your reasoning.

Go to *BigIdeasMath.com* to get HELP with solving the exercises.

▶ Review & Refresh

Find the missing values in the ratio table. Then write the equivalent ratios.

1.

Flour (cups)	$\frac{3}{4}$		3	1
Oats (cups)	$\frac{1}{3}$	$\frac{2}{3}$		

2.

Pages	$\frac{1}{4}$	$\frac{3}{4}$		5
Minutes	$\frac{1}{2}$		3	

Copy and complete the statement using <, >, or =.

3. $\dfrac{9}{2}$ ▢ $\dfrac{8}{3}$ **4.** $-\dfrac{8}{15}$ ▢ $\dfrac{10}{18}$ **5.** $\dfrac{-6}{24}$ ▢ $\dfrac{-2}{8}$

▶▶ Concepts, Skills, & Problem Solving

WRITING RATES **Find the number of degrees moved by the minute hand of a clock in the given amount of time. Explain your reasoning.** (See Exploration 1, p. 189.)

6. $\dfrac{2}{3}$ hour   **7.** $\dfrac{7}{12}$ hour   **8.** $1\dfrac{1}{4}$ hours

FINDING UNIT RATES **Find the unit rate.**

9. 180 miles in 3 hours

10. 256 miles per 8 gallons

11. $\dfrac{1}{2}$ pound : 5 days

12. 4 grams for every $\dfrac{3}{4}$ serving

13. $9.60 for 4 pounds

14. $4.80 for 6 cans

15. 297 words in 5.5 minutes

16. $\dfrac{1}{3}$ kilogram : $\dfrac{2}{3}$ foot

17. $\dfrac{5}{8}$ ounce per $\dfrac{1}{4}$ pint

18. $21\dfrac{3}{4}$ meters in $2\dfrac{1}{2}$ hours

MP USING TOOLS **Find the missing values in the ratio table. Then write the equivalent ratios.**

19.

Calories	25	50		
Servings	$\frac{1}{3}$		1	$\frac{4}{3}$

20.

Oxygen (liters)	4	$\frac{4}{3}$		16
Time (minute)	$\frac{3}{4}$		1	

21. **MP PROBLEM SOLVING** In January 2012, the U.S. population was about 313 million people. In January 2017, it was about 324 million. What was the average rate of population change per year?

22. **MODELING REAL LIFE** You can sand $\frac{4}{9}$ square yard of wood in $\frac{1}{2}$ hour. How many square yards can you sand in 3.2 hours? Justify your answer.

REASONING **Tell whether the rates are equivalent. Justify your answer.**

23. 75 pounds per 1.5 years
    38.4 ounces per 0.75 year

24. $7\frac{1}{2}$ miles for every $\frac{3}{4}$ hour

    $\frac{1}{2}$ mile for every 3 minutes

25. **PROBLEM SOLVING** The table shows nutritional information for three beverages.

    a. Which has the most calories per fluid ounce?

    b. Which has the least sodium per fluid ounce?

Beverage	Serving Size	Calories	Sodium
Whole milk	1 c	146	98 mg
Orange juice	1 pt	210	10 mg
Apple juice	24 fl oz	351	21 mg

26. **MODELING REAL LIFE** A shuttle leaving Earth's atmosphere travels 15 miles every 2 seconds. When entering the Earth's atmosphere, the shuttle travels $2\frac{3}{8}$ miles per $\frac{1}{2}$ second. Find the difference in the distances traveled after 15 seconds when leaving and entering the atmosphere.

27. **RESEARCH** Fire hydrants are one of four different colors to indicate the rate at which water comes from the hydrant.

    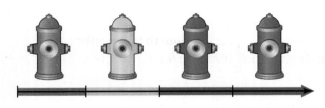

    a. Use the Internet to find the ranges of rates indicated by each color.

    b. Research why a firefighter needs to know the rate at which water comes out of a hydrant.

28. **DIG DEEPER!** You and a friend start riding bikes toward each other from opposite ends of a 24-mile biking route. You ride $2\frac{1}{6}$ miles every $\frac{1}{4}$ hour. Your friend rides $7\frac{1}{3}$ miles per hour.

    a. After how many hours do you meet?

    b. When you meet, who has traveled farther? How much farther?

5.3 Identifying Proportional Relationships

Learning Target: Determine whether two quantities are in a proportional relationship.

Success Criteria:
- I can determine whether ratios form a proportion.
- I can explain how to determine whether quantities are proportional.
- I can distinguish between proportional and nonproportional situations.

EXPLORATION 1

Determining Proportional Relationships

Work with a partner.

a. You can paint 50 square feet of a surface every 40 minutes. How long does it take you to paint the mural shown? Explain how you found your answer.

25 ft

9 ft

CREATIVITY

b. The number of square feet you paint is *proportional* to the number of minutes it takes you. What do you think it means for a quantity to be *proportional* to another quantity?

c. Assume your friends paint at the same rate as you. The table shows how long it takes you and different numbers of friends to paint a fence. Is x proportional to y in the table? Explain.

Painters, x	1	2	3	4
Hours, y	4	2	$\frac{4}{3}$	1

Math Practice

Look for Patterns
How can the table in part (c) help you answer the question in part (d)?

d. How long will it take you and four friends to paint the fence? Explain how you found your answer.

5.3 Lesson

Key Vocabulary 🔊
proportion, *p. 196*
cross products,
   p. 197
proportional, *p. 198*

🔑 Key Idea

Proportions

Words A **proportion** is an equation stating that the values of two ratios are equivalent.

Numbers Equivalent ratios: $2:3$ and $4:6$

Proportion: $\dfrac{2}{3} = \dfrac{4}{6}$

EXAMPLE 1 ## Determining Whether Ratios Form a Proportion

Tell whether the ratios form a proportion.

a. 6 : 4 and 8 : 12

Compare the values of the ratios.

$$\frac{6}{4} = \frac{6 \div 2}{4 \div 2} = \frac{3}{2}$$

$$\frac{8}{12} = \frac{8 \div 4}{12 \div 4} = \frac{2}{3}$$

> The values of the ratios are *not* equivalent.

▷ Because $\dfrac{3}{2} \neq \dfrac{2}{3}$, the ratios $6:4$ and $8:12$ do *not* form a proportion.

When you are determining whether ratios form a proportion, you are checking whether the ratios are equivalent.

b. 10 : 40 and 2.5 : 10

Compare the values of the ratios.

$$\frac{10}{40} = \frac{10 \div 10}{40 \div 10} = \frac{1}{4}$$

> The values of the ratios are equivalent.

$$\frac{2.5}{10} = \frac{2.5 \times 10}{10 \times 10} = \frac{25}{100} = \frac{25 \div 25}{100 \div 25} = \frac{1}{4}$$

▷ Because $\dfrac{1}{4} = \dfrac{1}{4}$, the ratios $10:40$ and $2.5:10$ form a proportion.

Try It **Tell whether the ratios form a proportion.**

1. $1:2$ and $5:10$

2. $4:6$ and $18:24$

3. 4.5 to 3 and 6 to 9

4. $\dfrac{1}{2}$ to $\dfrac{1}{4}$ and 8 to 4

🔊 Multi-Language Glossary at *BigIdeasMath.com*

 **Key Ideas**

Cross Products

In the proportion $\dfrac{a}{b} = \dfrac{c}{d}$, the products $a \cdot d$ and $b \cdot c$ are called **cross products**.

Cross Products Property

Words   The cross products of a proportion are equal.

You can use the Multiplication Property of Equality to show that the cross products are equal.

$$\dfrac{a}{b} = \dfrac{c}{d}$$

$$\cancel{bd} \cdot \dfrac{a}{\cancel{b}} = b\cancel{d} \cdot \dfrac{c}{\cancel{d}}$$

$$ad = bc$$

Numbers	**Algebra**
$\dfrac{2}{3} \bowtie \dfrac{4}{6}$	$\dfrac{a}{b} \bowtie \dfrac{c}{d}$
$2 \cdot 6 = 3 \cdot 4$	$ad = bc$, where $b \neq 0$ and $d \neq 0$

EXAMPLE 2 **Using Cross Products**

Tell whether the ratios form a proportion.

a.   6 : 9 and 12 : 18

Use the Cross Products Property to determine whether the ratios form a proportion.

$$\dfrac{6}{9} \overset{?}{=} \dfrac{12}{18} \qquad \text{Determine whether the values of the ratios are equivalent.}$$

$$6 \cdot 18 \overset{?}{=} 9 \cdot 12 \qquad \text{Find the cross products.}$$

$$108 = 108 \qquad \text{The cross products are equal.}$$

  So, the ratios 6 : 9 and 12 : 18 form a proportion.

b.   2 : 3 and 4 : 5

Use the Cross Products Property to determine whether the ratios form a proportion.

$$\dfrac{2}{3} \overset{?}{=} \dfrac{4}{5} \qquad \text{Determine whether the values of the ratios are equivalent.}$$

$$2 \cdot 5 \overset{?}{=} 3 \cdot 4 \qquad \text{Find the cross products.}$$

$$10 \neq 12 \qquad \text{The cross products are } not \text{ equal.}$$

  So, the ratios 2 : 3 and 4 : 5 do *not* form a proportion.

Try It **Tell whether the ratios form a proportion.**

5. 6 : 2 and 12 : 1

6. 8 : 12 and $\dfrac{2}{3}$: 1

Two quantities are **proportional** when all of the ratios relating the quantities are equivalent. These quantities are said to be in a *proportional relationship*.

EXAMPLE 3 **Determining Whether Two Quantities are Proportional**

Tell whether x and y are proportional.

Compare the values of the ratios x to y.

x	y
$\frac{1}{2}$	3
1	6
$\frac{3}{2}$	9
2	12

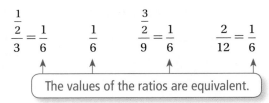

$$\frac{\frac{1}{2}}{3} = \frac{1}{6} \qquad \frac{1}{6} \qquad \frac{\frac{3}{2}}{9} = \frac{1}{6} \qquad \frac{2}{12} = \frac{1}{6}$$

The values of the ratios are equivalent.

Math Practice

Construct Arguments
Can you use the values of the ratios y to x in Example 3? Explain.

 So, x and y are proportional.

Try It **Tell whether x and y are proportional.**

7.

x	1	2	3	4
y	2	4	6	8

8.

x	2	4	6	8	10
y	4	2	1	$\frac{1}{2}$	$\frac{1}{4}$

 Self-Assessment for Concepts & Skills

Solve each exercise. Then rate your understanding of the success criteria in your journal.

PROPORTIONS **Tell whether the ratios form a proportion.**

9. $4 : 14$ and $12 : 40$ 10. $9 : 3$ and $45 : 15$

11. **VOCABULARY** Explain how to determine whether two quantities are proportional.

12. **WHICH ONE DOESN'T BELONG?** Which ratio does *not* belong with the other three? Explain your reasoning.

$4 : 10$ $2 : 5$

$3 : 5$ $6 : 15$

EXAMPLE 4 **Modeling Real Life**

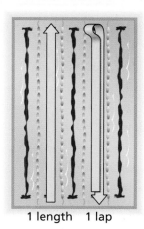

1 length   1 lap

You swim for 16 minutes and complete 20 laps. You swam your first 4 laps in 2.4 minutes. How long does it take you to swim 10 laps?

Compare unit rates to determine whether the number of laps is proportional to your time. If it is, then you can use ratio reasoning to find the time it takes you to swim 10 laps.

2.4 minutes for every 4 laps: $\dfrac{2.4}{4} = 0.6$ minute per lap

16 minutes for every 20 laps: $\dfrac{16}{20} = 0.8$ minute per lap

The number of laps is *not* proportional to the time. So, you *cannot* use ratio reasoning to determine the time it takes you to swim 10 laps.

Because you slowed down after your first 4 laps, you can estimate that you swim 10 laps in more than

$$\frac{0.6 \text{ minute}}{1 \text{ lap}} \cdot 10 \text{ laps} = 6 \text{ minutes},$$

but less than

$$\frac{0.8 \text{ minute}}{1 \text{ lap}} \cdot 10 \text{ laps} = 8 \text{ minutes}.$$

So, you can estimate that it takes you about 7 minutes to swim 10 laps.

Self-Assessment for *Problem Solving*

Solve each exercise. Then rate your understanding of the success criteria in your journal.

13. After making 20 servings of pasta, a chef has used 30 cloves of garlic. The chef used 6 cloves to make the first 4 servings. How many cloves of garlic are used to make 10 servings? Justify your answer.

14. **DIG DEEPER!** A runner completes a 25-mile race in 5 hours. The runner completes the first 7.5 miles in 1.5 hours.

    a. Do these rates form a proportion? Justify your answer.

    b. Can you determine, with certainty, the time it took the runner to complete 10 miles? Explain your reasoning.

5.3 Practice

? Go to *BigIdeasMath.com* to get HELP with solving the exercises.

▶ Review & Refresh

Find the unit rate.

1. 30 inches per 5 years

2. 486 games every 3 seasons

3. 8750 steps every 1.25 hours

4. 3.75 pints out of every 5 gallons

Add or subtract.

5. $-28 + 15$

6. $-6 + (-11)$

7. $-10 - 8$

8. $-17 - (-14)$

Solve the equation.

9. $\dfrac{x}{6} = 25$

10. $8x = 72$

11. $150 = 2x$

12. $35 = \dfrac{x}{4}$

▶▶ Concepts, Skills, & Problem Solving

MP REASONING **You can paint 75 square feet of a surface every 45 minutes. Determine how long it takes you to paint a wall with the given dimensions.** (See Exploration 1, p. 195.)

13. $8\,\text{ft} \times 5\,\text{ft}$

14. $7\,\text{ft} \times 6\,\text{ft}$

15. $9\,\text{ft} \times 9\,\text{ft}$

PROPORTIONS **Tell whether the ratios form a proportion.**

16. 1 to 3 and 7 to 21

17. $1 : 5$ and $6 : 30$

18. 3 to 4 and 24 to 18

19. $3.5 : 2$ and $14 : 8$

20. $24 : 30$ and $3 : \dfrac{7}{2}$

21. $\dfrac{21}{2} : 3$ and $16 : 6$

22. $0.6 : 0.5$ and $12 : 10$

23. 2 to 4 and 11 to $\dfrac{11}{2}$

24. $\dfrac{5}{8} : \dfrac{2}{3}$ and $\dfrac{1}{4} : \dfrac{1}{3}$

IDENTIFYING PROPORTIONAL RELATIONSHIPS **Tell whether x and y are proportional.**

25.

x	1	2	3
y	7	8	9

26.

x	2	4	6
y	5	10	15

27.

x	0.25	0.5	0.75
y	4	8	12

28.

x	$\dfrac{2}{3}$	1	$\dfrac{4}{3}$
y	$\dfrac{7}{10}$	$\dfrac{3}{5}$	$\dfrac{1}{2}$

MP YOU BE THE TEACHER Your friend determines whether *x* and *y* are proportional. Is your friend correct? Explain your reasoning.

29.

x	8	9
y	3	4

$$\frac{8+1}{3+1} = \frac{9}{4}$$

The values of the ratios *x* to *y* are equal. So, *x* and *y* are proportional.

30.

x	2	4	8
y	6	12	18

$$\frac{2}{6} = \frac{1}{3} \qquad \frac{4}{12} = \frac{1}{3}$$

The values of the ratios *x* to *y* are equal. So, *x* and *y* are proportional.

PROPORTIONS Tell whether the rates form a proportion.

31. 7 inches in 9 hours; 42 inches in 54 hours

32. 12 players from 21 teams; 15 players from 24 teams

33. 385 calories in 3.5 servings; 300 calories in 3 servings

34. 4.8 laps every 8 minutes; 3.6 laps every 6 minutes

35. $\frac{3}{4}$ pound for every 5 gallons; $\frac{4}{5}$ pound for every $5\frac{1}{3}$ gallons

36. **MP MODELING REAL LIFE** You do 90 sit-ups in 2 minutes. Your friend does 126 sit-ups in 2.8 minutes. Do these rates form a proportion? Explain.

37. **MP MODELING REAL LIFE** Find the heart rates of you and your friend. Do these rates form a proportion? Explain.

	Heartbeats	Seconds
You	22	20
Friend	18	15

38. **MP PROBLEM SOLVING** You earn $56 walking your neighbor's dog for 8 hours. Your friend earns $36 painting your neighbor's fence for 4 hours. Are the pay rates equivalent? Explain.

39. **GEOMETRY** Are the heights and bases of the two triangles proportional? Explain.

$h = 8$ cm
$h = 12$ cm
$b = 10$ cm
$b = 15$ cm

Session Number, *x*	Pitches, *y*	Curveballs, *z*
1	10	4
2	20	8
3	30	12
4	40	16

40. **MP REASONING** A pitcher coming back from an injury limits the number of pitches thrown in bullpen sessions as shown.

   a. Which quantities are proportional?

   b. How many pitches that are *not* curveballs will the pitcher likely throw in Session 5?

41. **(MP) STRUCTURE** You add the same numbers of pennies and dimes to the coins shown. Is the new ratio of pennies to dimes proportional to the original ratio of pennies to dimes? If so, illustrate your answer with an example. If not, show why with a counterexample.

a.

b.

42. **(MP) REASONING** You are 13 years old, and your cousin is 19 years old. As you grow older, is your age proportional to your cousin's age? Explain your reasoning.

43. **(MP) MODELING REAL LIFE** The shadow of the moon during a solar eclipse travels 2300 miles in 1 hour. In the first 20 minutes, the shadow traveled $766\frac{2}{3}$ miles. How long does it take for the shadow to travel 1150 miles? Justify your answer.

44. **(MP) MODELING REAL LIFE** In 60 seconds, a car in a parade travels 0.2 mile. The car traveled the last 0.05 mile in 12 seconds. How long did it take for the car to travel 0.1 mile? Justify your answer.

45. **OPEN-ENDED** Describe (a) a real-life situation where you expect two quantities to be proportional and (b) a real-life situation where you do *not* expect two quantities to be proportional. Explain your reasoning.

46. **(MP) PROBLEM SOLVING** A specific shade of red nail polish requires 7 parts red to 2 parts yellow. A mixture contains 35 quarts of red and 8 quarts of yellow. Is the mixture the correct shade? If so, justify your answer. If not, explain how you can fix the mixture to make the correct shade of red.

47. **(MP) LOGIC** The quantities x and y are proportional. Use each of the integers 1–5 to complete the table. Justify your answer.

x	10		6	
y				0.5

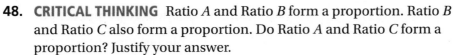

48. **CRITICAL THINKING** Ratio A and Ratio B form a proportion. Ratio B and Ratio C also form a proportion. Do Ratio A and Ratio C form a proportion? Justify your answer.

5.4 Writing and Solving Proportions

Learning Target: Use proportions to solve ratio problems.

Success Criteria:
- I can solve proportions using various methods.
- I can find a missing value that makes two ratios equivalent.
- I can use proportions to represent and solve real-life problems.

EXPLORATION 1

Solving a Ratio Problem

Work with a partner. A train travels 50 miles every 40 minutes. To determine the number of miles the train travels in 90 minutes, your friend creates the following table.

Miles	50	x
Minutes	40	90

a. Explain how you can find the value of x.

b. Can you use the information in the table to write a proportion? If so, explain how you can use the proportion to find the value of x. If not, explain why not.

c. How far does the train below travel in 2 hours?

Math Practice

Use Equations
What equation can you use to find the answer in part (c)?

30 miles every $\frac{1}{2}$ hour

d. Share your results in part (c) with other groups. Compare and contrast methods used to solve the problem.

You can solve proportions using various methods.

EXAMPLE 1 ## Solving a Proportion Using Mental Math

Solve $\dfrac{3}{2} = \dfrac{x}{8}$.

Step 1: Think: The product of 2 and what number is 8?

$$\dfrac{3}{2} = \dfrac{x}{8}$$

$2 \times ? = 8$

Step 2: Because the product of 2 and 4 is 8, multiply the numerator by 4 to find x.

$3 \times 4 = 12$

$$\dfrac{3}{2} = \dfrac{x}{8}$$

$2 \times 4 = 8$

 The solution is $x = 12$.

Try It Solve the proportion.

1. $\dfrac{5}{8} = \dfrac{20}{d}$

2. $\dfrac{7}{z} = \dfrac{14}{10}$

3. $\dfrac{21}{24} = \dfrac{x}{8}$

EXAMPLE 2 ## Solving a Proportion Using Multiplication

Solve $\dfrac{5}{7} = \dfrac{x}{21}$.

$$\dfrac{5}{7} = \dfrac{x}{21} \qquad \text{Write the proportion.}$$

$$21 \cdot \dfrac{5}{7} = 21 \cdot \dfrac{x}{21} \qquad \text{Multiplication Property of Equality}$$

$$15 = x \qquad \text{Simplify.}$$

 The solution is $x = 15$.

Try It Solve the proportion.

4. $\dfrac{w}{6} = \dfrac{6}{9}$

5. $\dfrac{12}{10} = \dfrac{a}{15}$

6. $\dfrac{y}{10} = \dfrac{3}{5}$

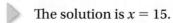

EXAMPLE 3 **Solving a Proportion Using Cross Products**

Solve each proportion.

a. $\dfrac{x}{8} = \dfrac{7}{10}$

$x \cdot 10 = 8 \cdot 7$ Cross Products Property

$10x = 56$ Multiply.

$x = 5.6$ Divide each side by 10.

▶ The solution is $x = 5.6$.

b. $\dfrac{9}{y} = \dfrac{3}{17}$

$9 \cdot 17 = y \cdot 3$ Cross Products Property

$153 = 3y$ Multiply.

$51 = y$ Divide each side by 3.

▶ The solution is $y = 51$.

Try It Solve the proportion.

7. $\dfrac{2}{7} = \dfrac{x}{28}$ **8.** $\dfrac{12}{5} = \dfrac{6}{y}$ **9.** $\dfrac{40}{z+1} = \dfrac{15}{6}$

EXAMPLE 4 **Writing and Solving a Proportion**

Find the value of x so that the ratios $3:8$ and $x:20$ are equivalent.

For the ratios to be equivalent, the values of the ratios must be equal. So, find the value of x for which $\dfrac{3}{8}$ and $\dfrac{x}{20}$ are equal by solving a proportion.

$\dfrac{3}{8} = \dfrac{x}{20}$ Write a proportion.

$20 \cdot \dfrac{3}{8} = 20 \cdot \dfrac{x}{20}$ Multiplication Property of Equality

$7.5 = x$ Simplify.

▶ So, $3:8$ and $x:20$ are equivalent when $x = 7.5$.

Try It Find the value of x so that the ratios are equivalent.

10. $2:4$ and $x:6$ **11.** $x:5$ and $8:2$ **12.** 4 to 3 and 10 to x

EXAMPLE 5 **Writing a Proportion**

A chef increases the amounts of ingredients in a recipe to make a proportional recipe. The new recipe has 6 cups of black beans. Which proportion can be used to find the number x of cups of water in the new recipe?

> **Black Bean Soup**
>
> 1.5 cups black beans
> 0.5 cup salsa
> 2 cups water
> 1 tomato
> 2 teaspoons seasoning

A. $\dfrac{2}{1.5} = \dfrac{6}{x}$ **B.** $\dfrac{1.5}{6} = \dfrac{x}{2}$

C. $\dfrac{1.5}{2} = \dfrac{x}{6}$ **D.** $\dfrac{1.5}{2} = \dfrac{6}{x}$

In the original recipe, the ratio of cups of black beans to cups of water is $1.5 : 2$. In the new recipe, the ratio is $6 : x$.

For the new recipe to be proportional to the original recipe, these ratios must be equivalent. So, the values of the ratios must be equal, $\dfrac{1.5}{2} = \dfrac{6}{x}$.

 The correct answer is **D**.

Try It

13. Write a proportion that can be used to find the number of tomatoes in the new recipe.

 ## Self-Assessment *for Concepts & Skills*

Solve each exercise. Then rate your understanding of the success criteria in your journal.

SOLVING A PROPORTION Solve the proportion.

14. $\dfrac{5}{12} = \dfrac{b}{36}$ **15.** $\dfrac{6}{p} = \dfrac{42}{35}$

16. WRITING AND SOLVING A PROPORTION Find the value of x so that the ratios $x : 9$ and $5 : 6$ are equivalent.

17. DIFFERENT WORDS, SAME QUESTION Which is different? Find "both" answers.

> Solve $\dfrac{3}{x} = \dfrac{12}{8}$.

> Find x so that $3 : x$ and $12 : 8$ are equivalent.

> Find x so that $3 : 12$ and $x : 8$ are equivalent.

> Solve $\dfrac{12}{x} = \dfrac{3}{8}$.

EXAMPLE 6 **Modeling Real Life**

A titanosaur's heart pumped 50 gallons of blood for every 2 heartbeats. How many heartbeats did it take to pump 1000 gallons of blood?

Understand the problem.

You are given the rate at which a titanosaur's heart pumped blood. Because all of the rates you can write using this relationship are equivalent, the amount of blood pumped is proportional to the number of heartbeats. You are asked to find how many heartbeats it took to pump 1000 gallons of blood.

Make a plan.

The ratio of heartbeats to gallons of blood is 2 : 50. The number x of heartbeats for every 1000 gallons of blood can be represented by the ratio $x : 1000$. Use a proportion to find the value of x for which $\dfrac{2}{50}$ and $\dfrac{x}{1000}$ are equal.

THE TITANOSAUR

Solve and check.

$$\frac{2}{50} = \frac{x}{1000} \qquad \text{Write a proportion.}$$

$$40 = x \qquad \text{Multiply each side by 1000.}$$

So, it took 40 heartbeats to pump 1000 gallons of blood.

Another Method
You can use a ratio table to solve the problem.

× 20

Heartbeats	2	40
Blood (gallons)	50	1000

✓

× 20

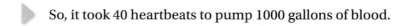

Self-Assessment for Problem Solving

Solve each exercise. Then rate your understanding of the success criteria in your journal.

18. You burn 35 calories every 3 minutes running on a treadmill. You want to run for at least 15 minutes, but no more than 30 minutes. What are the possible numbers of calories that you will burn? Justify your answer.

19. **DIG DEEPER!** Two boats travel at the same speed to different destinations. Boat A reaches its destination in 12 minutes. Boat B reaches its destination in 18 minutes. Boat B travels 3 miles farther than Boat A. How fast do the boats travel? Justify your answer.

5.4 Practice

? Go to *BigIdeasMath.com* to get HELP with solving the exercises.

▶ Review & Refresh

Tell whether *x* and *y* are proportional.

1.

x	4	6	8
y	6	8	10

2.

x	$\frac{2}{5}$	$\frac{4}{5}$	4
y	3	6	30

Plot the ordered pair in a coordinate plane.

3. $A(-5, -2)$ 4. $B(-3, 0)$ 5. $C(-1, 2)$ 6. $D(1, 4)$

7. Which expression is equivalent to $(3w - 8) - 4(2w + 3)$?

   A. $11w + 4$ B. $-5w - 5$ C. $-5w + 4$ D. $-5w - 20$

▶▶ Concepts, Skills, & Problem Solving

SOLVING A RATIO PROBLEM Determine how far the vehicle travels in 3 hours. (See Exploration 1, p. 203.)

8. A helicopter travels 240 miles every 2 hours.

9. A motorcycle travels 25 miles every 0.5 hour.

10. A train travels 10 miles every $\frac{1}{4}$ hour.

11. A ferry travels 45 miles every $1\frac{1}{2}$ hours.

SOLVING A PROPORTION Solve the proportion. Explain your choice of method.

12. $\dfrac{1}{4} = \dfrac{z}{20}$ 13. $\dfrac{3}{4} = \dfrac{12}{y}$ 14. $\dfrac{35}{k} = \dfrac{7}{3}$ 15. $\dfrac{b}{36} = \dfrac{5}{9}$

16. $\dfrac{x}{8} = \dfrac{3}{12}$ 17. $\dfrac{3}{4} = \dfrac{v}{14}$ 18. $\dfrac{15}{8} = \dfrac{45}{c}$ 19. $\dfrac{35}{28} = \dfrac{n}{12}$

20. $\dfrac{a}{6} = \dfrac{15}{2}$ 21. $\dfrac{y}{9} = \dfrac{44}{54}$ 22. $\dfrac{4}{24} = \dfrac{c}{36}$ 23. $\dfrac{20}{16} = \dfrac{d}{12}$

24. $\dfrac{10}{7} = \dfrac{8}{k}$ 25. $\dfrac{5}{n} = \dfrac{16}{32}$ 26. $\dfrac{9}{10} = \dfrac{d}{6.4}$ 27. $\dfrac{2.4}{1.8} = \dfrac{7.2}{k}$

28. **MP YOU BE THE TEACHER** Your friend solves the proportion $\dfrac{m}{8} = \dfrac{15}{24}$. Is your friend correct? Explain your reasoning.

$$\frac{m}{8} = \frac{15}{24}$$
$$m \cdot 24 = 8 \cdot 15$$
$$m = 5$$

29. **MP** **NUMBER SENSE** Without solving, determine whether $\frac{x}{4} = \frac{15}{3}$ and $\frac{x}{15} = \frac{4}{3}$ have the same solution. Explain your reasoning.

WRITING A PROPORTION Use the table to write a proportion.

30.

	Game 1	Game 2
Points	12	18
Shots	14	w

31.

	May	June
Winners	n	34
Entries	85	170

32.

	Today	Yesterday
Miles	15	m
Hours	2.5	4

33.

	Race 1	Race 2
Meters	100	200
Seconds	x	22.4

WRITING AND SOLVING A PROPORTION Find the value of x so that the ratios are equivalent.

34. $1 : 8$ and $4 : x$

35. 4 to 5 and x to 20

36. $3 : x$ and $12 : 40$

37. x to 0.25 and 6 to 1.5

38. $x : \frac{5}{2}$ and $8 : 10$

39. $\frac{7}{4}$ to 14 and x to 32

40. **WRITING A PROPORTION** Your science teacher has a photograph of the space shuttle *Atlantis*. Every 1 centimeter in the photograph represents 200 centimeters on the actual shuttle. Which of the proportions can you use to find the actual length x of *Atlantis*? Explain.

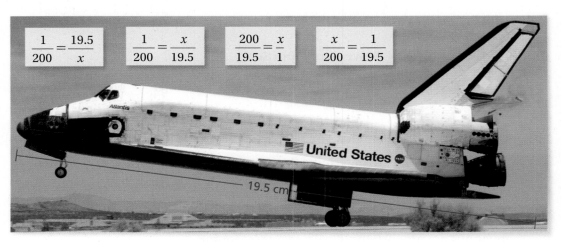

$$\frac{1}{200} = \frac{19.5}{x} \qquad \frac{1}{200} = \frac{x}{19.5} \qquad \frac{200}{19.5} = \frac{x}{1} \qquad \frac{x}{200} = \frac{1}{19.5}$$

41. **MP** **MODELING REAL LIFE** In an orchestra, the ratio of trombones to violas is 1 to 3. There are 9 violas. How many trombones are in the orchestra?

42. **MP** **MODELING REAL LIFE** A dance team has 80 dancers. The ratio of seventh-grade dancers to all dancers is $5 : 16$. Find the number of seventh-grade dancers on the team.

43. **MP MODELING REAL LIFE** There are 144 people in an audience. The ratio of adults to children is 5 to 3. How many are adults?

44. **MP PROBLEM SOLVING** You have $50 to buy T-shirts. You can buy 3 T-shirts for $24. Do you have enough money to buy 7 T-shirts? Justify your answer.

45. **MP PROBLEM SOLVING** You buy 10 vegetarian pizzas and pay with $100. How much change do you receive?

3 Vegetarian Pizzas for $25.50

46. **MP MODELING REAL LIFE** A person who weighs 120 pounds on Earth weighs 20 pounds on the Moon. How much does a 93-pound person weigh on the Moon?

47. **MP PROBLEM SOLVING** Three pounds of lawn seed covers 1800 square feet. How many bags are needed to cover 8400 square feet?

LAWN SEED 4 lb

48. **MP MODELING REAL LIFE** There are 180 white lockers in a school. There are 3 white lockers for every 5 blue lockers. How many lockers are in the school?

CONVERTING MEASURES Use a proportion to complete the statement. Round to the nearest hundredth if necessary.

49. $6 \text{ km} \approx$ ▢ mi   50. $2.5 \text{ L} \approx$ ▢ gal   51. $90 \text{ lb} \approx$ ▢ kg

SOLVING A PROPORTION Solve the proportion.

52. $\dfrac{2x}{5} = \dfrac{9}{15}$ 53. $\dfrac{5}{2} = \dfrac{d-2}{4}$ 54. $\dfrac{4}{k+3} = \dfrac{8}{14}$

55. **MP LOGIC** It takes 6 hours for 2 people to build a swing set. Can you use the proportion $\dfrac{2}{6} = \dfrac{5}{h}$ to determine the number of hours h it will take 5 people to build the swing set? Explain.

56. **MP STRUCTURE** The ratios $a : b$ and $c : d$ are equivalent. Which of the following equations are proportions? Explain your reasoning.

$$\frac{b}{a} = \frac{d}{c}$$ $$\frac{a}{c} = \frac{b}{d}$$ $$\frac{a}{d} = \frac{c}{b}$$ $$\frac{c}{a} = \frac{d}{b}$$

57. **CRITICAL THINKING** Consider the proportions $\dfrac{m}{n} = \dfrac{1}{2}$ and $\dfrac{n}{k} = \dfrac{2}{5}$. What is $\dfrac{m}{k}$? Explain your reasoning.

5.5 Graphs of Proportional Relationships

Learning Target: Represent proportional relationships using graphs and equations.

Success Criteria:
- I can determine whether quantities are proportional using a graph.
- I can find the unit rate of a proportional relationship using a graph.
- I can create equations to represent proportional relationships.

EXPLORATION 1

Representing Relationships Graphically

Work with a partner. The tables represent two different ways that red and blue food coloring are mixed.

Mixture 1

Drops of Blue, x	Drops of Red, y
1	2
2	4
3	6
4	8

Mixture 2

Drops of Blue, x	Drops of Red, y
0	2
2	4
4	6
6	8

a. Represent each table in the same coordinate plane. Which graph represents a proportional relationship? How do you know?

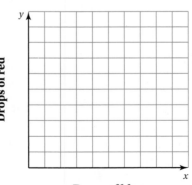

Drops of red

Drops of blue

Math Practice

Use a Graph
How is the graph of the proportional relationship different from the other graph?

b. Find the unit rate of the proportional relationship. How is the unit rate shown on the graph?

c. What is the multiplicative relationship between x and y for the proportional relationship? How can you use this value to write an equation that relates y and x?

Key Vocabulary
constant of
proportionality,
p. 212

The equation $y = kx$ can also be written as $\dfrac{y}{x} = k$. So, k is equal to the value of the ratio $y : x$.

 Key Idea

Graphs of Proportional Relationships

Words Two quantities x and y are proportional when $y = kx$, where k is a number and $k \neq 0$. The number k represents the multiplicative relationship between the quantities and is called the **constant of proportionality**.

Graph The graph of $y = kx$ is a line that passes through the origin.

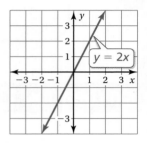

EXAMPLE 1 **Determining Whether Two Quantities are Proportional**

Tell whether x and y are proportional. Explain your reasoning.

a.

x	1	2	3	4
y	−2	0	2	4

Plot the points. Draw a line through the points.

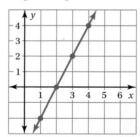

▷ The line does *not* pass through the origin. So, x and y are not proportional.

b.

x	0	2	4	6
y	0	2	4	6

Plot the points. Draw a line through the points.

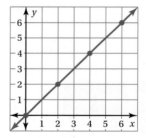

▷ The line passes through the origin. So, x and y are proportional.

Try It **Tell whether x and y are proportional. Explain your reasoning.**

1.

x	y
0	−2
1	1
2	4
3	7

2.

x	y
1	4
2	8
3	12
4	16

3.

x	y
−2	4
−1	2
0	0
1	2

◀)) *Multi-Language Glossary at BigIdeasMath.com*

EXAMPLE 2 **Finding a Unit Rate from a Graph**

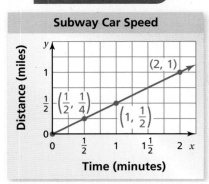

Subway Car Speed

Distance (miles) — *Time (minutes)*

The graph shows the speed of a subway car. Find the speed in miles per minute.

The graph is a line through the origin, so time and distance are proportional. To find the speed in miles per minute, use a point on the graph to find the unit rate.

One Way: Use the point $(2, 1)$ to find the speed.

> The point $(2, 1)$ indicates that the subway car travels 1 mile every 2 minutes. So, the unit rate is
>
> $$\frac{1}{2} \text{ mile per minute.}$$

▷ The speed of the subway car is $\frac{1}{2}$ mile per minute.

Another Way: Use the point $\left(1, \frac{1}{2}\right)$ to find the speed.

> The point $\left(1, \frac{1}{2}\right)$ indicates that the subway car travels $\frac{1}{2}$ mile every 1 minute. This is the unit rate.

▷ The speed of the subway car is $\frac{1}{2}$ mile per minute.

On the graph of a proportional relationship, the point $(1, k)$ indicates the unit rate, $k : 1$, and the constant of proportionality, k. This value is a measure of the steepness, or slope, of the line.

Try It

4. **WHAT IF?** Does your answer change when you use the point $\left(\frac{1}{2}, \frac{1}{4}\right)$ to find the speed of the subway car? Explain your reasoning.

Self-Assessment for Concepts & Skills

Solve each exercise. Then rate your understanding of the success criteria in your journal.

5. **IDENTIFYING A PROPORTIONAL RELATIONSHIP** Use the graph shown to tell whether x and y are proportional. Explain your reasoning.

6. **FINDING A UNIT RATE** Interpret each plotted point in the graph. Then identify the unit rate, if possible.

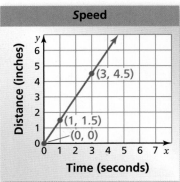

Speed

Distance (inches) — *Time (seconds)*

$(3, 4.5)$
$(1, 1.5)$
$(0, 0)$

EXAMPLE 3 **Modeling Real Life**

The graph shows the area y (in square feet) that a robotic vacuum cleans in x minutes. Find the area cleaned in 10 minutes.

The graph is a line through the origin, so x and y are proportional. You can write an equation to represent the relationship between area and time.

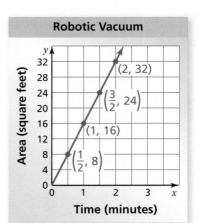

Robotic Vacuum

Because the graph passes through the point $(1, 16)$, the unit rate is 16 square feet per minute and the constant of proportionality is $k = 16$. So, an equation of the line is $y = 16x$. Substitute to find the area cleaned in 10 minutes.

$$y = 16x \qquad \text{Write the equation.}$$
$$= 16(10) \qquad \text{Substitute 10 for } x.$$
$$= 160 \qquad \text{Multiply.}$$

▷ So, the vacuum cleans 160 square feet in 10 minutes.

Self-Assessment for Problem Solving

Solve each exercise. Then rate your understanding of the success criteria in your journal.

7. The table shows the temperature y (in degrees Fahrenheit), x hours after midnight.

Hours, x	0	0.5	1	1.5
Temperature, y (°F)	42	44	46	48

a. Describe a proportional relationship between time and temperature shown by the table. Explain your reasoning.

b. Find the temperature 3.5 hours after midnight.

8. **DIG DEEPER!** Show how you can use a proportional relationship to plan the heights of the vertical supports of a waterskiing ramp. Then explain how increasing the steepness of the ramp affects the proportional relationship.

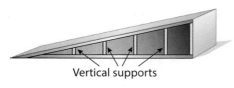

Vertical supports

Go to **BigIdeasMath.com** to get HELP with solving the exercises.

▶ Review & Refresh

Find the value of x so that the ratios are equivalent.

1. $2:7$ and $8:x$ **2.** 3 to 2 and x to 18 **3.** $9:x$ and $54:8$

Find the quotient, if possible.

4. $36 \div 4$ **5.** $42 \div (-6)$ **6.** $-39 \div 3$ **7.** $-44 \div (-4)$

Solve the inequality. Graph the solution.

8. $-\dfrac{x}{3} < 2$ **9.** $\dfrac{1}{3}p \geq 4$ **10.** $-8 < \dfrac{2}{3}n$ **11.** $-2w \leq 10$

▶▶ Concepts, Skills, & Problem Solving

REPRESENTING RELATIONSHIPS GRAPHICALLY **Represent the table graphically. Does the graph represent a proportional relationship? How do you know?**
(See Exploration 1, p. 211.)

12.

Hours, x	Miles, y
0	50
1	100
2	150

13.

Cucumbers, x	Tomatoes, y
2	4
3	6
4	8

IDENTIFYING A PROPORTIONAL RELATIONSHIP **Tell whether x and y are proportional. Explain your reasoning.**

14.

x	1	2	3	4
y	2	4	6	8

15.

x	-2	-1	0	1
y	0	2	4	6

16.

x	-1	0	1	2
y	-2	-1	0	1

17.

x	3	6	9	12
y	2	4	6	8

18.

x	1	2	3	4
y	3	4	5	6

19.

x	1	3	5	7
y	0.5	1.5	2.5	3.5

20. **MP YOU BE THE TEACHER** Your friend uses the graph to determine whether x and y are proportional. Is your friend correct? Explain your reasoning.

> The graph is a line, so x and y are proportional.

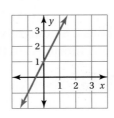

FINDING A UNIT RATE Interpret each plotted point in the graph. Then identify the unit rate.

21.

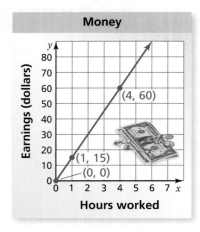

Money

22.

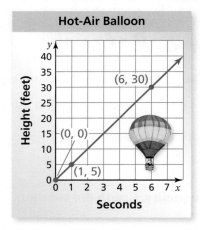

Hot-Air Balloon

IDENTIFYING A PROPORTIONAL RELATIONSHIP Tell whether x and y are proportional. If so, identify the constant of proportionality. Explain your reasoning.

23. $x - y = 0$ **24.** $\dfrac{x}{y} = 2$ **25.** $8 = xy$ **26.** $x^2 = y$

WRITING AN EQUATION The variables x and y are proportional. Use the values to find the constant of proportionality. Then write an equation that relates x and y.

27. When $y = 72$, $x = 3$.   **28.** When $y = 20$, $x = 12$.   **29.** When $y = 45$, $x = 40$.

30. **MP** **MODELING REAL LIFE** The table shows the profit y for recycling x pounds of aluminum. Find the profit for recycling 75 pounds of aluminum.

Aluminum (lb), x	10	20	30	40
Profit, y	$4.50	$9.00	$13.50	$18.00

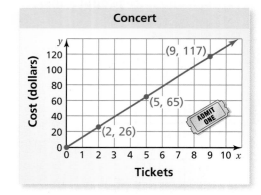

Concert

31. **MP** **MODELING REAL LIFE** The graph shows the cost of buying concert tickets. Tell whether x and y are proportional. If so, find and interpret the constant of proportionality. Then find the cost of 14 tickets.

32. **MP** **REASONING** The graph of a proportional relationship passes through (12, 16) and (1, y). Find y.

33. **MP** **PROBLEM SOLVING** The amount of chlorine in a swimming pool is proportional to the volume of water. The pool has 2.5 milligrams of chlorine per liter of water. How much chlorine is in the pool?

34. **DIG DEEPER!** A vehicle travels 250 feet every 3 seconds. Find the value of the ratio, the unit rate, and the constant of proportionality. How are they related?

8000 gallons

5.6 Scale Drawings

Learning Target: Solve problems involving scale drawings.

Success Criteria:
- I can find an actual distance in a scale drawing.
- I can explain the meaning of scale and scale factor.
- I can use a scale drawing to find the actual lengths and areas of real-life objects.

EXPLORATION **1**

Creating a Scale Drawing

Work with a partner. Several sections in a zoo are drawn on 1-centimeter grid paper as shown. Each centimeter in the drawing represents 4 meters.

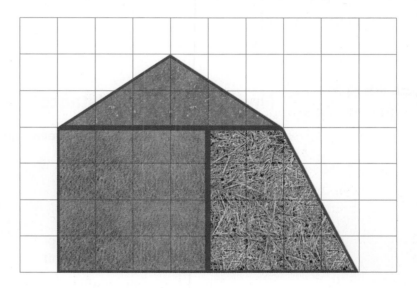

a. Describe the relationship between the lengths of the fences in the drawing and the actual side lengths of the fences.

b. Describe the relationship between the areas of the sections in the drawing and the actual areas of the sections.

c. Are the relationships in parts (a) and (b) the same? Explain your reasoning.

d. Choose a different distance to represent each centimeter on a piece of 1-centimeter grid paper. Then create a new drawing of the sections in the zoo using the distance you chose. Describe any similarities or differences in the drawings.

Math Practice

Analyze Givens

How does the information given about the drawing shown help you create an accurate drawing in part (d)?

Key Vocabulary
scale drawing, *p. 218*
scale model, *p. 218*
scale, *p. 218*
scale factor, *p. 219*

Recall that a ratio *a* : *b* is equivalent to $1 : \frac{b}{a}$.

A scale is usually written as a ratio where the first quantity is 1 unit.

Key Idea

Scale Drawings and Models

A **scale drawing** is a proportional, two-dimensional drawing of an object.
A **scale model** is a proportional, three-dimensional model of an object.

Scale

The measurements in scale drawings and models are proportional to the measurements of the actual object. The **scale** gives the ratio that compares the measurements of the drawing or model with the actual measurements.

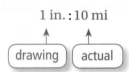

1 in. : 10 mi

drawing   actual

EXAMPLE 1 **Finding an Actual Distance**

What is the actual distance *d* between Cadillac and Detroit?

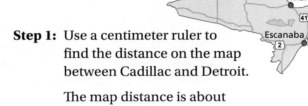

Step 1: Use a centimeter ruler to find the distance on the map between Cadillac and Detroit.

The map distance is about 3.5 centimeters.

Step 2: Use the scale 1 cm : 50 mi and the ratio 3.5 cm : *d* mi to write and solve a proportion.

$$\frac{1}{50} = \frac{3.5}{d}$$

map distance (cm)
actual distance (m)

$d = 50 \cdot 3.5$ Cross Products Property
$d = 175$ Multiply.

So, the distance between Cadillac and Detroit is about 175 miles.

Another Method
You can use a ratio table.

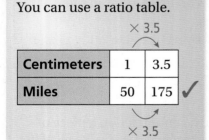

× 3.5

Centimeters	1	3.5
Miles	50	175

× 3.5

Try It

1. What is the actual distance between Traverse City and Marquette?

A scale can be written without units when the units are the same. The value of this ratio is called the **scale factor**. The scale factor describes the multiplicative relationship between the dimensions of a scale drawing or scale model and the dimensions of the actual object.

EXAMPLE 2 **Finding a Scale Factor**

A scale model of the Sergeant Floyd Monument is 10 inches tall. The actual monument is 100 feet tall.

a. What does 1 inch represent in the model? What is the scale?

The ratio of the model height to the actual height is 10 in. : 100 ft. Divide each quantity by 10 to determine the number of feet represented by 1 inch in the model.

$$\div 10 \overbrace{\binom{10 \text{ in.} : 100 \text{ ft}}{1 \text{ in.} : 10 \text{ ft}}} \div 10$$

▷ In the model, 1 inch represents 10 feet. So, the scale is 1 in. : 10 ft.

b. What is the scale factor of the model?

Write the scale with the same units. Use the fact that 1 ft = 12 in.

$$10 \text{ ft} = 10 \text{ ft} \times \frac{12 \text{ in.}}{1 \text{ ft}} = 120 \text{ in.}$$

▷ The scale is 1 in. : 120 in., or 1 : 120. So, the scale factor is $\frac{1}{120}$.

Try It

2. A drawing has a scale of 1 mm : 20 cm. What is the scale factor of the drawing?

Self-Assessment for Concepts & Skills

Solve each exercise. Then rate your understanding of the success criteria in your journal.

3. **VOCABULARY** In your own words, explain the meaning of the scale and scale factor of a drawing or model.

4. **FINDING AN ACTUAL DISTANCE** Consider the scale drawing of Balanced Rock in Arches National Park. What is the actual height of the structure?

5. **FINDING A SCALE FACTOR** A drawing has a scale of 3 in. : 2 ft. What is the scale factor of the drawing?

6. **MP REASONING** Describe the scale factor of a model that is (a) larger than the actual object and (b) smaller than the actual object.

1 cm : 32 ft

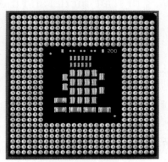

EXAMPLE 3 **Modeling Real Life**

The scale drawing of a square computer chip helps you see the individual components on the chip.

a. **Find the perimeter and the area of the computer chip in the scale drawing.**

When measured using a centimeter ruler, the scale drawing of the computer chip has a side length of 4 centimeters.

▶ So, the perimeter of the computer chip in the scale drawing is $4(4) = 16$ centimeters, and the area is $4^2 = 16$ square centimeters.

1 cm : 2 mm

b. **Find the actual perimeter and area of the computer chip.**

Multiplying each quantity in the scale by 4 shows that the actual side length of the computer chip is 8 millimeters.

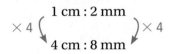

▶ So, the actual perimeter of the computer chip is $4(8) = 32$ millimeters, and the actual area is $8^2 = 64$ square millimeters.

c. **Compare the side lengths of the scale drawing with the actual side lengths of the computer chip.**

Find the scale factor. Use the fact that 1 cm = 10 mm.

Because the scale can be written as 10 mm : 2 mm, or 10 : 2, the scale factor is $\frac{10}{2} = 5$.

▶ So, the side lengths of the scale drawing are 5 times the actual side lengths of the computer chip.

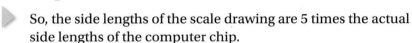

Self-Assessment for Problem Solving

Solve each exercise. Then rate your understanding of the success criteria in your journal.

9 ft

4 ft

Scale: 1 ft : 11.2 ft

7. A scale drawing of the Parthenon is shown. Find the actual perimeter and area of the rectangular face of the Parthenon. Then recreate the scale drawing with a scale factor of 0.2. Find the perimeter and area of the rectangular face in your drawing.

8. **DIG DEEPER!** You are in charge of creating a billboard advertisement that is 16 feet long and 8 feet tall. Choose a product. Create a scale drawing of the billboard using words and a picture. What is the scale factor of your design?

Go to *BigIdeasMath.com* to get HELP with solving the exercises.

▶ Review & Refresh

Tell whether x and y are proportional. Explain your reasoning.

1.

x	10	9	8	7
y	5	4	3	2

2.

x	6	12	18	24
y	7	14	21	28

Simplify the expression.

3. $7p + 6p$

4. $8 + 3d - 17$

5. $-2 + \frac{2}{5}b - \frac{1}{4}b + 6$

Write the word sentence as an inequality.

6. A number c is less than -3.

7. 7 plus a number z is more than 5.

8. The product of a number m and 6 is no less than 30.

▶▶ Concepts, Skills, & Problem Solving

CREATING A SCALE DRAWING Each centimeter on the 1-centimeter grid paper represents 8 inches. Create a proportional drawing of the figure that is larger or smaller than the figure shown. (See Exploration 1, p. 217.)

9.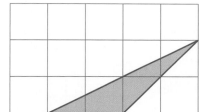

10.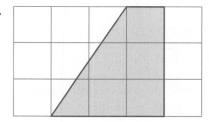

FINDING AN ACTUAL DISTANCE Use the map in Example 1 to find the actual distance between the cities.

11. Kalamazoo and Ann Arbor

12. Lansing and Flint

13. Grand Rapids and Escanaba

14. Saginaw and Alpena

USING A SCALE Find the missing dimension. Use the scale 1 : 12.

	Item	Model	Actual
15.	Mattress	Length: 6.25 in.	Length: in.
16.	Corvette	Length: in.	Length: 15 ft
17.	Water tower	Depth: 32 cm	Depth: m
18.	Wingspan	Width: 5.4 ft	Width: yd
19.	Football helmet	Diameter: mm	Diameter: 21 cm

FINDING A SCALE FACTOR Use a centimeter ruler to find the scale and the scale factor of the drawing.

20.

|← 120 m →|

21.

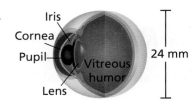

Iris
Cornea
Pupil
Vitreous humor
Lens
24 mm

22. CRITICAL THINKING You know the length and the width of a scale model. What additional information do you need to know to find the scale of the model? Explain.

23. (MP) MODELING REAL LIFE Central Park is a rectangular park in New York City.

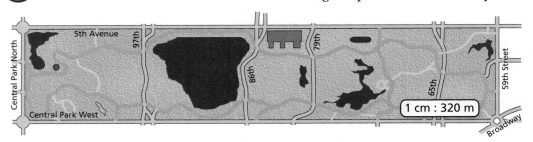

1 cm : 320 m

  a. Find the perimeter and the area of the scale drawing of Central Park.

  b. Find the actual perimeter and area of Central Park.

24. (MP) PROBLEM SOLVING In a blueprint, each square has a side length of $\frac{1}{4}$ inch.

  a. Ceramic tile costs $5 per square foot. How much does it cost to tile the bathroom?

  b. Carpet costs $18 per square yard. How much does it cost to carpet the bedroom and living room?

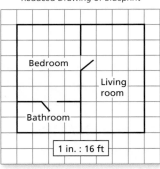

Reduced Drawing of Blueprint

Bedroom
Living room
Bathroom
1 in. : 16 ft

REPRODUCING A SCALE DRAWING Recreate the scale drawing so that it has a scale of 1 cm : 4 m.

25.

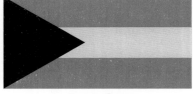

1 cm : 8 m

26.

1 cm : 2 m

27. **DIG DEEPER!** Make a conjecture about the relationship between the scale factor of a drawing and the quotients $\frac{\text{drawing perimeter}}{\text{actual perimeter}}$ and $\frac{\text{drawing area}}{\text{actual area}}$. Explain your reasoning.

Connecting Concepts

▶ *Using the Problem-Solving Plan*

1. The table shows the toll y (in dollars) for traveling x miles on a turnpike. You have $8.25 to pay your toll. How far can you travel on the turnpike?

Distance, x (miles)	25	30	35	40
Toll, y (dollars)	3.75	4.50	5.25	6.00

Understand the problem. The table shows the tolls for traveling several different distances on a turnpike. You have $8.25 to pay the toll. You are asked to find how far you can travel on the turnpike with $8.25 for tolls.

Make a plan. First, determine the relationship between x and y and write an equation to represent the relationship. Then use the equation to determine the distance you can travel.

Solve and check. Use the plan to solve the problem. Then check your solution.

2. A company uses a silo in the shape of a rectangular prism to store bird seed. The base of the silo is a square with side lengths of 20 feet. Are the height and the volume of the silo proportional? Justify your answer.

3. A rectangle is drawn in a coordinate plane as shown. In the same coordinate plane, create a scale drawing of the rectangle that has a vertex at $(0, 0)$ and a scale factor of 3.

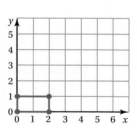

Performance Task

Mixing Paint

At the beginning of this chapter, you watched a STEAM Video called "Painting a Large Room." You are now ready to complete the performance task related to this video, available at *BigIdeasMath.com*. Be sure to use the problem-solving plan as you work through the performance task.

▶ Review Vocabulary

Write the definition and give an example of each vocabulary term.

ratio, *p. 184*
value of a ratio, *p. 184*
equivalent ratios, *p. 185*
ratio table, *p. 185*
rate, *p. 190*
unit rate, *p. 190*

equivalent rates, *p. 190*
proportion, *p. 196*
cross products, *p. 197*
proportional, *p. 198*
constant of proportionality, *p. 212*

scale drawing, *p. 218*
scale model, *p. 218*
scale, *p. 218*
scale factor, *p. 219*

▶ Graphic Organizers

You can use an **Example and Non-Example Chart** to list examples and non-examples of a concept. Here is an Example and Non-Example Chart for *scale factor*.

Scale factor

Examples	Non-Examples
$\frac{5}{1}$	1 cm : 2 mm
$\frac{1}{200}$	1 mm : 20 cm
$\frac{1}{1}$	12 in. : 1 ft
$\frac{3}{2}$	3 mi : 2 in.

Choose and complete a graphic organizer to help you study the concept.

1. ratio

2. equivalent ratios

3. rate

4. unit rate

5. equivalent rates

6. proportion

7. cross products

8. proportional

9. scale

"What do you think of my Example & Non-Example Chart for popular cat toys?"

Chapter Self-Assessment

As you complete the exercises, use the scale below to rate your understanding of the success criteria in your journal.

1	2	3	4
I do not understand.	I can do it with help.	I can do it on my own.	I can teach someone else.

5.1 Ratios and Ratio Tables (pp. 183–188)

Learning Target: Understand ratios of rational numbers and use ratio tables to represent equivalent ratios.

Write the ratio. Then find and interpret the value of the ratio.

1. salt : flour

2. water to flour

3. salt to water

Modeling Clay
Ingredients:
2 cups flour $\frac{1}{2}$ cup salt $\frac{3}{4}$ cup water

Find the missing values in the ratio table. Then write the equivalent ratios.

4.

Flour (cups)	$\frac{3}{2}$	3		
Milk (cups)	$\frac{1}{2}$		$\frac{3}{2}$	2

5.

Miles	45	135		90
Hours	0.75		3	

6. The cost for 16 ounces of cheese is $3.20. What is the cost for 20 ounces of cheese?

5.2 Rates and Unit Rates (pp. 189–194)

Learning Target: Understand rates involving fractions and use unit rates to solve problems.

Find the unit rate.

7. 289 miles on 10 gallons

8. $6\frac{2}{5}$ revolutions in $2\frac{2}{3}$ seconds

9. You can mow 23,760 square feet in $\frac{1}{2}$ hour. How many square feet can you mow in 2 hours? Justify your answer.

Tell whether the rates are equivalent. Justify your answer.

10. 60 centimeters every 2.5 years
    30 centimeters every 15 months

11. $2.56 per $\frac{1}{2}$ pound
    $0.48 per 6 ounces

5.3 Identifying Proportional Relationships (pp. 195–202)

Learning Target: Determine whether two quantities are in a proportional relationship.

Tell whether the ratios form a proportion.

12. 4 to 9 and 2 to 3

13. $12 : 22$ and $18 : 33$

14. $\dfrac{1}{2} : 2$ and $\dfrac{1}{4} : \dfrac{1}{10}$

15. 3.2 to 8 and 1.2 to 3

16. Tell whether x and y are proportional.

x	1	3	6	8
y	4	12	24	32

17. You can type 250 characters in 60 seconds. Your friend can type 375 characters in 90 seconds. Do these rates form a proportion? Explain.

5.4 Writing and Solving Proportions (pp. 203–210)

Learning Target: Use proportions to solve ratio problems.

Solve the proportion. Explain your choice of method.

18. $\dfrac{3}{8} = \dfrac{9}{x}$

19. $\dfrac{x}{4} = \dfrac{2}{5}$

20. $\dfrac{5}{12} = \dfrac{y}{15}$

21. $\dfrac{s+1}{4} = \dfrac{4}{8}$

Use the table to write a proportion.

22.

	Game 1	Game 2
Penalties	6	8
Minutes	12	m

23.

	Concert 1	Concert 2
Songs	15	18
Hours	2.5	h

24. Find the value of x so that the ratios $8 : 20$ and $6 : x$ are equivalent.

25. Swamp gas consists primarily of methane, a chemical compound consisting of a $1 : 4$ ratio of carbon to hydrogen atoms. If a sample of methane contains 1564 hydrogen atoms, how many carbon atoms are present in the sample?

5.5 Graphs of Proportional Relationships (pp. 211–216)

Learning Target: Represent proportional relationships using graphs and equations.

26. Tell whether x and y are proportional. Explain your reasoning.

x	−3	−1	1	3
y	6	2	−2	−6

27. The graph shows the number of visits your website received over the past 6 months. Interpret each plotted point in the graph. Then identify the unit rate.

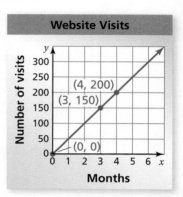

Website Visits

Tell whether x and y are proportional. If so, identify the constant of proportionality. Explain your reasoning.

28. $x + y = 6$ **29.** $y - x = 0$ **30.** $\dfrac{x}{y} = 20$ **31.** $x = y + 2$

32. The variables x and y are proportional. When $y = 4$, $x = \dfrac{1}{2}$. Find the constant of proportionality. Then write an equation that relates x and y.

5.6 Scale Drawings (pp. 217–222)

Learning Target: Solve problems involving scale drawings.

Find the missing dimension. Use the scale factor 1 : 20.

	Item	Model	Actual
33.	Basketball player	Height: in.	Height: 90 in.
34.	Dinosaur	Length: 3.75 ft	Length: ft

Use a centimeter ruler to find the scale and the scale factor of the drawing.

35. |———— 30 in. ————|

36. |—7.5 in.—|

37. A scale model of a lighthouse has a scale of 1 in. : 8 ft. The scale model is 20 inches tall. How tall is the lighthouse?

Find the unit rate.

1. 84 miles in 12 days

2. $2\frac{2}{5}$ kilometers in $3\frac{3}{4}$ minutes

Tell whether the ratios form a proportion.

3. 1 to 0.4 and 9 to 3.6

4. $2 : \frac{8}{3}$ and $\frac{2}{3} : 6$

Tell whether x and y are proportional. Explain your reasoning.

5.

x	2	4	6	8
y	10	20	30	40

6.

x	1	3	5	7
y	3	7	11	15

7. Use the table to write a proportion.

	Monday	Tuesday
Gallons	6	8
Miles	180	m

Solve the proportion.

8. $\dfrac{x}{8} = \dfrac{9}{4}$

9. $\dfrac{17}{4} = \dfrac{y}{6}$

Tell whether x and y are proportional. If so, identify the constant of proportionality. Explain your reasoning.

10. $xy - 11 = 5$

11. $\dfrac{y}{x} = 8$

12. A recipe calls for $\frac{2}{3}$ cup flour for every $\frac{1}{2}$ cup sugar. Write the ratio of sugar to flour. Then find and interpret the value of the ratio.

13. The graph shows the number of cycles of a crosswalk signal during the day and during the night.

   a. Write equations that relate x and y for both the day and night periods.

   b. Find how many more cycles occur during the day than during the night for a six-hour period.

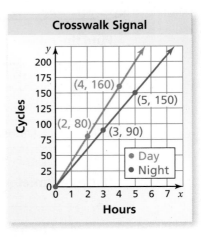

14. An engineer is using computer-aided design (CAD) software to design a component for a space shuttle. The scale of the drawing is 1 cm : 60 in. The actual length of the component is 12.75 feet. What is the length of the component in the drawing?

15. A specific shade of green glaze is made of 5 parts blue glaze to 3 parts yellow glaze. A glaze mixture contains 25 quarts of blue glaze and 9 quarts of yellow glaze. How can you fix the mixture to make the specific shade of green glaze?

Cumulative Practice

1. The school store sells 4 pencils for $0.80. What is the unit cost of a pencil?

    A. $0.20

    B. $0.80

    C. $3.20

    D. $5.00

2. What is the simplified form of the expression?

    $$3x - (2x - 5)$$

    F. $x - 5$

    G. $x + 5$

    H. $5x - 5$

    I. $-x - 5$

3. Which fraction is equivalent to -1.25?

    A. $-12\frac{1}{2}$

    B. $-1\frac{1}{4}$

    C. $-\frac{125}{1000}$

    D. $1\frac{1}{4}$

4. What is the value of x for the proportion $\frac{8}{12} = \frac{x}{18}$?

5. What inequality is represented by the graph?

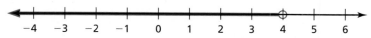

    F. $x - 3 < 7$

    G. $x + 6 \le 10$

    H. $-5 + x < -1$

    I. $x - 8 > -4$

6. What is the missing value in the ratio table?

x	$\frac{2}{3}$	$\frac{4}{3}$	$\frac{8}{3}$	$\frac{10}{3}$
y	6	12	24	

    A. $24\frac{2}{3}$

    B. 30

    C. 36

    D. 48

7. Which expression shows factoring $12x + 54$ using the GCF?

    F. $2(6x + 27)$ **G.** $3(4x + 18)$

    H. $6(2x + 9)$ **I.** $12\left(x + \dfrac{9}{2}\right)$

8. The distance traveled by a high-speed train is proportional to the number of hours traveled. Which of the following is *not* a valid interpretation of the graph?

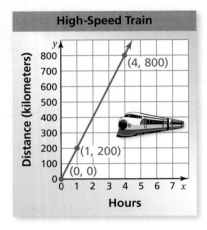

    A. The train travels 0 kilometers in 0 hours.

    B. The unit rate is 200 kilometers per hour.

    C. After 4 hours, the train is traveling 800 kilometers per hour.

    D. The train travels 800 kilometers in 4 hours.

9. Which graph represents a number that is at most -2?

    F.

    G.

    H.

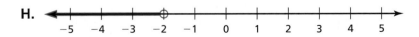

    I.

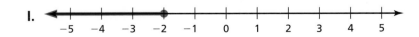

10. A map of the state where your friend lives has the scale $\frac{1}{2}$ in. : 10 mi.

Part A   Your friend measured the distance between her town and the state capital on the map. Her measurement was $4\frac{1}{2}$ inches. Based on your friend's measurement, what is the actual distance (in miles) between her town and the state capital? Show your work and explain your reasoning.

Part B   Your friend wants to mark her favorite campsite on the map. She knows that the campsite is 65 miles north of her town. What distance on the map (in inches) represents an actual distance of 65 miles? Show your work and explain your reasoning.

11. What is the value of the expression $-56 \div (-8)$?

12. The quantities x and y are proportional. What is the missing value in the table?

x	y
$\frac{5}{7}$	10
$\frac{9}{7}$	18
$\frac{15}{7}$	30
4	

A. 38   **B.** 42

C. 46   **D.** 56

13. To begin a board game, you place a playing piece at START. On your first three turns, you move ahead 8 spaces, move back 3 spaces, and then move ahead 2 spaces. How many spaces are you from START?

F. 2   **G.** 3

H. 7   **I.** 13

6 Percents

Chapter Learning Target:
Understand fractions, decimals, and percents.

Chapter Success Criteria:
- ▢ I can rewrite fractions, decimals, and percents.
- ▢ I can compare and order fractions, decimals, and percents.
- ■ I can use the percent proportion or percent equation to find a percent, a part, or a whole.
- ■ I can apply percents to solve real-life problems.

STEAM Video: "Tornado!"

Tornado!

More tornadoes occur each year in the United States than in any other country. How can you use a percent to describe the portion of tornadoes in the United States that occur in your state?

Watch the STEAM Video "Tornado!" Then answer the following questions.

1. The map below shows the average annual number of tornadoes in each state. Which regions have the most tornadoes? the fewest tornadoes?

2. Robert says that only Alaska, Hawaii, and Rhode Island average less than 1 tornado per year. What percent of states average *more* than 1 tornado per year?

Tornado Alley

After completing this chapter, you will be able to use the concepts you learned to answer the questions in the *STEAM Video Performance Task*. You will be given information about the average annual numbers of tornadoes in several states over a 25-year period. For example:

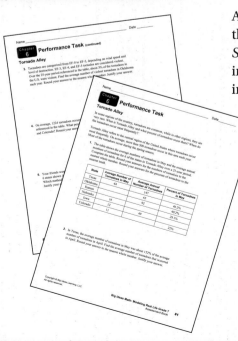

Texas: 147

Kansas: 92

Oklahoma: 65

Iowa: 49

You will be asked to solve various percent problems about tornadoes. Why is it helpful to know the percent of tornadoes that occur in each state?

Getting Ready for Chapter

Chapter Exploration

Work with a partner. Write the percent of the model that is shaded. Then write the percent as a decimal.

1.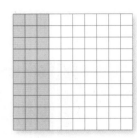

$$\boxed{}\ \% = \dfrac{\boxed{}}{\boxed{}}\ \longleftarrow \text{per}$$
$$\longleftarrow \text{cent}$$

$$= \dfrac{\boxed{}}{\boxed{}} \quad \text{Simplify.}$$

$$= \boxed{} \quad \text{Write the fraction as a decimal.}$$

2.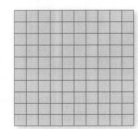

3.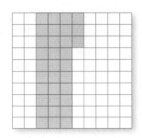

4.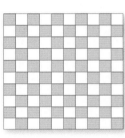

5.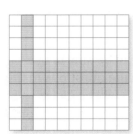

6.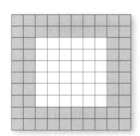

7.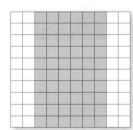

8. WRITE A PROCEDURE Work with a partner. Write a procedure for rewriting a percent as a decimal. Use examples to justify your procedure.

Vocabulary

The following vocabulary terms are defined in this chapter. Think about what each term might mean and record your thoughts.

percent of change	percent of decrease	discount
percent of increase	percent error	markup

6.1 Fractions, Decimals, and Percents

Learning Target: Rewrite fractions, decimals, and percents using different representations.

Success Criteria:
- I can write percents as decimals and decimals as percents.
- I can write fractions as decimals and percents.
- I can compare and order fractions, decimals, and percents.

EXPLORATION 1

Comparing Numbers in Different Forms

Work with a partner. Determine which number is greater. Explain your method.

a. 7% sales tax   or $\dfrac{1}{20}$ sales tax

b. 0.37 cup of flour   or $\dfrac{1}{3}$ cup of flour

c. $\dfrac{5}{8}$-inch wrench   or   0.375-inch wrench

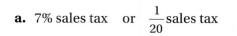

d. $12\dfrac{3}{5}$ dollars   or   12.56 dollars

e. $5\dfrac{5}{6}$ fluid ounces   or   5.6 fluid ounces

EXPLORATION 2

Ordering Fractions, Decimals, and Percents

Work with a partner and follow the steps below.

Math Practice

Make a Plan

Make a plan to order the numbers. How might having a plan help you to order numbers quickly?

- Write five different numbers on individual slips of paper. Include at least one decimal, one fraction, and one percent.

- On a separate sheet of paper, create an answer key that shows your numbers written from least to greatest.

- Exchange slips of paper with another group and race to order the numbers from least to greatest. Then exchange answer keys to check your orders.

Key Ideas

Writing Percents as Decimals

Words Remove the percent symbol. Then divide by 100, which moves the decimal point two places to the left.

Numbers $82\% = 82.\%= 0.82$ $2.\overline{45}\% = 02.\overline{45}\% = 0.02\overline{45}$

Writing Decimals as Percents

Words Multiply by 100, which moves the decimal point two places to the right. Then add a percent symbol.

Numbers $0.47 = 0.47 = 47\%$ $0.\overline{2} = 0.222\ldots = 22.\overline{2}\%$

> **Remember**
>
> Bar notation indicates one or more repeating digits.

EXAMPLE 1 **Converting Between Percents and Decimals**

Write each percent as a decimal or each decimal as a percent. Use a model to represent each number.

a. $61\% = 61.\%= 0.61$

b. $8\% = 08.\% = 0.08$

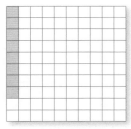

c. $0.27 = 0.27 = 27\%$

d. $0.\overline{3} = 0.333\ldots = 33.\overline{3}\%$

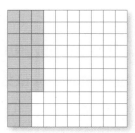
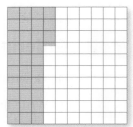

Try It Write the percent as a decimal or the decimal as a percent. Use a model to represent the number.

1. 39% **2.** $12.\overline{6}\%$ **3.** 0.05 **4.** 1.25

EXAMPLE 2 **Writing Fractions as Decimals and Percents**

Write each fraction as a decimal and a percent.

> **Remember**
>
> For a fraction with a denominator of 100, $\frac{n}{100} = n\%$.

a. $\frac{4}{5}$

$$\frac{4}{5} = \frac{4 \times 20}{5 \times 20} = \frac{80}{100} = 80\% = 0.8$$

▶ So, $\frac{4}{5}$ can be written as 0.8 or 80%.

b. $\frac{15}{11}$

Use long division to divide 15 by 11.

$$\frac{15}{11} = 1.\overline{36}$$

Write $1.\overline{36}$ as a percent.

$$1.\overline{36} = 1.3636\ldots = 136.\overline{36}\%$$

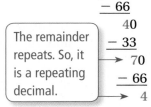

> The remainder repeats. So, it is a repeating decimal.

$$\begin{array}{r} 1.3636 \\ 11\overline{)15.0000} \\ -11 \\ \hline 40 \\ -33 \\ \hline 70 \\ -66 \\ \hline 40 \\ -33 \\ \hline 70 \\ -66 \\ \hline 4 \end{array}$$

▶ So, $\frac{15}{11}$ can be written as $1.\overline{36}$ or $136.\overline{36}\%$.

Try It **Write the fraction as a decimal and a percent.**

5. $\frac{5}{8}$ **6.** $\frac{1}{6}$ **7.** $\frac{11}{3}$ **8.** $\frac{3}{1000}$

 ## *Self-Assessment* for Concepts & Skills

Solve each exercise. Then rate your understanding of the success criteria in your journal.

CONVERTING BETWEEN PERCENTS AND DECIMALS **Write the percent as a decimal or the decimal as a percent. Use a model to represent the number.**

9. 46%   **10.** $66.\overline{6}\%$ **11.** 0.18   **12.** $2.\overline{3}$

WRITING FRACTIONS AS DECIMALS AND PERCENTS **Write the fraction as a decimal and a percent.**

13. $\frac{7}{10}$ **14.** $\frac{5}{9}$

15. $\frac{7}{2000}$ **16.** $\frac{17}{15}$

EXAMPLE 3 **Modeling Real Life**

An ice rink is open December through February. The table shows the attendance each month as a portion of the total attendance. How many times more guests visit the ice rink in the busiest month than in the least busy month?

Month	December	January	February
Portion of Guests	0.72	$\frac{3}{25}$	16%

Write $\frac{3}{25}$ and 16% as decimals.

January: $\frac{3}{25} = \frac{12}{100} = 0.12$ **February:** $16\% = 16.\%\!= 0.16$

The busiest month was December, the second busiest month was February, and the least busy month was January. So, divide 0.72 by 0.12.

$$0.12\overline{)0.72} \longrightarrow 12\overline{)72.}$$

$$\begin{array}{r} 6. \\ 12\overline{)72.} \\ -72 \\ \hline 0 \end{array}$$

Multiply each number by 100.

▷ So, 6 times more guests visit the ice rink in the busiest month than in the least busy month.

 Self-Assessment for Problem Solving

Solve each exercise. Then rate your understanding of the success criteria in your journal.

17. An astronaut spends 53% of the day working, 0.1 of the day eating, $\frac{3}{10}$ of the day sleeping, and the rest of the day exercising. Order the events by duration from least to greatest. Justify your answer.

18. **DIG DEEPER!** A band plays one concert in Arizona, one concert in California, and one concert in Georgia. In California, the band earned $\frac{3}{2}$ the profit that they earned in Arizona. Of the total profit earned by the band, 32% is earned in Arizona. How many times more money did the band earn at the most profitable concert than at the least profitable concert? Justify your answer.

6.1 Practice

? Go to *BigIdeasMath.com* to get
HELP with solving the exercises.

▶ Review & Refresh

Find the missing dimension. Use the scale 1 : 15.

	Item	Model	Actual
1.	Figure skater	Height: in.	Height: 67.5 in.
2.	Pipe	Length: 5 ft	Length: ft

Simplify the expression.

3. $2(3p - 6) + 4p$

4. $5n - 3(4n + 1)$

5. What is the solution of $2n - 4 > -12$?

     A. $n < -10$ **B.** $n < -4$ **C.** $n > -2$ **D.** $n > -4$

▶▶ Concepts, Skills, & Problem Solving

COMPARING NUMBERS IN DIFFERENT FORMS **Determine which number is greater. Explain your method.** (See Exploration 1, p. 235.)

6. $4\frac{2}{5}$ tons or 4.3 tons

7. 82% success rate or $\frac{5}{6}$ success rate

CONVERTING BETWEEN PERCENTS AND DECIMALS **Write the percent as a decimal or the decimal as a percent. Use a model to represent the number.**

8. 26%

9. 0.63

10. 9%

11. 0.6

12. 44.7%

13. 55%

14. $39.\overline{2}\%$

15. 3.554

16. 123%

17. 0.041

18. 0.122

19. $49.\overline{92}\%$

20. (MP) **YOU BE THE TEACHER** Your friend writes $4.\overline{8}\%$ as a decimal. Is your friend correct? Explain your reasoning.

$$4.\overline{8}\% = 4.888\ldots\% = 488.\overline{8}$$

WRITING FRACTIONS AS DECIMALS AND PERCENTS **Write the fraction as a decimal and a percent.**

21. $\frac{29}{100}$

22. $\frac{3}{4}$

23. $\frac{7}{8}$

24. $\frac{2}{3}$

25. $\frac{7}{9}$

26. $\frac{12}{5}$

27. $\frac{9}{2}$

28. $\frac{1}{1000}$

29. $\frac{17}{6}$

30. $\frac{3}{11}$

31. $\frac{1}{750}$

32. $\frac{22}{9}$

MP PRECISION Order the numbers from least to greatest.

33. 66.1%, 0.66, $\frac{2}{3}$, 0.667

34. $\frac{2}{9}$, 21%, $0.2\overline{1}$, $\frac{11}{50}$

MATCHING Tell which letter shows the graph of the number.

35. $\frac{7}{9}$ **36.** 0.812   **37.** $\frac{5}{6}$ **38.** 79.5%

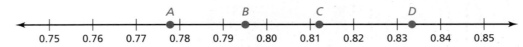

39. MP PROBLEM SOLVING The table shows the portion of students in each grade that participate in School Spirit Week. Order the grades by portion of participation from least to greatest.

Grade	Participation
6	0.64
7	$\frac{3}{5}$
8	65%

40. MP MODELING REAL LIFE The table shows the portion of gold medals that were won by the United States in five summer Olympic games. In what year did the United States win the least portion of gold medals? the greatest portion? Justify your answers.

Year	2000	2004	2008	2012	2016
Portion of Gold Medals Won	$12.\overline{3}\%$	$\frac{36}{301}$	$0.\overline{12}$	$\frac{23}{150}$	$\frac{46}{307}$

41. MP PROBLEM SOLVING You, your friend, and your cousin have a basketball competition where each person attempts the same number of shots. You make 70% of your shots, your friend makes $\frac{7}{9}$ of her shots, and your cousin makes $0.7\overline{2}$ of his shots. How many times more shots are made by the first place finisher than the third place finisher?

42. DIG DEEPER! Three different mixtures contain small amounts of acetic acid. Mixture A is 0.036 acetic acid, Mixture B is 4.2% acetic acid, and Mixture C is $\frac{1}{22}$ acetic acid. Explain how to use this information to determine which mixture contains the greatest amount of acetic acid.

43. MP MODELING REAL LIFE Over 44% of the 30 students in a class read a book last month. What are the possible numbers of students in the class who read a book last month? Justify your answer.

44. MP NUMBER SENSE Fill in the blanks using each of the numbers 0–7 exactly once, so that the percent, decimal, and fraction below are ordered from least to greatest. Justify your answer.

$$\boxed{}\boxed{}.\boxed{}\%\qquad\boxed{}.\boxed{}\boxed{}\qquad\frac{\boxed{}}{\boxed{}}$$

6.2 The Percent Proportion

Learning Target: Use the percent proportion to find missing quantities.

Success Criteria:
• I can write proportions to represent percent problems.
• I can solve a proportion to find a percent, a part, or a whole.

EXPLORATION 1

Using Percent Models

Work with a partner.

a. Complete each model. Explain what each model represents.

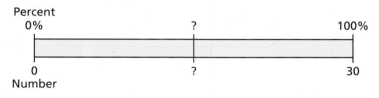

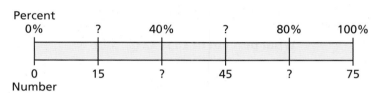

Math Practice

Use a Model
What quantities are given in each model? How can you use these quantities to answer the questions in part (b)?

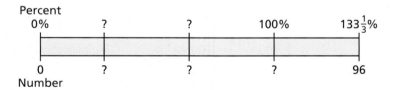

b. Use the models in part (a) to answer each question.

• What number is 50% of 30?

• 15 is what percent of 75?

• 96 is $133\frac{1}{3}$% of what number?

c. How can you use ratio tables to check your answers in part (b)? How can you use proportions? Provide examples to support your reasoning.

d. Write a question different from those in part (b) that can be answered using one of the models in part (a). Trade questions with another group and find the solution.

 **Key Idea**

The Percent Proportion

Words   You can represent "a is p percent of w" with the proportion

$$\frac{a}{w} = \frac{p}{100}$$

where a is part of the whole w, and $p\%$, or $\frac{p}{100}$, is the percent.

Numbers   3 out of 4 is 75%.

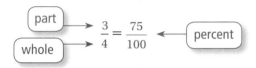

> *In percent problems, the word of is usually followed by the whole.*

EXAMPLE 1   **Finding a Percent**

What percent of 15 is 12?

$$\frac{a}{w} = \frac{p}{100}$$ Write the percent proportion.

$$\frac{12}{15} = \frac{p}{100}$$ Substitute 12 for a and 15 for w.

$$100 \cdot \frac{12}{15} = 100 \cdot \frac{p}{100}$$ Multiplication Property of Equality

$$80 = p$$ Simplify.

▷ So, 80% of 15 is 12.

Math Practice

Use a Table
Show how to use a ratio table to find the percent.

Check Use a model to check your answer.

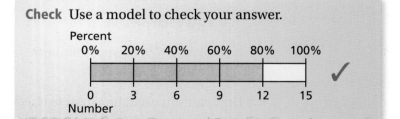

Try It Write and solve a proportion to answer the question.

1. What percent of 5 is 3?   **2.** 24 is what percent of 20?

EXAMPLE 2 **Finding a Part**

What number is 0.5% of 200?

$$\frac{a}{w} = \frac{p}{100}$$ Write the percent proportion.

$$\frac{a}{200} = \frac{0.5}{100}$$ Substitute 200 for w and 0.5 for p.

$$a = 1$$ Multiply each side by 200.

 So, 1 is 0.5% of 200.

Try It **Write and solve a proportion to answer the question.**

3. What number is 80% of 60?

4. 10% of 40.5 is what number?

EXAMPLE 3 **Finding a Whole**

150% of what number is 30?

$$\frac{a}{w} = \frac{p}{100}$$ Write the percent proportion.

$$\frac{30}{w} = \frac{150}{100}$$ Substitute 30 for a and 150 for p.

$$3000 = 150w$$ Cross Products Property

$$20 = w$$ Divide each side by 150.

 So, 150% of 20 is 30.

Try It **Write and solve a proportion to answer the question.**

5. 0.1% of what number is 4?

6. $\frac{1}{2}$ is 25% of what number?

 Self-Assessment *for Concepts & Skills*

Solve each exercise. Then rate your understanding of the success criteria in your journal.

7. USING THE PERCENT PROPORTION Write and solve a proportion to determine what percent of 120 is 54.

$$\frac{15}{w} = \frac{50}{100}$$

$$\frac{15}{50} = \frac{p}{100}$$

8. **MP** **CHOOSE TOOLS** Use a model to find 60% of 30.

$$\frac{15}{30} = \frac{p}{100}$$

$$\frac{a}{30} = \frac{50}{100}$$

9. WHICH ONE DOESN'T BELONG? Which proportion at the left does *not* belong with the other three? Explain your reasoning.

EXAMPLE 4 **Modeling Real Life**

The bar graph shows the strengths of tornadoes that occurred in a state in a recent year. What percent of the tornadoes were EF1s?

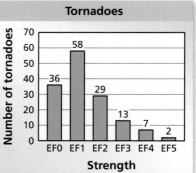

Understand the problem.

You are given a bar graph that shows the number of tornadoes in each strength category. You are asked to find the percent of the tornadoes that were EF1s.

Make a plan.

The total number of tornadoes, 145, is the whole, and the number of EF1 tornadoes, 58, is the part. Use the percent proportion to find the percent of the tornadoes that were EF1s.

Solve and check.

$$\frac{a}{w} = \frac{p}{100}$$ Write the percent proportion.

$$\frac{58}{145} = \frac{p}{100}$$ Substitute 58 for a and 145 for w.

$$100 \cdot \frac{58}{145} = 100 \cdot \frac{p}{100}$$ Multiplication Property of Equality

$$40 = p$$ Simplify.

So, 40% of the tornadoes were EF1s.

Check Reasonableness
The number of EF1 tornadoes, 58, is less than half the total number of tornadoes, 145. So, the percent of the tornadoes that were EF1s should be less than 50%. Because 40% < 50%, the answer is reasonable. ✓

 Self-Assessment for Problem Solving

Solve each exercise. Then rate your understanding of the success criteria in your journal.

10. An arctic woolly-bear caterpillar lives for 7 years and spends 90% of its life frozen. How many days of its life is the arctic woolly-bear frozen?

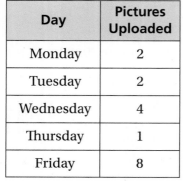

Day	Pictures Uploaded
Monday	2
Tuesday	2
Wednesday	4
Thursday	1
Friday	8

11. **DIG DEEPER!** The table shows the numbers of pictures you upload to a social media website for 5 days in a row. How many total pictures do you upload during the week when 32% of the total pictures are uploaded on Saturday and Sunday?

6.2 Practice

? Go to *BigIdeasMath.com* to get
HELP with solving the exercises.

▶ Review & Refresh

Write the fraction as a decimal and a percent.

1. $\dfrac{42}{100}$ **2.** $\dfrac{7}{1000}$ **3.** $\dfrac{13}{9}$ **4.** $\dfrac{41}{66}$

Evaluate the expression when $a = -15$ and $b = -5$.

5. $a \div b$ **6.** $\dfrac{b + 14}{a}$ **7.** $\dfrac{b^2}{a + 5}$

8. What is the solution of $9x = -1.8$?

 A. $x = -5$ **B.** $x = -0.2$ **C.** $x = 0.2$ **D.** $x = 5$

▶▶ Concepts, Skills, & Problem Solving

MP CHOOSE TOOLS **Use a model to answer the question. Use a proportion to
check your answer.** (See Exploration 1, p. 241.)

9. What number is 20% of 80?   **10.** 10 is what percent of 40?

11. 15 is 30% of what number?   **12.** What number is 120% of 70?

13. 20 is what percent of 50?   **14.** 48 is 75% of what number?

USING THE PERCENT PROPORTION **Write and solve a proportion to answer
the question.**

15. What percent of 25 is 12?   **16.** 14 is what percent of 56?

17. 25% of what number is 9?   **18.** 36 is 0.9% of what number?

19. 75% of 124 is what number?   **20.** 110% of 90 is what number?

21. What number is 0.4% of 40?   **22.** 72 is what percent of 45?

$$\dfrac{a}{w} = \dfrac{p}{100}$$
$$\dfrac{34}{w} = \dfrac{40}{100}$$
$$w = 85$$

23. **MP YOU BE THE TEACHER** Your friend uses the percent
proportion to answer the question below. Is your friend
correct? Explain your reasoning.

 "40% of what number is 34?"

24. **MP MODELING REAL LIFE** Of 140 seventh-grade students, 15%
earn the Presidential Youth Fitness Award. How many students
earn the award?

25. **MP MODELING REAL LIFE** A salesperson receives a
3% commission on sales. The salesperson receives $180
in commission. What is the amount of sales?

Section 6.2   The Percent Proportion   **245**

USING THE PERCENT PROPORTION Write and solve a proportion to answer the question.

26. 0.5 is what percent of 20?

27. 14.2 is 35.5% of what number?

28. $\frac{3}{4}$ is 60% of what number?

29. What number is 25% of $\frac{7}{8}$?

30. **MP MODELING REAL LIFE** You are assigned 32 math exercises for homework. You complete 75% of the exercises before dinner. How many exercises do you have left to do after dinner?

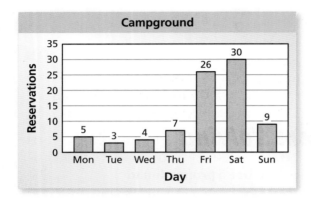

31. **MP MODELING REAL LIFE** Your friend earns $10.50 per hour, which is 125% of her hourly wage last year. How much did your friend earn per hour last year?

32. **MP MODELING REAL LIFE** The bar graph shows the numbers of reserved campsites at a campground for one week. What percent of the reservations were for Friday or Saturday?

33. **MP PROBLEM SOLVING** Your friend displays the results of a survey that asks several people to vote on a new school mascot.

    a. What is missing from the bar graph?

    b. What percent of the votes does the least popular mascot receive? Explain your reasoning.

    c. There are 124 votes total. How many votes does tiger receive?

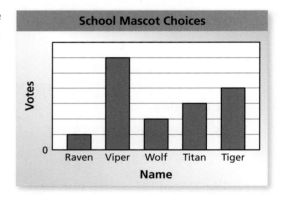

34. **DIG DEEPER!** A quarterback throw 33 passes in the first three quarters of a football game. The ratio of complete passes to incomplete passes during the first three quarters is 6 : 5. He completes every pass in the fourth quarter and 62.5% of his passes for the entire game. How many passes does the quarterback throw in the fourth quarter? Justify your answer.

35. **MP REASONING** 20% of a number is x. What is 100% of the number? Assume $x > 0$.

36. **MP STRUCTURE** Answer each question. Assume $x > 0$.

    a. What percent of $8x$ is $5x$?

    b. What is 65% of $80x$?

6.3 The Percent Equation

Learning Target: Use the percent equation to find missing quantities.

Success Criteria:
- I can write equations to represent percent problems.
- I can use the percent equation to find a percent, a part, or a whole.

EXPLORATION 1

Using Percent Equations

Work with a partner.

a. The circle graph shows the number of votes received by each candidate during a school election. So far, only half of the students have voted. Find the percent of students who voted for each candidate. Explain your method.

Votes Received by Each Candidate

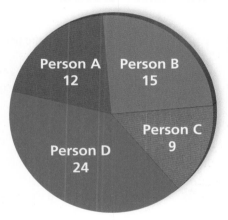

Math Practice

Use Equations
How does the equation you wrote in part (b) compare to the percent proportion? Explain.

b. You have learned that $\dfrac{\text{part}}{\text{whole}}$ = percent. Solve the equation for the "part." Explain your reasoning.

c. The circle graph shows the final results of the election after every student voted. Use the equation you wrote in part (b) to find the number of students who voted for each candidate.

Final Results

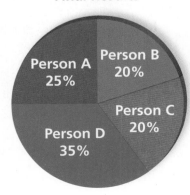

d. Use a different method to check your answers in part (c). Which method do you prefer? Explain.

Key Idea

The Percent Equation

Words To represent "*a* is *p* percent of *w*," use an equation.

percent

$$a = p\% \cdot w$$

part of the whole   whole

Numbers $\quad 15 = 50\% \cdot 30 \qquad 15 = 0.5 \cdot 30 \qquad 15 = \dfrac{1}{2} \cdot 30$

EXAMPLE 1 **Finding a Part of a Number**

What number is 24% of 50?   **Estimate**

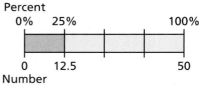

Common Error

Remember to convert a percent to a fraction or a decimal when using the percent equation. For Example 1, write 24% as $\dfrac{24}{100}$.

$a = p\% \cdot w$ $\qquad$ Write the percent equation.

$\quad = \dfrac{24}{100} \cdot 50$ $\qquad$ Substitute $\dfrac{24}{100}$ for $p\%$ and 50 for w.

$\quad = 12$ $\qquad$ Simplify.

So, 12 is 24% of 50. $\qquad$ **Reasonable?** $12 \approx 12.5$ ✓

Try It Write and solve an equation to answer the question.

1. What number is 10% of 20?

2. What number is 150% of 40?

EXAMPLE 2 **Finding a Percent**

9.5 is what percent of 25?

$\qquad a = p\% \cdot w$ $\qquad$ Write the percent equation.

$\qquad 9.5 = p\% \cdot 25$ $\qquad$ Substitute 9.5 for a and 25 for w.

$\qquad \dfrac{9.5}{25} = \dfrac{p\% \cdot 25}{25}$ $\qquad$ Division Property of Equality

$\qquad 0.38 = p\%$ $\qquad$ Simplify.

Because 0.38 equals 38%, 9.5 is 38% of 25.

Try It **Write and solve an equation to answer the question.**

3. 3 is what percent of 600?

4. 18 is what percent of 20?

EXAMPLE 3 **Finding a Whole**

39 is 52% of what number?

$$a = p\% \cdot w \qquad \text{Write the percent equation.}$$

$$39 = 0.52 \cdot w \qquad \text{Substitute 39 for } a \text{ and 0.52 for } p\%.$$

$$\frac{39}{0.52} = \frac{0.52 \cdot w}{0.52} \qquad \text{Division Property of Equality}$$

$$75 = w \qquad \text{Simplify.}$$

> So, 39 is 52% of 75.

Math Practice

Use a Table
Show how to use a ratio table to find the whole.

Try It **Write and solve an equation to answer the question.**

5. 8 is 80% of what number?

6. 90 is 180% of what number?

Self-Assessment *for Concepts & Skills*

Solve each exercise. Then rate your understanding of the success criteria in your journal.

7. VOCABULARY Write the percent equation in words.

USING THE PERCENT EQUATION **Write and solve an equation to answer the question.**

8. 14 is what percent of 70?

9. What number is 36% of 85?

10. 9 is 12% of what number?

11. 108 is what percent of 72?

12. DIFFERENT WORDS, SAME QUESTION Which is different? Find "both" answers.

What number is 20% of 55?	55 is 20% of what number?
20% of 55 is what number?	0.2 • 55 is what number?

EXAMPLE 4 **Modeling Real Life**

8th Street Cafe

DATE: MAY04   12:45PM
TABLE: 29
SERVER: JANE

Food Total	**27.50**
Tax	**1.65**
Subtotal	**29.15**

TIP: _____

TOTAL: _____

Thank You

You are paying for lunch and receive the bill shown.

a. **Find the percent of sales tax on the food total.**

Answer the question: $1.65 is what percent of $27.50?

$$a = p\% \cdot w$$ Write the percent equation.

$$1.65 = p\% \cdot 27.50$$ Substitute 1.65 for a and 27.50 for w.

$$0.06 = p\%$$ Divide each side by 27.50.

▷ Because 0.06 equals 6%, the percent of sales tax is 6%.

b. **You leave a 16% tip on the food total. Find the total amount you pay for lunch.**

Answer the question: What tip amount is 16% of $27.50?

$$a = p\% \cdot w$$ Write the percent equation.

$$= 0.16 \cdot 27.50$$ Substitute 0.16 for $p\%$ and 27.50 for w.

$$= 4.40$$ Multiply.

The amount of the tip is $4.40.

▷ So, you pay a total of $29.15 + $4.40 = $33.55.

 # Self-Assessment *for Problem Solving*

Solve each exercise. Then rate your understanding of the success criteria in your journal.

13. **DIG DEEPER!** A school offers band and chorus classes. The table shows the percents of the 1200 students in the school who are enrolled in band, chorus, or neither class. How many students are enrolled in both classes? Explain.

Class	Enrollment
Band	34%
Chorus	28%
Neither	42%

14. Water Tank A has a capacity of 550 gallons and is 66% full. Water Tank B is 53% full. The ratio of the capacity of Water Tank A to Water Tank B is 11 : 15.

   a. How much water is in each tank?

   b. What percent of the total volume of both tanks is filled with water?

6.3 Practice

Go to **BigIdeasMath.com** to get HELP with solving the exercises.

▶ Review & Refresh

Write and solve a proportion to answer the question.

1. 30% of what number is 9?

2. 42 is what percent of 80?

3. What percent of 36 is 20?

4. What number is 120% of 80?

Find the distance between the two numbers on a number line.

5. −4 and 10

6. $-\frac{2}{3}$ and $\frac{4}{3}$

7. $-5\frac{2}{5}$ and $-1\frac{3}{10}$

8. −4.3 and 7.5

9. There are 160 people in a grade. The ratio of boys to girls is 3 to 5. Which proportion can you use to find the number x of boys?

   A. $\frac{3}{8} = \frac{x}{160}$

   B. $\frac{3}{5} = \frac{x}{160}$

   C. $\frac{5}{8} = \frac{x}{160}$

   D. $\frac{3}{5} = \frac{160}{x}$

▶▶ Concepts, Skills, & Problem Solving

USING PERCENT EQUATIONS The circle graph shows the number of votes received by each candidate during a school election. Find the percent of students who voted for the indicated candidate. (See Exploration 1, p. 247.)

10. Candidate A

11. Candidate B

12. Candidate C

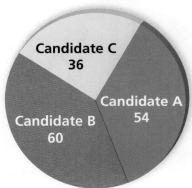

Votes Received by Each Candidate

Candidate C 36

Candidate A 54

Candidate B 60

USING THE PERCENT EQUATION Write and solve an equation to answer the question.

13. 20% of 150 is what number?

14. 45 is what percent of 60?

15. 35% of what number is 35?

16. 0.8% of 150 is what number?

17. 29 is what percent of 20?

18. 0.5% of what number is 12?

19. What percent of 300 is 51?

20. 120% of what number is 102?

MP YOU BE THE TEACHER Your friend uses the percent equation to answer the question. Is your friend correct? Explain your reasoning.

21. What number is 35% of 20?

$$a = p\% \cdot w$$
$$= 0.35 \cdot 20$$
$$= 7$$

22. 30 is 60% of what number?

$$a = p\% \cdot w$$
$$= 0.6 \cdot 30$$
$$= 18$$

23. **MP** **MODELING REAL LIFE** A salesperson receives a 2.5% commission on sales. What commission does the salesperson receive for $8000 in sales?

24. **MP** **MODELING REAL LIFE** Your school raised 125% of its fundraising goal. The school raised $6750. What was the goal?

25. **MP** **MODELING REAL LIFE** The sales tax on the model rocket shown is $1.92. What is the percent of sales tax?

PUZZLE There were *n* signers of the Declaration of Independence. The youngest was Edward Rutledge, who was *x* years old. The oldest was Benjamin Franklin, who was *y* years old.

26. *x* is 25% of 104. What was Rutledge's age?

27. 7 is 10% of *y*. What was Franklin's age?

28. *n* is 80% of *y*. How many signers were there?

Favorite Sport

Other

40.0%

37.5%

29. **MP** **LOGIC** How can you tell whether a percent of a number will be *greater than*, *less than*, or *equal to* the number? Give examples to support your answer.

30. **MP** **PROBLEM SOLVING** In a survey, a group of students is asked their favorite sport. Eighteen students choose "other" sports.

    a. How many students participate in the survey?

    b. How many choose football?

31. **TRUE OR FALSE?** Tell whether the statement is *true* or *false*. Explain your reasoning.

If *W* is 25% of *Z*, then *Z* : *W* is 75 : 25.

32. **DIG DEEPER!** At a restaurant, the amount of your bill before taxes and tip is $18.53. A 6% sales tax is applied to your bill, and you want to leave at least a 20% tip, but have only five-dollar bills. You plan to use any change you receive as part of the tip. What is the minimum percent that you can tip? Explain your reasoning.

33. **MP** **REASONING** The table shows your test results in a math class. What score do you need on the last test to earn 90% of the total points on the tests?

Test Score	Point Value
83%	100
91.6%	250
88%	150
?	300

6.4 Percents of Increase and Decrease

Learning Target: Find percents of change in quantities.

Success Criteria:
- I can explain the meaning of percent of change.
- I can find the percent of increase or decrease in a quantity.
- I can find the percent error of a quantity.

EXPLORATION 1

Exploring Percent of Change

Work with a partner.

Each year in the Columbia River Basin, adult salmon swim upriver to streams to lay eggs.

To go up the river, the adult salmon use fish ladders. But to go down the river, the young salmon must pass through several dams.

At one time, there were electric turbines at each of the eight dams on the main stem of the Columbia and Snake Rivers. About 88% of the young salmon pass through a single dam unharmed.

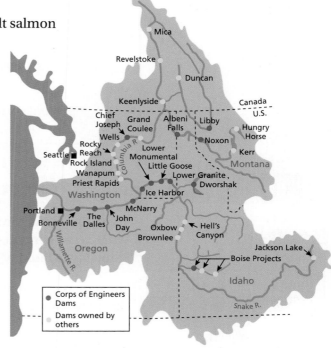

Math Practice

Check Progress
As the number of dams increases, what should be true about the number of young salmon that pass through unharmed?

a. One thousand young salmon pass through a dam. How many pass through unharmed?

b. One thousand young salmon pass through the river basin. How many pass through all 8 dams unharmed?

c. By what percent does the number of young salmon *decrease* when passing through a single dam?

d. Describe a similar real-life situation in which a quantity *increases* by a constant percent each time an event occurs.

A **percent of change** is the percent that a quantity changes from the original amount.

$$\text{percent of change} = \frac{\text{amount of change}}{\text{original amount}}$$

Key Idea

Percents of Increase and Decrease

When the original amount increases, the percent of change is called a **percent of increase**.

$$\text{percent of increase} = \frac{\text{new amount} - \text{original amount}}{\text{original amount}}$$

When the original amount decreases, the percent of change is called a **percent of decrease**.

$$\text{percent of decrease} = \frac{\text{original amount} - \text{new amount}}{\text{original amount}}$$

EXAMPLE 1 **Finding a Percent of Increase**

Day	Hours Online
Saturday	2
Sunday	4.5

The table shows the numbers of hours you spent online last weekend. What is the percent of change in your time spent online from Saturday to Sunday?

The time spent online Sunday is greater than the time spent online Saturday. So, the percent of change is a percent of increase.

$$\text{percent of increase} = \frac{\text{new amount} - \text{original amount}}{\text{original amount}}$$

$$= \frac{4.5 - 2}{2} \qquad \text{Substitute.}$$

$$= \frac{2.5}{2} \qquad \text{Subtract.}$$

$$= 1.25, \text{ or } 125\% \qquad \text{Write as a percent.}$$

▶ So, your time spent online increased 125% from Saturday to Sunday.

Try It **Find the percent of change. Round to the nearest tenth of a percent if necessary.**

1. 10 inches to 25 inches

2. 57 people to 65 people

EXAMPLE 2 **Finding a Percent of Decrease**

The bar graph shows a softball player's home run totals. What was the percent of change from 2016 to 2017?

The number of home runs decreased from 2016 to 2017. So, the percent of change is a percent of decrease.

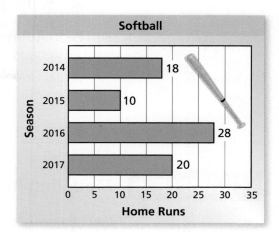

Softball

$$\text{percent of decrease} = \frac{\text{original amount} - \text{new amount}}{\text{original amount}}$$

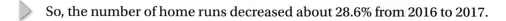

$$= \frac{28 - 20}{28} \qquad \text{Substitute.}$$

$$= \frac{8}{28} \qquad \text{Subtract.}$$

$$\approx 0.286, \text{ or } 28.6\% \qquad \text{Write as a percent.}$$

▷ So, the number of home runs decreased about 28.6% from 2016 to 2017.

Try It

3. In Example 2, what was the percent of change from 2014 to 2015?

Self-Assessment for Concepts & Skills

Solve each exercise. Then rate your understanding of the success criteria in your journal.

4. VOCABULARY What does it mean for a quantity to change by $n\%$?

5. MP NUMBER SENSE Without calculating, determine which situation has a greater percent of change. Explain.

- 5 bonus points added to 50 points
- 5 bonus points added to 100 points

FINDING A PERCENT OF CHANGE Identify the percent of change as an *increase* or a *decrease*. Then find the percent of change.

6. 8 feet to 24 feet

7. 300 miles to 210 miles

 **Key Idea**

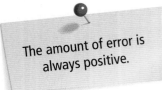

The amount of error is always positive.

Percent Error

A **percent error** is the percent that an estimated amount differs from the actual amount.

$$\text{percent error} = \frac{\text{amount of error}}{\text{actual amount}}$$

EXAMPLE 3 **Modeling Real Life**

Bag A: 15 ounces

Bag B: 16.5 ounces

You fill bags with about 16 ounces of homemade dog treats. The acceptable percent error when filling a bag is 5%. Tell whether each bag is acceptable.

Find the percent error for each bag.

Bag A: The amount of error is $16 - 15 = 1$ ounce.

$$\text{percent error} = \frac{\text{amount of error}}{\text{actual amount}}$$

$$= \frac{1}{16}$$

$$= 0.0625, \text{ or } 6.25\%$$

Bag B: The amount of error is $16.5 - 16 = 0.5$ ounce.

$$\text{percent error} = \frac{\text{amount of error}}{\text{actual amount}}$$

$$= \frac{0.5}{16}$$

$$= 0.03125, \text{ or } 3.125\%$$

Because 6.25% > 5%, Bag A is not acceptable. Because 3.125% < 5%, Bag B is acceptable.

 Self-Assessment *for Problem Solving*

Solve each exercise. Then rate your understanding of the success criteria in your journal.

8. In one round of a game, you are asked how many bones are in a human body. If the percent error of your answer is at most 5%, you earn two points. If the percent error is at most 10%, but greater than 5%, you earn one point. You guess 195 bones. The correct answer is 206 bones. How many points do you earn?

9. **DIG DEEPER!** The manager of a restaurant offers a 20% decrease in price to tennis teams. A cashier applies a 10% decrease and then another 10% decrease. Is this the same as applying a 20% decrease? If so, justify your answer. If not, explain how to achieve a 20% decrease after first applying a 10% decrease.

6.4 Practice

? Go to *BigIdeasMath.com* to get HELP with solving the exercises.

▶ Review & Refresh

Write and solve an equation to answer the question.

1. What number is 25% of 64?

2. 39.2 is what percent of 112?

3. 5 is 5% of what number?

4. 18 is 32% of what number?

Find the sum. Write fractions in simplest form.

5. $\frac{4}{7} + \left(-\frac{6}{7}\right)$

6. $-4.621 + 3.925$

7. $-\frac{5}{12} + \frac{3}{4}$

▶▶ Concepts, Skills, & Problem Solving

EXPLORING PERCENT CHANGE **You are given the percent of salmon that pass through a single dam unharmed. By what percent does the number of salmon decrease when passing through a single dam?** (See Exploration 1, p. 253.)

8. 75%

9. 80%

10. 62%

11. 94%

FINDING A PERCENT OF CHANGE **Identify the percent of change as an *increase* or a *decrease*. Then find the percent of change. Round to the nearest tenth of a percent if necessary.**

12. 12 inches to 36 inches

13. 75 people to 25 people

14. 50 pounds to 35 pounds

15. 24 songs to 78 songs

16. 10 gallons to 24 gallons

17. 72 paper clips to 63 paper clips

18. 16 centimeters to 44.2 centimeters

19. 68 miles to 42.5 miles

20. **MP YOU BE THE TEACHER** Your friend finds the percent increase from 18 to 26. Is your friend correct? Explain your reasoning.

$$\frac{26 - 18}{26} \approx 0.31 = 31\%$$

21. **MP MODELING REAL LIFE** Last week, you finished Level 2 of a video game in 32 minutes. Today, you finish Level 2 in 28 minutes. What is the percent of change?

22. **MP MODELING REAL LIFE** You estimate that a baby pig weighs 20 pounds. The actual weight of the baby pig is 16 pounds. Find the percent error.

Section 6.4 Percents of Increase and Decrease **257**

23. **MP** **PRECISION** A researcher estimates that a fossil is 3200 years old. Using *carbon-14 dating*, a procedure used to determine the age of an object, the researcher discovers that the fossil is 3600 years old.

  a. Find the percent error.

  b. What other estimate gives the same percent error? Explain your reasoning.

FINDING A PERCENT OF CHANGE Identify the percent of change as an *increase* or a *decrease*. Then find the percent of change. Round to the nearest tenth of a percent if necessary.

24. $\frac{1}{4}$ to $\frac{1}{2}$

25. $\frac{4}{5}$ to $\frac{3}{5}$

26. $\frac{3}{8}$ to $\frac{7}{8}$

27. $\frac{5}{4}$ to $\frac{3}{8}$

28. **CRITICAL THINKING** Explain why a change from 20 to 40 is a 100% increase, but a change from 40 to 20 is a 50% decrease.

29. **MP** **MODELING REAL LIFE** The table shows population data for a community.

Year	Population
2011	118,000
2017	138,000

  a. What is the percent of change from 2011 to 2017?

  b. Predict the population in 2023. Explain your reasoning.

30. **GEOMETRY** Suppose the length and the width of the sandbox are doubled.

  a. Find the percent of change in the perimeter.

  b. Find the percent of change in the area.

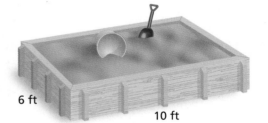

6 ft

10 ft

31. **MP** **MODELING REAL LIFE** A company fills boxes with about 21 ounces of cereal. The acceptable percent error in filling a box is 2.5%. Box A contains 20.4 ounces of cereal and Box B contains 21.5 ounces of cereal. Tell whether each box is an acceptable weight.

7:45
June

5:51
September

32. **MP** **PRECISION** Find the percent of change from June to September in the mile-run times shown.

33. **CRITICAL THINKING** A number increases by 10% and then decreases by 10%. Will the result be *greater than*, *less than*, or *equal to* the original number? Explain.

34. **MP** **PROBLEM SOLVING** You want to reduce your daily calorie consumption by about 9%. You currently consume about 2100 calories per day. Use mental math to estimate the number of calories you should consume in one week to meet your goal. Explain.

35. **DIG DEEPER!** Donations to an annual fundraiser are 15% greater this year than last year. Last year, donations were 10% greater than the year before. The amount raised this year is $10,120. How much was raised two years ago?

36. **MP** **REASONING** Forty students are in the science club. Of those, 45% are girls. This percent increases to 56% after more girls join the club. How many more girls join?

6.5 Discounts and Markups

Learning Target: Solve percent problems involving discounts and markups.

Success Criteria:
• I can use percent models to solve problems involving discounts and markups.
• I can write and solve equations to solve problems involving discounts and markups.

EXPLORATION 1

Comparing Discounts

Work with a partner.

a. The same pair of earrings is on sale at three stores. Which store has the best price? Use the percent models to justify your answer.

Store A:
Regular price: $45

40%
off

Store B:
Regular price: $49

50%
off

Store C:
Regular price: $39

20%
off

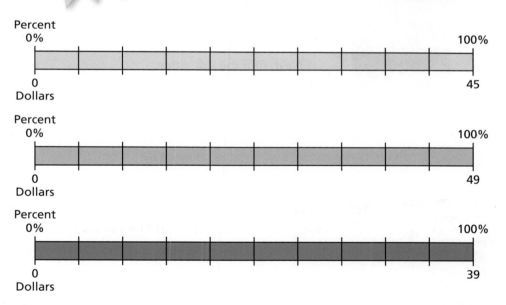

b. You buy the earrings on sale for 30% off at a different store. You pay $22.40. What was the original price of the earrings? Use the percent model to justify your answer.

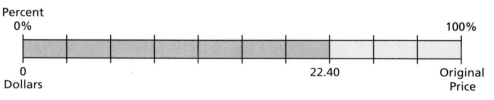

c. You sell the earrings in part (b) to a friend for 60% more than what you paid. What is the selling price? Use a percent model to justify your answer.

6.5 Lesson

Key Vocabulary
discount, *p. 260*
markup, *p. 260*

🔑 Key Ideas

Discounts

A **discount** is a decrease in the original price of an item.

Markups

To make a profit, stores charge more than what they pay. The increase from what the store pays to the selling price is called a **markup**.

EXAMPLE 1 | **Finding a Sale Price**

The original price of a video game is $35. What is the sale price?

Method 1: First, find the discount. The discount is 25% of $35.

$$a = p\% \cdot w \qquad \text{Write the percent equation.}$$

$$= 0.25 \cdot 35 \qquad \text{Substitute 0.25 for } p\% \text{ and 35 for } w.$$

$$= 8.75 \qquad \text{Multiply.}$$

Next, find the sale price.

Sale price	=	Original price	−	Discount
	=	35	−	8.75
	=	26.25		

 So, the sale price is $26.25.

Method 2: Use the fact that the sale price is 100% − 25% = 75% of the original price.

Find the sale price.

Sale price = 75% of $35

$$= 0.75 \cdot 35$$

$$= 26.25$$

 So, the sale price is $26.25.

> For an item with an original price of *p*, the price after a 25% discount is *p* − 0.25*p*, or 0.75*p*. So, a 25% discount is the same as paying 75% of the original price.

Check

Percent

0%	25%		75%	100%

| 0 | 8.75 | | 26.25 | 35 |

Number ✓

Try It

1. The original price of a skateboard is $50. The skateboard is on sale for 20% off. What is the sale price?

 Multi-Language Glossary at *BigIdeasMath.com*

EXAMPLE 2 **Finding an Original Price**

What is the original price of the cleats?

The sale price is $100\% - 40\% = 60\%$ of the original price.

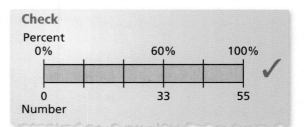

40% OFF NOW $33

Answer the question:

33 is 60% of what number?

$a = p\% \cdot w$ Write the percent equation.

$33 = 0.6 \cdot w$ Substitute 33 for a and 0.6 for $p\%$.

$55 = w$ Divide each side by 0.6.

▷ So, the original price of the cleats is $55.

Check

Percent

0%   60%   100%

0   33   55

Number ✓

Try It

2. The discount on a DVD is 50%. It is on sale for $10. What is the original price of the DVD?

Self-Assessment *for Concepts & Skills*

Solve each exercise. Then rate your understanding of the success criteria in your journal.

3. **WRITING** Describe how to find the sale price of an item that has a 15% discount.

FINDING A SALE PRICE **Find the sale price. Use a percent model to check your answer.**

4. A portable table tennis set costs $30 before a 30% discount.

5. The original price of an easel is $70. The easel is on sale for 20% off.

FINDING AN ORIGINAL PRICE **Find the original price. Use a percent model to check your answer.**

6. A bracelet costs $36 after a 25% discount.

7. The discount on a toy robot is 40%. The toy robot is on sale for $54.

EXAMPLE 3 **Modeling Real Life**

A store pays $70 for a bicycle. What is the selling price when the markup is 20%?

Method 1: First, find the markup. The markup is 20% of $70.

$$a = p\% \cdot w$$
$$= 0.20 \cdot 70$$
$$= 14$$

Next, find the selling price.

$$\boxed{\text{Selling price}} = \boxed{\text{Cost to store}} + \boxed{\text{Markup}}$$
$$= 70 + 14$$
$$= 84$$

▷ So, the selling price is $84.

Method 2: Use a ratio table. The selling price is 120% of the cost to the store.

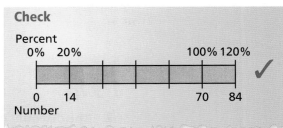

Percent	Dollars
100%	$70
20%	$14
120%	$84

$\div 5$ $\times 6$ $\div 5$ $\times 6$

▷ So, the selling price is $84.

Check

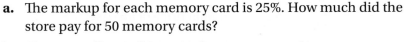

✓

 Self-Assessment *for Problem Solving*

Solve each exercise. Then rate your understanding of the success criteria in your journal.

8. You have two coupons for a store. The first coupon applies a $15 discount to a single purchase, and the second coupon applies a 10% discount to a single purchase. You can only use one coupon on a purchase. When should you use each coupon? Explain.

9. A store sells memory cards for $25 each.

   a. The markup for each memory card is 25%. How much did the store pay for 50 memory cards?

   b. The store offers a discount when a customer buys two or more memory cards. A customer pays $47.50 for two memory cards. What is the percent of discount?

   c. How much does a customer pay for three memory cards if the store increases the percent of discount in part (b) by 2%?

6.5 Practice

? Go to *BigIdeasMath.com* to get HELP with solving the exercises.

▶ Review & Refresh

Identify the percent of change as an *increase* or a *decrease*. Then find the percent of change. Round to the nearest tenth of a percent if necessary.

1. 16 meters to 20 meters

2. 9 points to 4 points

3. 15 ounces to 5 ounces

4. 38 staples to 55 staples

Find the product. Write fractions in simplest form.

5. $\dfrac{4}{7}\left(-\dfrac{1}{6}\right)$

6. $-1.58(6.02)$

7. $-3\left(-2\dfrac{1}{8}\right)$

▶▶ Concepts, Skills, & Problem Solving

COMPARING DISCOUNTS The same item is on sale at two stores. Which one is the better price? Use percent models to justify your answer. (See Exploration 1, p. 259.)

8. 60% off $60 or 55% off $50

9. 85% off $90 or 70% off $65

MP USING TOOLS Copy and complete the table.

	Original Price	Percent of Discount	Sale Price
10.	$80	20%	
11.	$42	15%	
12.	$120	80%	
13.	$112	32%	
14.	$69.80	60%	
15.		25%	$40
16.		5%	$57
17.		80%	$90
18.		64%	$72
19.		15%	$146.54
20.	$60		$45
21.	$82		$65.60
22.	$95		$61.75

FINDING A SELLING PRICE Find the selling price.

23. Cost to store: $50
Markup: 10%

24. Cost to store: $80
Markup: 60%

25. Cost to store: $140
Markup: 25%

26. **MP YOU BE THE TEACHER** A store pays $60 for an item. Your friend finds the selling price when the markup is 20%. Is your friend correct? Explain your reasoning.

> $0.2(\$60) = \$12$
> So, the selling price is $12.

27. **MP STRUCTURE** The scooter is being sold at a 10% discount. The original price is shown. Which methods can you use to find the new sale price? Which method do you prefer? Explain.

> Multiply $42.00 by 0.9.

> Multiply $42.00 by 0.1, then subtract from $42.00.

> Multiply $42.00 by 0.9, then add to $42.00.

> Multiply $42.00 by 0.9, then subtract from $42.00.

28. **MP NUMBER SENSE** The original price of an item is p dollars. Is the price of the item with an 18% markup the same as multiplying the original price by 1.18? Use two expressions to justify your answer.

29. **MP PROBLEM SOLVING** You are shopping for a video game system.

   a. At which store should you buy the system?

   b. Store A has a weekend sale. What discount must Store A offer for you to buy the system there?

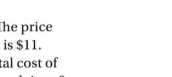

Store	Cost to Store	Markup
A	$162	40%
B	$155	30%
C	$160	25%

30. **DIG DEEPER!** A pool manager balances the pH level of a pool. The price of a bucket of chlorine tablets is $90, and the price of a pH test kit is $11. The manager uses a coupon that applies a 40% discount to the total cost of the two items. How much money does the pool manager pay for each item?

31. **MP PRECISION** You buy a pair of jeans at a department store.

   a. What is the percent of discount to the nearest percent?

   b. What is the percent of sales tax to the nearest tenth of a percent?

   c. The price of the jeans includes a 60% markup. After the discount, what is the percent of markup to the nearest percent?

> **Department Store**
>
> | Jeans | 39.99 |
> |-------|-------|
> | Discount | -10.00 |
> | Subtotal | 29.99 |
> | Sales Tax | 1.95 |
> | Total | 31.94 |
>
> *Thank You*

32. **CRITICAL THINKING** You buy a bicycle helmet for $22.26, which includes 6% sales tax. The helmet is discounted 30% off the selling price. What is the original price?

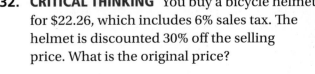

33. **MP REASONING** A drone that costs $129.50 is discounted 40%. The next month, the sale price is discounted an additional 60%. Is the drone now "free"? If so, explain. If not, find the sale price.

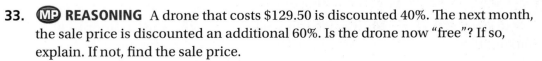

6.6 Simple Interest

Learning Target: Understand and apply the simple interest formula.

Success Criteria:
- I can explain the meaning of simple interest.
- I can use the simple interest formula to solve problems.

EXPLORATION 1

Understanding Simple Interest

Work with a partner. You deposit $150 in an account that earns 6% *simple interest per year*. You do not make any other deposits or withdrawals. The table shows the balance of the account at the end of each year.

Years	Balance
0	$150
1	$159
2	$168
3	$177
4	$186
5	$195
6	$204

a. Describe any patterns you see in the account balance.

b. How is the amount of interest determined each year?

c. How can you find the amount of simple interest earned when you are given an initial amount, an interest rate, and a period of time?

Math Practice

Look for Patterns

How does the pattern in the balances help you find the simple interest rate?

d. You deposit $150 in a different account that earns simple interest. The table shows the balance of the account each year. What is the interest rate of the account? What is the balance after 10 years?

Years	0	1	2	3
Balance	$150	$165	$180	$195

6.6 Lesson

Key Vocabulary
interest, *p. 266*
principal, *p. 266*
simple interest, *p. 266*

Interest is money paid or earned for using or lending money. The **principal** is the amount of money borrowed or deposited.

Key Idea

Simple Interest

Words **Simple interest** is money paid or earned only on the principal.

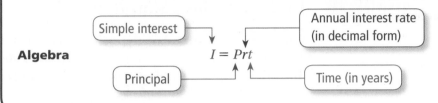

Algebra $I = Prt$

Reading
An interest rate per year is also called an annual interest rate.

EXAMPLE 1 Finding a Balance

You deposit $500 in a savings account. The account earns 3% simple interest per year. What is the balance after 3 years?

To find the balance, calculate the interest and add it to the principal.

$I = Prt$	Write the simple interest formula.
$= 500(0.03)(3)$	Substitute 500 for P, 0.03 for r, and 3 for t.
$= 45$	Multiply.

The interest earned is $45 after 3 years.

▸ So, the balance is $500 + $45 = $545 after 3 years.

Math Practice

Use a Formula
Write a formula that you can use to find the total balance B of an account. Explain your reasoning.

Try It

1. What is the balance of the account after 9 months?

EXAMPLE 2 Finding an Annual Interest Rate

You deposit $1000 in an account. The account earns $100 simple interest in 4 years. What is the annual interest rate?

$I = Prt$	Write the simple interest formula.
$100 = 1000(r)(4)$	Substitute 100 for I, 1000 for P, and 4 for t.
$100 = 4000r$	Simplify.
$0.025 = r$	Divide each side by 4000.

▸ So, the annual interest rate of the account is 0.025, or 2.5%.

 Multi-Language Glossary at *BigIdeasMath.com*

Try It

2. You deposit $350 in an account. The account earns $17.50 simple interest in 2.5 years. What is the annual interest rate?

EXAMPLE 3 **Finding an Amount of Time**

A bank offers three savings accounts. The simple annual interest rate is determined by the principal. How long does it take an account with a principal of $800 to earn $100 in interest?

The diagram shows that the interest rate for a principal of $800 is 2%.

$I = Prt$	Write the simple interest formula.
$100 = 800(0.02)(t)$	Substitute 100 for I, 800 for P, and 0.02 for r.
$100 = 16t$	Simplify.
$6.25 = t$	Divide each side by 16.

▷ So, the account earns $100 in interest in 6.25 years.

Try It

3. In Example 3, how long does it take an account with a principal of $10,000 to earn $750 in interest?

Self-Assessment for Concepts & Skills

Solve each exercise. Then rate your understanding of the success criteria in your journal.

4. **VOCABULARY** Explain the meaning of simple interest.

USING THE SIMPLE INTEREST FORMULA Use the simple interest formula.

5. You deposit $20 in a savings account. The account earns 4% simple interest per year. What is the balance after 4 years?

6. You deposit $800 in an account. The account earns $360 simple interest in 3 years. What is the annual interest rate?

7. You deposit $650 in a savings account. How long does it take an account with an annual interest rate of 5% to earn $178.25 in interest?

 **EXAMPLE 4** **Modeling Real Life** ⎯⎯⎯⎯⎯⎯⎯⎯⎯⎯

You borrow $600 to buy a violin. The simple annual interest rate is 15%. You pay off the loan after 2 years of equal monthly payments. How much is each payment?

Understand the problem. You are given the amount and simple annual interest rate of a loan that you pay back in 2 years. You are asked to find the monthly payment.

Make a plan. Use the simple interest formula to find the interest you pay on the loan. Then divide the total amount you pay by the number of months in 2 years.

Solve and check.

$I = Prt$	Write the simple interest formula.
$= 600(0.15)(2)$	Substitute 600 for P, 0.15 for r, and 2 for t.
$= 180$	Multiply.

You pay $600 + $180 = $780 for the loan.

 So, each monthly payment is $\dfrac{780}{24} = \$32.50$.

> **Look Back** When you substitute 600 for P and 0.15 for r, you obtain $I = 90t$. This indicates that you pay $90 in interest each year. So, in 2 years you pay $2(90) = \$180$ in interest. ✓

 ## Self-Assessment *for Problem Solving* ⎯⎯⎯⎯⎯⎯

Solve each exercise. Then rate your understanding of the success criteria in your journal.

8. You want to deposit $1000 in a savings account for 3 years. One bank adds a $100 bonus to your principal and offers a 2% simple annual interest rate. Another bank does not add a bonus, but offers 6% simple interest per year. Which bank should you choose? Explain.

9. Your cousin borrows $1125 to repair her car. The simple annual interest rate is 10%. She makes equal monthly payments of $25. How many years will it take to pay off the loan?

10. **DIG DEEPER!** You borrow $900 to buy a laptop. You plan to pay off the loan after 5 years of equal monthly payments. After 10 payments, you have $1200 left to pay. What is the simple annual interest rate of your loan?

6.6 Practice

Go to *BigIdeasMath.com* to get HELP with solving the exercises.

▶ Review & Refresh

Find the selling price.

1. A store pays $8 for a pool noodle. The markup is 20%.

2. A store pays $3 for a magazine. The markup is 5%.

Solve the inequality. Graph the solution.

3. $x + 5 < 2$

4. $b - 2 \geq -1$

5. $w + 6 \leq -3$

▶ Concepts, Skills, & Problem Solving

UNDERSTANDING SIMPLE INTEREST The table shows the balance of an account each year. What is the interest rate of the account? What is the balance after 10 years? (See Exploration 1, p. 265.)

6.

Years	Balance
0	$40
1	$42
2	$44
3	$46

7.

Years	Balance
0	$175
1	$189
2	$203
3	$217

FINDING INTEREST EARNED An account earns simple annual interest. **(a)** Find the interest earned. **(b)** Find the balance of the account.

8. $600 at 5% for 2 years

9. $1500 at 4% for 5 years

10. $350 at 3% for 10 years

11. $1800 at 6.5% for 30 months

12. $925 at 2.3% for 2.4 years

13. $5200 at 7.36% for 54 months

14. **MP YOU BE THE TEACHER** Your friend finds the simple interest earned on $500 at 6% for 18 months. Is your friend correct? Explain your reasoning.

$$I = (500)(0.06)(18)$$
$$= \$540$$

FINDING AN ANNUAL INTEREST RATE Find the annual interest rate.

15. $I = \$24, P = \$400, t = 2$ years

16. $I = \$562.50, P = \$1500, t = 5$ years

17. $I = \$54, P = \$900, t = 18$ months

18. $I = \$160, P = \$2000, t = 8$ months

FINDING AN AMOUNT OF TIME Find the amount of time.

19. $I = \$30, P = \$500, r = 3\%$

20. $I = \$720, P = \$1000, r = 9\%$

21. $I = \$54, P = \$800, r = 4.5\%$

22. $I = \$450, P = \$2400, r = 7.5\%$

23. **FINDING AN ACCOUNT BALANCE** A savings account earns 5% simple interest per year. The principal is $1200. What is the balance after 4 years?

24. **FINDING AN ANNUAL INTEREST RATE** You deposit $400 in an account. The account earns $18 simple interest in 9 months. What is the annual interest rate?

25. **FINDING AN AMOUNT OF TIME** You deposit $3000 in a CD (certificate of deposit) that earns 5.6% simple annual interest. How long will it take to earn $336 in interest?

FINDING AN AMOUNT PAID Find the amount paid for the loan.

26. $1500 at 9% for 2 years

27. $2000 at 12% for 3 years

28. $2400 at 10.5% for 5 years

29. $4800 at 9.9% for 4 years

USING THE SIMPLE INTEREST FORMULA Copy and complete the table.

	Principal	Annual Interest Rate	Time	Simple Interest
30.	$12,000	4.25%	5 years	
31.		6.5%	18 months	$828.75
32.	$15,500	8.75%		$5425.00
33.	$18,000		54 months	$4252.50

34. **MP MODELING REAL LIFE** A family borrows money for a rainforest tour. The simple annual interest rate is 12%. The loan is paid after 3 months. What is the total amount paid for the tour?

Rainforest Tour
Tickets $940
Food $170
Supplies $120

35. **MP MODELING REAL LIFE** You deposit $5000 in an account earning 7.5% simple interest per year. How long will it take for the balance of the account to be $6500?

36. **MP MODELING REAL LIFE** You borrow $1300 to buy a telescope. What is the monthly payment?

11.8% Simple Interest
Equal monthly
payments for 2 years

37. **MP REASONING** How many years will it take for $2000 to double at a simple annual interest rate of 8%? Explain how you found your answer.

38. **DIG DEEPER!** You take out two loans. After 2 years, the total interest for the loans is $138. On the first loan, you pay 7.5% simple annual interest on a principal of $800. On the second loan, you pay 3% simple annual interest. What is the principal for the second loan?

39. **MP REPEATED REASONING** You deposit $500 in an account that earns 4% simple annual interest. The interest earned each year is added to the principal to create a new principal. Find the total amount in your account after each year for 3 years.

40. **MP NUMBER SENSE** An account earns r% simple interest per year. Does doubling the initial principal have the same effect on the total interest earned as doubling the amount of time? Justify your answer.

Connecting Concepts

Using the Problem-Solving Plan

1. The table shows the percent of successful shots for each team in a hockey game. A total of 55 shots are taken in the game. The ratio of shots taken by the Blazers to shots taken by the Hawks is 6 : 5. How many goals does each team score?

Team	Percent of Successful Shots
Blazers	10%
Hawks	16%

Understand the problem. You know that 55 shots are taken in a hockey game and that the Blazers take 6 shots for every 5 shots taken by the Hawks. You also know the percent of successful shots for each team.

Make a plan. Use a ratio table to determine the number of shots taken by each team. Then use the percent equation to determine the number of successful shots for each team.

Solve and check. Use the plan to solve the problem. Then check your solution.

2. Fill in the blanks with positive numbers so that the sum of the fractions is 37.5% of the first fraction. Justify your answer.

$$\frac{\blacksquare}{5} + \left(-\frac{\blacksquare}{4} \right)$$

3. The graph shows the distance traveled by a motorcycle on a dirt road. After turning onto a paved road, the motorcycle travels $\frac{1}{5}$ mile every $\frac{1}{4}$ minute. Find the percent of change in the speed of the motorcycle. Round to the nearest tenth of a percent if necessary.

Motorcycle

Graph with x-axis "Time (minutes)" and y-axis "Distance (miles)". Points shown at $\left(1, \frac{7}{12}\right)$ and $\left(4, 2\frac{1}{3}\right)$.

Performance Task

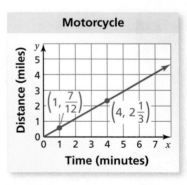

Tornado Alley

At the beginning of this chapter, you watched a STEAM Video called "Tornado!" You are now ready to complete the performance task related to this video, available at *BigIdeasMath.com*. Be sure to use the problem-solving plan as you work through the performance task.

▶ Review Vocabulary

Write the definition and give an example of each vocabulary term.

percent of change, *p. 254*   percent error, *p. 256*   interest, *p. 266*
percent of increase, *p. 254*   discount, *p. 260*   principal, *p. 266*
percent of decrease, *p. 254*   markup, *p. 260*   simple interest, *p. 266*

▶ Graphic Organizers

You can use a **Summary Triangle** to explain a concept. Here is an example of a Summary Triangle for *writing a percent as a decimal*.

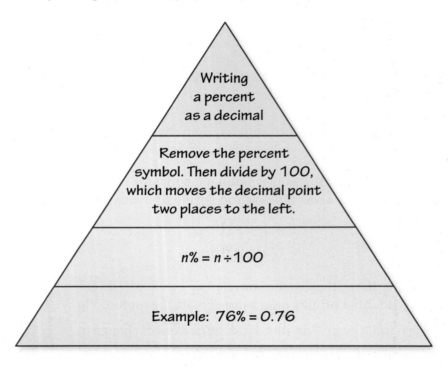

Writing a percent as a decimal

Remove the percent symbol. Then divide by 100, which moves the decimal point two places to the left.

$n\% = n \div 100$

Example: $76\% = 0.76$

Choose and complete a graphic organizer to help you study the concept.

1. writing a decimal as a percent

2. comparing and ordering fractions, decimals, and percents

3. the percent proportion

4. the percent equation

5. percent of change

6. discount

7. markup

I'm writing to Classy Calicos about this one.

Lonely? Buy a pet. Dogs are cool! Example: Beagles

"I found this great Summary Triangle in my Beautiful Beagle Magazine."

Chapter Self-Assessment

As you complete the exercises, use the scale below to rate your understanding of the success criteria in your journal.

1	2	3	4
I do not understand.	I can do it with help.	I can do it on my own.	I can teach someone else.

6.1 Fractions, Decimals, and Percents *(pp. 235–240)*

Learning Target: Rewrite fractions, decimals, and percents using different representations.

Write the percent as a decimal or the decimal as a percent. Use a model to represent the number.

1. 74%

2. 2%

3. 221%

4. 0.17

5. $4.\overline{3}$

6. 0.079

Write the fraction as a decimal and a percent.

7. $\dfrac{17}{20}$

8. $\dfrac{3}{8}$

9. $\dfrac{14}{9}$

10. For school spirit day, 11.875% of your class wears orange shirts, $\dfrac{5}{8}$ of your class wears blue shirts, 0.15625 of your class wears white shirts, and the rest of your class wears gold shirts. Order the portions of shirts of each color from least to greatest. Justify your answer.

6.2 The Percent Proportion *(pp. 241–246)*

Learning Target: Use the percent proportion to find missing quantities.

Write and solve a proportion to answer the question.

11. What percent of 60 is 18?

12. 40 is what percent of 32?

13. What number is 70% of 70?

14. $\dfrac{3}{4}$ is 75% of what number?

15. About 29% of the Earth's surface is covered by land. The total surface area of the Earth is about 510 million square kilometers. What is the area of the Earth's surface covered by land?

6.3 The Percent Equation (pp. 247–252)

Learning Target: Use the percent equation to find missing quantities.

Write and solve an equation to answer the question.

16. What number is 24% of 25?

17. 9 is what percent of 20?

18. 60.8 is what percent of 32?

19. 91 is 130% of what number?

20. 85% of what number is 10.2?

21. 83% of 20 is what number?

22. 15% of the parking spaces at a school are handicap spaces. The school has 18 handicap spaces. How many parking spaces are there in total?

23. Of the 25 students on a field trip, 16 bring cameras. What percent of the students bring cameras?

6.4 Percents of Increase and Decrease (pp. 253–258)

Learning Target: Find percents of change in quantities.

Identify the percent of change as an *increase* or a *decrease*. Then find the percent of change. Round to the nearest tenth of a percent if necessary.

24. 6 yards to 36 yards

25. 120 meals to 52 meals

26. You estimate that a jar contains 68 marbles. The actual number of marbles is 60. Find the percent error.

27. The table shows the numbers of skim boarders at a beach on Saturday and Sunday. What was the percent of change in boarders from Saturday to Sunday?

Day	Number of Skim Boarders
Saturday	12
Sunday	9

6.5 Discounts and Markups (pp. 259–264)

Learning Target: Solve percent problems involving discounts and markups.

Find the sale price or original price.

28. Original price: $50
Discount: 15%
Sale price: ?

29. Original price: ?
Discount: 20%
Sale price: $75

30% off
Now $21

SALE

30. What is the original price of the tennis racquet?

31. A store pays $50 for a pair of shoes. The markup is 25%.

   a. What is the selling price for the shoes?

   b. What is the total cost for a person to buy the shoes including a 6% sales tax?

6.6 Simple Interest (pp. 265–270)

Learning Target: Understand and apply the simple interest formula.

An account earns simple interest. (a) Find the interest earned. (b) Find the balance of the account.

32. $300 at 4% for 3 years

33. $2000 at 3.5% for 4 years

Find the annual interest rate.

34. $I = \$17$, $P = \$500$, $t = 2$ years

35. $I = \$426$, $P = \$1200$, $t = 5$ years

Find the amount of time.

36. $I = \$60$, $P = \$400$, $r = 5\%$

37. $I = \$237.90$, $P = \$1525$, $r = 2.6\%$

38. You deposit $100 in an account. The account earns $2 simple interest in 6 months. What is the annual interest rate?

39. Bank A is offering a loan with a simple interest rate of 8% for 2 years. Bank B is offering a loan with a simple interest rate of 6.5% for 3 years.

$5400

   a. Assuming the monthly payments are equal, what is the monthly payment for the four wheeler from Bank A? from Bank B?

   b. Give reasons for why a person might choose Bank A and why a person might choose Bank B for a loan to buy the four wheeler. Explain your reasoning.

Write the percent as a decimal, or the decimal as a percent. Use a model to represent the number.

1. 0.96%

2. 3%

3. 25.$\overline{5}$%

4. 0.$\overline{6}$

5. 7.88

6. 0.58

Order the numbers from least to greatest.

7. 86%, $\frac{15}{18}$, 0.84, $\frac{8}{9}$, 0.8$\overline{6}$

8. 91.6%, 0.91, $\frac{11}{12}$, 0.917, 9.2%

Write and solve a proportion or equation to answer the question.

9. What percent of 28 is 21?

10. 64 is what percent of 40?

11. What number is 80% of 45?

12. 0.8% of what number is 6?

Identify the percent of change as an *increase* or a *decrease*. Then find the percent of change. Round to the nearest tenth of a percent if necessary.

13. 4 strikeouts to 10 strikeouts

14. $24 to $18

Find the sale price or selling price.

15. Original price: $15
Discount: 5%
Sale price: ?

16. Cost to store: $5.50
Markup: 75%
Selling price: ?

An account earns simple interest. Find the interest earned or the principal.

17. Interest earned: ?
Principal: $450
Interest rate: 6%
Time: 8 years

18. Interest earned: $27
Principal: ?
Interest rate: 1.5%
Time: 2 years

19. You spend 8 hours each weekday at school. (a) Write the portion of a weekday spent at school as a fraction, a decimal, and a percent. (b) What percent of a week is spent at school if you go to school 4 days that week? Round to the nearest tenth.

20. Research indicates that 90% of the volume of an iceberg is below water. The volume of the iceberg above the water is 160,000 cubic feet. What is the volume of the iceberg below water?

21. You estimate that there are 66 cars in a parking lot. The actual number of cars is 75.

   a. Find the percent error.

   b. What other estimate gives the same percent error? Explain your reasoning.

Cumulative Practice

1. A movie theater offers 30% off the price of a movie ticket to students from your school. The regular price of a movie ticket is $8.50. What is the discounted price that you pay for a ticket?

   A. $2.55

   B. $5.50

   C. $5.95

   D. $8.20

2.  What is the least value of x for which the inequality is true?

$$16 \geq -2x$$

3. You are building a scale model of a park that is planned for a city. The model uses the scale 1 centimeter = 2 meters. The park will have a rectangular reflecting pool with a length of 20 meters and a width of 12 meters. In your scale model, what will be the area of the reflecting pool?

   F. 60 cm^2

   G. 120 cm^2

   H. 480 cm^2

   I. 960 cm^2

4. Which proportion represents the problem?

   "17% of a number is 43. What is the number?"

   A. $\dfrac{17}{43} = \dfrac{n}{100}$

   B. $\dfrac{n}{17} = \dfrac{43}{100}$

   C. $\dfrac{n}{43} = \dfrac{17}{100}$

   D. $\dfrac{43}{n} = \dfrac{17}{100}$

5. Which list of numbers is in order from least to greatest?

   F. $0.8, \dfrac{5}{8}, 70\%, 0.09$

   G. $0.09, \dfrac{5}{8}, 0.8, 70\%$

   H. $\dfrac{5}{8}, 70\%, 0.8, 0.09$

   I. $0.09, \dfrac{5}{8}, 70\%, 0.8$

6. What is the value of $\frac{9}{8} \div \left(-\frac{11}{4}\right)$?

7. The number of calories you burn by playing basketball is proportional to the number of minutes you play. Which of the following is a valid interpretation of the graph?

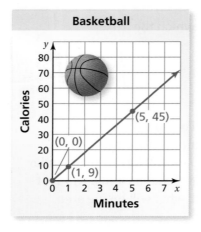

Basketball

A. The unit rate is $\frac{1}{9}$ calorie per minute.

B. You burn 5 calories by playing basketball for 45 minutes.

C. You do not burn any calories if you do not play basketball for at least 1 minute.

D. You burn an additional 9 calories for each minute of basketball you play.

8. A softball team is ordering uniforms. Each player receives one of each of the items shown in the table.

Item	Jersey	Pants	Hat	Socks
Price (dollars)	x	15.99	4.88	3.99

Which expression represents the total cost (in dollars) when there are 15 players on the team?

F. $x + 24.86$

G. $15x + 372.90$

H. $x + 372.90$

I. $x + 387.90$

9. Your friend solves the equation. What should your friend do to correct the error that he made?

$$-3(2 + w) = -45$$
$$2 + w = -15$$
$$w = -17$$

A. Multiply -45 by -3.

B. Add 3 to -45.

C. Add 2 to -15.

D. Divide -45 by -3.

10. You are comparing the costs of a certain model of ladder at a hardware store and at an online store.

Part A What is the total cost of buying the ladder at each of the stores? Show your work and explain your reasoning.

Part B Suppose that the hardware store is offering 10% off the price of the ladder and that the online store is offering free shipping and handling. Which store offers the lower total cost for the ladder? by how much? Show your work and explain your reasoning.

11. Which graph represents the inequality $-5 - 3x \geq -11$.

F.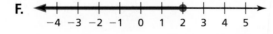

G.

H.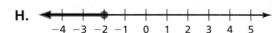

I.

7  Probability

7.1   Probability

7.2   Experimental and
        Theoretical Probability

7.3   Compound Events

7.4   Simulations

Chapter Learning Target:
Understand probability.

Chapter Success Criteria:
- ■ I can identify the possible outcomes of a situation.
- ■ I can explain the meaning of experimental and theoretical probability.
- ■ I can make predictions using probabilities.
- ■ I can solve real-life problems using probability.

THROW!

STEAM Video: "Massively Multiplayer
Rock Paper Scissors"

Massively Multiplayer Rock Paper Scissors

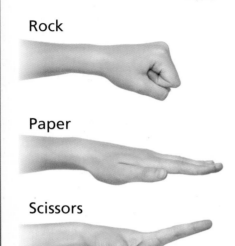

Rock

Paper

Scissors

You can use *experimental probability* to describe the percent of times that you win, lose, or tie in Rock Paper Scissors. Describe a real-life situation where it is helpful to describe the percent of times that a particular outcome occurs.

Watch the STEAM Video "Massively Multiplayer Rock Paper Scissors." Then answer the following questions.

1. The table shows the ways that you can win, lose, or tie in Rock Paper Scissors. You and your opponent throw the signs for rock, paper, or scissors at random. What percent of the time do you expect to win? lose? tie?

		Your Throw		
		Rock	**Paper**	**Scissors**
Opponent's Throw	**Rock**	tie	win	lose
	Paper	lose	tie	win
	Scissors	win	lose	tie

2. You play Rock Paper Scissors 15 times. About how many times do you expect to win? Explain your reasoning.

Fair and Unfair Carnival Games

After completing this chapter, you will be able to use the concepts you learned to answer the questions in the *STEAM Video Performance Task.*

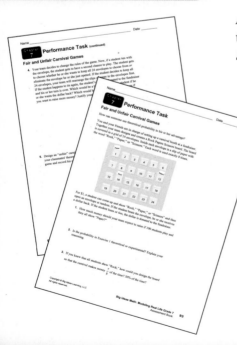

You will be given information about a version of Rock Paper Scissors used at a carnival. Then you will be asked to design your own "unfair" carnival game using a spinner or a number cube, and test your game with a classmate.

In what ways can a game of chance be considered fair? unfair? Explain your reasoning.

Getting Ready for Chapter

Chapter Exploration

Work with a partner.

1. Play Rock Paper Scissors 30 times. Tally your results in the table.

2. How many possible results are there?

3. Of the possible results, in how many ways can Player A win? In how many ways can Player B win? In how many ways can there be a tie?

4. Is one of the players more likely to win than the other player? Explain your reasoning.

GAME RULES
Rock **breaks** scissors.
Paper **covers** rock.
Scissors **cut** paper.

		Player A		
		Rock	Paper	Scissors
Player B	Rock			
	Paper			
	Scissors			

Vocabulary

The following vocabulary terms are defined in this chapter. Think about what each term might mean and record your thoughts.

probability	theoretical probability	simulation
relative frequency	sample space	
experimental probability	compound event	

7.1 Probability

Learning Target: Understand how the probability of an event indicates its likelihood.

Success Criteria:
- I can identify possible outcomes of an experiment.
- I can use probability and relative frequency to describe the likelihood of an event.
- I can use relative frequency to make predictions.

EXPLORATION 1

Determining Likelihood

Work with a partner. Use the spinners shown.

Spinner 1 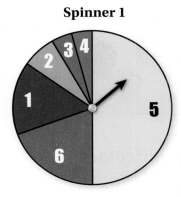 Spinner 2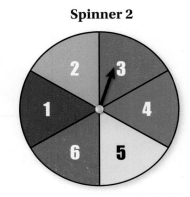

a. For each spinner, determine which numbers you are more likely to spin and which numbers you are less likely to spin. Explain your reasoning.

b. Spin each spinner 20 times and record your results in two tables. Do the data support your answers in part (a)? Explain why or why not.

Math Practice

Recognize Usefulness of Tools

How does organizing the data in tables help you to interpret the results?

Spinner 1	
Number	Frequency
1	
2	
3	
4	
5	
6	

Spinner 2	
Number	Frequency
1	
2	
3	
4	
5	
6	

c. How can you use percents to describe the likelihood of spinning each number? Explain.

Key Idea

Outcomes and Events

An **experiment** is an investigation or a procedure that has varying results. The possible results of an experiment are called **outcomes**. A collection of one or more outcomes is an **event**. The outcomes of a specific event are called **favorable outcomes**.

For example, randomly choosing a marble from a group of marbles is an experiment. Each marble in the group is an outcome. Selecting a green marble from the group is an event.

Possible outcomes

Event: Choosing a green marble
Number of favorable outcomes: 2

EXAMPLE 1 **Identifying Outcomes**

You spin the spinner.

a. **How many possible outcomes are there?**

The possible outcomes are spinning a 1, 2, 1, 3, 1, or 4. So, there are six possible outcomes.

b. **What are the favorable outcomes of spinning an even number?**

The favorable outcomes of spinning an even number are 2 and 4.

even	*not* even
2, 4	1, 1, 3, 1

c. **In how many ways can spinning a number less than 2 occur?**

The possible outcomes of spinning a number less than 2 are 1, 1, and 1. So, spinning a number less than 2 can occur in 3 ways.

less than 2	*not* less than 2
1, 1, 1	2, 3, 4

Try It

1. You randomly choose one of the tiles shown from a hat.

   a. How many possible outcomes are there?

   b. What are the favorable outcomes of choosing a vowel?

   c. In how many ways can choosing a consonant occur?

🔊 *Multi-Language Glossary at BigIdeasMath.com*

 **Key Idea**

Probability

The **probability** of an event is a number that represents the likelihood that the event will occur. Probabilities are between 0 and 1, including 0 and 1. The diagram relates likelihoods (above the diagram) and probabilities (below the diagram).

Probabilities can be written as fractions, decimals, or percents.

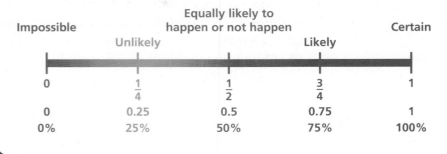

EXAMPLE 2 **Describing Likelihood**

There is an 80% chance of rain, a 50% chance of thunderstorms, and a 15% chance of hail tomorrow. Describe the likelihood of each event.

a. **There is rain tomorrow.**

The probability of rain tomorrow is 80%.

> Because 80% is close to 75%, it is *likely* that there will be rain tomorrow.

b. **There are thunderstorms tomorrow.**

The probability of thunderstorms tomorrow is 50%.

> Because the probability is 50%, thunderstorms are *equally likely to happen or not happen.*

c. **There is hail tomorrow.**

The probability of hail tomorrow is 15%.

> Because 15% is between 0% and 25%, it is *unlikely* that there will be hail tomorrow.

Try It **Describe the likelihood of the event given its probability.**

2. The probability that you land a jump on a snowboard is $\frac{1}{10}$.

3. There is a 100% chance that the temperature will be less than 120°F tomorrow.

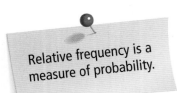

Relative frequency is a measure of probability.

When you conduct an experiment, the **relative frequency** of an event is the fraction or percent of the time that the event occurs.

$$\text{relative frequency} = \frac{\text{number of times the event occurs}}{\text{total number of times you conduct the experiment}}$$

EXAMPLE 3 ## Using Relative Frequencies

You flip a bottle and record the number of times it lands upright and the number of times it lands on its side. Describe the likelihood that the bottle lands upright on your next flip.

Upright	II
Side	ℍℾ ℍℾ ℍℾ ℍℾ III

The bottle landed upright 2 times in a total of 25 flips.

$$\text{relative frequency} = \frac{\text{number of times the event occurs}}{\text{total number of times you conduct the experiment}}$$

$$= \frac{2}{25}$$

The bottle landed upright 2 times.

There was a total of 25 flips.

▶ The relative frequency is $\frac{2}{25}$, or 8%. So, it is unlikely that the bottle lands upright.

Try It

Shots Made	ℍℾ IIII
Shots Missed	ℍℾ I

4. You attempt three-point shots on a basketball court and record the number of made and missed shots. Describe the likelihood of each event.

    a. You make your next shot.   **b.** You miss your next shot.

Self-Assessment *for Concepts & Skills*

Solve each exercise. Then rate your understanding of the success criteria in your journal.

5. IDENTIFYING OUTCOMES You roll a number cube. What are the possible outcomes?

6. USING RELATIVE FREQUENCIES A bag contains only red marbles and blue marbles. You randomly draw a marble from the bag and replace it. The table shows the results of repeating this experiment. Find the likelihood of each event.

Red	ℍℾ ℍℾ ℍℾ ℍℾ I
Blue	ℍℾ ℍℾ ℍℾ ℍℾ I

    a. The next marble you choose is red.

    b. The next marble you choose is neither red nor blue.

EXAMPLE 4 — Modeling Real Life

Each turn in a game, you randomly draw a token from a bag and replace it. The table shows the number of times you draw each type of token. How many times can you expect to draw a positive point value in 35 turns?

Token	Frequency
+3 points	卌 卌
+1 point	卌 II
−2 points	III

Understand the problem. You are given the number of times that you draw each type of token from a bag. You are asked to determine the number of times you can expect to draw a positive point value in 35 turns.

Make a plan. Find the relative frequency of drawing a positive point value. Then use the relative frequency and the percent equation to answer the question.

Solve and check. The favorable outcomes of drawing a positive point value are drawing a +3 token or a +1 token. So, the relative frequency of drawing a positive point value is $\frac{10 + 7}{20} = \frac{17}{20}$, or 85%.

To determine the number of times you can expect to draw a positive point value, answer the question "What is 85% of 35?"

$a = p\% \cdot w$	Write percent equation.
$= 0.85 \cdot 35$	Substitute 0.85 for $p\%$ and 35 for w.
$= 29.75$	Multiply.

Check Reasonableness
The table shows that positive point values are drawn 17 of 20 times. So, in 35 turns, you can expect to draw positive point values less than $17 \times 2 = 34$ times. ✓

▷ You can expect to draw a positive point value about 30 times.

Self-Assessment for Problem Solving

Solve each exercise. Then rate your understanding of the success criteria in your journal.

7. The table shows the number of days you have a pop quiz and the number of days you do not have a pop quiz in three weeks of school. How many days can you expect to have a pop quiz during a 180-day school year? Explain.

Pop Quiz	No Pop Quiz
II	卌 卌 III

8. In a football game, the teams pass the ball on 40% of the plays. Of the passes thrown, greater than 75% are completed. You watch the film of a randomly chosen play. Describe the likelihood that the play results in a complete pass. Explain your reasoning.

Go to *BigIdeasMath.com* to get HELP with solving the exercises.

▶ Review & Refresh

An account earns simple interest. Find the interest earned.

1. $700 at 3% for 4 years
2. $650 at 2% for 6 years
3. $480 at 1.5% for 5 years
4. $1200 at 2.8% for 30 months

Write the indicated ratio. Then find and interpret the value of the ratio.

5. rolled oats : chopped peanuts
6. sunflower seeds to pumpkin seeds
7. pumpkin seeds : rolled oats

Granola (dry ingredients)	
rolled oats	2 cups
chopped peanuts	1/2 cup
sunflower seeds	1/3 cup
pumpkin seeds	1/4 cup

Solve the inequality. Graph the solution.

8. $x + 5 < 9$
9. $b - 2 \geq -7$
10. $1 > -\dfrac{w}{3}$
11. $6 \leq -2g$

▶▶ Concepts, Skills, & Problem Solving

DETERMINING LIKELIHOOD Determine which numbers you are more likely to spin and which numbers you are less likely to spin. Explain your reasoning. (See Exploration 1, p. 283.)

12.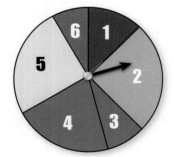

13.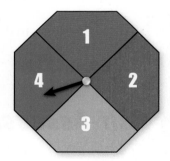

IDENTIFYING OUTCOMES You spin the spinner shown.

14. How many possible outcomes are there?

15. What are the favorable outcomes of spinning a number no greater than 3?

16. In how many ways can spinning an even number occur?

17. In how many ways can spinning a prime number occur?

IDENTIFYING OUTCOMES You randomly choose one marble from the bag. **(a)** Find the number of ways the event can occur. **(b)** Find the favorable outcomes of the event.

18. Choosing blue

19. Choosing green

20. Choosing purple

21. Choosing yellow

22. Choosing *not* red

23. Choosing *not* blue

24. 🅼🅿 **YOU BE THE TEACHER** Your friend finds the number of ways that choosing *not* purple can occur. Is your friend correct? Explain your reasoning.

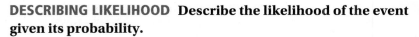

purple	*not* purple
purple	red, blue, green, yellow

Choosing not purple can occur in 4 ways.

CRITICAL THINKING Tell whether the statement is *true* or *false*. If it is false, change the italicized word to make the statement true.

25. Spinning blue and spinning *green* have the same number of favorable outcomes on Spinner A.

26. There are *three* possible outcomes of spinning Spinner A.

27. Spinning *red* can occur in four ways on Spinner B.

28. Spinning not green can occur in *three* ways on Spinner B.

Spinner A

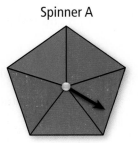

Spinner B

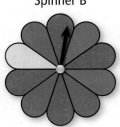

DESCRIBING LIKELIHOOD Describe the likelihood of the event given its probability.

29. Your soccer team wins $\frac{3}{4}$ of the time.

30. There is a 0% chance that you will grow 12 feet.

31. The probability that the sun rises tomorrow is 1.

32. It rains on $\frac{1}{5}$ of the days in June.

33. 🅼🅿 **MODELING REAL LIFE** You have a 50% chance of being chosen to explain a math problem in front of the class. Describe the likelihood that you are chosen.

34. 🅼🅿 **MODELING REAL LIFE** You roll a number cube and record the number of times you roll an even number and the number of times you roll an odd number. Describe the likelihood of each event.

Even	ⅢⅢ ⅢⅢ ⅢⅢ ⅢⅢ ⅢⅢ Ⅰ
Odd	ⅢⅢ ⅢⅢ ⅢⅢ ⅢⅢ ⅢⅢ

   a. You roll an even number on your next roll.

   b. You roll an odd number on your next roll.

35. **MP REASONING** You want to determine whether a coin is *fair*. You flip the coin and record the number of times you flip heads and the number of times you flip tails.

Heads	~~IIII~~ ~~IIII~~ ~~IIII~~ ~~IIII~~ II
Tails	III

a. Describe the likelihood that you flip heads on your next flip.

b. Describe the likelihood that you flip tails on your next flip.

c. Do you think the coin is a *fair* coin? Explain.

Win	~~IIII~~ I
Lose	~~IIII~~ ~~IIII~~ ~~IIII~~
Free Turn	IIII

36. **MP LOGIC** At a carnival, each guest randomly chooses 1 of 50 rubber ducks and then replaces it. The table shows the numbers of each type of duck that have been drawn so far. Out of 150 draws, how many can you expect to *not* be a losing duck? Justify your answer.

37. **CRITICAL THINKING** A dodecahedron has twelve sides numbered 1 through 12. Describe the likelihood that each event will occur when you roll the dodecahedron. Explain your reasoning.

a. rolling a 1

b. rolling a multiple of 3

c. rolling a number greater than 6

38. **DIG DEEPER!** A bargain bin contains classical CDs and rock CDs. There are 60 CDs in the bin. Choosing a rock CD and *not* choosing a rock CD have the same number of favorable outcomes. How many rock CDs are in the bin?

39. **MP REASONING** You randomly choose one of the cards and set it aside. Then you randomly choose a second card. Describe how the number of possible outcomes changes after the first card is chosen.

MP STRUCTURE A Punnett square is a grid used to show possible gene combinations for the offspring of two parents. In the Punnett square shown, a boy is represented by *XY*. A girl is represented by *XX*.

40. Complete the Punnett square. Explain why the events "having a boy" and "having a girl" are equally likely.

41. Two parents each have the gene combination *Cs*. The gene *C* is for curly hair. The gene *s* is for straight hair. Any gene combination that includes a *C* results in curly hair. When all outcomes are equally likely, what is the probability of a child having curly hair?

Mother's Genes

	X	X
X	XX	
Y		

Father's Genes

7.2 Experimental and Theoretical Probability

Learning Target: Develop probability models using experimental and theoretical probability.

Success Criteria:
- I can explain the meanings of experimental probability and theoretical probability.
- I can find experimental and theoretical probabilities.
- I can use probability to make predictions.

EXPLORATION 1

Conducting Experiments

Work with a partner. Conduct the following experiments and find the relative frequencies.

Experiment 1

- Flip a quarter 25 times and record whether each flip lands heads up or tails up.

Experiment 2

- Toss a thumbtack onto a table 25 times and record whether each toss lands point up or on its side.

a. Combine your results with those of your classmates. Do the relative frequencies change? What do you notice?

b. Everyone in your school conducts each experiment and you combine the results. How do you expect the relative frequencies to change? Explain.

c. How many times in 1000 flips do you expect a quarter to land heads up? How many times in 1000 tosses do you expect a thumbtack to land point up? Explain your reasoning.

d. In a *uniform probability model*, each outcome is equally likely to occur. Can you use a uniform probability model to describe either experiment? Explain.

Math Practice

Use Definitions
You know the number of possible outcomes in a uniform probability model. Can you find the probability of each outcome? Explain your reasoning.

Section 7.2 Experimental and Theoretical Probability **291**

Key Vocabulary
experimental
    probability, *p. 292*
theoretical
    probability, *p. 292*

Key Idea

Experimental Probability

Probability that is based on repeated trials of an experiment is called **experimental probability**.

$$P(\text{event}) = \frac{\text{number of times the event occurs}}{\text{total number of trials}}$$

EXAMPLE 1   Finding an Experimental Probability

Heads	Tails
6	19

The table shows the results of spinning a penny 25 times. What is the experimental probability of spinning heads?

Heads was spun 6 times in a total of $6 + 19 = 25$ spins.

$$P(\text{event}) = \frac{\text{number of times the event occurs}}{\text{total number of trials}}$$

Experimental probabilities are found the same way as relative frequencies.

$$P(\text{heads}) = \frac{6}{25}$$

Heads was spun 6 times.

There was a total of 25 spins.

▶ The experimental probability is $\frac{6}{25}$, 0.24, or 24%.

Try It **The table shows the results of rolling a number cube 50 times. Find the experimental probability of the event.**

Number Rolled	1	2	3	4	5	6
Frequency	10	4	8	11	11	6

1. rolling a 3

2. rolling an odd number

 ## Key Idea

Theoretical Probability

When all possible outcomes are equally likely, the **theoretical probability** of an event is the quotient of the number of favorable outcomes and the number of possible outcomes.

$$P(\text{event}) = \frac{\text{number of favorable outcomes}}{\text{number of possible outcomes}}$$

EXAMPLE 2 **Finding a Theoretical Probability**

You randomly choose one of the letters shown. What is the theoretical probability of choosing a vowel?

$$P(\text{vowel}) = \frac{\text{number of favorable outcomes}}{\text{number of possible outcomes}} = \frac{3}{7}$$

There are 3 vowels.

There is a total of 7 letters.

▷ The probability of choosing a vowel is $\frac{3}{7}$, or about 43%.

Try It

3. What is the theoretical probability of randomly choosing an X?

EXAMPLE 3 **Comparing Probabilities**

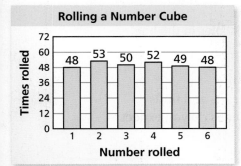

Rolling a Number Cube

Times rolled: 48, 53, 50, 52, 49, 48
Number rolled: 1, 2, 3, 4, 5, 6

The bar graph shows the results of rolling a number cube 300 times. How does the experimental probability of rolling an odd number compare with the theoretical probability?

Step 1: Find the experimental probability of rolling an odd number.

The bar graph shows 48 ones, 50 threes, and 49 fives. So, an odd number was rolled $48 + 50 + 49 = 147$ times in a total of 300 rolls.

$$P(\text{odd}) = \frac{\text{number of times an odd number was rolled}}{\text{total number of rolls}}$$

$$= \frac{147}{300}$$

$$= \frac{49}{100}, \text{ or } 49\%$$

In general, as the number of trials increases, the experimental probability gets closer to the theoretical probability.

Step 2: Find the theoretical probability of rolling an odd number.

$$P(\text{odd}) = \frac{\text{number of favorable outcomes}}{\text{number of possible outcomes}} = \frac{3}{6} = \frac{1}{2}, \text{ or } 50\%$$

▷ The experimental probability of rolling an odd number is 49%, which is close to the theoretical probability of 50%.

Try It

4. How does the experimental probability of rolling a number greater than 1 compare with the theoretical probability?

EXAMPLE 4 **Using an Experimental Probability**

Color	Frequency
Blue	3
Green	12
Red	9
Yellow	6

A bag contains 50 marbles. You randomly draw a marble from the bag, record its color, and then replace it. The table shows the results after 30 draws. Predict the number of red marbles in the bag.

Find the experimental probability of drawing a red marble.

$$P(\text{event}) = \frac{\text{number of times the event occurs}}{\text{total number of trials}}$$

$$P(\text{red}) = \frac{9}{30} = \frac{3}{10}$$

> You draw red 9 times.

> You draw a total of 30 marbles.

To make a prediction, multiply the probability of drawing red by the total number of marbles in the bag.

$$\frac{3}{10} \cdot 50 = 15$$

▷ So, you can predict that there are 15 red marbles in the bag.

Try It

5. An inspector randomly selects 200 pairs of jeans and finds 5 defective pairs. About how many pairs of jeans do you expect to be defective in a shipment of 5000?

Self-Assessment for Concepts & Skills

Solve each exercise. Then rate your understanding of the success criteria in your journal.

6. **VOCABULARY** Explain what it means for an event to have a theoretical probability of 0.25 and an experimental probability of 0.3.

7. **DIFFERENT WORDS, SAME QUESTION** You flip a coin and record the results in the table. Which is different? Find "both" answers.

Heads	Tails
32	28

> What is the experimental probability of flipping heads?

> What fraction of the flips can you expect a result of heads?

> What percent of the flips result in heads?

> What is the relative frequency of flipping heads?

EXAMPLE 5 **Modeling Real Life**

The theoretical probability of winning a bobblehead when spinning a prize wheel is $\frac{1}{6}$. The wheel has 18 sections.

a. **How many sections have a bobblehead as a prize?**

Use the equation for theoretical probability.

$$P(\text{bobblehead}) = \frac{\text{number of bobblehead sections}}{\text{total number of sections}}$$

$$\frac{1}{6} = \frac{s}{18} \qquad \text{Substitute. Let } s \text{ be the number of bobblehead sections.}$$

$$3 = s \qquad \text{Multiply each side by 18.}$$

▷ So, 3 sections have a bobblehead as a prize.

b. **The prize wheel is spun 540 times. About how many bobbleheads do you expect to be won?**

To make a prediction, multiply the probability of winning a bobblehead by the total number of times the wheel is spun.

$$\frac{1}{6} \cdot 540 = 90$$

▷ So, you can predict about 90 bobbleheads will be won.

 Self-Assessment for Problem Solving

Solve each exercise. Then rate your understanding of the success criteria in your journal.

Ticket	Frequency
Win	2
Lose	29
Draw again	9

8. Contestants randomly draw a ticket from a hat and replace it. The table shows the results after 40 draws. There are 7 winning tickets in the hat. Predict the total number of tickets in the hat. Explain.

9. **DIG DEEPER!** You randomly choose two different songs on a music playlist that has 80 songs. The probability that the first song is a hip-hop song is 45%. The first song you choose is a hip-hop song. What is the probability that the second song is also a hip-hop song? Explain your reasoning.

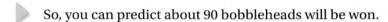

Go to *BigIdeasMath.com* to get HELP with solving the exercises.

▶ Review & Refresh

Describe the likelihood of the event given its probability.

1. You randomly guess the correct answer of a multiple choice question $\frac{1}{4}$ of the time.

2. There is a 95% chance that school will *not* be cancelled tomorrow.

Find the annual interest rate.

3. $I = \$16$, $P = \$200$, $t = 2$ years

4. $I = \$26.25$, $P = \$500$, $t = 18$ months

Tell whether x and y are proportional.

5.

x	1	3	9
y	8	24	75

6.

x	0.75	1.5	2.25
y	0.3	0.6	0.9

▶▶ Concepts, Skills, & Problem Solving

CONDUCTING AN EXPERIMENT **Use the bar graph below to find the relative frequency of the event.** (See Exploration 1, p. 291.)

7. spinning a 6

8. spinning an even number

FINDING AN EXPERIMENTAL PROBABILITY
Use the bar graph to find the experimental probability of the event.

9. spinning a number less than 3

10. *not* spinning a 1

11. spinning a 1 or a 3

12. spinning a 7

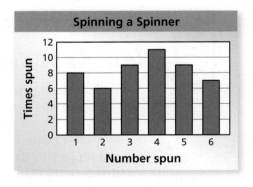

13. **MP YOU BE THE TEACHER** Your friend uses the bar graph above to find the experimental probability of spinning a 4. Is your friend correct? Explain your reasoning.

> There are 6 possible outcomes. So, the experimental probability of spinning a 4 is $\frac{1}{6}$.

14. **MP MODELING REAL LIFE** You check 20 laser pointers at random. Three of the laser pointers are defective. What is the experimental probability that a laser pointer is defective?

FINDING A THEORETICAL PROBABILITY Use the spinner to find the theoretical probability of the event.

15. spinning red

16. spinning a 1

17. spinning an odd number

18. spinning a multiple of 2

19. spinning a number less than 7

20. spinning a 9

21. **MP** **REASONING** Each letter of the alphabet is printed on an index card. What is the theoretical probability of randomly choosing any letter except Z?

COMPARING PROBABILITIES The bar graph shows the results of spinning the spinner below 200 times. Compare the theoretical and experimental probabilities of the event.

22. spinning a 4

23. spinning a 3

24. spinning a number greater than 4

25. spinning an odd number

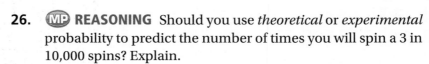

Spinning a Spinner

26. **MP** **REASONING** Should you use *theoretical* or *experimental* probability to predict the number of times you will spin a 3 in 10,000 spins? Explain.

27. **MP** **MODELING REAL LIFE** A board game uses a bag of 105 lettered tiles. You randomly choose a tile and then return it to the bag. The table shows the number of vowels and the number of consonants after 50 draws. Predict the number of vowels in the bag.

Vowel	Consonant
ⅢⅢⅢ III	ⅢⅢⅢⅢ ⅢⅢ II

28. **MP** **MODELING REAL LIFE** On a game show, a contestant randomly draws a chip from a bag and replaces it. Each chip says either *win* or *lose*. The theoretical probability of drawing a winning chip is $\frac{3}{10}$. The bag contains 9 winning chips.

a. How many chips are in the bag?

b. Out of 20 contestants, how many do you expect to draw a winning chip?

29. **MP** **PROBLEM SOLVING** There are 8 females and 10 males in a class.

a. What is the theoretical probability that a randomly chosen student is female?

b. One week later, there are 27 students in the class. The theoretical probability that a randomly chosen student is a female is the same as last week. How many males joined the class?

30. **MP** **NUMBER SENSE** The table at the right shows the results of flipping two coins 12 times each.

HH	HT	TH	TT
2	6	3	1

    a. What is the experimental probability of flipping two tails? Using this probability, how many times can you expect to flip two tails in 600 trials?

HH	HT	TH	TT
23	29	26	22

    b. The table at the left shows the results of flipping the same two coins 100 times each. What is the experimental probability of flipping two tails? Using this probability, how many times can you expect to flip two tails in 600 trials?

    c. Why is it important to use a large number of trials when using experimental probability to predict results?

31. **COMPARING PROBABILITIES** The table shows the possible outcomes of rolling a pair of number cubes. You roll a pair of number cubes 60 times and record your results in the bar graph shown.

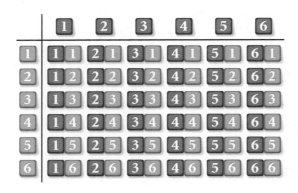

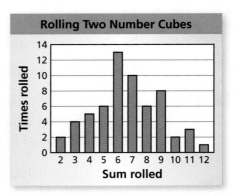

    a. Compare the theoretical and experimental probabilities of rolling each sum.

    b. Which sum do you expect to be most likely after 500 trials? 1000 trials? Explain your reasoning.

    c. Predict the experimental probability of rolling each sum after 10,000 trials. Explain your reasoning.

32. **PROJECT** When you toss a paper cup into the air, there are three ways for the cup to land: *open-end up*, *open-end down*, or *on its side*.

    a. Toss a paper cup 100 times and record your results. Do the outcomes for tossing the cup appear to be equally likely? Explain.

    b. Predict the number of times each outcome will occur in 1000 tosses. Explain your reasoning.

    c. Suppose you tape a quarter to the bottom of the cup. Do you think the cup will be *more likely* or *less likely* to land open-end up? Justify your answer.

7.3 Compound Events

Learning Target: Find sample spaces and probabilities of compound events.

Success Criteria:
- I can find the sample space of two or more events.
- I can find the total number of possible outcomes of two or more events.
- I can find probabilities of compound events.

EXPLORATION 1

Comparing Combination Locks

Work with a partner. You are buying a combination lock. You have three choices.

a. One lock has 3 wheels. Each wheel is numbered from 0 to 9. How many possible outcomes are there for each wheel? How many possible combinations are there?

b. How can you use the number of possible outcomes on each wheel to determine the number of possible combinations?

c. Another lock has one wheel numbered from 0 to 39. Each combination uses a sequence of three numbers. How many possible combinations are there?

Math Practice

View as Components

What is the number of possible outcomes for each wheel of the lock? Explain.

d. Another lock has 4 wheels as described. How many possible combinations are there?

Wheel 1: 0–9
Wheel 2: A–J
Wheel 3: K–T
Wheel 4: 0–9

e. For which lock are you least likely to guess the combination? Why?

The set of all possible outcomes of one or more events is called the **sample space**. You can use tables and tree diagrams to find the sample space of two or more events.

EXAMPLE 1 **Finding a Sample Space**

You randomly choose a bread and type of sandwich. Find the sample space. How many different sandwiches are possible?

Use a tree diagram to find the sample space.

Bread	Type	Outcome
Wheat	Ham	Wheat Ham
	Turkey	Wheat Turkey
	Steak	Wheat Steak
	Chicken	Wheat Chicken
Sourdough	Ham	Sourdough Ham
	Turkey	Sourdough Turkey
	Steak	Sourdough Steak
	Chicken	Sourdough Chicken

Bread
• Wheat
• Sourdough

Type
• Ham
• Turkey
• Steak
• Chicken

  There are 8 different outcomes in the sample space. So, there are 8 different sandwiches possible.

Try It

1. **WHAT IF?** The sandwich shop adds a multi-grain bread. Find the sample space. How many sandwiches are possible?

You can use the sample space or the **Fundamental Counting Principle** to find the total number of possible outcomes of two or more events.

The Fundamental Counting Principle can be extended to more than two events.

 Key Idea

Fundamental Counting Principle

An event *M* has *m* possible outcomes. An event *N* has *n* possible outcomes. The total number of outcomes of event *M* followed by event *N* is $m \times n$.

🔊 Multi-Language Glossary at *BigIdeasMath.com*

EXAMPLE 2 **Finding the Total Number of Possible Outcomes**

Find the total number of possible outcomes of rolling a number cube and flipping a coin.

Method 1: Use a table to find the sample space. Let H = heads and T = tails.

	1	**2**	**3**	**4**	**5**	**6**
(quarter heads)	1H	2H	3H	4H	5H	6H
(quarter tails)	1T	2T	3T	4T	5T	6T

▷ There are 12 possible outcomes.

Method 2: Use the Fundamental Counting Principle. Identify the number of possible outcomes of each event.

    Event 1: Rolling a number cube has 6 possible outcomes.

    Event 2: Flipping a coin has 2 possible outcomes.

$$6 \times 2 = 12 \qquad \text{Fundamental Counting Principle}$$

▷ There are 12 possible outcomes.

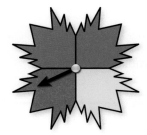

Try It

2. Find the total number of possible outcomes of spinning the spinner and randomly choosing a number from 1 to 5.

EXAMPLE 3 **Finding the Total Number of Possible Outcomes**

How many different outfits can you make from the T-shirts, jeans, and shoes in the closet?

Use the Fundamental Counting Principle. Identify the number of possible outcomes for each event.

    Event 1: Choosing a T-shirt has 7 possible outcomes.

    Event 2: Choosing jeans has 4 possible outcomes.

    Event 3: Choosing shoes has 3 possible outcomes.

$$7 \times 4 \times 3 = 84 \qquad \text{Fundamental Counting Principle}$$

▷ So, you can make 84 different outfits.

Try It

3. How many different outfits can you make from 4 T-shirts, 5 pairs of jeans, and 5 pairs of shoes?

A **compound event** consists of two or more events. As with a single event, the probability of a compound event is the quotient of the number of favorable outcomes and the number of possible outcomes.

EXAMPLE 4 **Finding the Probability of a Compound Event**

In Example 2, what is the probability of rolling a number greater than 4 and flipping tails?

There are two favorable outcomes in the sample space for rolling a number greater than 4 and flipping tails: 5T and 6T.

$$P(\text{event}) = \frac{\text{number of favorable outcomes}}{\text{number of possible outcomes}}$$

$$P(\text{greater than 4 and tails}) = \frac{2}{12} \qquad \text{Substitute.}$$

$$= \frac{1}{6} \qquad \text{Simplify.}$$

The probability is $\frac{1}{6}$, or $16\frac{2}{3}\%$.

Try It

4. In Example 2, what is the probability of rolling at most 4 and flipping heads?

Self-Assessment *for Concepts & Skills*

Solve each exercise. Then rate your understanding of the success criteria in your journal.

Flower
- Daffodil
- Hyacinth
- Tulip

Ornament
- Figurine
- Trophy

5. **FINDING THE SAMPLE SPACE** You randomly choose a flower and ornament for a display case. Find the sample space. How many different displays are possible?

6. **FINDING THE TOTAL NUMBER OF POSSIBLE OUTCOMES** You randomly choose a number from 1 to 5 and a letter from A to D. Find the total number of possible outcomes.

7. **WHICH ONE DOESN'T BELONG?** You roll a number cube and flip a coin. Which probability does *not* belong with the other three? Explain your reasoning.

$P(\text{less than 2 and heads})$ $P(\text{greater than 2 and tails})$

$P(\text{less than 2 and tails})$ $P(\text{greater than 5 and heads})$

EXAMPLE 5 **Modeling Real Life**

On a game show, you choose one box from each pair of boxes shown. In each pair, one box contains a prize and the other does not. What is the probability of winning at least one prize?

Choice 1

Use a tree diagram to find the sample space. Let P = prize and N = no prize. Circle the outcomes in which you win 1, 2, or 3 prizes.

Choice 2

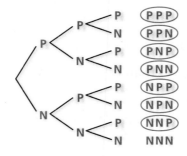

P < P < P (PPP)
            N (PPN)
       N < P (PNP)
            N (PNN)
N < P < P (NPP)
            N (NPN)
       N < P (NNP)
            N NNN

Choice 3

There are seven favorable outcomes in the sample space for winning at least one prize.

$$P(\text{event}) = \frac{\text{number of favorable outcomes}}{\text{number of possible outcomes}}$$

$P(\text{at least one prize}) = \dfrac{7}{8}$ Substitute.

▷ The probability of winning at least one prize is $\dfrac{7}{8}$, or 87.5%.

 Self-Assessment *for Problem Solving*

Solve each exercise. Then rate your understanding of the success criteria in your journal.

8. A tour guide organizes vacation packages at a beachside town. There are 7 hotels, 5 cabins, 4 meal plans, 3 escape rooms, and 2 amusement parks. The tour guide chooses either a hotel or a cabin and then selects one of each of the remaining options. Find the total number of possible vacation packages.

9. **DIG DEEPER!** A fitness club with 100 members offers one free training session per member in either running, swimming, or weightlifting. Thirty of the fitness center members sign up for the free session. The running and swimming sessions are each twice as popular as the weightlifting session. What is the probability that a randomly chosen fitness club member signs up for a free running session?

7.3 Practice

Go to *BigIdeasMath.com* to get HELP with solving the exercises.

▶ Review & Refresh

Use the bar graph to find the experimental probability of the event.

1. rolling a 5

2. rolling a 2 or 6

3. rolling at least a 3

4. rolling a number less than or equal to 4

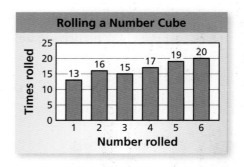

Find the product.

5. $3 \cdot 2$

6. $5(-3)$

7. $-6(-2)$

▶▶ Concepts, Skills, & Problem Solving

COMPARING PASSWORDS Determine which password is less likely to be guessed. (See Exploration 1, p. 299.)

8. a password with 3 numbers or a password with 3 capital letters

9. a password with 6 numbers or a password with 4 capital letters

USING A TREE DIAGRAM Use a tree diagram to find the sample space and the total number of possible outcomes.

10.

Birthday Party	
Activity	Miniature golf, Laser tag, Roller skating
Time	1:00 P.M.–3:00 P.M., 6:00 P.M.–8:00 P.M.

11.

New School Mascot	
Type	Lion, Bear, Hawk, Dragon
Style	Realistic, Cartoon

12.

Party Favor	
Item	Keychain, Magnet
Color	Blue, Green , Red

13.

Fidget Toy	
Type	Cube, Necklace, Spinner
Frame	Metal, Plastic, Rubber

14. **MP YOU BE THE TEACHER** Your friend finds the total number of ways that you can answer a quiz with five true-false questions. Is your friend correct? Explain your reasoning.

$2 + 2 + 2 + 2 + 2 = 10$

You can answer the quiz in 10 different ways.

USING THE FUNDAMENTAL COUNTING PRINCIPLE Use the Fundamental Counting Principle to find the total number of possible outcomes.

15.

Beverage	
Size	Small, Medium, Large
Flavor	Orange juice, Apple juice, Lemonade, Milk

16.

Fitness Tracker	
Battery	1 day, 3 days, 5 days, 7 days
Color	Silver, Green, Blue, Pink, Black

17.

Clown	
Suit	Dotted, Striped, Checkered
Wig	Single color, Multicolor
Talent	Balloon animals, Juggling, Unicycle, Magic

18.

Meal	
Appetizer	Soup, Spinach dip, Salad
Entrée	Chicken, Beef, Spaghetti, Fish
Dessert	Yogurt, Fruit, Rice pudding

19. **MP CHOOSE TOOLS** You randomly choose one of the marbles. Without replacing the first marble, you choose a second marble.

   a. Name two ways you can find the total number of possible outcomes.

   b. Find the total number of possible outcomes.

20. **FINDING A PROBABILITY** You roll two number cubes. What is the probability of rolling double threes?

FINDING THE PROBABILITY OF A COMPOUND EVENT You spin the spinner and flip a coin. Find the probability of the compound event.

21. spinning a 1 and flipping heads

22. spinning an even number and flipping heads

23. spinning a number less than 3 and flipping tails

24. spinning a 6 and flipping tails

25. *not* spinning a 5 and flipping heads

26. spinning a prime number and *not* flipping heads

FINDING THE PROBABILITY OF A COMPOUND EVENT You spin the spinner, flip a coin, and then spin the spinner again. Find the probability of the compound event.

27. spinning blue, flipping heads, then spinning a 1

28. spinning an odd number, flipping heads, then spinning yellow

29. spinning an even number, flipping tails, then spinning an odd number

30. *not* spinning red, flipping tails, then *not* spinning an even number

31. **MP REASONING** You randomly guess the answers to two questions on a multiple-choice test. Each question has three choices: A, B, and C.

   a. What is the probability that you guess the correct answers to both questions?

   b. Suppose you can eliminate one of the choices for each question. How does this change the probability that both of your guesses are correct?

32. **MP REASONING** You forget the last two digits of your cell phone password.

   a. What is the probability that you randomly choose the correct digits?

   b. Suppose you remember that both digits are even. How does this change the probability that you choose the correct digits?

33. **MP MODELING REAL LIFE** A combination lock has 3 wheels, each numbered from 0 to 9. You try to guess the combination by writing five different numbers from 0 to 999 on a piece of paper. Find the probability that the correct combination is written on the paper.

34. **MP MODELING REAL LIFE** A train has one engine and six train cars. Find the total number of ways an engineer can arrange the train. (The engine must be first.)

35. **MP REPEATED REASONING** You have been assigned a nine-digit identification number.

   a. Should you use the Fundamental Counting Principle or a tree diagram to find the total number of possible identification numbers? Explain.

   b. How many identification numbers are possible?

   c. **RESEARCH** Use the Internet to find out why the possible number of Social Security numbers is not the same as your answer to part (b).

36. **DIG DEEPER!** A social media account password includes a number from 0 to 9, an uppercase letter, a lowercase letter, and a special character, in that order.

   a. There are 223,080 password combinations. How many special characters are there?

   b. What is the probability of guessing the account password if you know the number and uppercase letter, but forget the rest?

37. **MP PROBLEM SOLVING** From a group of 5 scientists, an environmental committee of 3 people is selected. How many different committees are possible?

7.4 Simulations

Learning Target: Design and use simulations to find probabilities of compound events.

Success Criteria:
- I can design a simulation to model a real-life situation.
- I can recognize favorable outcomes in a simulation.
- I can use simulations to find experimental probabilities.

EXPLORATION 1

Using a Simulation

Work with a partner. A basketball player makes 80% of her free throw attempts.

a. Is she likely to make at least two of her next three free throws? Explain your reasoning.

b. The table shows 30 randomly generated numbers from 0 to 999. Let each number represent three shots. How can you use the digits of these numbers to represent made shots and missed shots?

838	617	282	341	785
747	332	279	082	716
937	308	800	994	689
198	025	853	591	813
672	289	518	649	540
865	631	227	004	840

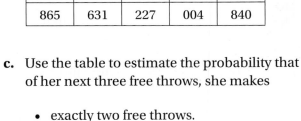

c. Use the table to estimate the probability that of her next three free throws, she makes

- exactly two free throws.

- at most one free throw.

- at least two free throws.

- at least two free throws in a row.

Math Practice

Choose Tools
What tools can you use to randomly generate data?

d. The experiment used in parts (b) and (c) is called a *simulation*. Another player makes $\frac{3}{5}$ of her free throws. Describe a simulation that can be used to estimate the probability that she makes three of her next four free throws.

Key Vocabulary 🔊
simulation, *p. 308*

A **simulation** is an experiment that is designed to reproduce the conditions of a situation or process. Simulations allow you to study situations that are impractical to create in real life.

EXAMPLE 1   Simulating Outcomes That Are Equally Likely

A dog has three puppies. The gender of each puppy is equally likely.

a. **Design a simulation involving 20 trials that you can use to model the genders of the puppies.**

Choose an experiment that has two equally likely outcomes for each event (gender), such as flipping three coins. Let heads (H) represent a male and tails (T) represent a female.

Math Practice

Communicate Precisely
Describe a simulation involving a number cube that you can use to find the probability in part (b).

b. **Use your simulation to find the experimental probability that all three puppies are males.**

To find the experimental probability, perform 20 trials of the simulation. The table shows the results. Find the number of outcomes that represent 3 males, HHH.

HTH	HTT	HTT	HTH	HTT
TTT	HTT	HHH	TTT	HTT
HTH	HTT	HHH	HTH	HTT
HTT	HTH	TTT	HTT	HTH

HHH occurred 2 times.

$$P(\text{three males}) = \frac{2}{20} = \frac{1}{10}$$

There is a total of 20 trials.

▷ The experimental probability is $\frac{1}{10}$, 0.1, or 10%.

Try It

1. You randomly guess the answers to four true-false questions.

   a. Design a simulation that you can use to model the answers.

   b. Use your simulation to find the experimental probability that you answer all four questions correctly.

🔊 Multi-Language Glossary at *BigIdeasMath.com*

EXAMPLE 2 **Simulating Outcomes That Are Not Equally Likely**

You have a 60% chance of winning a board game and a 20% chance of winning a card game. Design and use a simulation involving 50 randomly generated numbers to estimate the probability of winning both games.

The digits 1–6 and 1–2 are chosen because they have a 60% and 20% chance of being randomly generated for each digit.

Use a simulation with randomly generated numbers from 0 to 99. Let the digits 1 through 6 in the tens place represent winning the board game. Let the digits 1 and 2 in the ones place represent winning the card game.

Use the random number generator on a graphing calculator to generate the numbers. The table shows the results. Find the number of outcomes that represent winning both games.

```
randInt(0,99,50)
{52 66 73 68 75…
```

(52)	66	73	68	75	28	35	47	48	02
16	68	49	03	77	35	92	78	06	06
58	18	89	39	24	80	(32)	(41)	77	(21)
(32)	40	96	59	86	01	(12)	00	94	73
40	71	28	(61)	01	24	37	25	03	25

$$P(\text{win both games}) = \frac{7}{50}$$

> 7 numbers meet the criteria.

> There is a total of 50 trials.

▷ The experimental probability is $\frac{7}{50}$, 0.14, or 14%.

Try It

2. A baseball team wins 70% of the time. Design and use a simulation to estimate the probability that the team wins the next three games.

Self-Assessment *for Concepts & Skills*

Solve each exercise. Then rate your understanding of the success criteria in your journal.

3. **SIMULATING OUTCOMES** Four multiple-choice questions on a quiz each have five answer choices. You randomly guess the answer to each question. Design and use a simulation to find the experimental probability that you answer all of the questions correctly.

4. **SIMULATING OUTCOMES** You select a marble from a bag and a chip from a box. You have a 20% chance of choosing a green marble and a 90% chance of choosing a red chip. Estimate the probability that you choose a green marble and a red chip.

EXAMPLE 3 **Modeling Real Life** ─────────────

Each school year, there is a 40% chance that weather causes one or more days of school to be canceled. Estimate the probability that weather causes a cancellation at least 3 years in a row in the next 4 years.

Use a simulation involving 50 randomly generated four-digit numbers to estimate the probability. Let the digits 1 through 4 represent years with a cancellation.

Use a random number table in a spreadsheet to generate the numbers. The spreadsheet shows the results. Find the number of outcomes in which the digits 1 through 4 occur at least three times in a row.

To create a four-digit random number table in a spreadsheet, enter

=INT(RAND()*10000)

into each cell.

	A	B	C	D	E	F
1	6527	4621	7810	3510	1408	
2	8141	0676	2535	8172	4095	
3	3450	7780	6435	8672	7537	
4	5063	1925	5137	9485	9437	
5	3299	2364	8034	8063	1323	
6	2556	1519	2735	2796	3987	
7	3771	7417	9177	4308	2723	
8	7593	7289	5091	0351	2179	
9	1479	0511	4550	8242	9407	
10	6910	8079	6142	6823	6138	
11						

$$P\left(\begin{array}{c}\text{cancellation at least 3 years}\\ \text{in a row in the next 4 years}\end{array}\right) = \frac{4}{50} = \frac{2}{25}$$

4 numbers meet the criteria.

There is a total of 50 trials.

▶ The experimental probability is $\frac{2}{25}$, 0.08, or 8%.

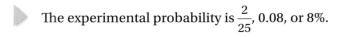

Self-Assessment for Problem Solving ───────

Solve each exercise. Then rate your understanding of the success criteria in your journal.

5. Each day there is a 50% chance that your tablet overheats. Estimate the probability that your tablet overheats on exactly 2 of the next 3 days.

6. **DIG DEEPER!** The probability that a homeowner needs a plumber this year is 22%. The probability that the homeowner needs a septic tank specialist is 14%. Estimate the probability that the homeowner needs a plumber, but not a septic tank specialist.

7.4 Practice

Go to *BigIdeasMath.com* to get HELP with solving the exercises.

▶ Review & Refresh

You flip a coin and roll the 20-sided figure. Find the probability of the compound event.

1. Flipping tails and rolling at least a 14

2. Flipping heads and rolling less than 3

Simplify the expression.

3. $5(a - 2)$　　　　4. $-7(1 + 3x)$　　　　5. $-1(3p - 8)$

▶▶ Concepts, Skills, & Problem Solving

USING A SIMULATION A medicine is effective for 80% of patients. The table shows 30 randomly generated numbers from 0 to 999. Use the table to estimate the probability of the event. (See Exploration 1, p. 307.)

463	013	231	898	139
365	492	565	188	465
438	751	961	646	598
045	241	940	901	467
151	774	538	380	509
251	924	401	549	859

6. The medicine is effective on each of three patients.

7. The medicine is effective on fewer than two of the next three patients.

SIMULATING OUTCOMES Design and use a simulation to find the experimental probability.

8. In your indoor garden, 50% of seeds sprout. What is the experimental probability that at least one of your next three seeds sprouts?

9. An archer hits a target 50% of the time. What is the experimental probability that the archer hits the target exactly four of the next five times?

10. A bank randomly selects one of four free gifts to send to each new customer. Gifts include a calculator, a keychain, a notepad, and a pen. What is the experimental probability that the next two new customers both receive calculators? that neither receives a calculator?

11. Employees spin a reward wheel. The wheel is equally likely to stop on each of six rewards labeled A–F. What is the experimental probability that fewer than two of the next three spins land on reward A?

USING NUMBER CUBES Design and use a simulation with number cubes to estimate the probability.

12. Your lawn mower does not start on the first try $\frac{1}{6}$ of the time. Estimate the probability that your lawn mower will not start on the first try exactly one of the next two times you mow the lawn.

13. An application on your phone correctly identifies four out of every six songs. Estimate the probability that at least three of the next four songs are correctly identified.

SIMULATING OUTCOMES Design and use a simulation to find the experimental probability.

14. Two beakers are used in a lab test. What is the experimental probability that there are reactions in both beakers during the lab test?

Probability of Reaction	
Beaker 1	80%
Beaker 2	50%

15. You use a stain remover on two separate stains on a shirt. What is the experimental probability that the stain remover removes both the mud stain and the food stain?

Probability of Stain Removal	
Mud	90%
Food	80%

16. **DIG DEEPER!** The probability that a computer crashes one or more times in a month is 10%. Estimate the probability that the computer crashes at least one or more times per month for two months in a row during the first half of the year.

17. **MP MODELING REAL LIFE** You visit an orchard. The probability that you randomly select a ripe apple is 92%. The probability that you randomly select a ripe cherry is 86%. Estimate the probability that you pick an apple that is ripe and a cherry that is not ripe.

18. **CRITICAL THINKING** You use a simulation to find an experimental probability. How does the experimental probability compare to the theoretical probability as the number of trials increases?

19. **MP LOGIC** At a restaurant, 30% of customers donate to charity in exchange for a coupon. Estimate the probability that it will take at least four customers to find one who donates.

7 Connecting Concepts

Using the Problem-Solving Plan

1. In an Internet contest, gift cards and bicycles are given as prizes in the ratio 9 : 1. Estimate the probability that at least two of three randomly selected winners receive bicycles.

Understand the problem. You know the ratio of gift cards to bicycles awarded in the contest. You want to find the probability that at least two of three randomly selected winners receive bicycles.

Make a plan. Use the ratio to find the theoretical probability that a randomly selected winner receives a bicycle. Then use a simulation involving 50 randomly generated three-digit numbers to estimate the probability that at least two of three randomly selected winners receive bicycles.

Solve and check. Use the plan to solve the problem. Then check your solution.

2. A board game uses the spinner shown.

   a. Use theoretical probability to predict the number of times you will spin a number greater than or equal to 8 in 30 spins.

   b. You play the game and record the results of 30 spins. Find the percent error of your prediction in part (a).

Number Spun	1	2	3	4	5	6	7	8	9	10
Frequency	2	2	3	1	3	3	4	3	4	5

3. The tiles shown are placed in a bag. You randomly select one of the tiles, return it to the bag, and then randomly select another tile. What is the probability that the product of the numbers on the tiles selected is greater than zero? Justify your answer.

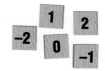

Performance Task

Fair and Unfair Carnival Games

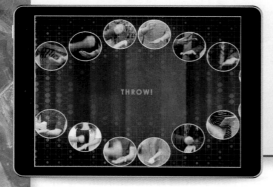

At the beginning of this chapter, you watched a STEAM Video called "Massively Multiplayer Rock Paper Scissors." You are now ready to complete the performance task related to this video, available at *BigIdeasMath.com*. Be sure to use the problem-solving plan as you work through the performance task.

7 Chapter Review

▶ Review Vocabulary

Write the definition and give an example of each vocabulary term.

outcomes, *p. 284*
event, *p. 284*
favorable outcomes, *p. 284*
probability, *p. 285*

relative frequency, *p. 286*
experimental probability, *p. 292*
theoretical probability, *p. 292*
sample space, *p. 300*

Fundamental Counting Principle, *p. 300*
compound event, *p. 302*
simulation, *p. 308*

▶ Graphic Organizers

You can use a **Four Square** to organize information about a concept. Each of the four squares can be a category, such as definition, vocabulary, example, non-example, words, algebra, table, numbers, visual, graph, or equation. Here is an example of a Four Square for *probability*.

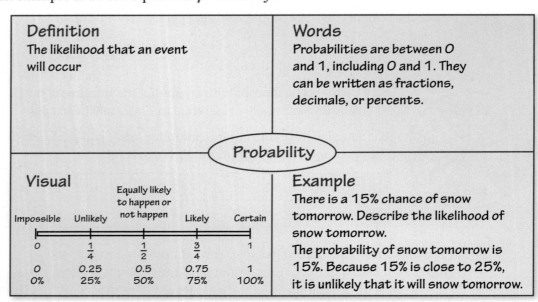

Choose and complete a graphic organizer to help you study the concept.

1. favorable outcomes
2. relative frequency
3. experimental probability
4. theoretical probability
5. Fundamental Counting Principle
6. compound event
7. simulation

"My **Four Square** shows that my new red skateboard is faster than my old blue skateboard."

314   Chapter 7   Probability

Chapter Self-Assessment

As you complete the exercises, use the scale below to rate your understanding of the success criteria in your journal.

1	2	3	4
I do not understand.	I can do it with help.	I can do it on my own.	I can teach someone else.

7.1 Probability *(pp. 283–290)*

Learning Target: Understand how the probability of an event indicates its likelihood.

You randomly choose one toy race car.

1. How many possible outcomes are there?

2. What are the favorable outcomes of choosing a car that is *not* green?

3. In how many ways can choosing a green car occur?

You spin the spinner. (a) Find the number of ways the event can occur. (b) Find the favorable outcomes of the event.

4. spinning a 1

5. spinning a 3

6. spinning an odd number

7. spinning an even number

8. spinning a number greater than 0

9. spinning a number less than 3

Describe the likelihood of the event given its probability.

10. There is a 0% chance of snow in July for Florida.

11. The probability that you are called on to answer a question in class is $\frac{1}{25}$.

12. There is an 85% chance the bus is on time.

13. The probability of flipping heads on a coin is 0.5.

14. During a basketball game, you record the number of rebounds from missed shots for each team.
(a) Describe the likelihood that your team rebounds the next missed shot. (b) How many rebounds should your team expect to have in 15 missed shots?

Your Team	⫲⫲ II
Opposing Team	III

7.2 Experimental and Theoretical Probability (pp. 291–298)

Learning Target: Develop probability models using experimental and theoretical probability.

The bar graph shows the results of spinning a spinner 100 times. Use the bar graph to find the experimental probability of the event.

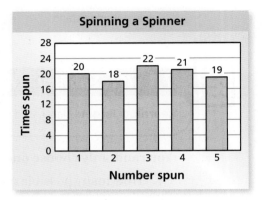

15. spinning a 2

16. spinning an even number

17. *not* spinning a 5

18. spinning a number less than 3

19. In Exercise 16, how does the experimental probability of spinning an even number compare with the theoretical probability?

Use the spinner to find the theoretical probability of the event.

20. spinning blue

21. spinning a 1

22. spinning an even number

23. spinning a 4

24. The theoretical probability of choosing a red grape from a bag of grapes is $\frac{2}{9}$. There are 8 red grapes in the bag. How many grapes are in the bag?

25. The theoretical probability of choosing Event A is $\frac{2}{7}$. What is the theoretical probability of *not* choosing Event A? Explain your reasoning.

7.3 Compound Events (pp. 299–306)

Learning Target: Find sample spaces and probabilities of compound events.

26. You have 6 bracelets and 15 necklaces. Find the number of ways you can wear one bracelet and one necklace.

27. Use a tree diagram to find how many different home theater systems you can make from 6 DVD players, 8 TVs, and 3 brands of speakers.

28. A red, green, and blue book are on a shelf. You randomly pick one of the books. Without replacing the first book, you choose another book. What is the probability that you picked the red and blue book?

29. You flip two coins and roll a number cube. What is the probability of flipping two tails and rolling an even number?

30. Describe a compound event that has a probability between 50% and 80%.

31. Your science teacher sets up six flasks. Two of the flasks contain water and four of the flasks contain hydrogen peroxide. A reaction occurs when you add yeast to hydrogen peroxide. You add yeast to two of the flasks. What is the probability that at least one reaction will occur?

7.4 Simulations *(pp. 307–312)*

Learning Target: Design and use simulations to find probabilities of compound events.

32. You select a marble from two different bags. You have a 30% chance of choosing a blue marble from the first bag and a 70% chance of choosing a blue marble from the second bag. Design and use a simulation to estimate the probability that you choose a blue marble from both bags.

33. A cereal company is including a prize in each box. There are 5 different prizes, all of which are equally likely.

   a. Describe a simulation involving 50 trials that you can use to model the prizes in the next 3 boxes of cereal you buy.

   b. Use your simulation to find the experimental probability that all three boxes contain a different prize.

34. In the past month, your cell phone has lost its entire charge on 40% of days. Design and use a simulation to estimate the experimental probability that your cell phone loses its entire charge on exactly 2 of the next 5 days.

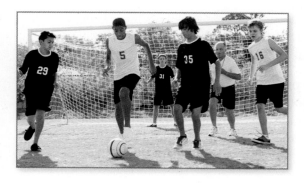

35. You and your friends form a team in gym class. You have an 80% chance of winning a game of basketball and a 10% chance of winning a game of soccer. Design and use a simulation involving 50 randomly generated numbers to estimate the probability of winning both games.

You randomly choose one game piece. (a) Find the number of ways the event can occur. (b) Find the favorable outcomes of the event.

1. choosing green

2. choosing *not* yellow

Find the sample space and the total number of possible outcomes.

3.

Sunscreen	
SPF	10, 15, 30, 45, 50
Type	Lotion, Spray, Gel

4.

Calculator	
Type	Basic display, Scientific, Graphing, Financial
Color	Black, White, Silver

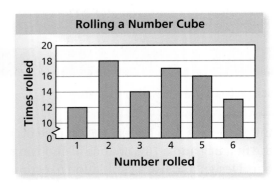

Rolling a Number Cube

Use the bar graph to find the experimental probability of the event.

5. rolling a 1 or a 2

6. rolling an odd number

7. *not* rolling a 5

8. rolling a number less than 7

Use the spinner to find the theoretical probability of the event(s).

9. spinning an even number

10. spinning a 1 and then a 2

11. You randomly choose one of the pens shown. What is the theoretical probability of choosing a black pen?

12. You randomly choose one of the pens shown. Your friend randomly chooses one of the remaining pens. What is the probability that you and your friend both choose a blue pen?

13. There is an 80% chance of a thunderstorm on Saturday. Describe the likelihood that there is *not* a thunderstorm on Saturday.

14. You are helping to remodel a bathroom. The probability that a randomly selected tile is cracked is 40%. For every 10 boards, there is 1 that is warped. Design and use a simulation to estimate the experimental probability that the next tile you select is cracked and the next board you select is *not* warped.

1. A school athletic director asked each athletic team member to name his or her favorite professional sports team. The results are below:

   - D.C. United: 3
   - Florida Panthers: 8
   - Jacksonville Jaguars: 26
   - Jacksonville Sharks: 7
   - Miami Dolphins: 22
   - Miami Heat: 15
   - Miami Marlins: 20
   - Minnesota Lynx: 4
   - New York Knicks: 5
   - Orlando Magic: 18
   - Tampa Bay Buccaneers: 17
   - Tampa Bay Lightning: 12
   - Tampa Bay Rays: 28
   - Other: 6

Test-Taking Strategy
Use Intelligent Guessing

What's the probability of drawing 1 hyena out of a bag with 2 hyenas and 3 mice?
(A) -10%   (B) 40%   (C) 60%   (D) 500%

40% < 60% I'm hoping 40%.

"You know it can't be -10% or 500%. So, you can intelligently guess between 40% and 60%."

One athletic team member is picked at random. What is the likelihood that this team member's favorite professional sports team is *not* located in Florida?

A. certain

B. likely, but not certain

C. unlikely, but not impossible

D. impossible

2. Each student in your class voted for his or her favorite day of the week. Their votes are shown in the circle graph:

Favorite Day of the Week

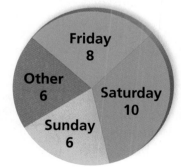

Friday 8

Other 6

Saturday 10

Sunday 6

A student from your class is picked at random. What is the probability that this student's favorite day of the week is Sunday?

3. What value makes the equation $11 - 3x = -7$ true?

    F. -6 **G.** $-\dfrac{4}{3}$

    H. 6 **I.** 54

4. Your friend solved the proportion in the box below.

$$\frac{16}{40} = \frac{p}{27}$$

$$16 \cdot p = 40 \cdot 27$$

$$16p = 1080$$

$$\frac{16p}{16} = \frac{1080}{16}$$

$$p = 67.5$$

What should your friend do to correct the error that he made?

    A. Add 40 to 16 and 27 to p.

    B. Subtract 16 from 40 and 27 from p.

    C. Multiply 16 by 27 and p by 40.

    D. Divide 16 by 27 and p by 40.

5. Which value is a solution of the inequality?

$$3 - 2y < 7$$

    F. -6 **G.** -3

    H. -2 **I.** -1

6. A spinner is divided into eight equal sections, as shown. You spin the spinner twice. What is the probability that the arrow will stop in a yellow section both times?

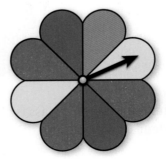

7. A pair of running shoes is on sale for 25% off the original price. Which price is closest to the sale price of the running shoes?

ORIGINAL PRICE $123.75

   A. $93   **B.** $99

   C. $124   **D.** $149

8. The value of a baseball card was $6 when it was sold. The value of this card is now $15. What is the percent increase in the value of the card?

   F. 40%   **G.** 90%

   H. 150%   **I.** 250%

9. You roll a number cube twice. You want to roll two even numbers.

Think
Solve
Explain

   Part A   Find the number of favorable outcomes and the number of possible outcomes of each roll.

   Part B   Find the probability of rolling two even numbers. Explain your reasoning.

10. You put $600 into an account. The account earns 5% simple interest per year. What is the balance after 4 years?

   A. $120   **B.** $720

   C. $1800   **D.** $12,600

11. You are comparing the prices of four boxes of cereal. Two of the boxes contain free extra cereal.

   • Box F costs $3.59 and contains 16 ounces.

   • Box G costs $3.79 and contains 16 ounces, plus an additional 10% for free.

   • Box H costs $4.00 and contains 500 grams.

   • Box I costs $4.69 and contains 500 grams, plus an additional 20% for free.

   Which box has the least unit cost?

   F. Box F   **G.** Box G

   H. Box H   **I.** Box I

Statistics

Chapter Learning Target:
Understand statistics.

Chapter Success Criteria:
- I can determine the validity of a conclusion.
- I can explain variability in samples of a population.
- I can solve a problem using statistics.
- I can compare populations.

STEAM Video: "Comparing Dogs"

Comparing Dogs

Although dogs and wolves are the same species, they can have very different characteristics. How are dogs and wolves similar?

Watch the STEAM Video "Comparing Dogs." Then answer the following questions.

1. In the video, the dogs Devo and Etta are walking in a park. Describe the *population* of the dogs shown in the video. Then describe a *sample* of the dogs shown in the video. Explain your reasoning.

2. Dogs, wolves, and dingos are all the same species. This species is called *Canis lupus.*

   a. Describe one possible sample of the *Canis lupus* species. Explain your reasoning.

   b. You want to know the average height of an animal in the Canis lupus species. Would you use the entire population of the species or would you use a sample to gather data? Explain.

   c. The entire *Canis lupus* species is a sample of what population? Explain.

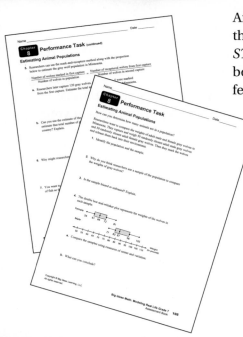

Estimating Animal Populations

After completing this chapter, you will be able to use the concepts you learned to answer the questions in the *STEAM Video Performance Task.* You will be given a double box-and-whisker plot that represents the weights of male and female gray wolves.

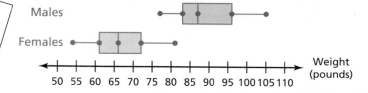

You will be asked to compare the weights of male and female gray wolves. Why might a researcher want to compare data from two different groups of wildlife?

323

Getting Ready for Chapter

Chapter Exploration

A **population** is an entire group of people or objects. A **sample** is a part of the population. You can use a sample to make an *inference*, or conclusion about a population.

Identify a population. → Select a sample. → Interpret the data in the sample. → Make an inference about the population.

Population → Sample → Interpretation → Inference

1. **Work with a partner. Identify the population and the sample in each pair.**

   a.

   The students in a school   The students in a math class

   b.

   The grizzly bears with GPS collars in a park   The grizzly bears in a park

   c.

   150 quarters   All quarters in circulation

   d.

   All fiction books in the library   10 fiction books in the library

2. **Work with a partner. When a sample is random, each member of the population is equally likely to be selected. You want to know the favorite activity of students at your school. Tell whether each sample is random. Explain your reasoning.**

   a. members of the school band

   b. students in your math class

   c. students who enter your school in a morning

   d. school newspaper readers

Vocabulary

The following vocabulary terms are defined in this chapter. Think about what each term might mean and record your thoughts.

population
sample

unbiased sample
biased sample

8.1 Samples and Populations

Learning Target: Understand how to use random samples to make conclusions about a population.

Success Criteria:
- I can explain why a sample is biased or unbiased.
- I can explain why conclusions made from a biased sample may not be valid.
- I can use an unbiased sample to make a conclusion about a population.

A **population** is an entire group of people or objects. A **sample** is a part of a population. You can gain information about a population by examining samples of the population.

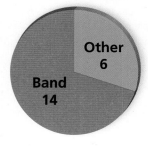

EXPLORATION 1

Using Samples of Populations

Work with a partner. You want to make conclusions about the favorite extracurricular activities of students at your school.

a. Identify the population. Then identify five samples of the population.

b. When a sample is selected *at random*, each member of the population is equally likely to be selected. Are any of the samples in part (a) selected at random? Explain your reasoning.

c. How are the samples below different? Is each conclusion valid? Explain your reasoning.

You ask 20 members of the school band about their favorite activity. The diagram shows the results. You conclude that band is the favorite activity of 70% of the students in your school.

Favorite Activity

Other 6

Band 14

You ask every eighth student who enters the school about their favorite activity. One student says glee club for every nine that name a different activity. You conclude that glee club is the favorite activity of 10% of the students in your school.

Math Practice

Maintain Oversight

Can the size of a sample affect the validity of a conclusion about a population? Explain.

d. (MP) **CHOOSE TOOLS** Write a survey question about a topic that interests you. How can you choose people to survey so that you can use the results to make a valid conclusion?

An **unbiased sample** is representative of a population. It is selected at random and is large enough to provide accurate data.

A **biased sample** is not representative of a population. One or more parts of the population are favored over others.

EXAMPLE 1 ## Identifying an Unbiased Sample

You want to estimate the number of students in a high school who ride a bus to school. Which sample is unbiased?

A. 4 students in the hallway

B. all students on the soccer team

C. 50 twelfth-grade students at random

D. 100 students at random during lunch

Choice A is not large enough to provide accurate data.

Choice B is not selected at random.

Choice C is not representative of the population because twelfth-grade students are favored over other students.

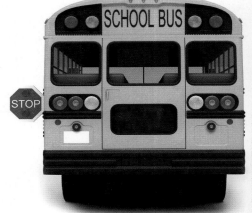

Choice D is representative of the population because it is selected at random and is large enough to provide accurate data.

> So, the correct answer is **D**.

Math Practice

Communicate Precisely
Explain why conclusions made from the sample in Choice C may be inaccurate. Is the sample biased for any possible population? Explain.

Try It

1. **WHAT IF?** You want to estimate the number of twelfth-grade students in a high school who ride a bus to school. Which sample is unbiased? Explain.

2. You want to estimate the number of eighth-grade students in your school who find it relaxing to listen to music. You consider two samples.

   • fifteen randomly selected members of the band

   • every fifth student whose name appears on an alphabetical list of eighth-grade students

   Which sample is unbiased? Explain.

The results of an unbiased sample are proportional to the results of the population. So, you can use unbiased samples to make conclusions about a population. Biased samples are not representative of a population. So, you should not use them to make conclusions about a population.

EXAMPLE 2 **Determining Whether Conclusions Are Valid**

You want to know how the residents of your town feel about adding a new landfill. Determine whether each conclusion is valid.

a. **You survey the 100 residents who live closest to the new landfill. The diagram shows the results. You conclude that 10% of the residents of your town support the new landfill.**

New Landfill

The sample is not representative of the population because residents who live close to the landfill may be less likely to support it.

> So, the sample is biased, and the conclusion is not valid.

New Landfill	
Support	40
Do Not Support	60

b. **You survey 100 residents at random. The table shows the results. You conclude that 60% of the residents of your town do not support the new landfill.**

The sample is representative of the population because it is selected at random and is large enough to provide accurate data.

> So, the sample is unbiased, and the conclusion is valid.

Try It

3. Four out of five randomly chosen teenagers support the new landfill. So, you conclude that 80% of the residents of your town support the new landfill. Is the conclusion valid? Explain.

Self-Assessment for Concepts & Skills

Solve each exercise. Then rate your understanding of the success criteria in your journal.

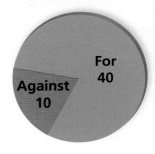

New Musical

4. **WRITING** You want to estimate the number of students in your school who play a school sport. You ask 40 honors students at random whether they play a school sport. Is this sample biased or unbiased? Explain.

5. **ANALYZING A CONCLUSION** You survey 50 randomly chosen audience members at a theater about whether the theater should produce a new musical. The diagram shows the results. You conclude that 80% of the audience members support production of a new musical. Is your conclusion valid? Explain.

EXAMPLE 3 **Modeling Real Life**

You ask 75 randomly chosen students at a school how many movies they watch each week. There are 1200 students in the school. Estimate the number of students in the school who watch one movie each week.

Movies per Week

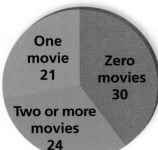

One movie 21
Zero movies 30
Two or more movies 24

Understand the problem.

You are given the numbers of movies watched each week by a sample of 75 students. You are asked to make an estimate about the population, all students in the school.

Make a plan.

The sample is representative of the population because it is selected at random and is large enough to provide accurate data. So, the sample is unbiased and its results are proportional to the results of the population. Use a ratio table to estimate the number of students in the school who watch one movie each week.

Solve and check.

$\times 4 \qquad \times 4$

Students (one movie)	21	84	336
Total Students	75	300	1200

$\times 4 \qquad \times 4$

Another Method
Use a proportion.
$$\frac{21}{75} = \frac{n}{1200}$$
$$336 = n \checkmark$$

So, about 336 students in the school watch one movie each week.

Self-Assessment for Problem Solving

Solve each exercise. Then rate your understanding of the success criteria in your journal.

Books per Month

Zero books 14
One book 19
Three or more books 10
Two books 7

6. You want to estimate the mean photo size on your cell phone. You choose 30 photos at random from your phone. The total size of the sample is 186 megabytes. Explain whether you can use the sample to estimate the mean size of photos on your cell phone. If so, what is your estimate?

7. **DIG DEEPER!** You ask 50 randomly chosen employees of a company how many books they read each month. The diagram shows the results. There are 600 people employed by the company. Estimate the number of employees who read at least one book each month.

8.1 Practice

 Go to *BigIdeasMath.com* to get HELP with solving the exercises.

▶ Review & Refresh

Design a simulation that you can use to model the situation. Then use your simulation to find the experimental probability.

1. The probability that a meal at a restaurant is overcooked is 10%. Estimate the probability that exactly 1 of the next 2 meals is overcooked.

2. The probability that you see a butterfly during a nature center tour is 80%. The probability that you see a turtle is 40%. What is the probability of seeing both?

Solve the inequality. Graph the solution.

3. $2x - 5 < 9$

4. $5q + 2 \geq -13$

5. $2 > 6 - 3r$

▶ Concepts, Skills, & Problem Solving

USING SAMPLES OF POPULATIONS **You ask 50 randomly chosen artists in your town about their favorite art form. Determine whether your conclusion is valid. Justify your answer.** (See Exploration 1, p. 325.)

6. You conclude that drawing is the favorite art form of 60% of artists in your town.

7. You conclude that ceramics is the favorite art form of 10% of people in your town.

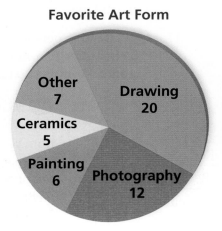

Favorite Art Form

Other 7
Drawing 20
Ceramics 5
Painting 6
Photography 12

IDENTIFYING POPULATIONS AND SAMPLES **Identify the population and the sample.**

8.
Residents of New Jersey | Residents of Ocean County

9.
4 cards

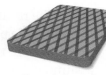
All cards in a deck

IDENTIFYING BIASED AND UNBIASED SAMPLES **Determine whether the sample is *biased* or *unbiased*. Explain.**

10. You want to estimate the number of books students in your school read over the summer. You survey every fourth student who enters the school.

11. You want to estimate the number of people in a town who think that a park needs to be remodeled. You survey every 10th person who enters the park.

12. **MP MODELING REAL LIFE** You want to determine the number of students in your school who have visited a science museum. You survey 50 students at random. Twenty have visited a science museum, and thirty have not. So, you conclude that 40% of the students in your school have visited a science museum. Is your conclusion valid? Explain.

13. **USING A SAMPLE** Which sample is better for making an estimate? Explain.

Estimate the number of defective pencils produced per day.	
Sample A	A random sample of 500 pencils from 20 machines
Sample B	A random sample of 500 pencils from 1 machine

CONDUCTING SURVEYS Determine whether you should survey the population or a sample. Explain.

14. You want to know the average height of seventh graders in the United States.

15. You want to know the favorite types of music of students in your homeroom.

16. **CRITICAL THINKING** Does increasing the size of a sample necessarily make the sample more representative of a population? Give an example to support your explanation.

17. **MP LOGIC** A person surveys residents of a town to determine whether a skateboarding ban should be overturned. Describe how the person can conduct the survey so that the sample is biased toward overturning the ban.

Favorite Way to Eliminate Waste	
Reducing	14
Reusing	4
Recycling	2

18. **MP MODELING REAL LIFE** You ask 20 randomly chosen environmental scientists from your state to name their favorite way to eliminate waste. There are 200 environmental scientists in your state. Estimate the number of environmental scientists in your state whose favorite way to eliminate waste is recycling.

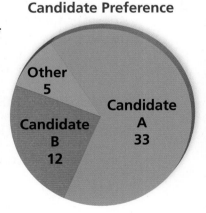

Candidate Preference

19. **MP MODELING REAL LIFE** To predict the result of a mayoral election, you survey 50 likely voters at random. The diagram shows the results. Describe whether the sample can be used to predict the outcome of the election. If so, what is your prediction for the number of votes received by the winner assuming that 500 people vote?

Number of Dogs	Frequency
1	54
2	38
3	3
4	1
5	4

20. **DIG DEEPER!** You ask 100 randomly chosen dog owners in your town how many dogs they own. The results are shown in the table. There are 500 dog owners in your town.

   a. Estimate the median number of dogs per dog owner in your town. Justify your answer.

   b. Estimate the mean number of dogs per dog owner in your town. Justify your answer.

8.2 Using Random Samples to Describe Populations

Learning Target: Understand variability in samples of a population.

Success Criteria:
• I can use multiple random samples to make conclusions about a population.
• I can use multiple random samples to examine variation in estimates.

EXPLORATION 1

Exploring Variability in Samples

Work with a partner. Sixty percent of all seventh graders have visited a planetarium.

a. Design a simulation using packing peanuts. Mark 60% of the packing peanuts and put them in a paper bag. What does choosing a marked peanut represent?

Math Practice

Make Conjectures
How many marked peanuts do you expect to draw in 30 trials? Explain your reasoning.

b. Simulate a sample of 25 students by choosing peanuts from the bag, replacing the peanut each time. Record the results.

c. Find the percent of students in the sample who have visited a planetarium. Compare this value to the actual percent of all seventh graders who have visited a planetarium.

d. Record the percent in part (c) from each pair in the class. Use a dot plot to display the data. Describe the variation in the data.

You have used unbiased samples to make conclusions about populations. Different samples often give slightly different conclusions due to variability in the sample data.

EXAMPLE 1 **Using Multiple Random Samples**

You and a group of friends want to know how many students in your school prefer pop music. There are 840 students in your school. Each person in the group randomly surveys 20 students. The table shows the results.

Favorite Type of Music			
	Country	Pop	Rock	Rap
You	2	13	4	1
Friend A	3	8	7	2
Friend B	4	10	5	1
Friend C	5	10	4	1
Friend D	5	9	3	3

a. **Use each sample to make an estimate for the number of students in your school who prefer pop music.**

In your sample, 13 out of 20, or 65% of the students chose pop music. So, you can estimate that 0.65(840) = 546 students in your school prefer pop music. Make estimates for the other samples.

	You	Friend A	Friend B	Friend C	Friend D
Estimate	546	336	420	420	378

> So, the estimates are that 336, 378, 420, 420, and 546 students prefer pop music.

b. **Describe the center and the variation of the estimates.**

> The estimates have a median of 420 students and a range of 546 − 336 = 210 students.

Try It

1. Use each sample to make an estimate for the number of students in your school who prefer rap music. Describe the center and the variation of the estimates.

EXAMPLE 2 **Estimating an Average of a Population**

You want to know the mean number of hours students with part-time jobs work each week. At each of six schools you randomly survey 10 students with part-time jobs. Your results are shown.

Hours Worked Each Week

A: 6, 8, 6, 6, 7, 4, 10, 8, 7, 8

B: 10, 4, 4, 6, 8, 6, 7, 12, 8, 8

C: 10, 9, 8, 6, 5, 8, 6, 6, 9, 10

D: 4, 8, 4, 4, 5, 4, 4, 6, 5, 6

E: 6, 8, 8, 6, 12, 4, 10, 8, 6, 12

F: 10, 4, 8, 9, 6, 8, 7, 12, 16, 10

a. Use each sample to make an estimate for the mean number of hours students with part-time jobs work each week. Describe the variation of the estimates.

Find the mean of each sample.

Sample	A	B	C	D	E	F
Mean	$\frac{70}{10} = 7$	$\frac{73}{10} = 7.3$	$\frac{77}{10} = 7.7$	$\frac{50}{10} = 5$	$\frac{80}{10} = 8$	$\frac{90}{10} = 9$

> So, the six estimates are that students with part-time jobs work 5, 7, 7.3, 7.7, 8, and 9 hours each week. The estimates have a range of $9 - 5 = 4$ hours.

b. Use all six samples to make one estimate for the mean number of hours students with part-time jobs work each week.

The mean of all sample data is $\frac{440}{60} = 7.\overline{3}$ hours.

> So, you can estimate that students with part-time jobs work $7.\overline{3}$ hours each week.

Try It

2. Repeat Example 2, but estimate the medians instead of the means.

Self-Assessment for Concepts & Skills

Solve each exercise. Then rate your understanding of the success criteria in your journal.

3. **USING MULTIPLE RANDOM SAMPLES** Use each sample in Example 1 to make an estimate for the number of students in your school who prefer rock music. Describe the variation of the estimates.

4. **ESTIMATING AN AVERAGE OF A POPULATION** You want to know the mean number of hours music students at your school practice each week. At each of three music classes you randomly survey 10 students. Your results are shown. Use all three samples to make one estimate for the mean number of hours music students practice each week.

Hours Practiced Each Week

A: 6, 5, 5, 6, 4, 6, 8, 5, 2, 6

B: 0, 6, 6, 5, 4, 5, 6, 3, 4, 9

C: 4, 5, 6, 4, 3, 2, 2, 3, 12, 1

Section 8.2 Using Random Samples to Describe Populations **333**

You can use technology to perform simulations with large numbers of trials.

EXAMPLE 3 **Modeling Real Life**

As stated in Exploration 1, 60% of all seventh graders have visited a planetarium. Use technology to simulate choosing 200 random samples of 50 students each. How closely do the samples estimate the percent of all seventh graders who have visited a planetarium?

The actual percentage is 60%, the number of samples is 200, and the sample size is 50. Use technology to run the simulation.

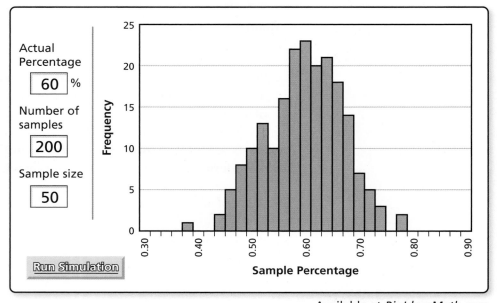

Actual Percentage
60 %

Number of samples
200

Sample size
50

Run Simulation

Available at *BigIdeasMath.com*

The estimates are clustered around 60%. Most are between 45% and 70%.

So, most of the samples are within 15% of the actual percentage.

 Self-Assessment for Problem Solving

Solve each exercise. Then rate your understanding of the success criteria in your journal.

5. Repeat Example 3 with the assumption that 50% of all seventh graders have visited a planetarium.

6. Forty percent of all seventh graders have visited a state park. How closely do 200 random samples of 50 students estimate the percent of seventh graders who have visited a state park? Use a simulation to support your answer.

8.2 Practice

Go to *BigIdeasMath.com* to get HELP with solving the exercises.

▶ Review & Refresh

You ask 100 randomly chosen high school students whether they support a new college in your town. Determine whether your conclusion is valid.

1. You conclude that 85% of high school students in your town support the new college.

2. You conclude that 15% of residents in your town do not support the new college.

New College	
Support	85
Do not support	15

Write and solve a proportion to answer the question.

3. What percent of 30 is 12?

4. 17 is what percent of 68?

▶▶ Concepts, Skills, & Problem Solving

EXPLORING VARIABILITY IN SAMPLES **Thirty percent of all seventh graders own a bracelet. Explain whether the sample closely estimates the percentage of seventh graders who own a bracelet.** (See Exploration 1, p. 331.)

5. 50 seventh graders, 14 own a bracelet

6. 30 seventh graders, 3 own a bracelet

Vegetable Preference		
	Fresh	**Canned**
A	11	9
B	14	6
C	12	8

7. **USING MULTIPLE RANDOM SAMPLES** A store owner wants to know how many of her 600 regular customers prefer canned vegetables. Each of her three cashiers randomly surveys 20 regular customers. The table shows the results.

   a. Use each sample to make an estimate for the number of regular customers of the store who prefer fresh vegetables.

   b. Describe the variation of the estimates.

8. **USING MULTIPLE RANDOM SAMPLES**
   An arcade manager wants to know how many of his 750 regular customers prefer to visit in the winter. Each of five staff members randomly surveys 25 regular customers. The table shows the results.

   a. Use each sample to make an estimate for the number of regular customers who prefer to visit in the winter.

   b. Describe the variation of the estimates.

Preferred Season to Visit the Arcade				
	Spring	**Summer**	**Fall**	**Winter**
A	4	4	6	11
B	5	3	7	10
C	6	5	5	9
D	4	5	6	10
E	4	4	5	12

9. **ESTIMATING A MEAN OF A POPULATION** A park ranger wants to know the mean number of nights students in your school plan to camp next summer. The park ranger randomly surveys 10 students from each class. The results are shown.

Nights Camping

A: 0, 5, 2, 3, 0, 6, 0, 10, 3, 0
B: 14, 0, 0, 6, 5, 0, 1, 2, 2, 5
C: 8, 8, 2, 3, 4, 1, 0, 0, 0, 6
D: 10, 10, 5, 6, 1, 0, 0, 0, 4, 0

a. Use each sample to make an estimate for the mean number of nights students in your school plan to camp next summer. Describe the variation of the estimates.

b. Use all four samples to make one estimate for the mean number of nights students plan to camp next summer.

10. **ESTIMATING A MEDIAN OF A POPULATION** Repeat Exercise 9, but estimate the medians instead of the means.

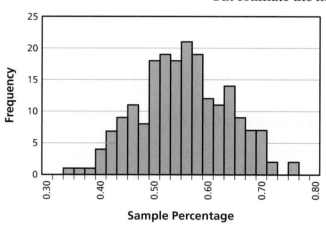

Sample Percentage

11. **DESCRIBING SAMPLE VARIATION** Fifty-five percent of doctors at a hospital prescribe a particular medication. A simulation with 200 random samples of 50 doctors each is shown. Describe how the sample percentages vary.

12. **MP MODELING REAL LIFE** Sixty percent of vacationers enjoy water parks. Use technology to generate 20 samples of size 100. How closely do the samples estimate the percent of all vacationers who enjoy water parks?

13. **MP MODELING REAL LIFE** Thirty percent of all new wooden benches have a patch of chipped paint. Use technology to simulate 100 random samples of 10 wooden benches. How closely do the samples estimate the percent of all wooden benches with a patch of chipped paint?

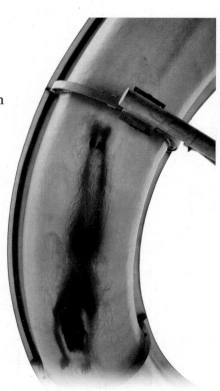

14. **DIG DEEPER!** You want to predict whether a proposal will be accepted by likely voters. You randomly sample 3 different groups of 100 likely voters. The results are shown. Do you expect the proposal to be accepted? Justify your answer.

	Proposal	
	Support	Oppose
Sample A	48	52
Sample B	52	48
Sample C	47	53

15. **CRITICAL THINKING** Explain why public opinion polls use sample sizes of more than 1000 people instead of using a smaller sample size.

8.3 Comparing Populations

Learning Target: Compare populations using measures of center and variation.

Success Criteria:
- I can find the measures of center and variation of a data set.
- I can describe the visual overlap of two data distributions numerically.
- I can determine whether there is a significant difference in the measures of center of two data sets.

EXPLORATION 1   Comparing Two Data Distributions

Work with a partner.

a. Does each data display show *overlap*? Explain.

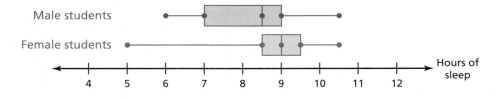

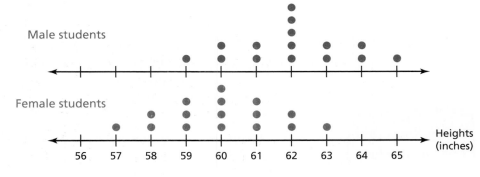

Math Practice

Recognize Usefulness of Tools

What are the advantages of each type of data display? Which do you prefer? Explain.

Ages of People in Two Exercise Classes

10:00 A.M. Class							8:00 P.M. Class
						1	8 9
						2	1 2 2 7 9 9
						3	0 3 4 5 7
9	7 3 2 2 2					4	0
	7 5 4 3 1					5	
		7 0 0				6	
			0			7	

Key: 2 | 4 | 0 = 42 and 40 years

b. How can you describe the overlap of two data distributions using words? How can you describe the overlap numerically?

c. In which pair of data sets is the difference in the measures of center the most significant? Explain your reasoning.

Use the mean and the mean absolute deviation (MAD) to compare two populations when both distributions are symmetric. Use the median and the interquartile range (IQR) when either one or both distributions are skewed.

EXAMPLE 1 **Comparing Populations**

Two data sets contain an equal number of values. The double box-and-whisker plot represents the values in the data sets.

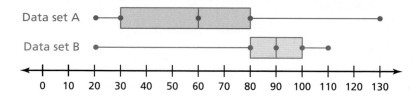

a. **Compare the data sets using measures of center and variation.**

Both distributions are skewed. Use the median and the IQR.

Data set A	**Data set B**
Median = 60	Median = 90
IQR = $80 - 30 = 50$	IQR = $100 - 80 = 20$

 So, Data set B has a greater measure of center, and Data set A has a greater measure of variation.

b. **Which data set is more likely to contain a value of 95?**

About 25% of the data values in Data set A are between 80 and 130. About 50% of the data values in Data set B are between 80 and 100.

 So, Data set B is more likely to contain a value of 95.

c. **Which data set is more likely to contain a value that differs from the center by at least 30?**

The IQR of Data set A is 50 and the IQR of Data set B is 20. This means it is more common for a value to differ from the center by 30 in Data set A than in Data set B.

 So, Data set A is more likely to contain a value that differs from the center by at least 30.

Math Practice

Look for Structure
Explain how you know that about 50% of the data values in Data set B are between 80 and 100.

Try It

1. Which data set is more likely to contain a value of 70?

2. Which data set is more likely to contain a value that differs from the center by no more than 3?

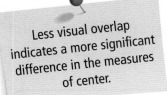

Less visual overlap indicates a more significant difference in the measures of center.

When two populations have similar variabilities, the visual overlap of the data can be described by writing the difference in the measures of center as a multiple of the measure of variation. Greater values indicate less visual overlap.

EXAMPLE 2 Describing Visual Overlap

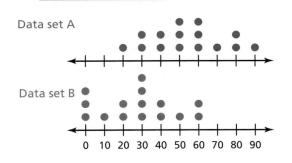

The double dot plot shows two data sets. Express the difference in the measures of center as a multiple of the measure of variation.

Both distributions are approximately symmetric. Use the mean and the MAD to describe the centers and variations.

Data set A

$$\text{Mean} = \frac{810}{15} = 54$$

$$\text{MAD} = \frac{244}{15} \approx 16$$

$$\frac{\text{difference in means}}{\text{MAD}} = \frac{26}{16} \approx 1.6$$

Data set B

$$\text{Mean} = \frac{420}{15} = 28$$

$$\text{MAD} = \frac{236}{15} \approx 16$$

 So, the difference in the means is about 1.6 times the MAD.

Try It

3. **WHAT IF?** Each value in the dot plot for Data set A increases by 30. How does this affect your answers? Explain.

Self-Assessment for Concepts & Skills

Solve each exercise. Then rate your understanding of the success criteria in your journal.

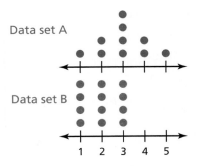

4. **COMPARING POPULATIONS** The double dot plot shows two data sets. Compare the data sets using measures of center and variation. Then express the difference in the measures of center as a multiple of the measure of variation.

5. **WHICH ONE DOESN'T BELONG?** You want to compare two populations represented by skewed distributions. Which measure does *not* belong with the other three? Explain your reasoning.

Median of first data set	Median of second data set
IQR of first data set	MAD of second data set

When the difference in the measures of center is at least 2 times the measure of variation, the difference is significant.

EXAMPLE 3 **Modeling Real Life**

The double box-and-whisker plot represents the heights of rollercoasters at two amusement parks. Are the rollercoasters significantly taller at one park than at the other park?

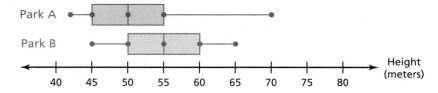

The distribution for Park A is skewed, so use the median and the IQR to describe the centers and variations.

Park A	Park B
Median = 50	Median = 55
IQR = 55 − 45 = 10	IQR = 60 − 50 = 10

Because the variabilities are similar, you can describe the visual overlap by expressing the difference in the medians as a multiple of the IQR.

$$\frac{\text{difference in medians}}{\text{IQR}} = \frac{5}{10} = 0.5$$

Because the quotient is less than 2, the difference in the medians is not significant.

▷ The rollercoasters are not significantly taller at one park than at the other park.

 Self-Assessment for Problem Solving

Solve each exercise. Then rate your understanding of the success criteria in your journal.

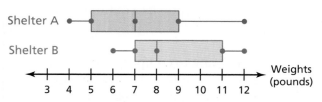

6. The double box-and-whisker plot represents the weights of cats at two shelters. Are the cats significantly heavier at one shelter than at the other? Explain.

7. **DIG DEEPER!** Tornadoes in Region A travel significantly farther than tornadoes in Region B. The tornadoes in Region A travel a median of 10 miles. Create a double box-and-whisker plot that can represent the distances traveled by the tornadoes in the two regions.

▶ Review & Refresh

Twenty percent of all seventh graders have watched a horse race. Explain whether the sample closely estimates the percentage of seventh graders who have watched a horse race.

1. In a sample of 15 seventh graders, 4 have watched a horse race.

2. In a sample of 10 seventh graders, 6 have watched a horse race.

Find the unit rate.

3. 60 kilometers in 2 hours

4. $11.40 for 5 cans

▶▶ Concepts, Skills, & Problem Solving

COMPARING TWO DATA DISTRIBUTIONS **The double box-and-whisker plot represents the values in two data sets.** (See Exploration 1, p. 337.)

5. Does the data display show *overlap*? Explain.

6. Is there a significant difference in the measures of center for the pair of data sets? Explain.

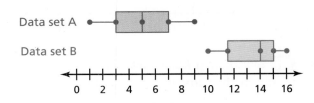

COMPARING POPULATIONS **Two data sets contain an equal number of values. The double box-and-whisker plot represents the values in the data sets.**

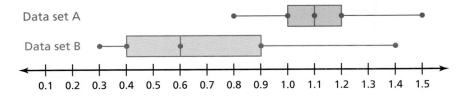

7. Compare the data sets using measures of center and variation.

8. Which data set is more likely to contain a value of 1.1?

9. Which data set is more likely to contain a value that differs from the center by 0.3?

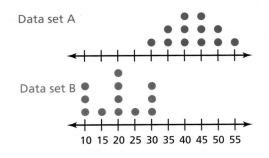

10. **DESCRIBING VISUAL OVERLAP** The double dot plot shows the values in two data sets. Express the difference in the measures of center as a multiple of the measure of variation.

11. **(MP) YOU BE THE TEACHER** The distributions of attendance at basketball games and volleyball games at your school are symmetric. Your friend makes a conclusion based on the calculations shown below. Is your friend correct? Explain your reasoning.

> Volleyball Game Attendance: Mean = 80, MAD = 20
>
> Basketball Game Attendance: Mean = 160, MAD = 20
>
> The difference in means is four times the MAD, so attendance at basketball games is significantly greater than attendance at volleyball games.

12. **(MP) MODELING REAL LIFE** The double box-and-whisker plot represents the goals scored per game by two hockey teams during a 20-game season. Is the number of goals scored per game significantly greater for one team than the other? Explain.

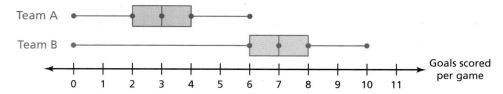

13. **(MP) MODELING REAL LIFE** The dot plots show the test scores for two classes taught by the same teacher. Are the test scores significantly greater for one class than the other? Explain.

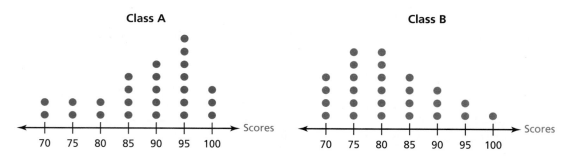

14. **(MP) PROBLEM SOLVING** A scientist experiments with mold colonies of equal area. She adds a treatment to half of the colonies. After a week, she measures the area of each colony. If the areas are significantly different, the scientist will repeat the experiment. The results are shown. Should the scientist repeat the experiment? Justify your answer.

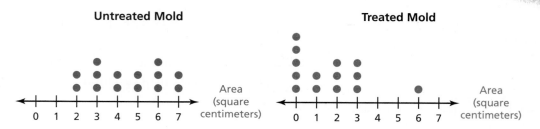

8.4 Using Random Samples to Compare Populations

Learning Target: Use random samples to compare populations.

Success Criteria:
- I can compare random samples using measures of center and variation.
- I can recognize whether random samples are likely to be representative of a population.
- I can compare populations using multiple random samples.

EXPLORATION 1

Using Random Samples

Work with a partner. You want to compare the numbers of hours spent on homework each week by male and female students in your state. You take a random sample of 15 male students and 15 female students throughout the state.

Male Students				
1.5	3	0	2.5	1
8	2.5	1	3	0
6.5	1	5	0	5

Female Students				
4	0	3	1	1
5	1	3	5.5	10
2	0	6	3.5	2

a. Compare the data in each sample.

b. Are the samples likely to be representative of all male and female students in your state? Explain.

c. You take 100 random samples of 15 male students in your state and 100 random samples of 15 female students in your state and record the median of each sample. The double box-and-whisker plot shows the distributions of the sample medians. Compare the distributions in the double box-and-whisker plot with the distributions of the data in the tables.

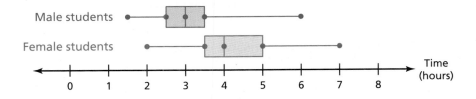

Math Practice

Build Arguments

How does taking multiple random samples allow you to make conclusions about two populations?

d. What can you conclude from the double box-and-whisker plot? Explain.

e. How can you use random samples to make accurate comparisons of two populations?

You do not need to have all of the data from two populations to make comparisons. You can use random samples to make comparisons.

EXAMPLE 1 **Comparing Random Samples**

Two bags each contain 1000 numbered tiles. The double box-and-whisker plot represents a random sample of 12 numbers from each bag. Compare the samples using measures of center and variation. Can you determine which bag contains tiles with greater numbers?

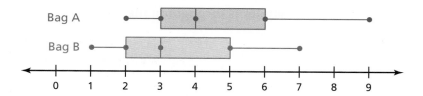

Both distributions are skewed right, so use the median and the IQR.

Bag A

Median = 4

IQR = 6 − 3 = 3

Bag B

Median = 3

IQR = 5 − 2 = 3

> You are more likely to make valid comparisons when the sample size is large and there is little variability in the data.

The variation in the samples is about the same, but the sample from Bag A has a greater median. The sample size is too small, however, to conclude that tiles in Bag A generally have greater numbers than tiles in Bag B.

Try It

1. The double dot plot shows the weekly reading habits of a random sample of 10 students in each of two schools. Compare the samples using measures of center and variation. Can you determine which school's students read less? Explain.

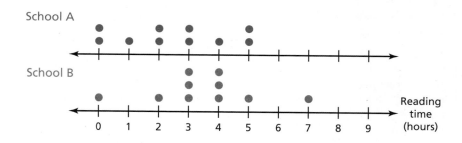

EXAMPLE 2 **Using Multiple Random Samples**

The double box-and-whisker plot represents the medians of 50 random samples of 12 numbers from each bag in Example 1. Compare the variability of the sample medians to the variability of the samples in Example 1. Can you determine which bag contains tiles with greater numbers?

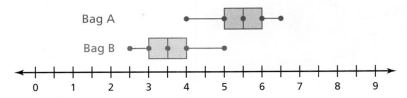

Bag A	**Bag B**
Median = 5.5	Median = 3.5
IQR = 6 − 5 = 1	IQR = 4 − 3 = 1

▷ The IQR of the sample medians for each bag is 1, which is less than the IQR of the samples in Example 1. Most of the sample medians for Bag A are greater than the sample medians for Bag B. So, tiles in Bag A generally have greater numbers than tiles in Bag B.

Try It

2. **WHAT IF?** Each value in the box-and-whisker plot of the sample medians for Bag A decreases by 2. Does this change your answer?

Self-Assessment *for Concepts & Skills*

Solve each exercise. Then rate your understanding of the success criteria in your journal.

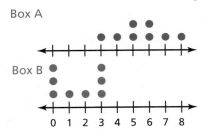

3. **COMPARING RANDOM SAMPLES** Two boxes each contain 600 numbered tiles. The double dot plot shows a random sample of 8 numbers from each box. Compare the samples using measures of center and variation. Can you determine which box contains tiles with greater numbers? Explain.

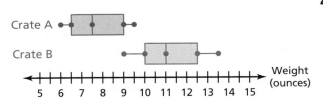

4. **USING MULTIPLE RANDOM SAMPLES** Two crates each contain 750 objects. The double box-and-whisker plot shows the median weights of 50 random samples of 10 objects from each crate. Can you determine which crate weighs more? Explain.

EXAMPLE 3 **Modeling Real Life**

The double box-and-whisker plot represents the medians of 50 random samples of 10 speeding tickets issued in two states. Compare the costs of speeding tickets in the two states.

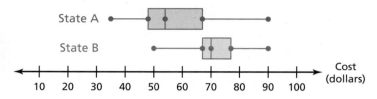

There is enough data to draw conclusions about the costs of speeding tickets in the two states. Find the measures of center and variation for the sample medians from each state. Then compare the data.

State A	State B
Median ≈ 54	Median $= 70$
IQR $\approx 67 - 48 = 19$	IQR $\approx 77 - 67 = 10$

The variation for State A is greater than the variation for State B, and the measure of center for State B is greater than the measure of center for State A.

> So, you can conclude that the cost of speeding tickets varies more in State A, but speeding tickets generally cost more in State B.

Self-Assessment for Problem Solving

Solve each exercise. Then rate your understanding of the success criteria in your journal.

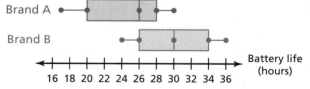

5. The double box-and-whisker plot represents the medians of 100 random samples of 20 battery lives for two cell phone brands. Compare the battery lives of the two brands.

6. The double box-and-whisker plot represents the medians of 50 random samples of 10 wait times at two patient care facilities. Which facility should you choose? Explain your reasoning.

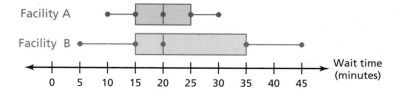

Go to **BigIdeasMath.com** to get HELP with solving the exercises.

▶ Review & Refresh

The double dot plot shows the values in two data sets.

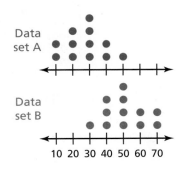

1. Compare the data sets using measures of center and variation.

2. Are the values of one data set significantly greater than the values of the other data set? Explain.

Solve the equation. Check your solution.

3. $5b - 3 = 22$

4. $1.5d + 3 = -4.5$

5. $4 = 9z - 2$

▶▶ Concepts, Skills, & Problem Solving

USING RANDOM SAMPLES You want to compare the numbers of hours spent on recreation each week by teachers and non-teachers in your state. You take 100 random samples of 15 teachers and 100 random samples of 15 non-teachers throughout the state and record the median value of each sample. The double box-and-whisker plot shows the distributions of sample medians. (See Exploration 1, p. 343.)

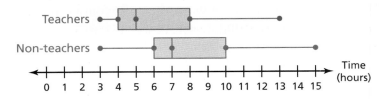

6. Are the samples likely to be representative of all teachers and non-teachers in your state?

7. What can you conclude from the double box-and-whisker plot? Explain.

8. **COMPARING RANDOM SAMPLES** The double dot plot shows the weekly running habits of athletes at two colleges. Compare the samples using measures of center and variation. Can you determine which college's athletes spend more time running? Explain.

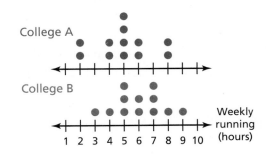

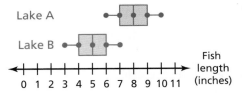

9. **USING MULTIPLE RANDOM SAMPLES** Two lakes each contain about 2000 fish. The double box-and-whisker plot shows the medians of 50 random samples of 14 fish lengths from each lake. Can you determine which lake contains longer fish? Explain.

10. **MP MODELING REAL LIFE** Two laboratories each produce 800 chemicals. A chemist takes 10 samples of 15 chemicals from each lab, and records the number that pass an inspection. Are the samples likely to be representative of all the chemicals for each lab? If so, which lab has more chemicals that will pass the inspection? Justify your answer.

Research Lab A				
14	13	15	15	14
14	15	15	13	12

Research Lab B				
12	10	12	14	11
9	14	11	11	15

11. **MP MODELING REAL LIFE** A farmer grows two types of corn seedlings. There are 1000 seedlings of each type. The double box-and-whisker plot represents the median growths of 50 random samples of 7 corn seedlings of each type. Compare the growths of each type of corn seedling. Justify your result.

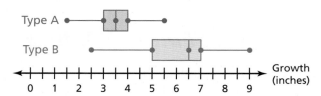

12. **DIG DEEPER!** You want to compare the number of words per sentence in a sports magazine to the number of words per sentence in a political magazine.

   a. The data represent random samples of the number of words in 10 sentences from each magazine. Compare the samples using measures of center and variation. Can you use the data to make a valid comparison about the magazines? Explain.

   Sports magazine: 9, 21, 15, 14, 25, 26, 9, 19, 22, 30
   Political magazine: 31, 22, 17, 5, 23, 15, 10, 20, 20, 17

   b. The double box-and-whisker plot represents the means of 200 random samples of 20 sentences from each magazine. Compare the variability of the sample means to the variability of the sample numbers of words in part (a).

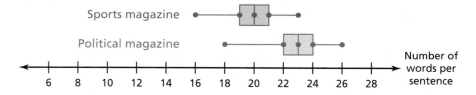

   c. Make a conclusion about the numbers of words per sentence in each magazine.

13. **PROJECT** You want to compare the average amounts of time students in sixth, seventh, and eighth grade spend on homework each week.

   a. Design an experiment involving random sampling that can help you make a comparison.

   b. Perform the experiment. Can you make a conclusion about which grade spends the most time on homework? Explain your reasoning.

8 Connecting Concepts

▶ *Using the Problem-Solving Plan*

1. In a city, 1500 randomly chosen residents are asked how many sporting events they attend each month. The city has 80,000 residents. Estimate the number of residents in the city who attend at least one sporting event each month.

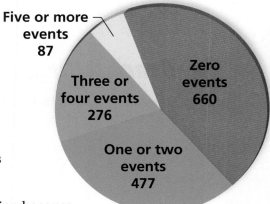

Sporting Events per Month

Five or more events 87

Three or four events 276

Zero events 660

One or two events 477

Understand the problem. ▶ You are given the numbers of sporting events attended each month by a sample of 1500 residents. You are asked to make an estimate about the population, all residents of the city.

Make a plan. ▶ The sample is representative of the population because it is selected at random and is large enough to provide accurate data. So, find the percent of people in the survey that attend at least one sporting event each month, and use the percent equation to make an estimate.

Solve and check. ▶ Use the plan to solve the problem. Then check your solution.

2. The dot plots show the values in two data sets. Is the difference in the measures of center for the data sets significant?

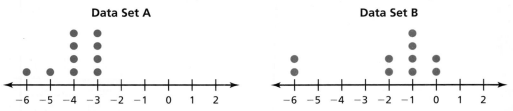

Data Set A

Data Set B

Yes	No
42	18

3. You ask 60 randomly chosen students whether they support a later starting time for school. The table shows the results. Estimate the probability that at least two out of four randomly chosen students do not support a later starting time.

Performance Task

Estimating Animal Populations

At the beginning of the this chapter, you watched a STEAM Video called "Comparing Dogs." You are now ready to complete the performance task related to this video, available at *BigIdeasMath.com*. Be sure to use the problem-solving plan as you work through the performance task.

▶ Review Vocabulary

Write the definition and give an example of each vocabulary term.

population, *p. 325*   unbiased sample, *p. 326*
sample, *p. 325*   biased sample, *p. 326*

▶ Graphic Organizers

You can use a **Definition and Example Chart** to organize information about a concept. Here is an example of a Definition and Example Chart for the vocabulary term *sample*.

> Sample: part of a population
>
> Example
> *unbiased sample*: 100 seventh-grade students selected randomly during lunch
>
> Example
> *biased sample*: the seventh-grade students at your lunch table

Choose and complete a graphic organizer to help you study each topic.

1. population
2. shape of a distribution
3. mean absolute deviation (MAD)
4. interquartile range (IQR)
5. double box-and-whisker plot
6. double dot plot

"Here is my Definition and Example Chart. I read in the news that a cat once floated over this waterfall in a barrel."

Chapter Self-Assessment

As you complete the exercises, use the scale below to rate your understanding of the success criteria in your journal.

1 I do not understand.

2 I can do it with help.

3 I can do it on my own.

4 I can teach someone else.

8.1 Samples and Populations (pp. 325–330)

Learning Target: Understand how to use random samples to make conclusions about a population.

1. You want to estimate the number of students in your school whose favorite subject is biology. You survey the first 10 students who arrive at biology club. Determine whether the sample is *biased* or *unbiased*. Explain.

2. You want to estimate the number of athletes who play soccer. Give an example of a biased sample. Give an example of an unbiased sample.

3. You want to know how the residents of your town feel about building a new baseball stadium. You randomly survey 100 people who enter the current stadium. Eighty support building a new stadium, and twenty do not. So, you conclude that 80% of the residents of your town support building a new baseball stadium. Is your conclusion valid? Explain.

4. Which sample is better for making an estimate? Explain.

Predict the number of students in a school who like gym class.	
Sample A	A random sample of 8 students from the yearbook
Sample B	A random sample of 80 students from the yearbook

5. You ask 125 randomly chosen students to name their favorite beverage. There are 1500 students in the school. Predict the number of students in the school whose favorite beverage is a sports drink.

6. You want to know the number of students in your state who have summer jobs. Determine whether you should survey the population or a sample. Explain.

Favorite Beverage	
Sports drink	58
Soda	36
Water	14
Other	17

8.2 Using Random Samples to Describe Populations *(pp. 331–336)*

Learning Target: Understand variability in samples of a population.

7. To pass a quality control inspection, the products at a factory must contain no critical defects, no more than 2.5% of products can contain major defects, and no more than 4% of products can contain minor defects. There are 40,000 products being shipped from a factory. Each inspector randomly samples 125 products. The table shows the results.

    a. Use each sample to make an estimate for the number of products with minor defects at the factory. Describe the center and the variation of the estimates.

    b. Use the samples to make an estimate for the percent of products with minor defects, with major defects, and with critical defects at the factory. Does the factory pass inspection? Explain.

	Type of Defect		
	Critical	**Major**	**Minor**
Inspector A	0	2	5
Inspector B	0	1	6
Inspector C	0	3	3
Inspector D	0	5	6

8. A scientist determines that 35% of packages of a food product contain a specific bacteria. Use technology to simulate choosing 100 random samples of 20 packages. How closely do the samples estimate the percent of all packages with the specific bacteria?

8.3 Comparing Populations *(pp. 337–342)*

Learning Target: Compare populations using measures of center and variation.

9. The double box-and-whisker plot represents the points scored per game by two football teams during the regular season.

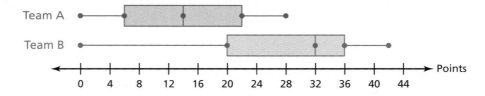

    a. Compare the data sets using measures of center and variation.

    b. Which team is more likely to score 18 points in a game?

10. The dot plots show the ages of campers at two summer camps.

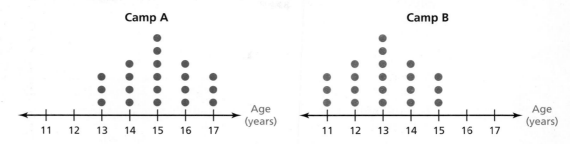

Camp A

Age (years)
11 12 13 14 15 16 17

Camp B

Age (years)
11 12 13 14 15 16 17

a. Express the difference in the measures of center as a multiple of the measure of variation.

b. Are the ages of campers at one camp significantly greater than at the other? Explain.

8.4 Using Random Samples to Compare Populations *(pp. 343–348)*

Learning Target: Use random samples to compare populations.

11. The double dot plot shows the median gas mileages of 10 random samples of 50 vehicles for two car models. Compare the samples using measures of center and variation. Can you determine which car model has a better gas mileage? Explain.

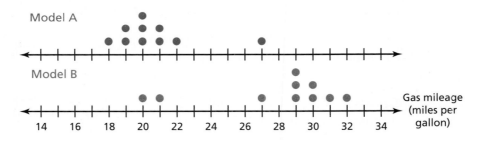

Model A

Model B

Gas mileage (miles per gallon)
14 16 18 20 22 24 26 28 30 32 34

12. You compare the average amounts of time people in their twenties and thirties spend driving each week. The double box-and-whisker plot represents the medians of 100 random samples of 8 people from each age group. Can you determine whether one age group drives more than the other? Explain.

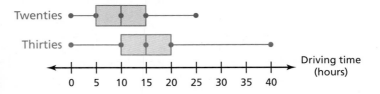

Twenties

Thirties

Driving time (hours)
0 5 10 15 20 25 30 35 40

1. You want to estimate the number of students in your school who prefer to bring a lunch from home rather than buy one at school. You survey five students who are standing in the lunch line. Determine whether the sample is *biased* or *unbiased*. Explain.

2. You want to predict which candidate will likely be voted Seventh Grade Class President. There are 560 students in the seventh grade class. You randomly sample 3 different groups of 50 seventh-grade students. The results are shown.

	Candidate Preference	
	Candidate A	Candidate B
Sample 1	27	23
Sample 2	22	28
Sample 3	15	35

    a. Use each sample to make an estimate for the number of students in seventh grade that vote for Candidate A.

    b. Who do you expect to be voted Seventh Grade Class President? Explain.

3. Of 60 randomly chosen students from a school surveyed, 16 chose the aquarium as their favorite field trip. There are 720 students in the school. Predict the number of students in the school who choose the aquarium as their favorite field trip.

4. The double box-and-whisker plot shows the ages of the viewers of two television shows in a small town.

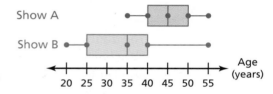

    a. Compare the data sets using measures of center and variation.

    b. Which show is more likely to have a 44-year-old viewer?

5. The double box-and-whisker plot shows the test scores for two French classes taught by the same teacher.

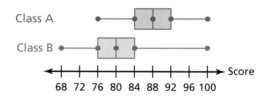

    a. Express the difference in the measures of center as a multiple of the measure of variation.

    b. Are the scores for one class significantly greater than for the other? Explain.

6. Two airplanes each hold about 400 pieces of luggage. The double dot plot shows a random sample of 8 pieces of luggage from each plane. Compare the samples using measures of center and variation. Can you determine which plane has heavier luggage? Explain.

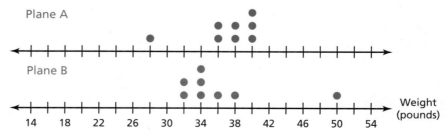

8 Cumulative Practice

1. Which of the ratios form a proportion?

   A. 5 to 2 and 4 to 10

   B. 2 : 3 and 7 : 8

   C. 3 to 2 and 15 to 10

   D. 12 : 8 and 8 : 4

Test-Taking Strategy
Solve Problem before Looking at Choices

A sample of 20 reef fish has 15 fish that love their school. How many of 200 reef fish love their school?
Ⓐ 50   Ⓑ 100   Ⓒ 150   Ⓓ 200

Do fish stay in school ALL year long?

"Solve the problem before looking at the choices. The sample has 75%. So, 75% of 200 is 150."

2. A student scored 600 the first time she took the mathematics portion of a college entrance exam. The next time she took the exam, she scored 660. Her second score represents what percent increase over her first score?

   F. 9.1%   **G.** 10%

   H. 39.6%   **I.** 60%

3. You ask 100 randomly chosen students to name their favorite food. There are 1250 students in the school. Based on this sample, what is the number of students in the school whose favorite food is chicken?

Favorite Food	
Pizza	38
Tacos	36
Chicken	8
Other	18

   A. 100   **B.** 225

   C. 450   **D.** 475

4. Which value of p makes the equation $p + 6 = 5$ true?

   F. -1 **G.** 1

   H. 11   **I.** 30

5. The table shows the costs for four cans of tomato soup. Which can has the lowest cost per ounce?

	Cost (dollars)	Number of Ounces
Can A	1.95	26
Can B	0.72	8
Can C	0.86	10.75
Can D	2.32	23.2

A. Can A

B. Can B

C. Can C

D. Can D

6. What value of y makes the equation $-3y = -18$ true?

7. The double dot plot shows the values in two data sets. Which sentence best represents the difference in the measures of center as a multiple of the measure of variation?

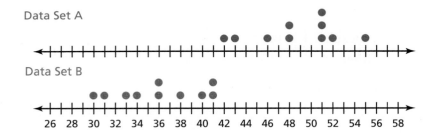

F. The difference of the means is about 3.3 times the MAD.

G. The difference of the means is about 3.8 times the MAD.

H. The difference of the means is 36 times the MAD.

I. The difference of the means is 48.7 times the MAD.

8. What is the missing value in the ratio table?

x	y
$\frac{2}{3}$	5
2	15
$\frac{8}{3}$	
8	60

$4 per pound

9. You are selling tomatoes. What is the minimum number of pounds of tomatoes you need to sell to earn at least $44?

A. 11

B. 12

C. 40

D. 176

Think Solve Explain

10. You and a group of friends want to know how many students in your school prefer science. There are 900 students in your school. Each person randomly surveys 20 students. The table shows the results. Which subject do students at your school prefer?

	Favorite Subject			
	English	**Math**	**Science**	**History**
You	4	5	6	5
Friend A	2	4	7	7
Friend B	7	4	8	1
Friend C	3	6	5	6
Friend D	6	7	2	5

Part A Use each sample to make an estimate for the number of students in your school who prefer science.

Part B Describe the variation of the estimates.

Part C Use the samples to make one estimate for the number of students who prefer science in your school.

Geometric Shapes and Angles

Chapter Learning Target:
Understand geometry.

Chapter Success Criteria:
- ☐ I can explain how to find the circumference of a circle.
- ☐ I can find the areas of circles and composite figures.
- ☐ I can solve problems involving angle measures.
- ☐ I can construct a polygon.

STEAM Video: "Track and Field"

Track and Field

Different lanes on a race track have different lengths.
How can competitors run in different lanes and have the
same finish line?

**Watch the STEAM Video "Track and Field." Then answer
the following questions.**

1. A track consists of a rectangle and two semicircles. The
   dimensions of the rectangle formed by the innermost
   lane are shown. What is the distance around each
   semicircle on the 400-meter, innermost lane?

2. How does the width of the rectangle, 63.7 meters,
   compare to the distance around each semicircle?
   Explain.

Finding the Area and Perimeter of a Track

After completing this chapter, you will be able to use
the concepts you learned to answer the questions in the
STEAM Video Performance Task. You will be given the
dimensions of a race track.

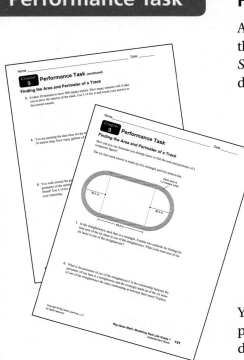

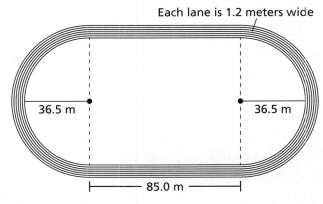

Each lane is 1.2 meters wide

36.5 m   36.5 m

85.0 m

You will be asked to solve various perimeter and area
problems about the track. Given a race track, what measures
do you need to find the outer perimeter?

Getting Ready for Chapter

Chapter Exploration

Work with a partner.

1. Perform the steps for each of the figures.

   - Measure the perimeter of the larger polygon to the nearest millimeter.
   - Measure the diameter of the circle to the nearest millimeter.
   - Measure the perimeter of the smaller polygon to the nearest millimeter.
   - Calculate the value of the ratio of the two perimeters to the diameter.
   - Take the average of the ratios. This average is the approximation of π (the Greek letter *pi*).

a.

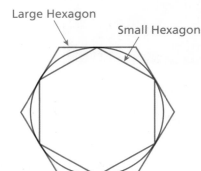

b.

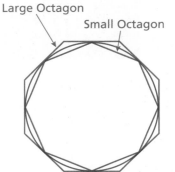

c.

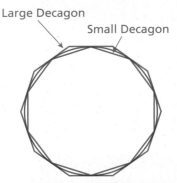

Sides	Large Perimeter	Diameter of Circle	Small Perimeter	$\dfrac{\text{Large Perimeter}}{\text{Diameter}}$	$\dfrac{\text{Small Perimeter}}{\text{Diameter}}$	Average of Ratios
6						
8						
10						

2. Based on the table, what can you conclude about the value of π? Explain your reasoning.

3. The Greek mathematician Archimedes used the above procedure to approximate the value of π. He used polygons with 96 sides. Do you think his approximation was more or less accurate than yours? Explain your reasoning.

Vocabulary

The following vocabulary terms are defined in this chapter. Think about what each term might mean and record your thoughts.

diameter of a circle   semicircle   adjacent angles
circumference   composite figure   vertical angles

9.1 Circles and Circumference

Learning Target: Find the circumference of a circle.

Success Criteria:
- I can explain the relationship between the diameter and circumference of a circle.
- I can use a formula to find the circumference of a circle.

EXPLORATION 1

Using a Compass to Draw a Circle

Work with a partner. Set a compass to 2 inches and draw a circle.

a. Draw a line from one side of the circle to the other that passes through the center. What is the length of the line? This is called the *diameter* of the circle.

b. **MP CHOOSE TOOLS** Estimate the distance around the circle. This is called the *circumference* of the circle. Explain how you found your answer.

EXPLORATION 2

Exploring Diameter and Circumference

Work with a partner.

Math Practice

Calculate Accurately
What other methods can you use to calculate the circumference of a circle? Which methods are more accurate?

a. Roll a cylindrical object on a flat surface to find the circumference of the circular base.

b. Measure the diameter of the circular base. Which is greater, the diameter or the circumference? how many times greater?

c. Compare your answers in part (b) with the rest of the class. What do you notice?

d. Without measuring, how can you find the circumference of a circle with a given diameter? Use your method to estimate the circumference of the circle in Exploration 1.

Key Vocabulary
circle, *p. 362*
center, *p. 362*
radius, *p. 362*
diameter, *p. 362*
circumference, *p. 363*
pi, *p. 363*
semicircle, *p. 364*

A **circle** is the set of all points in a plane that are the same distance from a point called the **center**.

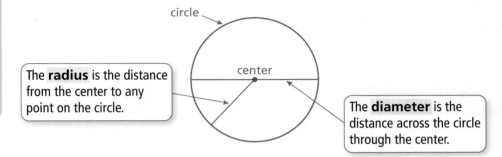

circle

center

The **radius** is the distance from the center to any point on the circle.

The **diameter** is the distance across the circle through the center.

Key Idea

Radius and Diameter

Words The diameter d of a circle is twice the radius r. The radius r of a circle is one-half the diameter d.

Algebra   **Diameter:** $d = 2r$ **Radius:** $r = \dfrac{d}{2}$

EXAMPLE 1   Finding a Radius and a Diameter

a. The diameter of a circle is 20 feet. Find the radius.

b. The radius of a circle is 7 meters. Find the diameter.

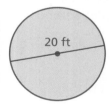

20 ft

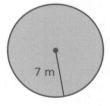

7 m

$r = \dfrac{d}{2}$ Radius of a circle

$= \dfrac{20}{2}$ Substitute 20 for *d*.

$= 10$ Divide.

The radius is 10 feet.

$d = 2r$ Diameter of a circle

$= 2(7)$ Substitute 7 for *r*.

$= 14$ Multiply.

The diameter is 14 meters.

Try It

1. The diameter of a circle is 16 centimeters. Find the radius.

2. The radius of a circle is 9 yards. Find the diameter.

The distance around a circle is called the **circumference**. The ratio of the circumference to the diameter is the same for *every* circle and its value is represented by the Greek letter π, called **pi**. Two approximations for the value of π are 3.14 and $\frac{22}{7}$.

When the radius or diameter is a multiple of 7, it is easier to use $\frac{22}{7}$ as the estimate of π.

 Key Idea

Circumference of a Circle

Words   The circumference C of a circle is equal to π times the diameter d or π times twice the radius r.

Algebra $C = \pi d$ or $C = 2\pi r$

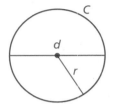

EXAMPLE 2   **Finding Circumferences of Circles**

a. Find the circumference of the flying disc. Use 3.14 for π.

$$C = 2\pi r \qquad \text{Write formula for circumference.}$$
$$\approx 2 \cdot 3.14 \cdot 5 \qquad \text{Substitute 3.14 for } \pi \text{ and 5 for } r.$$
$$= 31.4 \qquad \text{Multiply.}$$

The circumference is about 31.4 inches.

b. Find the circumference of the watch face. Use $\frac{22}{7}$ for π.

$$C = \pi d \qquad \text{Write formula for circumference.}$$
$$\approx \frac{22}{7} \cdot 28 \qquad \text{Substitute } \frac{22}{7} \text{ for } \pi \text{ and 28 for } d.$$
$$= 88 \qquad \text{Multiply.}$$

The circumference is about 88 millimeters.

Try It   Find the circumference of the object. Use 3.14 or $\frac{22}{7}$ for π.

3.

2 cm

4.

14 ft

5.

9 in.

EXAMPLE 3 **Finding the Perimeter of a Semicircular Region**

A semicircle is one-half of a circle. Find the perimeter of the semicircular region.

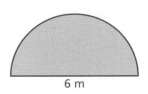

The straight side is 6 meters long. The distance around the curved part is one-half the circumference of a circle with a diameter of 6 meters.

6 m

$$\frac{C}{2} = \frac{\pi d}{2}$$ Divide the circumference by 2.

$$\approx \frac{3.14 \cdot 6}{2}$$ Substitute 3.14 for π and 6 for d.

$$= \frac{18.84}{2}$$ Multiply.

$$= 9.42$$ Divide.

▷   So, the perimeter is about $6 + 9.42 = 15.42$ meters.

 Try It   **Find the perimeter of the semicircular region.**

6.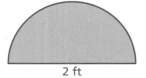

2 ft

7. 7 cm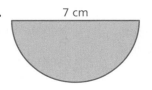

8.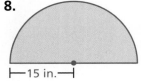

├─ 15 in. ─┤

 Self-Assessment for *Concepts & Skills*

Solve each exercise. Then rate your understanding of the success criteria in your journal.

9. WRITING Are there circles for which the value of the ratio of circumference to diameter is not equal to π? Explain.

10. FINDING A PERIMETER Find the perimeter of a semicircular region with a straight side that is 8 yards long.

11. DIFFERENT WORDS, SAME QUESTION Which is different? Find "both" answers.

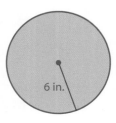

6 in.

> What is the distance around the circle?

> What is π times the radius?

> What is the circumference of the circle?

> What is π times the diameter?

EXAMPLE 4 **Modeling Real Life**

The circumference of the roll of caution tape decreases 10.5 inches after a firefighter uses some of the tape. What is the radius of the roll after the firefighter uses the tape?

C = 31.4 in.

The radius and circumference of the roll are the radius and circumference of the circular bases of the roll. After the decrease, the circumference is $31.4 - 10.5 = 20.9$ inches.

Use the formula for the circumference of a circle to find the radius of a circle with a circumference of 20.9 inches.

$C = 2\pi r$	Write formula for circumference.
$20.9 \approx 2(3.14)r$	Substitute 20.9 for C and 3.14 for π.
$20.9 = 6.28r$	Multiply.
$3.3 \approx r$	Divide each side by 6.28.

▶ So, the radius of the roll is about 3.3 inches.

Self-Assessment for Problem Solving

Solve each exercise. Then rate your understanding of the success criteria in your journal.

12. The wheels of a monster truck are 66 inches tall. Find the distance the monster truck travels when the tires make one 360-degree rotation.

66 in.

13. **DIG DEEPER!** The radius of a dog's collar should be at least 0.5 inch larger than the radius of the dog's neck. A dog collar adjusts to a circumference of 10 to 14 inches. Should the collar be worn by a dog with a neck circumference of 12.5 inches? Explain.

14. You resize a picture so that the radius of the midday Sun appears four times larger. How much larger does the circumference of the Sun appear? Explain.

9.1 Practice

 Go to *BigIdeasMath.com* to get HELP with solving the exercises.

▶ Review & Refresh

Two jars each contain 1000 numbered tiles. The double box-and-whisker plot represents a random sample of 10 numbers from each jar.

1. Compare the samples using measures of center and variation.

2. Can you determine which jar contains greater numbers? Explain.

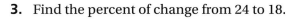

3. Find the percent of change from 24 to 18.

   A. 25% decrease   **B.** 25% increase   **C.** 75% increase   **D.** 75% decrease

▶▶ Concepts, Skills, & Problem Solving

EXPLORING DIAMETER AND CIRCUMFERENCE **Estimate the circumference of the circular base of the object.** (See Exploration 2, p. 361.)

4. tube of lip balm with radius 0.5 mm   5. D battery with radius 0.65 in.

FINDING A RADIUS **Find the radius of the button.**

6.  5 cm

7. 28 mm

8. 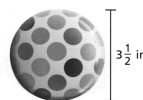 $3\frac{1}{2}$ in.

FINDING A DIAMETER **Find the diameter of the object.**

9. 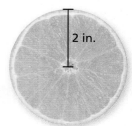 2 in.

10.  0.8 ft

11.  $\frac{3}{5}$ cm

FINDING A CIRCUMFERENCE **Find the circumference of the object. Use 3.14 or $\frac{22}{7}$ for π.**

12. 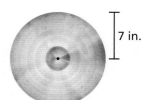 7 in.

13. 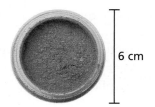 6 cm

14. 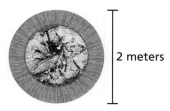 2 meters

FINDING THE PERIMETER OF A SEMICIRCULAR REGION Find the perimeter of the window.

15.

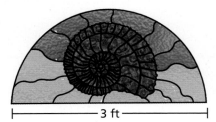

├────── 3 ft ──────┤

16.

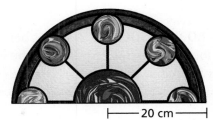

├──── 20 cm ────┤

ESTIMATING A RADIUS Estimate the radius of the object.

17.

C = 8.9 mm

18.

C = 122 in.

19. (MP) **MODELING REAL LIFE** A circular sinkhole has a circumference of 75.36 meters. A week later, it has a circumference of 150.42 meters.

    a. Estimate the diameter of the sinkhole each week.

    b. How many times greater is the diameter of the sinkhole a week later?

20. (MP) **REASONING** Consider the circles *A*, *B*, *C*, and *D*.

A.   **B.**   **C.**   **D.**

8 ft

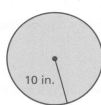
10 in.

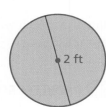
2 ft

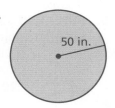
50 in.

    a. Without calculating, which circle has the greatest circumference? Explain.

    b. Without calculating, which circle has the least circumference? Explain.

FINDING CIRCUMFERENCES Find the circumferences of both circles.

21.

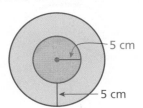
5 cm
5 cm

22.

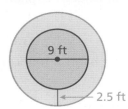
9 ft
2.5 ft

23.

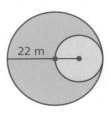
22 m

24. (MP) **MODELING REAL LIFE** A satellite is in an approximately circular orbit 36,000 kilometers from Earth's surface. The radius of Earth is about 6400 kilometers. What is the circumference of the satellite's orbit?

25. **(MP) STRUCTURE** The ratio of circumference to diameter is the same for every circle. Is the ratio of circumference to radius the same for every circle? Explain.

26. **(MP) PROBLEM SOLVING** A wire is bent to form four semicircles. How long is the wire? Justify your answer.

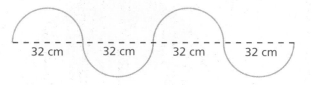

32 cm   32 cm   32 cm   32 cm

27. **CRITICAL THINKING** Explain how to draw a circle with a circumference of π^2 inches. Then draw the circle.

28. **DIG DEEPER!** "Lines" of latitude on Earth are actually circles. The Tropic of Cancer is the northernmost line of latitude at which the Sun appears directly overhead at noon. The Tropic of Cancer has a radius of 5854 kilometers.

To qualify for an around-the-world speed record, a pilot must cover a distance no less than the circumference of the Tropic of Cancer, cross all meridians, and land on the same airfield where the flight began.

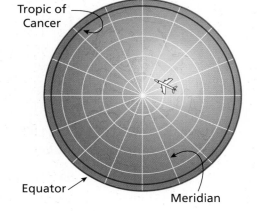

Tropic of Cancer

Equator

Meridian

   a. What is the minimum distance that a pilot must fly to qualify for an around-the-world speed record?

   b. **RESEARCH** Estimate the time it will take for a pilot to qualify for the speed record. Explain your reasoning.

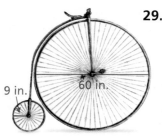

9 in.   60 in.

29. **(MP) PROBLEM SOLVING** Bicycles in the late 1800s looked very different than they do today.

   a. How many rotations does each tire make after traveling 600 feet? Round your answers to the nearest whole number.

   b. Would you rather ride a bicycle made with two large wheels or two small wheels? Explain.

30. **(MP) LOGIC** The length of the minute hand is 150% of the length of the hour hand.

   a. What distance will the tip of the minute hand move in 45 minutes? Justify your answer.

   b. In 1 hour, how much farther does the tip of the minute hand move than the tip of the hour hand? Explain how you found your answer.

36 mm

9.2 Areas of Circles

Learning Target: Find the area of a circle.

Success Criteria:
- I can estimate the area of a circle.
- I can use a formula to find the area of a circle.

EXPLORATION 1

Estimating the Area of a Circle

Work with a partner. Each grid contains a circle with a diameter of 4 centimeters. Use each grid to estimate the area of the circle. Which estimate should be closest to the actual area? Explain.

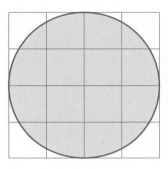 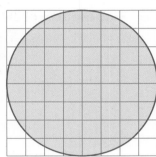 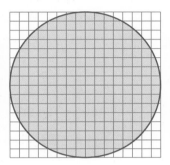

EXPLORATION 2

Writing a Formula for the Area of a Circle

Work with a partner. A student draws a circle with radius r and divides the circle into 24 equal sections. The student cuts out each section and arranges the sections to form a shape that resembles a parallelogram.

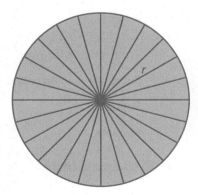 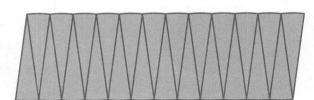

Math Practice

Interpret a Solution

Describe the relationship between the radius and the area of a circle.

a. Use the diagram to write a formula for the area A of a circle in terms of the radius r. Explain your reasoning.

b. Use the formula to check your estimates in Exploration 1.

 **Key Idea**

Area of a Circle

Words The area A of a circle is the product of π and the square of the radius r.

Algebra $A = \pi r^2$

EXAMPLE 1 **Finding Areas of Circles**

a. **Find the area of the circle. Use $\dfrac{22}{7}$ for π.**

Estimate
$3 \times 7^2 \approx 3 \times 50$
$\qquad\qquad = 150$

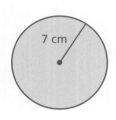

7 cm

$A = \pi r^2$ — Write formula for area.

$\approx \dfrac{22}{7} \cdot 7^2$ — Substitute $\dfrac{22}{7}$ for π and 7 for r.

$= \dfrac{22}{\cancel{7}_1} \cdot \cancel{49}^{\,7}$ — Evaluate 7^2. Divide out the common factor.

$= 154$ — Multiply.

▷ The area is about 154 square centimeters.

Reasonable?
$154 \approx 150$ ✓

b. **Find the area of the circle. Use 3.14 for π.**

The radius is $26 \div 2 = 13$ inches.

Estimate
$3 \times 13^2 \approx 3 \times 170$
$\qquad\qquad = 510$

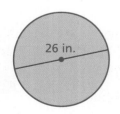

26 in.

$A = \pi r^2$ — Write formula for area.

$\approx 3.14 \cdot 13^2$ — Substitute 3.14 for π and 13 for r.

$= 3.14 \cdot 169$ — Evaluate 13^2.

$= 530.66$ — Multiply.

▷ The area is about 530.66 square inches.

Reasonable?
$530.66 \approx 510$ ✓

Try It

1. Find the area of a circle with a radius of 6 feet. Use 3.14 for π.

2. Find the area of a circle with a diameter of 28 meters. Use $\dfrac{22}{7}$ for π.

EXAMPLE 2 **Finding the Area of a Semicircle**

Find the area of the semicircle.

The area of the semicircle is one-half the area of a circle with a diameter of 30 feet. The radius of the circle is $30 \div 2 = 15$ feet.

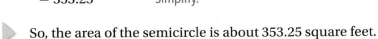

$$\frac{A}{2} = \frac{\pi r^2}{2} \qquad \text{Divide the area by 2.}$$

$$\approx \frac{3.14 \cdot 15^2}{2} \qquad \text{Substitute 3.14 for } \pi \text{ and 15 for } r.$$

$$= \frac{3.14 \cdot 225}{2} \qquad \text{Evaluate } 15^2.$$

$$= 353.25 \qquad \text{Simplify.}$$

30 ft

So, the area of the semicircle is about 353.25 square feet.

Math Practice

Find General Methods
How can you find the area of one-fourth of a circle? three-fourths of a circle?

Try It **Find the area of the semicircle.**

3.
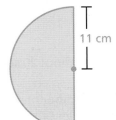
11 cm

4.
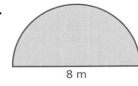
8 m

5.
5 yd
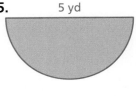

Self-Assessment *for Concepts & Skills*

Solve each exercise. Then rate your understanding of the success criteria in your journal.

6. **ESTIMATING AN AREA** The grid contains a circle with a diameter of 2 centimeters. Use the grid to estimate the area of the circle. How can you change the grid to improve your estimate? Explain.

7. **WRITING** Explain the relationship between the circumference and area of a circle.

8. **DIFFERENT WORDS, SAME QUESTION** Which is different? Find "both" answers.

What is the area of a circle with a diameter of 1 m?	What is the area of a circle with a diameter of 100 cm?
What is the area of a circle with a radius of 100 cm?	What is the area of a circle with a radius of 500 mm?

EXAMPLE 3 **Modeling Real Life**

A tsunami warning siren can be heard up to 2.5 miles away in all directions. From how many square miles can the siren be heard?

 Understand the problem.

You are given the description of a region in which a siren can be heard. You are asked to find the number of square miles within the range of the siren.

 Make a plan.

Two and a half miles from the siren in all directions is a circular region with a radius of 2.5 miles. So, find the area of a circle with a radius of 2.5 miles.

Solve and check.

$A = \pi r^2$	Write formula for area.
$\approx 3.14 \cdot 2.5^2$	Substitute 3.14 for π and 2.5 for r.
$= 3.14 \cdot 6.25$	Evaluate 2.5^2.
$= 19.625$	Multiply.

▷ So, the siren can be heard from about 20 square miles.

Check Reasonableness The number of square miles should be greater than $3 \cdot 2^2 = 12$, but less than $4 \cdot 3^2 = 36$.

Because $12 < 20 < 36$, the answer is reasonable. ✓

 Self-Assessment for Problem Solving

Solve each exercise. Then rate your understanding of the success criteria in your journal.

9. A local event planner wants to cover a circular region with mud for an obstacle course. The region has a circumference of about 157 feet. The cost to cover 1 square foot with mud is $1.50. Approximate the cost to cover the region with mud.

10. **DIG DEEPER!** A manufacturer recommends that you use a frying pan with a radius that is within 1 inch of the radius of your stovetop burner. The area of the bottom of your frying pan is 25π square inches. The circumference of your cooktop burner is 9π inches. Does your frying pan meet the manufacturer's recommendation?

372 Chapter 9 Geometric Shapes and Angles

Go to *BigIdeasMath.com* to get HELP with solving the exercises.

▶ Review & Refresh

Find the circumference of the object. Use 3.14 or $\frac{22}{7}$ for π.

1.

9 cm

2.
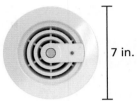
7 in.

You spin the spinner shown.

3. How many possible outcomes are there?

4. In how many ways can spinning an odd number occur?

▶▶ Concepts, Skills, & Problem Solving

ESTIMATING AN AREA **Use the grid to estimate the area of the circle.** (See Exploration 1, p. 369.)

5. diameter of 3 centimeters

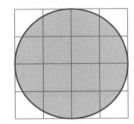

6. diameter of 1.6 inches

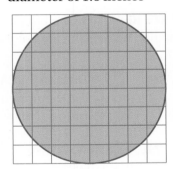

FINDING AN AREA **Find the area of the circle. Use 3.14 or $\frac{22}{7}$ for π.**

7.

9 mm

8.

14 cm

9.
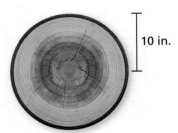
10 in.

10.

3 in.

11.
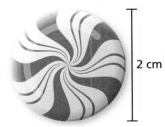
2 cm

12.

1.5 ft

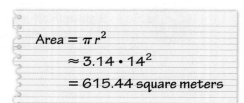

Area = πr^2

$\approx 3.14 \cdot 14^2$

$= 615.44$ square meters

13. **MP YOU BE THE TEACHER** Your friend finds the area of a circle with a diameter of 7 meters. Is your friend correct? Explain.

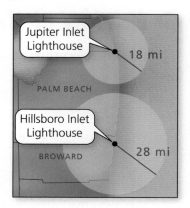

Jupiter Inlet Lighthouse — 18 mi

PALM BEACH

Hillsboro Inlet Lighthouse — 28 mi

BROWARD

14. **MP MODELING REAL LIFE** The diameter of a flour tortilla is 12 inches. What is the total area of two tortillas?

15. **MP MODELING REAL LIFE** The diameter of a coaster is 7 centimeters. What is the total area of five coasters?

16. **MP PROBLEM SOLVING** The Hillsboro Inlet Lighthouse lights up how much more area than the Jupiter Inlet Lighthouse?

FINDING THE AREA OF A SEMICIRCLE **Find the area of the semicircle.**

17.

18.

19.

├── 20 cm ──┤

├──── 24 in. ────┤

├──── 2 ft ────┤

20. **MP MODELING REAL LIFE** The plate for a microscope has a circumference of 100π millimeters. What is the area of the plate?

20 ft

21. **MP MODELING REAL LIFE** A dog is leashed to the corner of a house. How much running area does the dog have? Explain how you found your answer.

22. **MP REASONING** Target A has a circumference of 20 feet. Target B has a diameter of 3 feet. Both targets are the same distance away. Which target is easier to hit? Explain your reasoning.

23. **MP MODELING REAL LIFE** A circular oil spill has a radius of 2 miles. After a day, the radius of the oil spill increases by 3 miles. By how many square miles does the area of the oil spill increase?

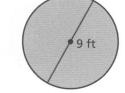

9 ft

24. **FINDING AN AREA** Find the area of the circle in square yards.

25. **MP REPEATED REASONING** What happens to the circumference and the area of a circle when you double the radius? triple the radius? Justify your answer.

26. **CRITICAL THINKING** Is the area of a semicircle with a diameter of *x greater than, less than,* or *equal to* the area of a circle with a diameter of $\frac{1}{2}x$? Explain.

9.3 Perimeters and Areas of Composite Figures

Learning Target: Find perimeters and areas of composite figures.

Success Criteria:
- I can use a grid to estimate perimeters and areas.
- I can identify the shapes that make up a composite figure.
- I can find the perimeters and areas of shapes that make up composite figures.

EXPLORATION 1

Submitting a Bid

Work with a partner. You want to bid on a project for the pool shown. The project involves ordering and installing the brown tile that borders the pool, and ordering a custom-made tarp to cover the surface of the pool. In the figure, each grid square represents 1 square foot.

- **You pay $5 per linear foot for the tile.**
- **You pay $4 per square foot for the tarp.**
- **It takes you about 15 minutes to install each foot of tile.**

a. Estimate the total cost for the tile and the tarp.

b. Write a bid for how much you will charge for the project. Include the hourly wage you will receive. Estimate your total profit.

Math Practice

Simplify a Situation

How does using a grid help you make approximations for the perimeter and area of the pool?

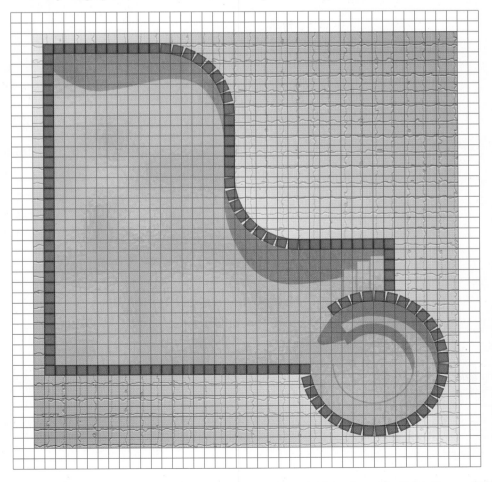

Key Vocabulary 🔊
composite figure,
p. 376

A **composite figure** is made up of triangles, squares, rectangles, semicircles, and other two-dimensional figures.

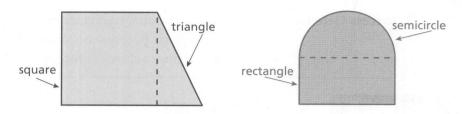

To find the perimeter of a composite figure, find the distance around the figure. To find the area of a composite figure, separate it into figures with areas you know how to find. Then find the sum of the areas of those figures.

EXAMPLE 1 **Estimating Perimeter and Area**

Estimate (a) the perimeter and (b) the area of the arrow.

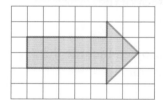

a.

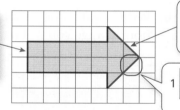

Count the number of grid square lengths around the arrow. There are 14.

Count the number of diagonal lengths around the arrow. There are 4.

Estimate the diagonal length to be 1.5 units.

Length of 14 grid square lengths: $14 \times 1 = 14$ units

Length of 4 diagonal lengths: $4 \times 1.5 = 6$ units

▷ So, the perimeter is about $14 + 6 = 20$ units.

b.

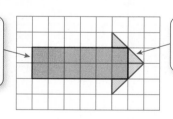

Count the number of squares that lie entirely in the figure. There are 12.

Count the number of half squares in the figure. There are 4.

Area of 12 squares: $12 \times 1 = 12$ square units

Area of 4 half squares: $4 \times 0.5 = 2$ square units

▷ So, the area is $12 + 2 = 14$ square units.

Try It

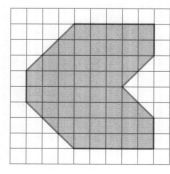

1. Estimate the perimeter and the area of the figure.

🔊 *Multi-Language Glossary at BigIdeasMath.com*

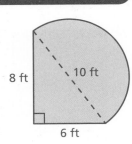

EXAMPLE 2 **Finding Perimeter and Area**

Find (a) the perimeter and (b) the area of the figure.

a. The figure is made up of a triangle and a semicircle.

The distance around the triangular part of the figure is $6 + 8 = 14$ feet. The distance around the semicircle is one-half the circumference of a circle with a diameter of 10 feet.

$$\frac{C}{2} = \frac{\pi d}{2}$$ Divide the circumference by 2.

$$\approx \frac{3.14 \cdot 10}{2}$$ Substitute 3.14 for π and 10 for d.

$$= 15.7$$ Simplify.

▷ So, the perimeter is about $14 + 15.7 = 29.7$ feet.

b. Find the area of the triangle and the area of the semicircle.

Area of Triangle

$$A = \frac{1}{2}bh$$

$$= \frac{1}{2}(6)(8)$$

$$= 24$$

Area of Semicircle

$$A = \frac{\pi r^2}{2}$$

$$\approx \frac{3.14 \cdot 5^2}{2}$$

$$= 39.25$$

The semicircle has a radius of $\frac{10}{2} = 5$ feet.

▷ So, the area is about $24 + 39.25 = 63.25$ square feet.

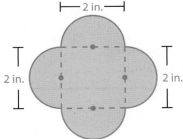

Try It

2. Find the perimeter and the area of the figure.

 Self-Assessment for Concepts & Skills

Solve each exercise. Then rate your understanding of the success criteria in your journal.

3. ESTIMATING PERIMETER AND AREA
Estimate the perimeter and area of the figure at the right.

4. FINDING PERIMETER AND AREA Identify the shapes that make up the figure at the left. Then find the perimeter and area of the figure.

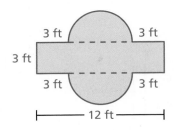

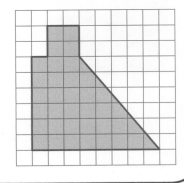

EXAMPLE 3 **Modeling Real Life**

The center circle of the basketball court has a radius of 3 feet and is painted blue. The rest of the court is stained brown. One gallon of wood stain covers 150 square feet. How many gallons of wood stain do you need to cover the brown portions of the court?

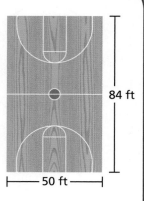

84 ft

50 ft

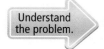 **Understand the problem.**

You are given dimensions of a basketball court. You are asked to determine the number of gallons of wood stain needed to stain the brown portions of the court when one gallon of wood stain covers 150 square feet.

Make a plan.

Find the entire area of the rectangular court. Then subtract the area of the center circle and divide by 150.

 **Solve and check.**

Area of Rectangle	*Area of Circle*
$A = \ell w$	$A = \pi r^2$
$= 84(50)$	$\approx 3.14 \cdot 3^2$
$= 4200$	$= 28.26$

The area that is stained is about $4200 - 28.26 = 4171.74$ square feet.

Because one gallon of wood stain covers 150 square feet, you need $4171.74 \div 150 \approx 27.8$ gallons of wood stain.

Check Reasonableness
The circle covers a small area of the court. So, it makes sense that you need just less than $\dfrac{84(50)}{150} = 28$ gallons of wood stain. ✓

 Self-Assessment *for Problem Solving*

Solve each exercise. Then rate your understanding of the success criteria in your journal.

5. A farmer wants to seed and fence a section of land. Fencing costs $27 per yard. Grass seed costs $2 per square foot. How much does it cost to fence and seed the pasture?

255 ft   255 ft
120 ft
450 ft   450 ft
450 ft

6. **DIG DEEPER!** In each room shown, you plan to put down carpet and add a wallpaper border around the ceiling. Which room needs more carpeting? more wallpaper?

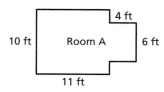

4 ft
10 ft   Room A   6 ft
11 ft

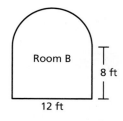

Room B
8 ft
12 ft

9.3 Practice

 Go to *BigIdeasMath.com* to get HELP with solving the exercises.

▶ Review & Refresh

Find the area of the circle. Use 3.14 or $\frac{22}{7}$ for π.

1.

4 mm

2.
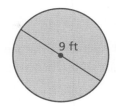
9 ft

Find the missing dimension. Use the scale 1 : 5.

	Item	Model	Actual
3.	House	Height: 6 ft	Height: ___ ft
4.	Garden hose	Length: ___ ft	Length: 20 yd
5.	Fountain	Depth: 20 cm	Depth: ___ m
6.	Bicycle wheel	Diameter: ___ in.	Diameter: 2 ft

▶▶ Concepts, Skills, & Problem Solving

ESTIMATING PERIMETER AND AREA **You build a patio with a brick border.** (See Exploration 1, p. 375.)

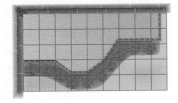

7. Estimate the perimeter of the patio.

8. Estimate the area of the patio.

ESTIMATING PERIMETER AND AREA **Estimate the perimeter and the area of the shaded figure.**

9.
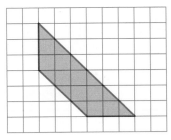

10.
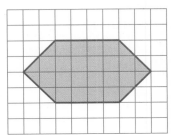

11.
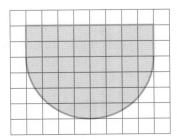

12.
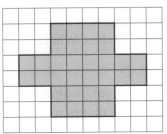

13.
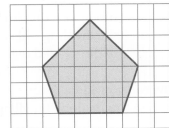

14.
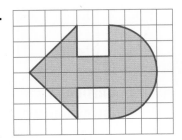

FINDING PERIMETER AND AREA Find the perimeter and the area of the figure.

15.
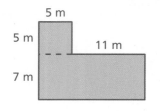

16.
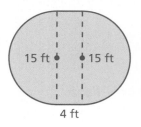

17.
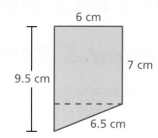

18. MP **YOU BE THE TEACHER** Your friend finds the perimeter of the figure. Is your friend correct? Explain your reasoning.

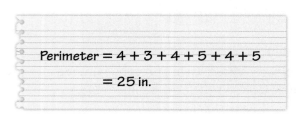

Perimeter = 4 + 3 + 4 + 5 + 4 + 5

= 25 in.

19. MP **LOGIC** A running track has six lanes. Explain why the starting points for the six runners are staggered. Draw a diagram as part of your explanation.

20. MP **PROBLEM SOLVING** You run around the perimeter of the baseball field at a rate of 9 feet per second. How long does it take you to run around the baseball field?

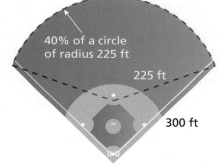

21. MP **STRUCTURE** The figure at the right is made up of a square and a rectangle. Find the area of the shaded region.

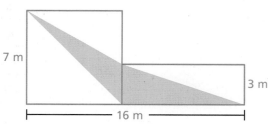

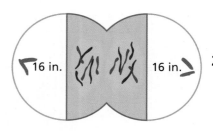

22. **DIG DEEPER!** Your friend makes a two-dimensional model of a dividing cell as shown. The total area of the dividing cell is 350 square inches. What is the area of the shaded region?

23. **CRITICAL THINKING** How can you add a figure to a composite figure without increasing its perimeter? Can this be done for all figures? Draw a diagram to support your answer.

9.4 Constructing Polygons

Learning Target: Construct a polygon with given measures.

Success Criteria:
- I can use technology to draw polygons.
- I can determine whether given measures result in one triangle, many triangles, or no triangle.
- I can draw polygons given angle measures or side lengths.

EXPLORATION 1

Using Technology to Draw Polygons

Work with a partner.

a. Use geometry software to draw each polygon with the given side lengths or angle measures, if possible. Complete the table.

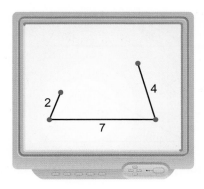

Side Lengths or Angle Measures	How many figures are possible?
i. 4 cm, 6 cm, 7 cm	
ii. 2 cm, 6 cm, 7 cm	
iii. 2 cm, 4 cm, 7 cm	
iv. 2 cm, 4 cm, 6 cm	
v. 2 in., 3 in., 3 in., 5 in.	
vi. 1 in., 1 in., 3 in., 6 in.	
vii. 1 in., 1 in., 3 in., 4 in.	
viii. 90°, 60°, 30°	
ix. 100°, 40°, 20°	
x. 50°, 60°, 70°	
xi. 20°, 80°, 100°	
xii. 20°, 50°, 50°, 60°	
xiii. 30°, 80°, 120°, 130°	
xiv. 60°, 60°, 120°, 120°	

Math Practice

Use Technology to Explore

How does geometry software help you learn about characteristics of triangles and quadrilaterals?

b. Without constructing, how can you tell whether it is possible to draw a triangle given three angle measures? three side lengths? Explain your reasoning.

c. Without constructing, how can you tell whether it is possible to draw a quadrilateral given four angle measures? four side lengths? Explain your reasoning.

You can draw a triangle with three given angle measures when the sum of the angle measures is 180°.

EXAMPLE 1 Constructing Triangles Using Angle Measures

Draw a triangle with angle measures of 30°, 60°, and 90°, if possible.

Because 30° + 60° + 90° = 180°, you can draw a triangle with the given angle measures.

Step 1: Draw the 30° angle.   **Step 2:** Draw the 60° angle.

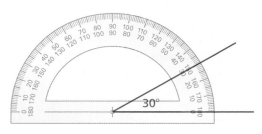   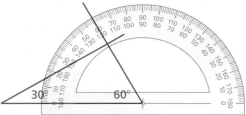

Step 3: Measure the remaining angle.
The angle measure is 90°.

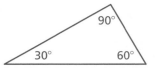

Try It **Draw a triangle with the given angle measures, if possible.**

1. 45°, 45°, 90°   **2.** 100°, 55°, 25°   **3.** 60°, 60°, 80°

EXAMPLE 2 Constructing Triangles Using Angles and Sides

Draw a triangle with side lengths of 3 centimeters and 4 centimeters that meet at a 20° angle.

Step 1: Draw a 20° angle.

Step 2: Use a ruler to mark 3 centimeters on one ray and 4 centimeters on the other ray.

Step 3: Draw the third side to form the triangle.

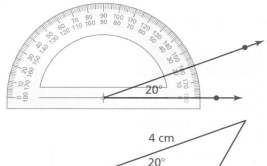

> In Example 1, you can change the lengths of the sides to create many different triangles that meet the criteria. In Example 2, only one triangle is possible.

Try It

4. Draw a triangle with side lengths of 1 inch and 2 inches that meet at a 60° angle.

You can draw a triangle with three given side lengths when the sum of the lengths of any two sides is greater than the length of the third side.

EXAMPLE 3 Constructing Triangles Using Side Lengths

Draw a triangle with the given side lengths, if possible.

a. **4 cm, 2 cm, 3 cm**

The sum of the lengths of any two sides is greater than the length of the third side.

$$4 \text{ cm} + 2 \text{ cm} > 3 \text{ cm} \qquad 4 \text{ cm} + 3 \text{ cm} > 2 \text{ cm} \qquad 2 \text{ cm} + 3 \text{ cm} > 4 \text{ cm}$$

So, you can draw a triangle with the given side lengths.

Step 1: Draw a 4-centimeter side.

Step 2: Use a compass to determine where the 2-centimeter side and the 3-centimeter side meet.

Step 3: The third vertex can be at either intersection point. Draw the triangle.

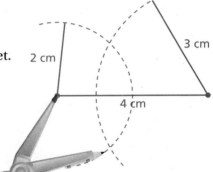

> In Example 3, only one triangle is possible. You can start with a different side length in Step 1, but the resulting triangle will have the same size and shape.

b. **2.5 in., 1 in., 1 in.**

Because 1 in. + 1 in. < 2.5 in., it is not possible to draw the triangle.

Check Try to draw the triangle. Draw a 2.5-inch side. Use a compass to show that the 1-inch sides cannot intersect.

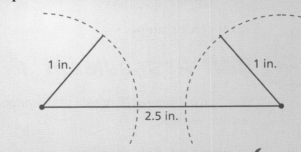

So, it is not possible to draw the triangle. ✓

Math Practice

Look for Structure
How can you change one of the side lengths in part (b) so that they form a triangle? Compare answers with a classmate.

Try It **Draw a triangle with the given side lengths, if possible.**

5. 2 cm, 2 cm, 5 cm   **6.** 4 cm, 3 cm, 3 cm   **7.** 1 cm, 4 cm, 5 cm

You can draw a quadrilateral with four given angle measures when the sum of the angle measures is 360°.

EXAMPLE 4 **Constructing a Quadrilateral**

Draw a quadrilateral with angle measures of 60°, 120°, 70°, and 110°, if possible.

Because 60° + 120° + 70° + 110° = 360°, you can draw a quadrilateral with the given angle measures.

Step 1: Draw a 60° angle and a 120° angle that each have one side on a line.

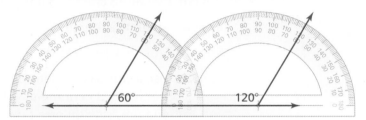

Step 2: Draw the remaining side at a 70° angle.

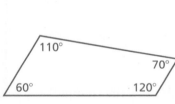

Step 3: Measure the remaining angle. The angle measure is 110°.

> **Try It** Draw a quadrilateral with the given angle measures, if possible.
>
> **8.** 100°, 90°, 65°, 105°   **9.** 100°, 40°, 20°, 20°

Self-Assessment for Concepts & Skills

Solve each exercise. Then rate your understanding of the success criteria in your journal.

DRAWING POLYGONS Draw a polygon with the given side lengths or angle measures, if possible.

10. 25 mm, 36 mm, 38 mm   **11.** 10°, 15°, 155°

12. 20°, 45°, 50°, 65°   **13.** 50°, 90°, 110°, 110°

14. USING SIDE LENGTHS Can you construct *one*, *many*, or *no* triangle(s) with side lengths of 3 inches, 4 inches, and 8 inches? Explain.

EXAMPLE 5 **Modeling Real Life**

You enclose a flower bed using landscaping boards with lengths of 3 yards, 4 yards, and 5 yards. Estimate the area of the flower bed.

Understand the problem.
You know the lengths of boards used to enclose a triangular region. You are asked to estimate the area of the triangular region.

Make a plan.
Draw a triangle with side lengths of 3 yards, 4 yards, and 5 yards using a scale of 1 cm : 1 yd. Use the drawing to estimate the base and height of the flower bed. Then use the formula for the area of a triangle to estimate the area.

Solve and check.
Draw the triangle.

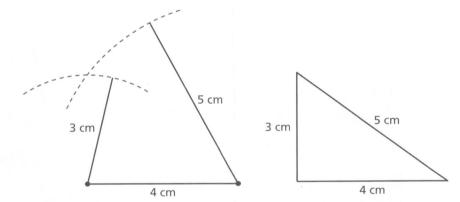

Another Method
Using a ruler, the height from the largest angle to the 5-centimeter side is about 2.4 centimeters. So, the area is about $\frac{1}{2}(2.4)(5) = 6$ yd². ✓

The shape of the flower bed appears to be a right triangle with a base length of 4 yards and a height of 3 yards.

▶ So, the area of the flower bed is about $A = \frac{1}{2}(4)(3) = 6$ square yards.

 Self-Assessment for Problem Solving

Solve each exercise. Then rate your understanding of the success criteria in your journal.

15. A triangular pen has fence lengths of 6 feet, 8 feet, and 10 feet. Create a scale drawing of the pen.

16. The front of a cabin is the shape of a triangle. The angles of the triangle are 40°, 70°, and 70°. Can you determine the height of the cabin? If not, what information do you need?

17. **DIG DEEPER!** Two rooftops have triangular patios. One patio has side lengths of 9 meters, 10 meters, and 11 meters. The other has side lengths of 6 meters, 10 meters, and 15 meters. Which patio has a greater area? Explain.

Go to *BigIdeasMath.com* to get HELP with solving the exercises.

▶ Review & Refresh

Find the perimeter and area of the figure.

1. 2 in.
2 in. 2 in.
2 in.
1 in.

2.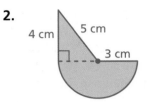
4 cm   5 cm
3 cm

Use a tree diagram to find the sample space and the total number of possible outcomes of the indicated event.

3. choosing a toothbrush

Toothbrush	
Type	Electric, Traditional
Strength	Extra soft, Soft, Medium

4. choosing a toy hoop

Toy Hoop	
Size	Small, Medium, Large
Color	Blue, Green, Orange, Pink, Purple, Yellow

▶▶ Concepts, Skills, & Problem Solving

USING TECHNOLOGY TO DRAW POLYGONS **Use geometry software to draw the polygon with the given side lengths or angle measures, if possible.** (See Exploration 1, p. 381.)

5. 30°, 65°, 85°

6. 2 in., 3 in., 5 in.

7. 80°, 90°,100°, 110°

8. 2 cm, 2 cm, 5 cm, 5 cm

CONSTRUCTING TRIANGLES USING ANGLE MEASURES **Draw a triangle with the given angle measures, if possible.**

9. 40°, 50°, 90°

10. 20°, 40°, 120°

11. 38°, 42°, 110°

12. 54°, 60°, 66°

13. **ⓂⓅ YOU BE THE TEACHER** Your friend determines whether he can draw a triangle with angle measures of 10°, 40°, and 130°. Is your friend correct? Explain your reasoning.

> 10° + 40° < 130°
>
> Because the sum of the measure of two angles is not greater than the measure of the third angle, you cannot draw a triangle.

CONSTRUCTING TRIANGLES USING ANGLES AND SIDES Draw a triangle with the given description.

14. side lengths of 1 inch and 2 inches meet at a 50° angle

15. side lengths of 7 centimeters and 9 centimeters meet at a 120° angle

16. a 95° angle connects to a 15° angle by a side of length 2 inches

17. a 70° angle connects to a 70° angle by a side of length 4 centimeters

CONSTRUCTING TRIANGLES USING SIDE LENGTHS Draw a triangle with the given side lengths, if possible.

18. 4 in., 5 in., 10 in.

19. 10 mm, 30 mm, 50 mm

20. 5 cm, 5 cm, 8 cm

21. 8 mm, 12 mm, 13 mm

22. **MP MODELING REAL LIFE** Can you construct a triangular case using two pieces of wood that are 12 inches long and one piece of wood that is 25 inches long? Explain.

23. **MP MODELING REAL LIFE** Can you construct a warning triangle using three pieces of plastic that are each 6 inches long? Explain.

24. **MP LOGIC** You are constructing a triangle. You draw the first angle, as shown. Your friend says that you must be constructing an acute triangle. Is your friend correct? Explain your reasoning.

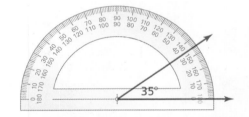

35°

USING ANGLES AND SIDES Determine whether you can construct *one, many,* or *no* triangle(s) with the given description. Explain your reasoning.

25. a triangle with one angle measure of 60° and one side length of 4 centimeters

26. a scalene triangle with side lengths of 3 centimeters and 7 centimeters

27. an isosceles triangle with two side lengths of 4 inches that meet at an 80° angle

28. a triangle with one angle measure of 60°, one angle measure of 70°, and a side length of 10 centimeters between the two angles

29. a triangle with one angle measure of 20°, one angle measure of 35°, and a side of length 3 inches that is between the two angles

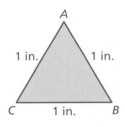

A

1 in.   1 in.

C   1 in.   B

30. **MP REASONING** A triangle is shown.

    a. Construct a triangle with side lengths twice those of the triangle shown. Does the new triangle have the same angle measures?

    b. How can you change the side lengths of the triangle so that the measure of $\angle A$ increases?

CONSTRUCTING QUADRILATERALS Draw a quadrilateral with the given angle measures, if possible.

31. 60°, 60°, 120°, 120°

32. 50°, 60°, 110°, 150°

33. 20°, 30°, 150°, 160°

34. 10°, 10°, 10°, 150°

CONSTRUCTING SPECIAL QUADRILATERALS Construct a quadrilateral with the given description.

35. a rectangle with side lengths of 1 inch and 2 inches

36. a kite with side lengths of 4 centimeters and 7 centimeters

37. a trapezoid with base angles of 40°

38. a rhombus with side lengths of 10 millimeters

39. **MP** **REASONING** A quadrilateral has side lengths of 6 units, 2 units, and 3 units as shown. How many quadrilaterals can be formed given a fourth side with a fixed length? Explain.

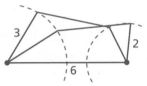

40. **MP** **REASONING** What types of quadrilaterals can you form using four side lengths of 7 units? Use drawings to support your conclusion.

41. **MP** **MODELING REAL LIFE** A triangular section of a farm is enclosed by fences that are 2 meters, 6 meters, and 7 meters long. Estimate the area of the section.

42. **MP** **MODELING REAL LIFE** A chemical spill expert sets up a triangular caution zone using cones. Cones A and B are 14 meters apart. Cones B and C are 22 meters apart. Cones A and C are 34 meters apart. Estimate the area of the caution zone.

43. **MP** **MODELING REAL LIFE** A search region is in the shape of an equilateral triangle. The measure of one side of the region is 20 miles. Make a scale drawing of the search region. Estimate the area of the search region.

44. **MP** **REASONING** A triangle has fixed side lengths of 2 and 14.

a. How many triangles can you construct? Use the figure below to explain your reasoning.

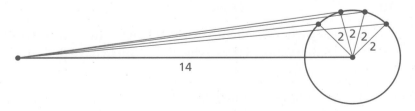

b. Is the unknown side length of the triangle also fixed? Explain.

9.5 Finding Unknown Angle Measures

Learning Target: Use facts about angle relationships to find unknown angle measures.

Success Criteria:
- I can identify adjacent, complementary, supplementary, and vertical angles.
- I can use equations to find unknown angle measures.
- I can find unknown angle measures in real-life situations.

EXPLORATION 1

Using Rules About Angles

Work with a partner. The diagram shows pairs of *adjacent* angles and *vertical* angles. Vertical angles cannot be adjacent.

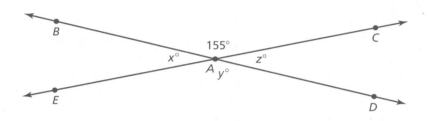

a. Which pair(s) of angles are adjacent angles? Explain.

b. Which pair(s) of angles are vertical angles? Explain.

c. Without using a protractor, find the values of x, y, and z. Explain your reasoning.

d. Make a conjecture about the measures of any two vertical angles.

e. Test your conjecture in part (d) using the diagram below. Explain why your conjecture is or is *not* true.

Math Practice

Use Definitions
How can you use the definition of supplementary angles to explain why your conjecture is or is *not* true?

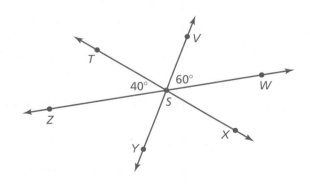

Key Ideas

Adjacent Angles

Words Two angles are **adjacent angles** when they share a common side and have the same vertex.

Complementary Angles

Words Two angles are **complementary angles** when the sum of their measures is 90°.

Supplementary Angles

Words Two angles are **supplementary angles** when the sum of their measures is 180°.

Vertical Angles

Words Two angles are **vertical angles** when they are opposite angles formed by the intersection of two lines. Vertical angles have the same measure because they are both supplementary to the same angle.

Reading

Angles that have the same measures are called *congruent angles.*

EXAMPLE 1   **Naming Angles**

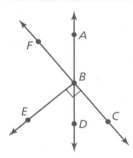

Name a pair of (a) adjacent angles, (b) complementary angles, (c) supplementary angles, and (d) vertical angles in the figure.

a. $\angle ABC$ and $\angle ABF$ share a common side and have the same vertex B.

▶ So, $\angle ABC$ and $\angle ABF$ are adjacent angles.

b. $\angle EBC$ is a right angle. This means that the sum of the measure of $\angle EBD$ and the measure of $\angle CBD$ is 90°.

▶ So, $\angle EBD$ and $\angle CBD$ are complementary angles.

c. $\angle ABC$ and $\angle DBC$ make up a straight angle. This means that the sum of the measure of $\angle ABC$ and the measure of $\angle DBC$ is 180°.

▶ So, $\angle ABC$ and $\angle DBC$ are supplementary angles.

d. $\angle ABF$ and $\angle CBD$ are opposite angles formed by the intersection of two lines.

▶ So, $\angle ABF$ and $\angle CBD$ are vertical angles.

Try It

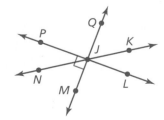

1. Name a pair of (a) adjacent angles, (b) complementary angles, (c) supplementary angles, and (d) vertical angles in the figure.

🔊 *Multi-Language Glossary at BigIdeasMath.com*

EXAMPLE 2 **Using Pairs of Angles**

Classify each pair of angles. Then find the value of x.

a.

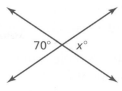

The angles are vertical angles. Vertical angles have the same measure.

▷ So, the value of x is 70.

> **Remember**
>
> When two or more adjacent angles form a larger angle, the sum of the measures of the smaller angles is equal to the measure of the larger angle.

b.

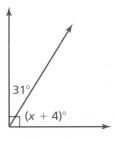

The angles are adjacent angles. Because the angles make up a right angle, the angles are also complementary angles, and the sum of their measures is 90°.

$(x + 4) + 31 = 90$ Write equation.

$x + 35 = 90$ Combine like terms.

$x = 55$ Subtract 35 from each side.

▷ So, the value of x is 55.

c.

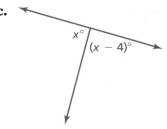

The angles are adjacent angles. Because the angles make up a straight angle, the angles are also supplementary angles, and the sum of their measures is 180°.

$x + (x - 4) = 180$ Write equation.

$2x - 4 = 180$ Combine like terms.

$2x = 184$ Add 4 to each side.

$x = 92$ Divide each side by 2.

▷ So, the value of x is 92.

Try It **Classify the pair of angles. Then find the value of x.**

2.

3.

4.

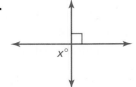

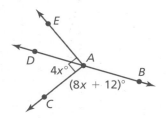

EXAMPLE 3 **Finding an Angle Measure**

Find the measure of ∠EAB.

To find the measure of ∠EAB, subtract the sum of the measures of ∠BAC and ∠EAC from 360°.

To find the measure of ∠BAC, find the value of x. ∠DAC and ∠BAC are supplementary angles. So, the sum of their measures is 180°.

$4x + (8x + 12) = 180$	Write equation.
$12x + 12 = 180$	Combine like terms.
$12x = 168$	Subtract 12 from each side.
$x = 14$	Divide each side by 12.

So, the measure of ∠BAC is 8(14) + 12 = 124°.

Because ∠EAC is a right angle, it has a measure of 90°.

▶ So, the measure of ∠EAB is 360 − (124 + 90) = 146°.

> **Remember**
>
> The sum of the measures of the angles around a point is equal to 360°.

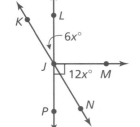

Try It **Find the measure of the indicated angle in the diagram.**

5. ∠NJM   **6.** ∠KJP   **7.** ∠KJM

Self-Assessment *for Concepts & Skills*

Solve each exercise. Then rate your understanding of the success criteria in your journal.

8. NAMING ANGLES Name a pair of (a) adjacent angles, (b) complementary angles, (c) supplementary angles, and (d) vertical angles in the figure at the left.

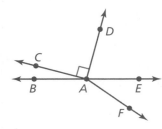

FINDING ANGLE MEASURES **Find the value of x.**

9.

10.

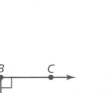

11. WHICH ONE DOESN'T BELONG? Which pair of angles does *not* belong with the other three? Explain your reasoning.

| ∠FBA, ∠FBE | ∠CBD, ∠DBF | ∠DBE, ∠DBC | ∠FBA, ∠EBD |

EXAMPLE 4 **Modeling Real Life**

A city worker designs an intersection of three roads that will be constructed next year. The measure of the angle between any two roads must be at least 60° in order for vehicles to turn safely. Does the design shown meet the requirement?

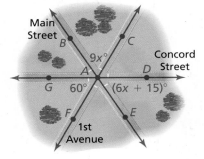

Main Street
B
C
9x°
A
D Concord Street
G 60° (6x + 15)°
F E
1st Avenue

Because ∠GAF and ∠DAC are vertical angles, you know that the measure of ∠DAC is 60°. Because ∠BAC, ∠DAC, and ∠EAD make up a straight angle, you know that the sum of their measures is 180°. Use this information to write and solve an equation for x. Then determine whether any of the angle measures between two roads is less than 60°.

$9x + 60 + (6x + 15) = 180$	Write equation.
$15x + 75 = 180$	Combine like terms.
$15x = 105$	Subtract 75 from each side.
$x = 7$	Divide each side by 15.

∠EAD has a measure of $6(7) + 15 = 57°$.

▷ So, the measure of ∠EAD is less than 60°, and the design does not meet the requirement.

Self-Assessment for Problem Solving

Solve each exercise. Then rate your understanding of the success criteria in your journal.

x°
x° x°

12. What is the angle between any two windmill blades in the windmill at the left? Justify your answer.

13. A hockey puck strikes a wall at an angle of 30°. The puck then travels away from the wall at the same angle. Find the value of *y*. Explain your reasoning.

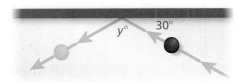

y°   30°

14. The laptop screen turns off when the angle between the keyboard and the screen is less than 20°. How many more degrees can the laptop screen close before the screen turns off?

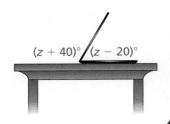

$(z + 40)°$ $(z - 20)°$

Section 9.5 Finding Unknown Angle Measures **393**

Go to *BigIdeasMath.com* to get HELP with solving the exercises.

▶ Review & Refresh

Draw a triangle with the given side lengths, if possible.

1. 1 in., 3 in., 4 in.

2. 4 cm, 4 cm, 7 cm

Solve the inequality. Graph the solution.

3. $-8y \leq 40$

4. $1.1z > -3.3$

5. $\frac{1}{3}x \geq 2.5$

▶▶ Concepts, Skills, & Problem Solving

USING RULES ABOUT ANGLES **The diagram shows pairs of** *adjacent* **angles and** *vertical* **angles.** (See Exploration 1, p. 389.)

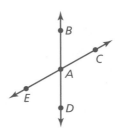

6. Which pair(s) of angles are adjacent angles? Explain.

7. Which pair(s) of angles are vertical angles? Explain.

NAMING ANGLES **Use the figure shown.**

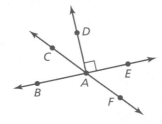

8. Name a pair of adjacent angles.

9. Name a pair of complementary angles.

10. Name a pair of supplementary angles.

11. Name a pair of vertical angles.

12. **MP YOU BE THE TEACHER** Your friend names a pair of angles with the same measure. Is your friend correct? Explain your reasoning.

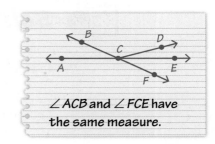

∠ACB and ∠FCE have the same measure.

ADJACENT AND VERTICAL ANGLES **Tell whether the angles are** *adjacent*, *vertical*, **or** *neither*. **Explain.**

13.

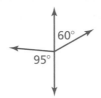

14.

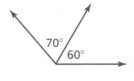

15.

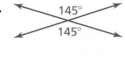

COMPLEMENTARY AND SUPPLEMENTARY ANGLES **Tell whether the angles are** *complementary*, *supplementary*, **or** *neither*. **Explain.**

16.

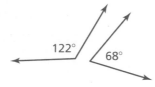

17.

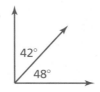

18.

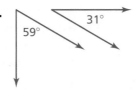

19. **MP YOU BE THE TEACHER**
Your friend names a pair of supplementary angles. Is your friend correct? Explain.

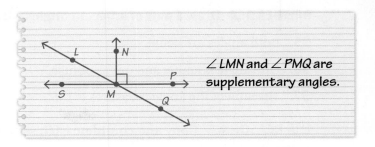

∠LMN and ∠PMQ are supplementary angles.

USING PAIRS OF ANGLES Classify the pair of angles. Then find the value of x.

20.

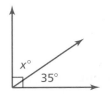

$x°$
$35°$

21.

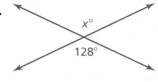

$x°$
$128°$

22.

$117°$ $x°$

23.

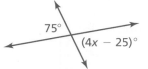

$75°$
$(4x - 25)°$

24.

$4x°$
$2x°$

25.

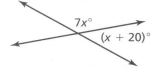

$7x°$
$(x + 20)°$

26.

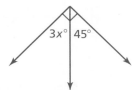

$3x°$ $45°$

27.

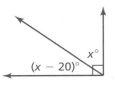

$(x - 20)°$
$x°$

28.

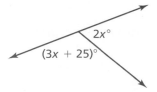

$2x°$
$(3x + 25)°$

29. **MP MODELING REAL LIFE** What is the measure of each angle formed by the intersection? Explain.

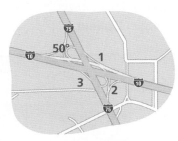

30. **MP MODELING REAL LIFE** A tributary joins a river at an angle. Find the value of x. Explain.

$x°$ $(2x + 21)°$

31. **MP MODELING REAL LIFE** The iron cross is a skiing trick in which the tips of the skis are crossed while the skier is airborne. Find the value of x in the iron cross shown.

$127°$ $(2x + 41)°$

FINDING ANGLE MEASURES Find all angle measures in the diagram.

32.

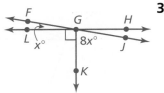

$x°$
$8x°$

33.

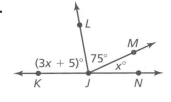

$(3x + 5)°$ $75°$
$x°$

34.

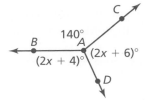

$140°$
B $(2x + 6)°$
$(2x + 4)°$

OPEN-ENDED Draw a pair of adjacent angles with the given description.

35. Both angles are acute.

36. One angle is acute, and one is obtuse.

37. The sum of the angle measures is 135°.

MP REASONING Copy and complete each sentence with *always, sometimes,* or *never.*

38. If *x* and *y* are complementary angles, then both *x* and *y* are_____ acute.

39. If *x* and *y* are supplementary angles, then *x* is_____ acute.

40. If *x* is a right angle, then *x* is_____ acute.

41. If *x* and *y* are complementary angles, then *x* and *y* are _____ adjacent.

42. If *x* and *y* are supplementary angles, then *x* and *y* are_____vertical.

43. **MP REASONING** Draw a figure in which ∠1 and ∠2 are acute vertical angles, ∠3 is a right angle adjacent to ∠2, and the sum of the measure of ∠1 and the measure of ∠4 is 180°.

44. **MP STRUCTURE** Describe the relationship between the two angles represented by the graph shown at the right.

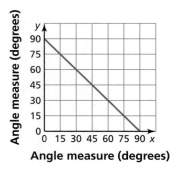

45. **MP STRUCTURE** Consider the figure shown at the left. Use a ruler to extend both rays into lines. What do you notice about the three new angles that are formed?

46. **OPEN-ENDED** Give an example of an angle that can be a supplementary angle but cannot be a complementary angle to another angle. Explain.

47. **MP MODELING REAL LIFE** The *vanishing point* of the picture is represented by point *B*.

   a. The measure of ∠*ABD* is 6.2 times greater than the measure of ∠*CBD*. Find the measure of ∠*CBD*.

   b. ∠*FBE* and ∠*EBD* are congruent. Find the measure of ∠*FBE*.

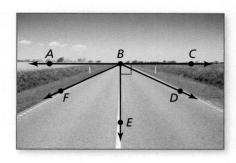

48. **CRITICAL THINKING** The measures of two complementary angles have a ratio of 3 : 2. What is the measure of the larger angle?

49. **MP REASONING** Two angles are vertical angles. What are their measures if they are also complementary angles? supplementary angles?

50. **MP PROBLEM SOLVING** Find the values of *x* and *y*.

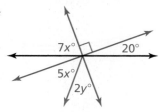

Connecting Concepts

▶ *Using the Problem-Solving Plan*

1. A dart is equally likely to hit any point on the board shown. Find the theoretical probability that a dart hitting the board scores 100 points.

25
50
100

4 in.

Understand the problem. ➤ You are given the dimensions of a circular dart board. You are asked to find the theoretical probability of hitting the center circle.

Make a plan. ➤ Find the area of the center circle and the area of the entire dart board. To find the theoretical probability of scoring 100 points, divide the area of the center circle by the area of the entire dart board.

Solve and check. ➤ Use the plan to solve the problem. Then check your solution.

2. A scale drawing of a window is shown. Find the perimeter and the area of the actual window. Justify your answer.

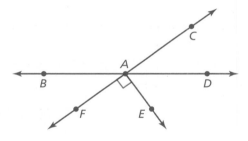

1 cm : 2 ft

3. $\angle CAD$ makes up 20% of a pair of supplementary angles. Find the measure of $\angle DAE$. Justify your answer.

C
A
B
D
F
E

Performance Task

Finding the Area and Perimeter of a Track

At the beginning of the this chapter, you watched a STEAM video called "Track and Field". You are now ready to complete the performance task related to this video, available at *BigIdeasMath.com*. Be sure to use the problem-solving plan as you work through the performance task.

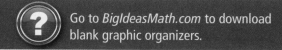
▶ Review Vocabulary

Write the definition and give an example of each vocabulary term.

circle, *p. 362*

center, *p. 362*

radius, *p. 362*

diameter, *p. 362*

circumference, *p. 363*

pi, *p. 363*

semicircle, *p. 364*

composite figure, *p. 376*

adjacent angles, *p. 390*

complementary angles, *p. 390*

supplementary angles, *p. 390*

vertical angles, *p. 390*

▶ Graphic Organizers

You can use a **Four Square** to organize information about a concept. Each of the four squares can be a category, such as definition, vocabulary, example, non-example, words, algebra, table, numbers, visual, graph, or equation. Here is an example of a Four Square for *circumference*.

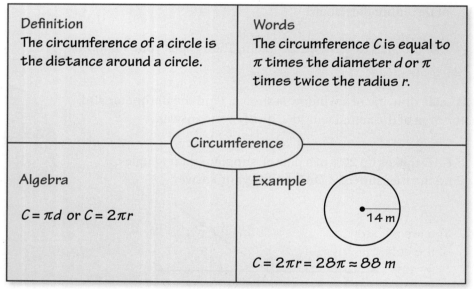

Choose and complete a graphic organizer to help you study each topic.

1. area of a circle

2. semicircle

3. composite figure

4. constructing triangles

5. constructing quadrilaterals

6. complementary angles

7. supplementary angles

8. vertical angles

"How do you like my Four Square on rubber duckies? Whenever I have my doggy bath, I insist that my ducky is with me."

Chapter Self-Assessment

As you complete the exercises, use the scale below to rate your understanding of the success criteria in your journal.

1	2	3	4
I do not understand.	I can do it with help.	I can do it on my own.	I can teach someone else.

9.1 Circles and Circumference (pp. 361–368)

Learning Target: Find the circumference of a circle.

1. What is the radius of a circular lid with a diameter of 5 centimeters?

2. The radius of a circle is 25 millimeters. Find the diameter.

Find the circumference of the object. Use 3.14 or $\frac{22}{7}$ for π.

3.
6 mm

4.
1.5 ft

5.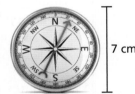
7 cm

6. You are placing non-slip tape along the perimeter of the bottom of a semicircle-shaped doormat. How much tape will you save applying the tape to the perimeter of the inside semicircle of the doormat? Justify your answer.

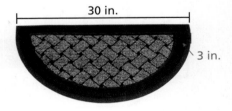
30 in.
3 in.

7. You need to carry a circular cake through a 32-inch wide doorway without tilting it. The circumference of the cake is 100 inches. Will the cake fit through the doorway? Explain.

C = 44 m

8. Estimate the radius of the Big Ben clock face in London.

9. Describe and solve a real-life problem that involves finding the circumference of a circle.

9.2 Areas of Circles *(pp. 369–374)*

Learning Target: Find the area of a circle.

Find the area of the circle. Use 3.14 or $\frac{22}{7}$ for π.

10.

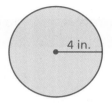

4 in.

11.

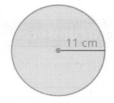

11 cm

12.

42 mm

13. A desktop is shaped like a semicircle with a diameter of 28 inches. What is the area of the desktop?

14. An ecologist is studying an algal bloom that has formed on the entire surface of a circular pond. What is the area of the surface of the pond covered by the algal bloom?

28 ft

15. A knitted pot holder is shaped like a circle. Its radius is 3.5 inches. What is its area?

9.3 Perimeters and Areas of Composite Figures *(pp. 375–380)*

Learning Target: Find perimeters and areas of composite figures.

Find the perimeter and the area of the figure.

16.

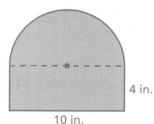

4 in.

10 in.

17.

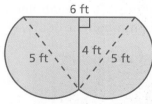

6 ft

5 ft 4 ft 5 ft

18. GARDEN You want to fence part of a yard to make a vegetable garden. How many feet of fencing do you need to surround the garden?

12 ft

14 ft

8 ft

10 ft

18 ft

9.4 Constructing Polygons (pp. 381–388)

Learning Target: Construct a polygon with given measures.

Draw a triangle with the given description, if possible.

19. a triangle with angle measures of 15°, 75°, and 90°

20. a triangle with a 3-inch side and a 4-inch side that meet at a 30° angle

21. a triangle with side lengths of 5 centimeters, 8 centimeters, and 2 centimeters

Draw a quadrilateral with the given angle measures, if possible.

22. 110°, 80°, 70°, 100°

23. 105°, 15°, 20°, 40°

9.5 Finding Unknown Angle Measures (pp. 389–396)

Learning Target: Use facts about angle relationships to find unknown angle measures.

Use the figure shown.

24. Name a pair of adjacent angles.

25. Name a pair of complementary angles.

26. Name a pair of supplementary angles.

27. Name a pair of vertical angles.

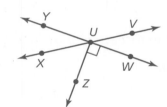

Classify the pair of angles. Then find the value of x.

28.

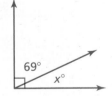

29.

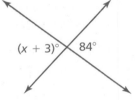

30.

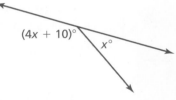

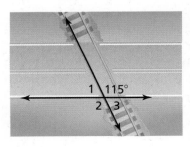

31. Describe two ways to find the measure of $\angle 2$.

32. Using the diagram from Exercises 24–27, find all the angle measures when $\angle XUY = 40°$.

1. Find the radius of a circle with a diameter of 17 inches.

Find (a) the circumference and (b) the area of the circle. Use 3.14 or $\frac{22}{7}$ for π.

2.
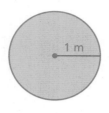
1 m

3.
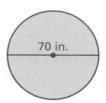
70 in.

Find (a) the perimeter and (b) the area of the figure. Use 3.14 or $\frac{22}{7}$ for π.

4.
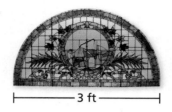
3 ft

5.
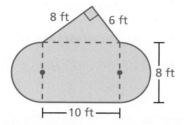
8 ft   6 ft
8 ft
10 ft

Draw a figure with the given description, if possible.

6. a triangle with sides of length 5 inches and 6 inches that meet at a 50° angle

7. a triangle with side lengths of 3 inches, 4 inches, and 5 inches

8. a quadrilateral with angle measures of 90°, 110°, 40°, and 120°

Classify each pair of angles. Then find the value of x.

9.
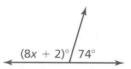
$(8x + 2)°$ / 74°

10.

$(x + 6)°$
56°

11.

113°
$x°$

12. A museum plans to rope off the perimeter of the L-shaped exhibit. How much rope does it need?

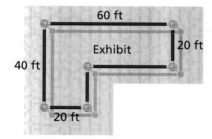
60 ft
20 ft
Exhibit
40 ft
20 ft

13. Draw a pair of adjacent angles that are neither complementary nor supplementary.

14. The circumference of a circle is 36.2 centimeters. What is the length of the diameter of the circle?

15 ft

15. The circular rug is placed on a square floor. The rug touches all four walls. How much of the floor space is *not* covered by the rug?

1. To make 6 servings of soup, you need 5 cups of chicken broth. You want to know how many servings you can make with 2 quarts of chicken broth. Which proportion should you use?

   A. $\dfrac{6}{5} = \dfrac{2}{x}$

   B. $\dfrac{6}{5} = \dfrac{x}{2}$

   C. $\dfrac{6}{5} = \dfrac{x}{8}$

   D. $\dfrac{5}{6} = \dfrac{x}{8}$

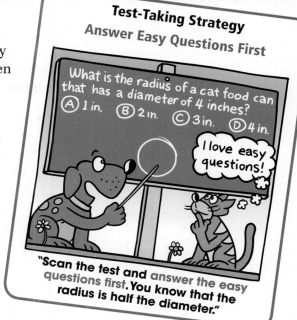

Test-Taking Strategy
Answer Easy Questions First

What is the radius of a cat food can that has a diameter of 4 inches?
 (A) 1 in.   (B) 2 in.   (C) 3 in.   (D) 4 in.

I love easy questions!

"Scan the test and answer the easy questions first. You know that the radius is half the diameter."

2. What is the value of x?

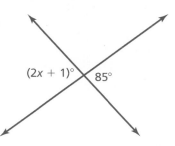

$(2x + 1)°$ $85°$

3. Your mathematics teacher described an inequality in words.

   > "5 less than the product of 7 and an unknown number is greater than 42."

   Which inequality matches your mathematics teacher's description?

   F. $7n - 5 < 42$

   G. $(7 - 5)n > 42$

   H. $5 - 7n > 42$

   I. $7n - 5 > 42$

4. What is the approximate area of the circle below? $\left(\text{Use } \dfrac{22}{7} \text{ for } \pi.\right)$

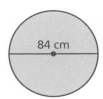

84 cm

   A. 132 cm^2

   B. 264 cm^2

   C. 5544 cm^2

   D. $22{,}176 \text{ cm}^2$

5. You have a 50% chance of selecting a blue marble from Bag A and a 20% chance of selecting a blue marble from Bag B. Use the provided simulation to answer the question, "What is the estimated probability of selecting a blue marble from both bags?"

> The digits 1 through 5 in the tens place represent selecting a blue marble from Bag A. The digits 1 and 2 in the ones place represent selecting a blue marble from Bag B.

52	66	73	68	75	28	35	47	48	02
16	68	49	03	77	35	92	78	06	06
58	18	89	39	24	80	32	41	77	21
32	40	96	59	86	01	12	00	94	73
40	71	28	61	01	24	37	25	03	25

F. 12% **G.** 16%

H. 24% **I.** 88%

6. Which proportion represents the problem?

"What number is 12% of 125?"

A. $\dfrac{n}{125} = \dfrac{12}{100}$ **B.** $\dfrac{12}{125} = \dfrac{n}{100}$

C. $\dfrac{125}{n} = \dfrac{12}{100}$ **D.** $\dfrac{12}{n} = \dfrac{125}{100}$

7. What is the approximate perimeter of the figure below? (Use 3.14 for π.)

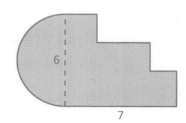

8. A savings account earns 2.5% simple interest per year. The principal is $850. What is the balance after 3 years?

F. $63.75 **G.** $871.25

H. $913.75 **J.** $7225

9. Two ponds each contain about 400 fish. The double box-and-whisker plot represents the weights of a random sample of 12 fish from each pond. Which statement about the measures of center and variation is true?

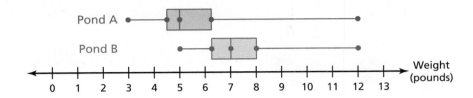

A. The variation in the samples is about the same, but the sample from Pond A has a greater median.

B. The variation in the samples is about the same, but the sample from Pond B has a greater median.

C. The measures of center and variation are about the same for both samples.

D. Neither the measures of center nor variation are the same for the samples.

10. A lawn sprinkler sprays water onto part of a circular region, as shown below.

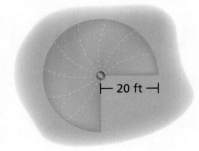

Part A What is the area, in square feet, of the region that the sprinkler sprays with water? Explain your reasoning. (Use 3.14 for π.)

Part B What is the perimeter, in feet, of the region that the sprinkler sprays with water? Explain your reasoning. (Use 3.14 for π.)

11. What is the least value of x for which $x - 12 \geq -8$ is true?

F. -20 G. -4

H. 4   I. 5

10 Surface Area and Volume

Chapter Learning Target:
Understand surface area and volume.

Chapter Success Criteria:
- ☐ I can describe the surface area and volume of different shapes.
- ☐ I can use formulas to find surface areas and volumes of solids.
- ■ I can solve real-life problems involving surface area and volume.
- ■ I can describe cross sections of solids.

STEAM Video: "Paper Measurements"

Paper Measurements

The thickness of a single piece of paper cannot be precisely measured using a ruler. What other method can you use to measure the thickness of a piece of paper?

**Watch the STEAM Video "Paper Measurements."
Then answer the following questions.**

1. A stack of 500 pieces of paper is 2 inches tall. How tall is a stack of 250 pieces? 100 pieces? 10 pieces? How thick is a single piece of paper?

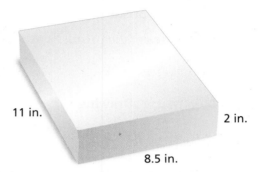

2. You have a circular notepad. How can you find the volume of one piece of paper in the notepad?

Performance Task

Volumes and Surface Areas of Small Objects

After completing this chapter, you will be able to use the concepts you learned to answer the questions in the *STEAM Video Performance Task*. You will be given the dimensions of a shipping box and the number of bouncy balls that fit in the box.

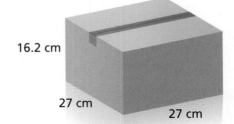

You will be asked to use the box to estimate the volume of each bouncy ball. Why might it be helpful to use the volume of a container of objects to estimate the volume of one of the objects?

Getting Ready for Chapter

Chapter Exploration

1. Work with a partner. Perform each step for each of the given dimensions.

   - Use 24 one-inch cubes to form a rectangular prism that has the given dimensions.
   - Make a sketch of the prism.
   - Find the surface area of the prism.

   a. $4 \times 3 \times 2$ **Drawing**   **Surface Area**

   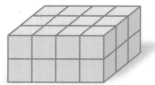   in.^{2}

   b. $1 \times 1 \times 24$ **c.** $1 \times 2 \times 12$ **d.** $1 \times 3 \times 8$

   e. $1 \times 4 \times 6$ **f.** $2 \times 2 \times 6$ **g.** $2 \times 4 \times 3$

2. **MP REASONING** Work with a partner. If two blocks of ice have the same volume, the block with the greater surface area will melt faster. The blocks below have equal volumes. Which block will melt faster? Explain your reasoning.

   1 ft

   1 ft   1 ft

   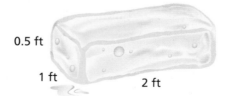

   0.5 ft

   1 ft   2 ft

Vocabulary

The following vocabulary terms are defined in this chapter. Think about what each term might mean and record your thoughts.

lateral surface area   slant height of a pyramid
regular pyramid   cross section

10.1 Surface Areas of Prisms

Learning Target: Find the surface area of a prism.

Success Criteria:
• I can use a formula to find the surface area of a prism.
• I can find the lateral surface area of a prism.

EXPLORATION 1

Writing a Formula for Surface Area

Work with a partner.

a. Use the diagrams to write a formula for the surface area of a rectangular prism. Explain your reasoning.

Math Practice

View as Components

Explain the meaning of each term in your formula.

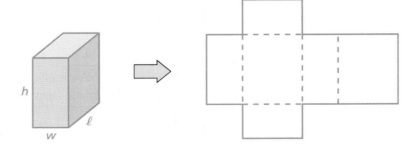

b. Choose dimensions for a rectangular prism. Then draw the prism and use your formula in part (a) to find the surface area.

EXPLORATION 2

Surface Areas of Prisms

Work with a partner.

a. Identify the solid represented by the net. Then find the surface area of the solid.

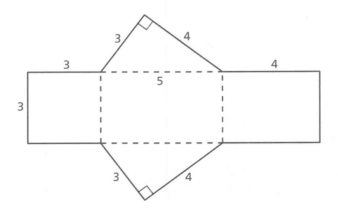

b. Describe a method for finding the surface area of any prism.

Key Vocabulary 🔊
lateral surface area,
p. 412

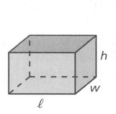 **Key Idea**

Surface Area of a Rectangular Prism

Words The surface area S of a rectangular prism is the sum of the areas of the bases and the lateral faces.

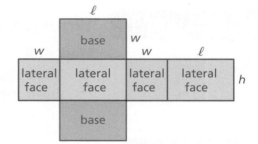

Algebra $S = 2\ell w + 2\ell h + 2wh$

Areas of bases

Areas of lateral faces

EXAMPLE 1 **Finding the Surface Area of a Rectangular Prism**

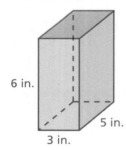

Find the surface area of the prism.

Draw a net.

$$S = 2\ell w + 2\ell h + 2wh$$
$$= 2(3)(5) + 2(3)(6) + 2(5)(6)$$
$$= 30 + 36 + 60$$
$$= 126$$

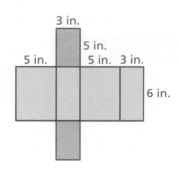

▷ The surface area is 126 square inches.

Try It **Find the surface area of the prism.**

1.
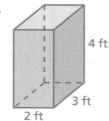

2.
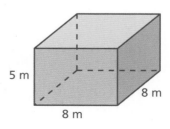

🔊 Multi-Language Glossary at *BigIdeasMath.com*

Key Idea

Surface Area of a Prism

The surface area S of any prism is the sum of the areas of the bases and the lateral faces.

$$S = \text{areas of bases} + \text{areas of lateral faces}$$

EXAMPLE 2 | **Finding the Surface Area of a Prism**

Find the surface area of the prism.

Draw a net.

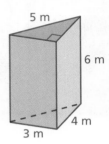

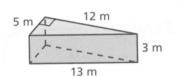

Area of a Base

Red base: $\dfrac{1}{2} \cdot 3 \cdot 4 = 6$

Areas of Lateral Faces

Green lateral face: $3 \cdot 6 = 18$

Purple lateral face: $5 \cdot 6 = 30$

Blue lateral face: $4 \cdot 6 = 24$

$S = \text{areas of bases} + \text{areas of lateral faces}$

$= \underbrace{6 + 6} + 18 + 30 + 24 = 84$

> There are two identical bases. Count the area twice.

▷ The surface area is 84 square meters.

Try It

3. Find the surface area of the prism at the left.

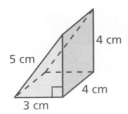

Self-Assessment for Concepts & Skills

Solve each exercise. Then rate your understanding of the success criteria in your journal.

4. WRITING Explain the meaning of each term in the formula for the surface area of a rectangular prism.

5. DIFFERENT WORDS, SAME QUESTION Which is different? Find "both" answers.

Find the surface area of the prism.	Find the area of the bases of the prism.
Find the area of the net of the prism.	Find the sum of the areas of the bases and the lateral faces of the prism.

The **lateral surface area** of a solid is the sum of the areas of each lateral face.

EXAMPLE 3 **Modeling Real Life**

The outsides of purple traps are coated with glue to catch emerald ash borers. You make your own trap in the shape of a rectangular prism with an open top and bottom. What is the surface area that you need to coat with glue?

Use the formula for the surface area of a rectangular prism. To find the lateral surface area, do not include the areas of the bases in the formula.

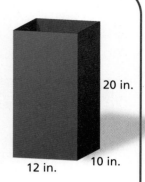

$$S = 2\ell h + 2wh \qquad \text{Write the formula.}$$
$$= 2(12)(20) + 2(10)(20) \qquad \text{Substitute.}$$
$$= 480 + 400 \qquad \text{Multiply.}$$
$$= 880 \qquad \text{Add.}$$

▷ So, you need to coat 880 square inches with glue.

Self-Assessment for Problem Solving

Solve each exercise. Then rate your understanding of the success criteria in your journal.

6. You want to stain the lateral faces of the wooden chest shown. Find the area that you want to stain in *square inches*.

7. One can of frosting covers about 280 square inches. Is one can of frosting enough to frost the cake? Explain.

8. **DIG DEEPER!** Find the surface area of the bench shown. Justify your answer.

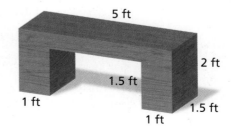

10.1 Practice

Go to *BigIdeasMath.com* to get
HELP with solving the exercises.

Review & Refresh

Classify the pair of angles. Then find the value of *x*.

1.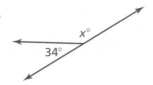

2.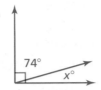

3.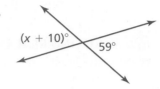

Find the area of a circle with the indicated dimensions. Use 3.14 or $\frac{22}{7}$ for π.

4. radius: 21 in.

5. diameter: 36 mm

6. radius: 8.5 m

Concepts, Skills, & Problem Solving

SURFACE AREA OF A PRISM Identify the solid represented by the net. Then find the surface area of the solid. (See Explorations 1 & 2, p. 409.)

7.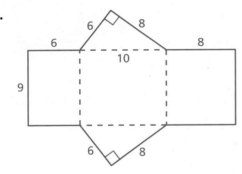

8.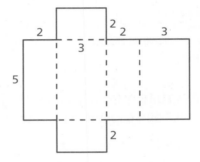

FINDING THE SURFACE AREA OF A PRISM Find the surface area of the prism.

9.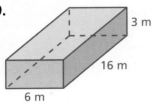

10.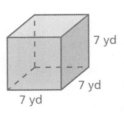

11.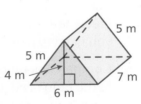

12.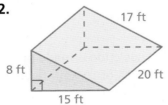

13.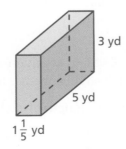

14.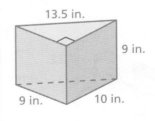

15. **MP** **YOU BE THE TEACHER** Your friend finds the surface area of the prism. Is your friend correct? Explain your reasoning.

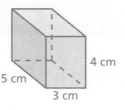
4 cm
5 cm
3 cm

$S = 2(5)(3) + 2(3)(4) + 2(5)(3)$
$= 30 + 24 + 30$
$= 84 \text{ cm}^2$

16. **MP** **MODELING REAL LIFE** A cube-shaped satellite has side lengths of 10 centimeters. What is the least amount of aluminum needed to cover the satellite?

FINDING SURFACE AREA **Find the surface area of the prism.**

17.
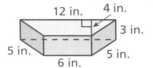
12 in.   4 in.
3 in.
5 in.   5 in.
6 in.

18.
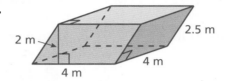
2 m
2.5 m
4 m
4 m

19. **OPEN-ENDED** Draw and label a rectangular prism that has a surface area of 158 square yards.

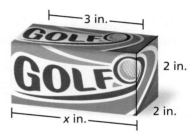
3 in.
2 in.
x in.
2 in.

20. **DIG DEEPER!** A label that wraps around a box of golf balls covers 75% of its lateral surface area. What is the value of x?

21. **MP** **STRUCTURE** You are painting the prize pedestals shown (including the bottoms). You need 0.5 pint of paint to paint the red pedestal.

a. The edge lengths of the green pedestal are one-half the edge lengths of the red pedestal. How much paint do you need to paint the green pedestal?

b. The edge lengths of the blue pedestal are triple the edge lengths of the green pedestal. How much paint do you need to paint the blue pedestal?

c. Compare the ratio of paint volumes to the ratio of edge lengths for the green and red pedestals. Repeat for the green and blue pedestals. What do you notice?

24 in.
16 in.
16 in.
16 in.

22. **MP** **NUMBER SENSE** A keychain-sized puzzle cube is made up of small cubes. Each small cube has a surface area of 1.5 square inches.

a. What is the edge length of each small cube?

b. What is the surface area of the entire puzzle cube?

10.2 Surface Areas of Cylinders

Learning Target: Find the surface area of a cylinder.

Success Criteria:
- I can use a formula to find the surface area of a cylinder.
- I can find the lateral surface area of a cylinder.

A *cylinder* is a solid that has two parallel, identical circular bases.

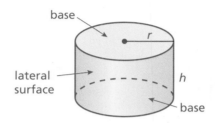

base
r
lateral surface
h
base

EXPLORATION 1

Finding the Surface Area of a Cylinder

Work with a partner.

a. Make a net for the can. Name each shape in the net.

b. How are the dimensions of the paper related to the dimensions of the can?

c. Write a formula that represents the surface area of a cylinder with a height of h and bases with a radius of r.

d. Estimate the dimensions of each can. Then use your formula in part (c) to estimate the surface area of each can.

Math Practice

Specify Units
What units did you use in your estimations in part (d)? What are the units for the surface areas of the cans?

Key Idea

Surface Area of a Cylinder

Words The surface area S of a cylinder is the sum of the areas of the bases and the lateral surface.

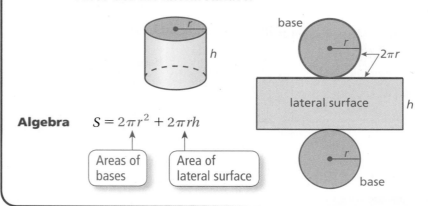

Algebra $S = 2\pi r^2 + 2\pi rh$

Areas of bases — Area of lateral surface

Remember

Pi can be approximated as 3.14 or $\frac{22}{7}$.

EXAMPLE 1 **Finding the Surface Area of a Cylinder**

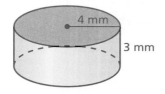

Find the surface area of the cylinder.

Draw a net.

$$S = 2\pi r^2 + 2\pi rh$$
$$= 2\pi(4)^2 + 2\pi(4)(3)$$
$$= 32\pi + 24\pi$$
$$= 56\pi$$
$$\approx 176$$

▶ The surface area is about 176 square millimeters.

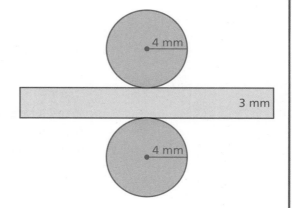

Try It Find the surface area of the cylinder. Round your answer to the nearest tenth if necessary.

1.
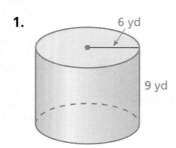

2.
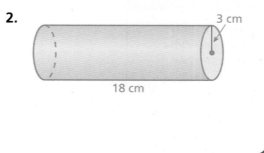

EXAMPLE 2 **Finding the Lateral Surface Area of a Cylinder**

Find the lateral surface area of the cylinder.

Use the formula for the surface area of a cylinder. To find the lateral surface area, do not include the areas of the circular bases in the formula.

The radius is $8 \div 2 = 4$ feet.

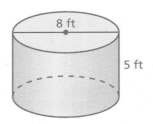

$$S = 2\pi rh \qquad \text{Write the formula.}$$
$$= 2\pi(4)(5) \qquad \text{Substitute 4 for } r \text{ and 5 for } h.$$
$$= 40\pi \qquad \text{Multiply.}$$
$$\approx 125.6 \qquad \text{Use 3.14 for } \pi.$$

▶ The lateral surface area is about 125.6 square feet.

Math Practice

Look for Structure
Explain why the area of the lateral face is the product of the height of the cylinder and the circumference of the base.

Try It **Find the lateral surface area of the cylinder. Round your answer to the nearest tenth.**

3.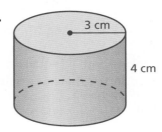

3 cm

4 cm

4.

3 yd

8 yd

Self-Assessment for Concepts & Skills

Solve each exercise. Then rate your understanding of the success criteria in your journal.

5. **WRITING** Which part of the formula $S = 2\pi r^2 + 2\pi rh$ represents the lateral surface area of a cylinder? the areas of the bases?

6. **CRITICAL THINKING** You are given the height of a cylinder and the circumference of its base. Describe how to find the surface area of the cylinder.

10 in.

4 in.

7. **FINDING A SURFACE AREA** Find the surface area of the cylinder at the left. Round your answer to the nearest tenth.

8. **FINDING A LATERAL SURFACE AREA** Find the lateral surface area of the cylinder at the right. Round your answer to the nearest tenth.

2 cm

2 cm

EXAMPLE 3 **Modeling Real Life**

The iced tea can is made from a sheet of aluminum that weighs 0.01 ounce per square inch. You receive $0.40 per pound of aluminum that you recycle. How much do you earn for recycling 24 iced tea cans?

1.5 in.

7 in.

12 FL OZ

Understand the problem.

You are given a unit rate in dollars per pound for recycled aluminum, the weight of one square inch of an aluminum can, and the dimensions of the can. You are asked to find how much you earn for recycling 24 cans.

Make a plan.

Find the surface area of one can and use it to find the weight of 24 cans. Then use the unit rate given in dollars per pound to find the value of the cans.

Solve and check.

$$S = 2\pi r^2 + 2\pi rh \qquad \text{Write the formula.}$$
$$= 2\pi(1.5)^2 + 2\pi(1.5)(7) \qquad \text{Substitute 1.5 for } r \text{ and 7 for } h.$$
$$= 4.5\pi + 21\pi \qquad \text{Simplify.}$$
$$= 25.5\pi \qquad \text{Add.}$$
$$\approx 80 \qquad \text{Use 3.14 for } \pi.$$

Check Reasonableness
19.2 ounces is greater than 16 ounces, or 1 pound, so the value should be greater than $0.40. Because $0.48 > $0.40, the answer is reasonable. ✓

The surface area of one can is about 80 square inches. So, 24 cans weigh about $24(80)(0.01) = 19.2$ ounces. This has a value of

$$19.2 \text{ oz} \times \frac{1 \text{ lb}}{16 \text{ oz}} \times \frac{\$0.40}{1 \text{ lb}} = \$0.48.$$

▷ So, you earn about $0.48 for recycling 24 cans.

Self-Assessment for Problem Solving

Solve each exercise. Then rate your understanding of the success criteria in your journal.

9. You remove the lid of the can. What is the percent of change in the surface area of the can?

40 mm

85 mm

10. After burning half of a cylindrical candle, the surface area is 176 square inches. The radius of the candle is 2 inches. What was the original height of the candle?

11. **DIG DEEPER!** The area of the sheet of wrapping paper is equal to the lateral surface area of a cylindrical tube. The tube is 14 inches tall. What is the surface area of the tube, including the bases? Explain your reasoning.

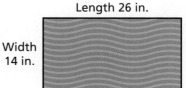

Length 26 in.

Width 14 in.

Go to *BigIdeasMath.com* to get HELP with solving the exercises.

▶ Review & Refresh

Find the surface area of the prism.

1.

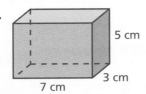

5 cm
3 cm
7 cm

2.

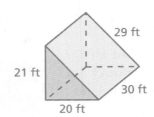

29 ft
21 ft
30 ft
20 ft

3. Which of the following is equivalent to 0.625?

A. $\frac{5}{8}$ **B.** $\frac{625}{100}$ **C.** 0.625%   **D.** 6.25%

▶▶ Concepts, Skills, & Problem Solving

FINDING SURFACE AREA **Find the surface area of the cylinder.**
(See Exploration 1, p. 415.)

4. a can with a radius of 60 millimeters and a height of 160 millimeters

5. a hay bale with a diameter of 30 inches and a height of 72 inches

FINDING SURFACE AREA **Find the surface area of the cylinder. Round your answer to the nearest tenth if necessary.**

6.

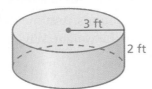

3 ft
2 ft

7.

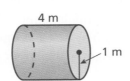

4 m
1 m

8.

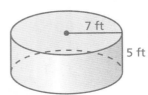

7 ft
5 ft

9.

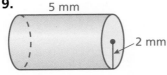

5 mm
2 mm

10.

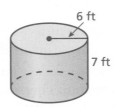

6 ft
7 ft

11.

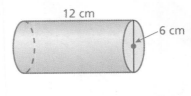

12 cm
6 cm

FINDING LATERAL SURFACE AREA **Find the lateral surface area of the cylinder. Round your answer to the nearest tenth if necessary.**

12.

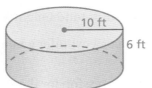

10 ft
6 ft

13.

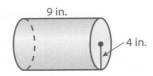

9 in.
4 in.

14.

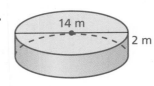

14 m
2 m

15. **MP** **YOU BE THE TEACHER**
Your friend finds the
surface area of the cylinder.
Is your friend correct?
Explain your reasoning.

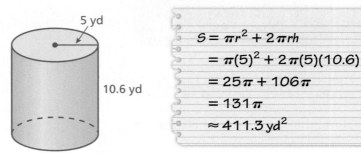

$$S = \pi r^2 + 2\pi rh$$
$$= \pi(5)^2 + 2\pi(5)(10.6)$$
$$= 25\pi + 106\pi$$
$$= 131\pi$$
$$\approx 411.3 \text{ yd}^2$$

16. **MP** **MODELING REAL LIFE**
The tank of a tanker truck is a
stainless steel cylinder. Find
the surface area of the tank.

radius = 4 ft

17. **MP** **MODELING REAL LIFE** The Petri dish shown has no lid.
What is the surface area of the outside of the Petri dish?

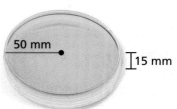

18. **MP** **REASONING** You have two 8.5-by-11-inch pieces of paper.
You form the lateral surfaces of two different cylinders by taping
together a pair of opposite sides on each piece of paper so that
one cylinder has a height of 8.5 inches and the other has a height
of 11 inches. Without calculating, compare the surface areas of
the cylinders (including the bases). Explain.

19. **DIG DEEPER!** A *ganza* is a percussion instrument
used in samba music.

   a. Find the surface area of each of the two labeled ganzas.

   b. The smaller ganza weighs 1.1 pounds. Assume that the
   surface area is proportional to the weight. What is the
   weight of the larger ganza?

20. **MP** **PROBLEM SOLVING** The wedge
is one-eighth of the wheel of cheese.

   a. Find the surface area of
   the cheese before it is cut.

   b. Find the surface area of the
   remaining cheese after
   the wedge is removed.
   Did the surface area increase,
   decrease, or remain the same?

21. **MP** **REPEATED REASONING** A cylinder has radius r and height h.

   a. How many times greater is the surface area of a cylinder when both
   dimensions are multiplied by 2? 3? 5? 10?

   b. Describe the pattern in part (a). Write an expression for the surface area
   of the cylinder when both dimensions are multiplied by a number x.

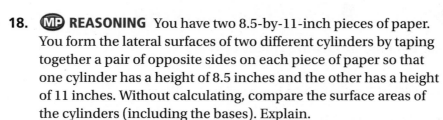

10.3 Surface Areas of Pyramids

Many well-known pyramids have square bases, however, the base of a pyramid can be any polygon.

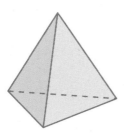

Triangular Base

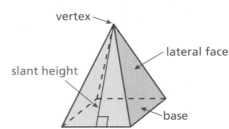

vertex

lateral face

slant height

base

Square Base

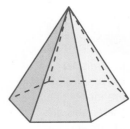

Hexagonal Base

EXPLORATION 1

Making a Scale Model

Work with a partner. Each pyramid below has a square base.

Cheops Pyramid in Egypt

Side ≈ 230 m, Slant height ≈ 186 m

Louvre Pyramid in Paris

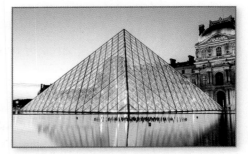

Side ≈ 35 m, Slant height ≈ 28 m

Math Practice

Analyze Relationships

What is the relationship between the lateral surface area of your scale model and the lateral surface area of the real-life pyramid?

a. Draw a net for a scale model of one of the pyramids. Describe the scale factor.

b. Find the lateral surface area of the real-life pyramid that you chose in part (a). Explain how you found your answer.

c. Draw a net for a pyramid with a non-rectangular base and find its lateral surface area. Explain how you found your answer.

10.3 Lesson

Key Vocabulary
regular pyramid, *p. 422*
slant height, *p. 422*

A **regular pyramid** is a pyramid whose base is a regular polygon. The lateral faces are triangles. The height of each triangle is the **slant height** of the pyramid.

Key Idea

Surface Area of a Pyramid

The surface area S of a pyramid is the sum of the areas of the base and the lateral faces.

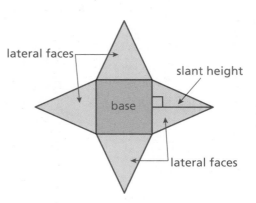

S = area of base + areas of lateral faces

Remember

In a regular polygon, all the sides are identical and all the angles are identical.

EXAMPLE 1 **Finding the Surface Area of a Square Pyramid**

Find the surface area of the regular pyramid.

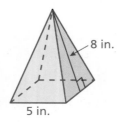

Draw a net.

Area of Base	**Area of a Lateral Face**
$5 \cdot 5 = 25$	$\frac{1}{2} \cdot 5 \cdot 8 = 20$

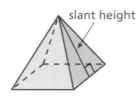

Find the sum of the areas of the base and the lateral faces.

$$S = \text{area of base} + \text{areas of lateral faces}$$
$$= 25 + \underbrace{20 + 20 + 20 + 20}$$
$$= 105$$

> There are 4 identical lateral faces. Count the area 4 times.

▷ The surface area is 105 square inches.

Try It

1. What is the surface area of a square pyramid with a base side length of 9 centimeters and a slant height of 7 centimeters?

Multi-Language Glossary at *BigIdeasMath.com*

10.5 Practice

Go to **BigIdeasMath.com** to get HELP with solving the exercises.

▶ Review & Refresh

Find the volume of the prism.

1.
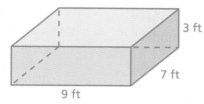
3 ft
7 ft
9 ft

2.
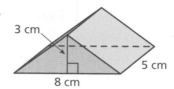
3 cm
5 cm
8 cm

Solve the inequality. Graph the solution.

3. $r + 0.5 < -0.4$ **4.** $z - 2.4 \geq -0.6$ **5.** $h - 5 \leq -3.7$

▶▶ Concepts, Skills, & Problem Solving

VOLUMES OF PYRAMIDS The rectangular prism is cut to form three pyramids. Show that the sum of the volumes of the three pyramids is equal to the volume of the prism. (See Exploration 1, p. 433.)

6.
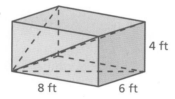
4 ft
8 ft   6 ft

7.
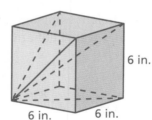
6 in.
6 in.   6 in.

FINDING THE VOLUME OF A PYRAMID Find the volume of the pyramid.

8.
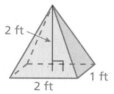
2 ft
2 ft   1 ft

9.
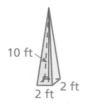
10 ft
2 ft   2 ft

10.
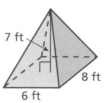
7 ft
6 ft   8 ft

11.
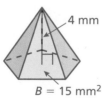
4 mm
$B = 15 \text{ mm}^2$

12.
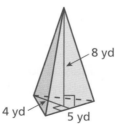
8 yd
4 yd   5 yd

13.
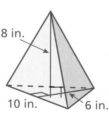
8 in.
10 in.   6 in.

14.
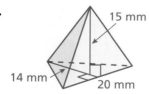
15 mm
14 mm   20 mm

15.
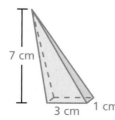
7 cm
3 cm   1 cm

16.
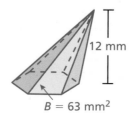
12 mm
$B = 63 \text{ mm}^2$

Section 10.5   Volumes of Pyramids   **437**

17. **MP** **YOU BE THE TEACHER** Your friend finds the volume of the pyramid. Is your friend correct? Explain your reasoning.

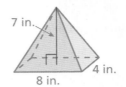
7 in.
8 in.
4 in.

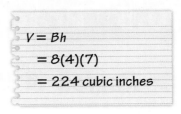
$V = Bh$
$= 8(4)(7)$
$= 224$ cubic inches

18. **MP** **MODELING REAL LIFE** A researcher develops a cage for a living cell in the shape of a square-based pyramid. A scale model of the cage is shown. What is the volume of the model?

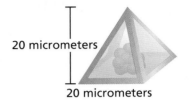
20 micrometers
20 micrometers

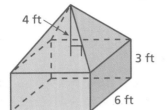
4 ft
3 ft
6 ft
6 ft

19. **FINDING VOLUME** Find the volume of the composite solid. Justify your answer.

20. **MP** **MODELING REAL LIFE** In 1483, Leonardo da Vinci designed a parachute. It is believed that this was the first parachute ever designed. In a notebook, he wrote, "If a man is provided with a length of gummed linen cloth with a length of 12 yards on each side and 12 yards high, he can jump from any great height whatsoever without injury." Find the volume of air inside Leonardo's parachute.

Not drawn to scale

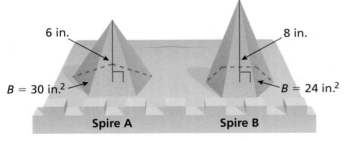
6 in.
8 in.
$B = 30$ in.^{2}
$B = 24$ in.^{2}
Spire A
Spire B

21. **MP** **MODELING REAL LIFE** Which sandcastle spire has a greater volume? How much more sand do you need to make the spire with the greater volume?

22. **MP** **PROBLEM SOLVING** Use the photo of the tepee.

   a. What is the shape of the base? How can you tell?

   b. The tepee's height is about 10 feet. Estimate the volume of the tepee.

23. **OPEN-ENDED** A rectangular pyramid has a volume of 40 cubic feet and a height of 6 feet. Find one possible set of dimensions of the base.

24. **MP** **REASONING** Do the two solids have the same volume? Explain.

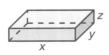
z
y
x

3z
y
x

10.6 Cross Sections of Three-Dimensional Figures

Learning Target: Describe the cross sections of a solid.

Success Criteria:
- I can explain the meaning of a cross section.
- I can describe cross sections of prisms and pyramids.
- I can describe cross sections of cylinders and cones.

EXPLORATION 1

Describing Cross Sections

Work with a partner. A baker is thinking of different ways to slice zucchini bread that is in the shape of a rectangular prism. The shape that is formed by the cut is called a *cross section*.

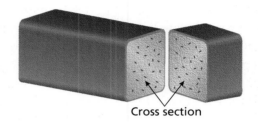

Cross section

a. What is the shape of the cross section when the baker slices the bread vertically, as shown above?

b. What is the shape of the cross section when the baker slices the bread horizontally?

c. What is the shape of the cross section when the baker slices off a corner of the bread?

Math Practice

Justify Conclusions

How can you use real-life objects to justify your conclusions in parts (d) and (e)?

d. Is it possible to obtain a cross section that is a trapezoid? Explain.

e. Name at least 3 cross sections that are possible to obtain from a rectangular pyramid. Explain your reasoning.

Key Vocabulary 🔊
cross section, *p. 440*

Consider a plane "slicing" through a solid. The intersection of the plane and the solid is a two-dimensional shape called a **cross section**. For example, the diagram shows that the intersection of the plane and the rectangular prism is a rectangle.

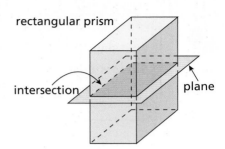

rectangular prism

intersection

plane

EXAMPLE 1 **Describing Cross Sections of Prisms and Pyramids**

Describe the intersection of the plane and the solid.

a.

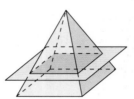

> The diagram shows the intersection of a plane and a rectangular pyramid. The intersection is a rectangle.

b.

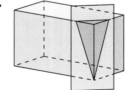

> The diagram shows the intersection of a plane and a rectangular prism. The intersection is a triangle.

Try It **Describe the intersection of the plane and the solid.**

1.

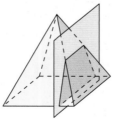

2.

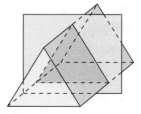

🔊 *Multi-Language Glossary at BigIdeasMath.com*

Example 1 shows how a plane intersects a polyhedron. Now consider the intersection of a plane and a solid having a curved surface, such as a cylinder or cone. As shown, a *cone* is a solid that has one circular base and one vertex.

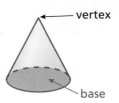

EXAMPLE 2 **Describing Cross Sections of Cylinders and Cones**

Describe the intersection of the plane and the solid.

a.

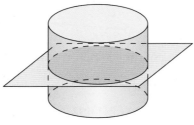

▷ The diagram shows the intersection of a plane and a cylinder. The intersection is a circle.

b.

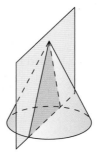

▷ The diagram shows the intersection of a plane and a cone. The intersection is a triangle.

Math Practice

Communicate Precisely

Can a cross section be three dimensional? Explain your reasoning.

Try It **Describe the intersection of the plane and the solid.**

3.

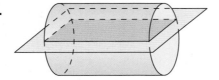

4.

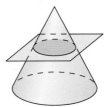

 Self-Assessment *for Concepts & Skills*

Solve each exercise. Then rate your understanding of the success criteria in your journal.

5. **VOCABULARY** What is a cross section?

6. **DESCRIBING CROSS SECTIONS** Describe the intersection of the plane and the solid at the left.

7. **(MP) REASONING** Name all possible cross sections of a cylinder.

8. **WHICH ONE DOESN'T BELONG?** You slice a square prism. Which cross section does *not* belong with the other three? Explain your reasoning.

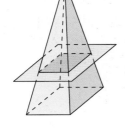

| circle | square | triangle | rectangle |

EXAMPLE 3 **Modeling Real Life**

An ice sculptor cuts the block of ice into 3 identical pieces. What is the percent of increase in the surface area of the ice?

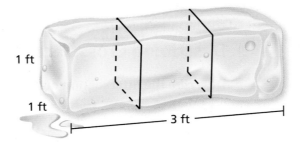

1 ft

1 ft

3 ft

Find the surface area of the ice before it is cut.

$S = 2\ell w + 2\ell h + 2wh$ Write the formula.

$= 2(1)(1) + 2(1)(3) + 2(1)(3)$ Substitute 1 for ℓ, 1 for w, and 3 for h.

$= 2 + 6 + 6$ Simplify.

$= 14 \text{ ft}^2$ Add.

When the ice is cut, the cross sections are squares with side lengths of 1 foot. The ice is cut into three cubes, each with edge lengths of 1 foot. Find the total surface area of the three cubes.

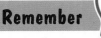

Remember

The surface area S of a cube with an edge length of s is $S = 6s^2$.

$S = 3(6s^2)$

$= 3(6 \cdot 1^2)$

$= 3(6)$

$= 18 \text{ ft}^2$

1 ft

1 ft

1 ft

▷ So, the percent of increase in the surface area of the ice is $\dfrac{18 - 14}{14} \approx 29\%$.

Self-Assessment for Problem Solving

Solve each exercise. Then rate your understanding of the success criteria in your journal.

9. A steel beam that is 12 meters long is cut into four equal parts. The cross sections are rectangles with side lengths of 1 meter and 2 meters.

 a. What is the perimeter of each cross section?

 b. What is the area of each cross section?

 c. What is the volume of the original beam?

10. **DIG DEEPER!** A lumberjack saws a cylindrical tree trunk at an angle. Is the cross section a circle? Explain your reasoning.

10.6 Practice

? Go to *BigIdeasMath.com* to get HELP with solving the exercises.

▶ Review & Refresh

Find the volume of the pyramid.

1.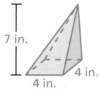
7 in.
4 in.
4 in.

2.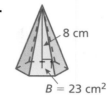
8 cm
$B = 23$ cm^2

Find the sum.

3. $(w - 7) + (-6w - 5)$

4. $(8 - b) + (5b + 6)$

▶▶ Concepts, Skills, & Problem Solving

DESCRIBING CROSS SECTIONS **Determine whether it is possible to obtain the cross section from a cube.** (See Exploration 2, p. 439.)

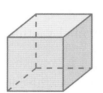

5. circle

6. square

7. equilateral triangle

8. pentagon

9. non-rectangular parallelogram

10. octagon

DESCRIBING CROSS SECTIONS OF PRISMS AND PYRAMIDS **Describe the intersection of the plane and the solid.**

11.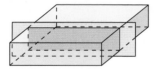

12.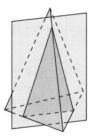

13.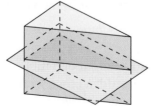

14.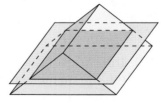

DESCRIBING CROSS SECTIONS OF CYLINDERS AND CONES **Describe the intersection of the plane and the solid.**

15.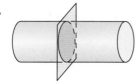

16.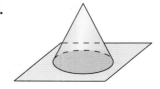

DESCRIBING CROSS SECTIONS Describe the shape that is formed by the cut in the food.

17.  **18.**  **19.**

20. **DESCRIBING CROSS SECTIONS** Describe the intersection of the plane and the cylinder.

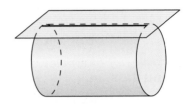

MP REASONING Determine whether the given intersection is possible. If so, draw the solid and the cross section.

21. The intersection of a plane and a cone is a rectangle.

22. The intersection of a plane and a square pyramid is a triangle.

23. **MP REASONING** A plane that intersects a prism is parallel to the bases of the prism. Describe the intersection of the plane and the prism.

24. **MP REASONING** Explain how a plane can be parallel to the base of a cone and intersect the cone at exactly one point.

25. **MP MODELING REAL LIFE** An artist plans to paint bricks.

   a. Find the surface area of the brick.

   b. The artist cuts along the length of the brick to form two bricks, each with a width of 2 inches. What is the percent of increase in the surface area? Justify your answer.

3 in.
10 in.
4 in.

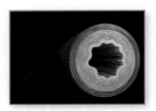

26. **MP MODELING REAL LIFE** A cross section of an artery is shown.

   a. Describe the cross section of the artery.

   b. The radius of the artery is 0.22 millimeter. What is the circumference of the artery?

27. **MP REASONING** Three identical square pyramids each with a height of h meters and a base area of 100 square meters are shown. For each pyramid, a cross section parallel to the base is shown. Describe the relationship between the area of the base and the area of any cross section parallel to the base.

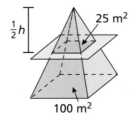

$\frac{1}{2}h$ 25 m² 100 m²

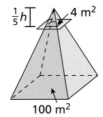

$\frac{1}{5}h$ 4 m² 100 m²

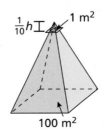

$\frac{1}{10}h$ 1 m² 100 m²

▶ *Using the Problem-Solving Plan*

1. A store pays $2 per pound for popcorn kernels. One cubic foot of kernels weighs about 45 pounds. What is the selling price of the container shown when the markup is 30%?

6 in.

4 in.

4 in.

 Understand the problem.

You are given the dimensions of a container of popcorn kernels and the price that a store pays for the kernels. You also know the weight of one cubic foot of popcorn kernels. You are asked to find the selling price of the container when the markup is 30%.

Make a plan.

Use the volume of the container to find the weight of the kernels. Then use the weight of the kernels to find the cost to the store. Finally, use the percent markup to find the selling price of the container.

Solve and check.

Use the plan to solve the problem. Then check your solution.

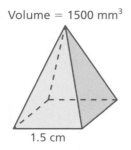

Volume = 1500 mm³

1.5 cm

2. The pyramid shown has a square base. What is the height of the pyramid? Justify your answer.

3. A cylindrical can of soup has a height of 7 centimeters and a lateral surface area of 63π square centimeters. The can is redesigned to have a lateral surface area of 45π square centimeters without changing the radius of the can. What is the height of the new design? Justify your answer.

Performance Task

WIDTH 8.5IN. LENGTH 11IN HEIGHT 2IN

Volumes and Surface Areas of Small Objects

At the beginning of this chapter, you watched a STEAM Video called "Paper Measurements." You are now ready to complete the performance task related to this video, available at *BigIdeasMath.com*. Be sure to use the problem-solving plan as you work through the performance task.

▶ Review Vocabulary

Write the definition and give an example of each vocabulary term.

lateral surface area, *p. 412*   slant height, *p. 422*
regular pyramid, *p. 422*   cross section, *p. 440*

▶ Graphic Organizers

You can use an **Information Frame** to help organize and remember a concept. Here is an example of an Information Frame for *Surface Areas of Rectangular Prisms*.

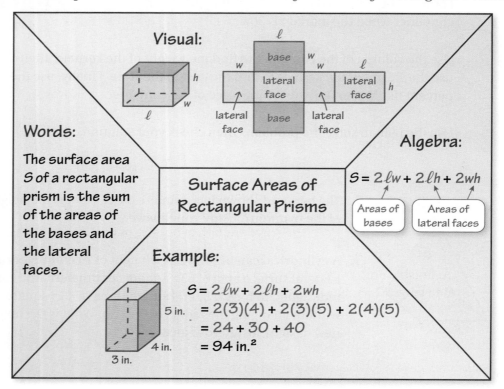

Visual:

Words:

The surface area S of a rectangular prism is the sum of the areas of the bases and the lateral faces.

Surface Areas of Rectangular Prisms

Algebra:

$S = 2\ell w + 2\ell h + 2wh$

Areas of bases   Areas of lateral faces

Example:

$S = 2\ell w + 2\ell h + 2wh$
$\quad = 2(3)(4) + 2(3)(5) + 2(4)(5)$
$\quad = 24 + 30 + 40$
$\quad = 94 \text{ in.}^2$

Choose and complete a graphic organizer to help you study the concept.

1. surface areas of prisms

2. surface areas of cylinders

3. surface areas of pyramids

4. volumes of prisms

5. volumes of pyramids

6. cross sections of three-dimensional figures

"I'm having trouble thinking of a good title for my **Information Frame**."

▶ Chapter Self-Assessment

As you complete the exercises, use the scale below to rate your understanding of the success criteria in your journal.

1	**2**	**3**	**4**
I do not understand.	I can do it with help.	I can do it on my own.	I can teach someone else.

10.1 Surface Areas of Prisms (pp. 409–414)

Learning Target: Find the surface area of a prism.

Find the surface area of the prism.

1.
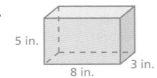
5 in.
8 in.
3 in.

2.
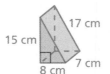
17 cm
15 cm
7 cm
8 cm

3.
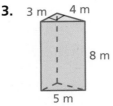
3 m 4 m
8 m
5 m

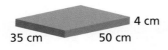
4 cm
35 cm 50 cm

4. You want to wrap the box using a piece of wrapping paper that is 76 centimeters long by 56 centimeters wide. Do you have enough wrapping paper to wrap the box? Explain.

5. To finish a project, you need to paint the lateral surfaces of a cube with side length 2.5 inches. Find the area that you need to paint.

10.2 Surface Areas of Cylinders (pp. 415–420)

Learning Target: Find the surface area of a cylinder.

Find the surface area and lateral surface area of the cylinder. Round your answers to the nearest tenth.

6.
3 yd
6 yd

7. 1.6 cm
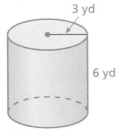

Lip Balm
Protects your lips from the sun and wind
Lip Balm
6 cm

8. The label covers the entire lateral surface area of the can. How much of the can is *not* covered by the label?

4 cm
Sunnyview Farms
Mandarin
ORANGE SEGMENTS
11 cm
NET WT. 16 OZ.

10.3 Surface Areas of Pyramids (pp. 421–426)

Learning Target: Find the surface area of a pyramid.

Find the surface area of the regular pyramid.

9.
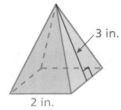
3 in.
2 in.

10.
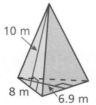
10 m
8 m   6.9 m

11.
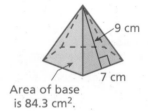
9 cm
7 cm
Area of base is 84.3 cm².

6 ft
3 ft

12. The tent is shaped like a square pyramid. There is no fabric covering the ground.

   a. Estimate the amount of fabric needed to make the tent.

   b. Fabric costs $5.25 per square yard. How much will it cost to make the tent?

10.4 Volumes of Prisms (pp. 427–432)

Learning Target: Find the volume of a prism.

Find the volume of the prism.

13.
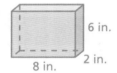
6 in.
2 in.
8 in.

14.
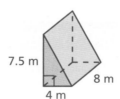
7.5 m
8 m
4 m

15.
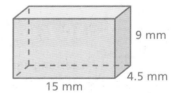
9 mm
15 mm
4.5 mm

16.
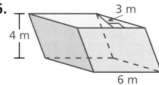
3 m
4 m
6 m

17.
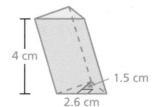
4 cm
1.5 cm
2.6 cm

18.
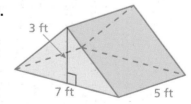
3 ft
7 ft   5 ft

19. Two cereal boxes each hold exactly 192 cubic inches of cereal. Which box should a manufacturer choose to minimize the amount of cardboard needed to make the cereal boxes?

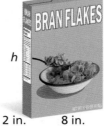
h
2 in.   8 in.

h
3 in.   8 in.

10.5 Volumes of Pyramids (pp. 433–438)

Learning Target: Find the volume of a pyramid.

Find the volume of the pyramid.

20.

20 ft

17 ft   15 ft

21.

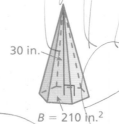

30 in.

$B = 210$ in.^{2}

22.

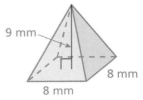

9 mm

8 mm

8 mm

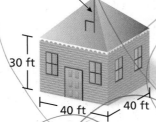

20 ft

30 ft

40 ft   40 ft

23. A pyramid-shaped hip roof is a good choice for a house in an area with many hurricanes.

    a. What is the volume of the roof to the nearest tenth of a foot?

    b. What is the volume of the entire house, including the roof?

24. A laboratory creates calcite crystals for use in the study of light. The crystal is made up of two pieces of calcite that form a square pyramid. The base length of the top piece is 2 inches.

    a. Find the volume of the entire pyramid.

    b. Find the volume of each piece of the pyramid.

1.75 in.

1.25 in.

3.5 in.

10.6 Cross Sections of Three-Dimensional Figures (pp. 439–444)

Learning Target: Describe the cross sections of a solid.

Describe the intersection of the plane and the solid.

25.

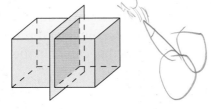

26.

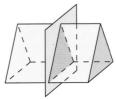

Sketch how a plane can intersect with a cylinder to form a cross section of the given shape.

27. rectangle   **28.** circle   **29.** line segment

Find the surface area of the prism or regular pyramid.

1.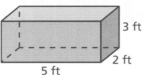
3 ft
2 ft
5 ft

2.
2 in.
1 in.

3.
15 m
11 m
9.5 m

Find the surface area and lateral surface area of the cylinder. Round your answers to the nearest tenth.

4.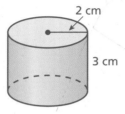
2 cm
3 cm

5.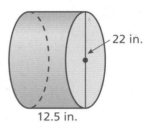
22 in.
12.5 in.

Find the volume of the solid.

6.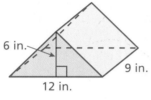
6 in.
9 in.
12 in.

7.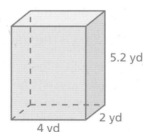
5.2 yd
4 yd
2 yd

8.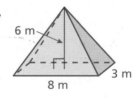
6 m
3 m
8 m

9. A quart of paint covers 80 square feet. How many quarts should you buy to paint the ramp with two coats? (Assume you will not paint the bottom of the ramp.)

15.2 ft
6 ft
19.5 ft
14 ft

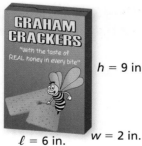
GRAHAM CRACKERS
"With the taste of REAL honey in every bite"
$h = 9$ in.
$\ell = 6$ in.
$w = 2$ in.

10. A manufacturer wants to double the volume of the graham cracker box. The manufacturer will either double the height or double the width.

a. What is the volume of the new graham cracker box?

b. Which option uses less cardboard? Justify your answer.

c. A graham cracker takes up about 1.5 cubic inches of space. Write an inequality that represents the numbers of graham crackers that can fit in the new box.

11. The label on the can of soup covers about 354.2 square centimeters. What is the height of the can? Round your answer to the nearest whole number.

4.7 cm
TOMATO SOUP

12. A lumberjack splits the cylindrical log from top to bottom with an ax, dividing it in half. Describe the shape that is formed by the cut.

1. A gift box and its dimensions are shown.

2 in.

8 in. 4 in.

What is the least amount of wrapping paper that you need to wrap the box?

A. 20 in.^{2}

B. 56 in.^{2}

C. 64 in.^{2}

D. 112 in.^{2}

Test-Taking Strategy

After Answering Easy Questions, Relax

Find the surface area.
(A) 10 ft   (C) 10 ft^2
(B) 10 ft^3 (D) 2 ft^3

2 ft
1 ft   1 ft

Neat! Didn't even use a formula.

"After answering the easy questions, relax and try the harder ones. For this, you know area is measured in square units."

2. James is getting ready for wrestling season. As part of his preparation, he plans to lose 5% of his body weight. James currently weighs 160 pounds. How much will he weigh, in pounds, after he loses 5% of his weight?

3. How far will the tip of the hour hand of the clock travel in 2 hours? (Use $\frac{22}{7}$ for π.)

84 mm

F. 44 mm

G. 88 mm

H. 264 mm

I. 528 mm

4. Which value of x makes the equation true?

$$5x - 3 = 11$$

A. 1.6   **B.** 2.8

C. 40   **D.** 70

5. A hockey rink contains 5 face-off circles. Each of these circles has a radius of 15 feet. What is the total area of all the face-off circles? (Use 3.14 for π.)

F. 706.5 ft^2 **G.** 2826 ft^2

H. 3532.5 ft^2 **I.** 14,130 ft^2

6. How much material is needed to make the popcorn container?

4 in.

9.5 in.

A. 76π in.^{2} **B.** 84π in.^{2}

C. 92π in.^{2} **D.** 108π in.^{2}

7. What is the surface area of the square pyramid?

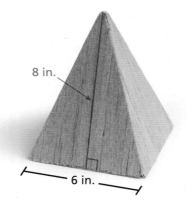

8 in.

6 in.

F. 24 in.^{2} **G.** 96 in.^{2}

H. 132 in.^{2} **I.** 228 in.^{2}

8. A rectangular prism and its dimensions are shown.

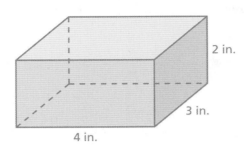

2 in.

3 in.

4 in.

What is the volume, in cubic inches, of a rectangular prism whose dimensions are three times greater?

9. What is the value of x?

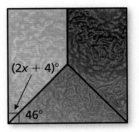

$(2x + 4)°$

46°

A. 20

B. 43

C. 44

D. 65

10. Which of the following are possible angle measures of a triangle?

F. 60°, 50°, 20°

G. 40°, 80°, 90°

H. 30°, 60°, 90°

I. 0°, 90°, 90°

11. The table shows the costs of buying matinee movie tickets.

Matinee Tickets, x	2	3	4	5
Cost, y	$9	$13.50	$18	$22.50

Part A   Graph the data.

Part B   Find and interpret the constant of proportionality for the graph of the line.

Part C   How much does it cost to buy 8 matinee movie tickets?

Selected Answers

Chapter 1

Section 1.1
Review & Refresh
1. $6 : 4$
3. $4 : 10$
5. 4
7. 7

Concepts, Skills, & Problem Solving
9. $4; -6$; *Sample answer:* 4 is farther right,
$$|-6| > |4|$$

11. $-\dfrac{4}{5}; -1.3$; *Sample answer:* $-\dfrac{4}{5}$ is farther right,
$$|-1.3| > \left|-\dfrac{4}{5}\right|$$

13. 2
15. 10
17. $\dfrac{1}{3}$
19. $\dfrac{5}{9}$
21. 3.8
23. $\dfrac{15}{4}$
25. 18.26
27. $5\dfrac{1}{6}$
29. $<$
31. $>$
33. $<$
35. $>$
37. no; The absolute value of a number cannot be negative.
39. *Sample answer:* -4
41. **a.** airplane fuel **b.** butter
43. $-7.2, -6.3, |5|, |-6.3|, 8$
45. $-\dfrac{1}{2}, \left|\dfrac{1}{4}\right|, \dfrac{5}{8}, \left|-\dfrac{3}{4}\right|, \left|-\dfrac{7}{8}\right|$
47. 3:00 P.M.; 12:00 P.M.
49. $n \leq 0$
51. false; The absolute value of zero is zero, which is neither positive nor negative.

Section 1.2
Review & Refresh
1. $<$
3. $>$
5. 6.406
7. $\dfrac{5}{8}$

9.

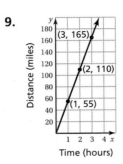

Concepts, Skills, & Problem Solving
11. integers with the same sign; -10; negative
13. $(-2) + 4; 2$
15. $-5 + 2; -3$
17. -10
19. 7
21. 0
23. 10
25. -4
27. -11
29. -4
31. -34
33. no; $-10 + (-10) = -20$
35. $48
37. *Sample answer:* $-26 + 1; -12 + (-13)$
39. Use the Associative Property to add 13 and -13 first. -8
41. *Sample answer:* Use the Commutative Property to switch the last two terms. -12
43. *Sample answer:* Use the Commutative Property to switch the last two terms. 11
45. -4
47. 21
49. -85
51. 7 units to the left of p
53. a distance of q units away from p
55. -3
57. yes; $650 + 530 + 52 + (-28) + (-75) = 1129$
59. *Sample answer:* You filled your water bottle with 12 ounces of water this morning and then drank 12 ounces.
61. $d = -10$
63. $m = -7$
65. **a.** $p = -q$; *Sample answer:* Subtract q from each side.
b. $p < -q$; *Sample answer:* Subtract q from each side.
c. $p > -q$; *Sample answer:* Subtract q from each side.

Section 1.3

Review & Refresh

1. 15

3. −5

5. 31

7. 114

9. D

Concepts, Skills, & Problem Solving

11. *Sample answer:* $\frac{1}{3}$; $\frac{5}{3}+\left(-\frac{4}{3}\right)=\frac{1}{3}$

13. $-1\frac{4}{5}$

15. $-\frac{5}{14}$

17. $-2\frac{5}{6}$

19. -57.19

21. no; The sum is -3.95.

23. *Sample answer:* You earn $1.25 doing chores and buy a sandwich for $1.25. You have no money left.

25. $-\$5.35$

27. The sum will be positive when the addend with the greater absolute value is positive. The sum will be negative when the addend with the greater absolute value is negative. The sum will be zero when the numbers are opposites.

29. *Sample answer:* Use the Commutative Property to switch the last two terms; -6.21

31. *Sample answer:* Use the Commutative Property to switch the last two terms and the Associative Property to regroup; $4\frac{1}{10}$

33. *Sample answer:*

$$-4.3 + \frac{4}{5} + 12$$

$$= -4.3 + 12 + \frac{4}{5} \quad \text{Comm. Prop. of Add.}$$

$$= 7.7 + \frac{4}{5} \quad \text{Add } -4.3 \text{ and } 12.$$

$$= 7.7 + 0.8 \quad \text{Write } \frac{4}{5} \text{ as a decimal.}$$

$$= 8.5 \quad \text{Add.}$$

35. 8

37. $\frac{1}{2}$

Section 1.4

Review & Refresh

1. $\frac{1}{3}$

3. $-5\frac{1}{2}$

5. 19.923

7. $-1 + (-3)$

Concepts, Skills, & Problem Solving

9. 2

11. 4

13. $-2 + 5$; $-2 - (-5)$; 3

15. 13

17. -5

19. -10

21. 3

23. 17

25. 1

27. -22

29. 20

31. $-2 - 9$; *Sample answer:* The air temperature is 9°C colder, so subtract 9.

33. -14 m

35. *Sample answer:* Write the subtraction as addition. Then use the Commutative Property to switch the last two terms; -7

37. Use the Associative Property to add 8 and -8 first; -5

39. *Sample answer:* Use the Commutative Property to switch the first two terms and the Associative Property to regroup; -28

41. -5

43. -17

45. **a.** February   **b.** 130°F

47. always; It's always positive because the first integer is always greater.

49. never; It's never positive because the first integer is never greater.

51. when a and b have the same sign and $|a| \geq |b|$ or $b = 0$

Section 1.5

Review & Refresh

1. 4

3. -19

5. 64 ft³

7. $-2, 1, |3|, |-4|, 6$

Concepts, Skills, & Problem Solving

9. $\frac{1}{9}; \frac{3}{9} - \frac{1}{9}; \frac{2}{9}$

11. $1\frac{1}{2}$

13. -3.5

15. -2.6

17. $-18\frac{13}{24}$

19. $\frac{1}{18}$

21. 14.963

23. no; $\frac{3}{2} - \frac{9}{2} = \frac{3}{2} + \left(-\frac{9}{2}\right) = -3$

25. *Sample answer:* A judge deducts $\frac{5}{8}$ point from an athlete's score, then removes the deduction after watching a tape of the athlete from another angle.

27. no; $\frac{1}{12}$ oz

29. *Sample answer:* Use the Commutative Property to switch the first two numbers; $\frac{2}{3}$

31. *Sample answer:* Write the subtraction as addition. Then use the Commutative Property to switch the middle two numbers and the Associative Property to add the first two numbers and the last two numbers; 7

33. *Sample answer:* Write the subtraction as addition. Then use the Commutative Property to switch the last two numbers and the Associative Property to regroup; 3.8

35. 3.2

37. 10.6

39. 9.21

41. 5.556

43. $13\frac{11}{12}$

45. $-1\frac{7}{8}$ mi

47. 4.48

49. $7\frac{5}{9}$

51. $2\frac{7}{10}$

53. **a.** 4.03 in.

   b. The rainfall is 1.73 inches below the historical average for the year.

55. sometimes; It is positive only if the first fraction is greater.

57. 2; 8; 85

Chapter 2

Section 2.1
Review & Refresh

1. 5.1

3. $1\frac{3}{5}$

5. 8

7. 19.125

Concepts, Skills, & Problem Solving

9. -8

11. -20

13. -21

15. 12

17. 27

19. 12

21. 0

23. -30

25. 78

27. 121

29. $-320{,}000$

31. -36

33. 0

35. -59

37. 54

39. 12

41. -3

43. yes; The opposite of 10^2 is -100.

45. 1792, -7168

47. about 45.83 min; *Sample answer:* Solve $22{,}000 + (-480t) = 0$.

49. -25

Section 2.2
Review & Refresh

1. 80

3. 28

5. 0.24, $\frac{1}{4}$, 28%

7. 0.69, $\frac{7}{10}$, 71%, 0.84, $\frac{9}{10}$

9. $-3 + 3$; $-3 - (-3)$; 0

Concepts, Skills, & Problem Solving

11. integers with different signs; -2; negative

13. -2

15. -5

17. -7

19. 3

21. -3

23. 0

25. -4

27. -13

29. no; The quotient should be positive.

31. 15

33. 4

35. -2

37. -2

39. -8

41. 65

43. 5

45. **a.** -2

   b. Score -6 or less in round 4.

47. *Sample answer:* $-20, -15, -10, -5, 0$; Start with -10, then pair -15 with -5 and -20 with 0. The sum of the integers must be $5(-10) = -50$.

Section 2.3
Review & Refresh

1. -2

3. 6

5. 35.28

7. 74.16441

9.

Hours	2	8	$\frac{4}{3}$
Dollars Earned	18	72	12

$2:18$; $8:72$; $\frac{4}{3}:12$

Concepts, Skills, & Problem Solving

11. repeats; 7 is not a factor of a power of 10

13. repeats; 24 is not a factor of a power of 10

15. $0.\overline{09}$

17. $-0.\overline{7}$

19. $1.8\overline{3}$

21. $1.041\overline{6}$

23. $-2.9\overline{4}$

25. $8.68\overline{1}$

27. $-\dfrac{9}{10}$ **29.** $-\dfrac{129}{500}$

31. $-2\dfrac{8}{25}$ **33.** $6\dfrac{3}{250}$

35. a. 0.55 **b.** $\dfrac{11}{20}$

37. $<$

39. no; $9\dfrac{5}{6} = 9.8\overline{3}$ **41.** $-\dfrac{7}{3}, -\dfrac{3}{4}, 0.5, \dfrac{2}{3}, 1.2$

43. $-\dfrac{8}{5}, -1.4, -0.9, \dfrac{1}{4}, 0.6$

45. $-\dfrac{7}{2}, -2.8, -\dfrac{5}{4}, 1.3, \dfrac{4}{3}$

47. $-1\dfrac{91}{200}, -1\dfrac{5}{11}, -1.45, -\dfrac{7}{5}$

49. math quiz

51. a. when a is negative, and a is not a factor of a power of 10

     b. when a and b have the same sign, $a \neq 0 \neq b$, and a and b are factors of a power of 10

Section 2.4
Review & Refresh
1. 0.3125 **3.** $6.\overline{72}$

5. 36 in.^{2} **7.** 121 ft^2

Concepts, Skills, & Problem Solving
9. *Sample answer:* $0.7 \cdot 0.5$; 0.35

11. negative; The numbers have different signs.

13. $\dfrac{1}{3}$ **15.** $2\dfrac{1}{2}$

17. -0.012 **19.** 0.36

21. $-4\dfrac{17}{27}$

23. no; $-2.2 \times (-3.7) = 8.14$

25. $3\dfrac{5}{8}$ gal   **27.** $-\dfrac{3}{8}$

29. -172 **31.** $-1\dfrac{1}{14}$

33. \$4951.45; The total length is $191\dfrac{11}{12}$ yards.

35. $1\dfrac{1}{5}$ **37.** $-2\dfrac{1}{10}$

39. $-5\dfrac{11}{24}$

41. *Sample answer:* $\dfrac{1}{2} \times \left(-\dfrac{5}{4}\right) \times \dfrac{-2}{5}$

Section 2.5
Review & Refresh
1. -0.655 **3.** $\dfrac{1}{8}$

5. Terms: 14, z, $6f$; Coefficients: 1, 6; Constant: 14

7. Terms: $42m$, 18, $12c^2$; Coefficients: 42, 12; Constant: 18

Concepts, Skills, & Problem Solving
9. *Sample answer:* $0.06 \div 0.6$; $0.06 \div 0.1$; 0.1; 0.6

11. -6 **13.** $3.\overline{63}$

15. -2.45 **17.** $\dfrac{2}{5}$

19. no; $-\dfrac{2}{3} \div \dfrac{4}{5} = -\dfrac{2}{3} \times \dfrac{5}{4}$

21. 6 **23.** $-1\dfrac{47}{100}$

25. 1.3 **27.** $\dfrac{1}{9}$

29. a. -0.02 in.

     b. 0.03 in.; $\dfrac{-0.05 + 0.09 + (-0.04) + (-0.08) + 0.03}{5}$ $= -0.01$

31. a. always; *Sample answer:* The number of decimal places in the product is the sum of the numbers of decimal places in the factors.

     b. sometimes; *Sample answer:* $0.5 \div 0.25 = 2$, $0.5 \div 0.3 = 1.\overline{6}$

Chapter 3

Section 3.1
Review & Refresh
1. $-\dfrac{1}{2}$ **3.** $-6\dfrac{1}{2}$

5. 15%, 1450%, 14.8, $15\dfrac{4}{5}$

Concepts, Skills, & Problem Solving
7. no; Expression 2 simplifies to $-5x$.

9. Terms: t, 8, $3t$; Like terms: t and $3t$

11. Terms: $2n$, $-n$, -4, $7n$; Like terms: $2n$, $-n$ and $7n$

13. Terms: $1.4y$, 5, -4.2, $-5y^2$, z; Like terms: 5 and -4.2

15. no; The terms are $3x$, -5, $-2x$, and $9x$ and the like terms are $3x$, $-2x$, and $9x$.

17. $11x + 2$

19. $4b - 5$

21. $-2.3v - 5$

23. $3 - \dfrac{1}{2}y$

25. $10.2x$; each hiker carries 10.2 pounds of equipment; 40.8 lbs

27. *Sample answer:* $15x^2 - 6x^2 + 2x^2 + 2y + y$;

$15x^2 - 6x^2 + 2x^2 + 2y + y$
$= \left[15x^2 + (-6x^2) + 2x^2 \right] + (2y + y)$
$= 11x^2 + 3y$, and $8x^2 + 3x^2 + 3y = 11x^2 + 3y$

29. Find the difference of the two distances. Divide the difference by 60 minutes to determine the distance per minute. This difference of the distances traveled in miles per minute can be multiplied by the number of minutes to find the difference of the distances traveled.

31. a. 153 in.²;
Area $= 240 - 32x + x^2 = 240 - 32(3) + 3^2$
$= 240 - 96 + 9 = 153$ in.²

b. *Sample answer:* England

Section 3.2
Review & Refresh

1. $15f$

3. $-11z - 3$

5. $\dfrac{2}{5}$

7. D

Concepts, Skills, & Problem Solving

9. $(2x + 7) - (2x - 4) = 11$

11. $2b + 9$

13. $6x - 18$

15. $-3\dfrac{3}{10}z - 11$

17. $\dfrac{3}{2}x + 2y - 3.5$

19. $-3g - 4$

21. $-7y + 20$

23. $-3\dfrac{1}{8}c + 15\dfrac{5}{8}$

25. $-6m - \dfrac{1}{4}n + 8\dfrac{1}{3}$

27. no; Your friend dropped the second set of parentheses instead of adding the opposite of the second expression.

29. no; If the variable terms are opposites, the sum is a numerical expression.

31. a. $(55w + 145)$ dollars;
$(10w + 120) + (45w + 25) = 55w + 145$

b. $145; $55

c. *Sample answer:* You would need to have a total of $650 in the accounts.
$55w + 145 = 650$
$55w = 505$
$w = 9.\overline{18}$
After 10 weeks, you can buy the new phone.

Section 3.3
Review & Refresh

1. $6b - 1$

3. $-6z - 5$

5. -36

7. -56

9. $\left|3.5\right| < \left|-5.8\right|$

Concepts, Skills, & Problem Solving

11. $6.5(3x + 4) - 6.5(x + 2), 6.5(2x + 2)$;
$6.5(3x + 4) - 6.5(x + 2) = 19.5x + 26 - 6.5x - 13$
$= 13x + 13$;
$6.5(2x + 2) = 13x + 13$

13. $3a - 21$

15. $-15m + 20$

17. $13.5s + 27$

19. $-2p + 2\dfrac{2}{5}$

21. $8y + 16$

23. $6d + 49.8$

25. $1\dfrac{1}{2}y - \dfrac{3}{8}z$

27. $3\dfrac{1}{3}a + 15b$

29. no; $-3(4 - 5b + 7) = -3(11 - 5b)$
$= -3(11) - (-3)(5b)$
$= -33 + 15b$

31. $-20a - 28$

33. $-4\dfrac{1}{4}p + 25$

35. $\dfrac{2}{7}n - 1\dfrac{4}{7}$

37. $7200 + 57d$; For the 6 snow fans, it costs $7200 to buy them and $57 per day to operate them.

39. *Sample answer:*

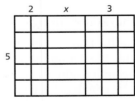

$5x + 25$

41. a. $8s + 16$; *Sample answer:*

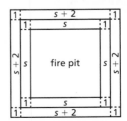

b. $4s + 8n - 4$; Row 1 is $4s + 4$ and row 2 is
$4(s + 2) + 4 = 4s + 12$, so row n is
$4\bigl(s + 2(n - 1)\bigr) + 4$.

Section 3.4

Review & Refresh

1. $8k - 40$

3. $\frac{1}{2}g + 1\frac{1}{2}$

5. -10.3

7. 2

9. -8

Concepts, Skills, & Problem Solving

11. *Sample answer:* $\frac{2}{3}\left(\frac{5}{4}m + n\right)$; Factor out $\frac{2}{3}$ from each area. Because $\frac{2}{3}$ is the width of the smaller rectangles, the two lengths are $\frac{5}{4}m$ and n.

13. $16(2z - 3)$

15. $3(y - 8)$

17. $2(3 + 8k)$

19. $4(5z - 2)$

21. $4(9a + 4b)$

23. $3(4 + 3g - 10h)$

25. $\frac{1}{3}(b - 1)$

27. $2.2(x + 2)$

29. $0.8(w + 4.5)$

31. $4\left(h - \frac{3}{4}\right)$

33. $\frac{3}{8}\left(z + \frac{8}{3}\right)$

35. $\frac{5}{2}\left(k - \frac{4}{5}\right)$

37. yes; Your friend factored out the $\frac{2}{3}$ properly from the sum and correctly rewrote the expression.

39. $-6\left(-3z + \frac{5}{2}\right)$

41. $-\frac{1}{2}(x - 12)$

43. $-\frac{1}{4}(2x + 5y)$

45. *Sample answer:* Because the mat is a square, all sides are the same length. The perimeter is $12x - 32$, and to find the dimension of each side, divide each term by 4. The length of each side is $3x - 8$ and $4(3x - 8) = 12x - 32$.

47. $30 + 9.75p$; For each kit, the pen costs $30 and each package of plastic costs $9.75.

Chapter 4

Section 4.1

Review & Refresh

1. $4(x - 5)$

3. $-\frac{2}{5}(w - 2)$

5. -56

7. -9

9. B

Concepts, Skills, & Problem Solving

11. $x = -2$; Add three $+1$ tiles to each side of the equation.

13. $a = 19$

15. $k = -20$

17. $g = -10$

19. $w = -15.4$

21. $p = \frac{2}{3}$

23. $y = -2.08$

25. $q = \frac{5}{18}$

27. $w = -1\frac{13}{24}$

29. $n - 4 = -15; n = -11$

31. $y + (-3) = -8; y = -5$

33. $t - 184.9 = -109.3; 75.6°F$

35. $10\frac{3}{4}$ m; The solution of $h - \left(-7\frac{3}{4}\right) = 18\frac{1}{2}$ is $h = 10\frac{3}{4}$.

37. 3.8 in.

39. 152 ft; The solution of $305 = h + 153$ is $152 = h$.

41. $41\frac{4}{15}$ km; The solution of $65\frac{3}{5} = d + 24\frac{1}{3}$ is $41\frac{4}{15} = d$.

43. 74.36

45. $2, -2$

47. $13, -13$

Section 4.2

Review & Refresh

1. $n = -3$

3. $h = -15.1$

5. -9

7. -9

Concepts, Skills, & Problem Solving

9. $x = -4$; Divide each side into 4 equal groups.

11. $x = 4$; Divide each side into 5 equal groups, then add a $+$ variable and four $+1$ tiles to each side of the equation.

13. $t = 9$

15. $k = -27$

17. $t = -4$

19. $b = 40$

21. $d = -9$

23. $p = 24$

25. $c = -20$

27. $y = -16\frac{1}{4}$

29. $\frac{x}{-9} = -16; x = 144$

31. $15x = -75; x = -5$

33. $0.75n = 36$; 48 bracelets

35 and 37. Sample answers are given.

35. a. $3x = -9$

b. $\frac{x}{2} = -1.5$

37. a. $5x = -\frac{5}{2}$

b. $\frac{x}{2} = -\frac{1}{4}$

39. All of them except "multiply each side by $-\frac{2}{3}$."

41. 1952 students; The solution of $\frac{3}{4}s = 1464$ is $s = 1952$.

43. $30.12; The solution of $150.60 = \frac{5}{6}x$ is $180.72 = x$ and $180.72 - 150.60 = \$30.12$.

45. $1\frac{3}{5}$ days; The solution of $\frac{5}{7}d = 4$ is $d = 5\frac{3}{5}$ and $5\frac{3}{5} - 4 = 1\frac{3}{5}$.

Section 4.3
Review & Refresh
1. $z = 6$ **3.** $m = -20$

5. -34.72 **7.** $-3\frac{1}{8}$

9. C

Concepts, Skills, & Problem Solving
11. $-3x + 4 = -11; x = 5$

13. $b = -3$ **15.** $t = -4$

17. $g = 4.22$ **19.** $p = 3\frac{1}{2}$

21. $h = -8.5$ **23.** $y = -6.4$

25. no; *Sample answer:* Use the Distributive Property first.

27. $a = 1\frac{1}{3}$ **29.** $b = 13\frac{1}{2}$

31. $v = -\frac{1}{30}$ **33.** $v = -5$

35. $d = -12$

37. 3 games; The solution of $2.5 + 2.25x = 9.25$ is $x = 3$.

39. $h = 9$

41. a. $\frac{x-5}{3} = 9$; 32 insects

  b. 32 insects; *Sample answer:* $3 \cdot 9 + 5 = 32$

  c. *Sample answers:* The length of a rectangle is 3 inches more than 2 times the width. The perimeter is 52 inches. Find the length; You currently have 13 coins after a classmate gave you 5 coins. How many coins did you start with?

Section 4.4
Review & Refresh
1. $p = 11$ **3.** $x = -7$

5. $n = 5$ **7.** C

Concepts, Skills, & Problem Solving
9. *Sample answer:* 21; all integers greater than or equal to 20

11. *Sample answer:* -600; all values less than -400

13. $w + 2.3 > 18$ **15.** $b - 4.2 < -7.5$

17. yes; The inequality is correct.

19. no **21.** yes

23. no

25.

27.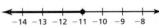

29. no **31.** no

33. a. $1.25x > 35$

  b. yes; It cost $56.25 for 45 trips, which is more than the $35 monthly pass.

35.

Section 4.5
Review & Refresh
1. $p > 5$ **3.** $n + \frac{2}{3} \geq 5\frac{1}{3}$

5. $w = -27$ **7.** $h = 80$

Concepts, Skills, & Problem Solving
9. $-1 < 4$; yes; $1 < 6$

11. $-4 < -1$; yes; $-2 < 1$

13. $a > 6$

15. $k \leq -11$

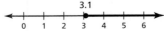

17. $n < 9$

19. $p \geq 1\frac{3}{4}$

21. $z \geq 3.1$

23. $-\dfrac{4}{5} > s$

25. $r < -0.9$

27. no; The graph should have an open circle at 5.

29. **a.** $15 + p \le 44$; $p \le 29$ passengers

    b. no; Only 29 more passengers can board the plane.

31. $x > 5$ in.   **33.** 4

35. **a.** $x \le 1350$ watts

    b. *Sample answer:* aquarium and television; yes;
    $200 + 150 = 350$ watts,
    $200 + 1100 = 1300$ watts

Section 4.6
Review & Refresh

1. $h < 2$

3. $n \ge -\dfrac{1}{10}$

5. $v = 45$ **7.** $m = 4$

Concepts, Skills, & Problem Solving

9. $-2 < 5$; yes; no; $-4 < 10$, $4 \not< -10$

11. $6 > -3$; yes; no; $12 > -6$, $-12 \not> 6$

13. $c \le -36$

15. $x < -32$

17. $k > 2$

19. $y \le -3$

21. $9.2x \ge 299$; $x \ge 32.5$ h

23. $n \ge -3$

25. $h \le -24$

27. $y > \dfrac{14}{3}$

29. $m < -27$

31. $b > 6$

33. yes; The properties of inequalities were all used correctly to find the solution.

35. $\dfrac{p}{7} < -3$; $p < -21$ **37.** $-2x > 30$; $x < -15$

39. $-2.5s < -20$; $s > 8$ sec

41. $10x \ge 120$; $x \ge 12$ cm

43. at least 5 days; The solution of $37d \ge 185$ is $d \ge 5$.

45. **a–c.** Answers will vary.

47. $m > -1$ and $m < 5$

49. $x \ge 3$

Section 4.7
Review & Refresh

1. $x \le -6$

3. $g \ge -8$

5.

Boys	6	3	30
Girls	10	5	50

    $6:10$, $3:5$, $30:50$

Concepts, Skills, & Problem Solving

7. $2x + 4 \ge -6$; $x \ge -5$

9. $y < 1$

11. $h > \dfrac{9}{2}$

13. $b \le -6$

15. $g > -1$

17. $k \ge -18$

19. $n < -0.6$

21. no; *Sample answer:* 4 should be multiplied by 3.

23. $n \ge 8$ additional jumps

25. $d > 6$

27. at least 6 lb

29. a. $150x + 450 \le 1000$; $x \le 3\frac{2}{3}$

   b. 0, 1, 2, 3; *Sample answer:* Only nonnegative integers make sense for the problem.

Chapter 5

Section 5.1
Review & Refresh

1. $p \ge 3$

3. $d \ge -7$

5. 0.84   **7.** D

Concepts, Skills, & Problem Solving

9. *Sample answer:*

x	$\frac{4}{5}$	8	2	$\frac{14}{5}$
y	$\frac{1}{2}$	5	$\frac{5}{4}$	$\frac{7}{4}$

yes; The values of the ratios are $\frac{8}{5}$.

11. $\frac{1}{2} : 3$; $\frac{1}{6}$; The amount of mint leaves is $\frac{1}{6}$ the amount of chopped watermelon.

13. $\frac{3}{4} : \frac{1}{2}$; $1\frac{1}{2}$; The amount of lime juice is $1\frac{1}{2}$ the amount of mint leaves.

15. 80, $\frac{1}{12}$, $\frac{3}{4}$; 20 : $\frac{1}{6}$; 80 : $\frac{2}{3}$; 10 : $\frac{1}{12}$; 90 : $\frac{3}{4}$

17. $\frac{1}{12}$, $1\frac{1}{2}$, $\frac{1}{48}$; $\frac{1}{24} : \frac{1}{2}$; $\frac{1}{12} : 1$; $\frac{1}{8} : 1\frac{1}{2}$; $\frac{1}{48} : \frac{1}{4}$

19. yes; There are 2 boys for every 3 girls.

21. 300 m^2

23. 108 pounds of mulch; 72 pounds of gravel

Section 5.2
Review & Refresh

1. $\frac{3}{2}$, $\frac{4}{3}$, $\frac{4}{9}$; $\frac{3}{4} : \frac{1}{3}$; $\frac{3}{2} : \frac{2}{3}$; $3 : \frac{4}{3}$; $1 : \frac{4}{9}$

3. $>$ **5.** $=$

Concepts, Skills, & Problem Solving

7. $210°$; $\frac{360°}{h} \times \frac{7}{12} h = 210°$

9. 60 mi : 1 h   **11.** $\frac{1}{10}$ lb : 1 day

13. $2.40 : 1$ lb   **15.** 54 words : 1 min

17. $2\frac{1}{2}$ oz : 1 pt

19. 75, 100, $\frac{2}{3}$; 25 : $\frac{1}{3}$; 50 : $\frac{2}{3}$; 75 : 1; 100 : $\frac{4}{3}$

21. 2.2 million people per year

23. no; $75 \div 1.5 = 50$ lb per yr; $38.4 \div 0.75 = 51.2$ oz per yr

25. a. whole milk   **b.** orange juice

27. a. Blue: more than 1500 gallons per minute
   Green: 1000–1499 gallons per minute
   Yellow: 500–999 gallons per minute
   Red: less than 500 gallons per minute

   b. *Sample answer:* If a firefighter pumps water out at too high a rate, the pipes in the ground could burst.

Section 5.3
Review & Refresh

1. 6 in. : 1 yr   **3.** 7000 steps : 1 h

5. -13 **7.** -18

9. $x = 150$ **11.** $x = 75$

Concepts, Skills, & Problem Solving

13. 24 min   **15.** 48.6 min

17. yes   **19.** yes

21. no   **23.** no

25. no   **27.** yes

29. no; $\frac{8}{3} \neq \frac{9}{4}$ **31.** yes

33. no **35.** yes

37. you: 1.1 beats per second, friend: 1.2 beats per second; No, the rates are not equivalent.

39. yes; The value of the ratio of height to base for both triangles is $\frac{4}{5}$.

41. **a.** no; *Sample answer:* Adding two pennies and two dimes to the coins will give a ratio of 5 pennies : 4 dimes. This ratio is not equivalent to 3 pennies : 2 dimes.

b. yes; *Sample answer:* Adding two pennies and two dimes to the coins will give a ratio of 6 pennies : 6 dimes. This ratio is equivalent to 4 pennies : 4 dimes.

43. 30 min; $\frac{60}{2300} = \frac{x}{1150}$, $x = 30$

45. **a.** *Sample answer:* Machines at a factory that produce an output of a certain amount per unit of time.

b. *Sample answer:* Running 10 laps during gym class. The time it takes to run each lap is rarely exactly the same.

47.

x	10	4	6	1
y	5	2	3	0.5

$\frac{10}{5} = \frac{4}{2} = \frac{6}{3} = \frac{1}{0.5}$

Section 5.4
Review & Refresh

1. no

3 and 5.

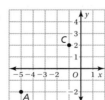

7. D

Concepts, Skills, & Problem Solving

9. 150 mi **11.** 90 mi

13–27. Explanations will vary.

13. $y = 16$ **15.** $b = 20$

17. $v = 10.5$ **19.** $n = 15$

21. $y = 7\frac{1}{3}$ **23.** $d = 15$

25. $n = 10$ **27.** $k = 5.4$

29. yes; Both cross products give the equation $3x = 60$.

31. 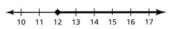 $\frac{n \text{ winners}}{85 \text{ entries}} = \frac{34 \text{ winners}}{170 \text{ entries}}$

33.  $\frac{100 \text{ meters}}{x \text{ seconds}} = \frac{200 \text{ meters}}{22.4 \text{ seconds}}$

35. $x = 16$ **37.** $x = 1$

39. $x = 4$ **41.** 3 trombones

43. 90 adults **45.** $15

47. 4 bags **49.** about 3.72

51. about 40.5 **53.** $d = 12$

55. no; The relationship is not proportional. It should take more people less time to build the swing set.

57. $\frac{1}{5}$; $\frac{m}{k} = \frac{\frac{n}{2}}{\frac{5n}{2}} = \frac{n}{2} \cdot \frac{2}{5n} = \frac{1}{5}$

Section 5.5
Review & Refresh

1. $x = 28$ **3.** $x = 1\frac{1}{3}$

5. -7 **7.** 11

9. $p \geq 12$

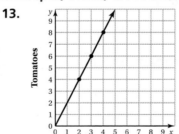

11. $w \geq -5$

Concepts, Skills, & Problem Solving

13.

yes; The line passes through the origin.

15. no; The line does not pass through the origin.

17. yes; The line passes through the origin.

19. yes; The line passes through the origin.

21. (0, 0): You earn $0 for working 0 hours;
(1, 15): You earn $15 for working 1 hour;
(4, 60): You earn $60 for working 4 hours;
$15 : 1 h

23. yes; $k = 1$; The equation can be written as $y = kx$.

25. no; The equation cannot be written as $y = kx$.

27. $k = 24$; $y = 24x$ **29.** $k = \frac{9}{8}$; $y = \frac{9}{8}x$

31. yes; $k = 13$; The cost of 1 ticket is $13; $182

33. about 76,000 mg

Section 5.6

Review & Refresh

1. no; The line does not pass through the origin.

3. $13p$ **5.** $\frac{3}{20}b + 4$

7. $7 + z > 5$

Concepts, Skills, & Problem Solving

9. *Sample answer:*

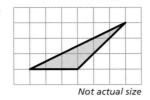

Not actual size

11. 100 mi   **13.** 200 mi

15. 75 in.   **17.** 3.84 m

19. 17.5 mm   **21.** 1 cm : 10 mm; 1

23. **a.** 30 cm; 31.25 cm²   **b.** 9600 m; 3,200,000 m²

25.

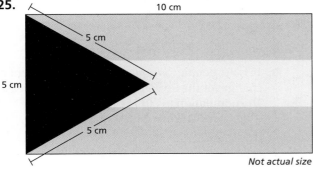

Not actual size

27. The value of the ratio of the perimeters is the scale factor and the value of the ratio of the areas is the square of the scale factor. *Sample answer:* If 2 similar figures have a scale of $a : b$, then the ratio of their perimeters is $a : b$ and the ratio of their areas is $a^2 : b^2$.

Chapter 6

Section 6.1

Review & Refresh

1. 4.5 in.   **3.** $10p - 12$

5. D

Concepts, Skills, & Problem Solving

7. $\frac{5}{6}$; *Sample answer:* convert both to decimals, $0.8\overline{3} > 0.82$

9. 63%   **11.** 60%

13. 0.55

15. 355.4%

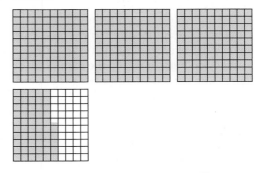

17. 4.1%   **19.** $0.49\overline{92}$

21. 0.29, 29%   **23.** 0.875, 87.5%

25. $0.\overline{7}$, $77.\overline{7}\%$ **27.** 4.5, 450%

29. $2.8\overline{3}$, $283.\overline{3}\%$ **31.** $0.001\overline{3}$, $0.1\overline{3}\%$

33. 0.66, 66.1%, $\frac{2}{3}$, 0.667

35. A   **37.** D

39. Grade 7, Grade 6, Grade 8

41. $1.\overline{1}$ times more shots

43. 14 or more students; $0.44 \times 30 = 13.2$. Because 13.2 is a decimal and over 44% of students read a book last month, round the value up to 14.

Section 6.2

Review & Refresh

1. 0.42, 42%   **3.** $1.\overline{4}$, $144.\overline{4}\%$

5. 3   **7.** -2.5

Concepts, Skills, & Problem Solving

9. 16

11. 50

13. 40%

15. $\dfrac{12}{25} = \dfrac{p}{100}; p = 48$

17. $\dfrac{9}{w} = \dfrac{25}{100}; w = 36$

19. $\dfrac{a}{124} = \dfrac{75}{100}; a = 93$

21. $\dfrac{a}{40} = \dfrac{0.4}{100}; a = 0.16$

23. yes; Your friend wrote and solved the correct percent proportion.

25. $6000

27. $\dfrac{14.2}{w} = \dfrac{35.5}{100}; w = 40$

29. $\dfrac{a}{\frac{7}{8}} = \dfrac{25}{100}; a = \dfrac{7}{32}$

31. $8.40

33. a. a scale along the vertical axis

 b. 6.25%; *Sample answer:* Although you do not know the actual number of votes, you can visualize each bar as a model with the horizontal lines breaking the data into equal parts. The sum of all the parts is 16. Raven has the least parts with 1, which is $100\% \div 16 = 6.25\%$.

 c. 31 votes

35. $5x$

Section 6.3

Review & Refresh

1. $\dfrac{30}{100} = \dfrac{9}{w}; w = 30$

3. $\dfrac{p}{100} = \dfrac{20}{36}; p = 55.\overline{5}$

5. 14

7. $4\dfrac{1}{10}$

9. A

Concepts, Skills, & Problem Solving

11. 40%

13. $a = 0.2 \cdot 150; 30$

15. $35 = 0.35 \cdot w; 100$

17. $29 = p\% \cdot 20; 145\%$

19. $51 = p\% \cdot 300; 17\%$

21. yes; The percent was converted to a decimal and multiplied by the "whole".

23. $200

25. 8%

27. 70 years old

29. If the percent is less than 100%, the percent of a number is less than the number; 50% of 80 is 40; If the percent is equal to 100%, the percent of a number is equal to the number; 100% of 80 is 80; If the percent is greater than 100%, the percent of a number is greater than the number; 150% of 80 is 120.

31. false; If W is 25% of Z, then $Z : W$ is $100 : 25$, because Z represents the whole.

33. 92%

Section 6.4

Review & Refresh

1. $a = 0.25 \cdot 64; 16$

3. $5 = 0.05 \cdot w; 100$

5. $-\dfrac{2}{7}$

7. $\dfrac{1}{3}$

Concepts, Skills, & Problem Solving

9. 20%

11. 6%

13. decrease; 66.7%

15. increase; 225%

17. decrease; 12.5%

19. decrease; 37.5%

21. 12.5% decrease

23. a. $11.\overline{1}\%$

 b. 4000 years old; *Sample answer:* The amount of the error and the original amount are the same, giving the same percent of error.

25. decrease; 25%

27. decrease; 70%

29. a. about 16.95% increase

 b. 161,391 people; *Sample answer:* The percent of change for the 6-year span is a 16.95% increase. The population in 2017 is 138,000, so $138,000 \times 0.1695 = 23,391$ increase in population for 2023. $138,000 + 23,391 = 161,391$ people

31. Box B is acceptable, Box A is unacceptable

33. less than; *Sample answer:* Let x represent the number. A 10% increase is equal to $x + 0.1x$, or $1.1x$. A 10% decrease of this new number is equal to $1.1x - 0.1(1.1x)$, or $0.99x$. Because $0.99x < x$, the result is less than the original number.

35. $8000

Section 6.5

Review & Refresh

1. increase; 25%

3. decrease; about 66.7%

5. $-\dfrac{2}{21}$

7. $6\dfrac{3}{8}$

Concepts, Skills, & Problem Solving

9. 85% off $90;

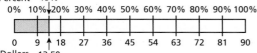

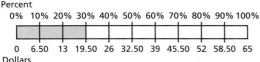

11. $35.70
13. $76.16

15. $53.33
17. $450

19. $172.40
21. 20%

23. $55
25. $175

27. "Multiply $42 by 0.9" and "Multiply $42 by 0.1, then subtract from $42." The first method is easier because it is only one step.

29. a. Store C   **b.** at least 11.82%

31. a. 25%   **b.** 6.5%   **c.** 20%

33. no; $31.08

Section 6.6

Review & Refresh

1. $9.60

3. $x < -3$

5. $w \leq -9$

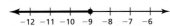

Concepts, Skills, & Problem Solving

7. 8%; $315

9. a. $300   **b.** $1800

11. a. $292.50   **b.** $2092.50

13. a. $1722.24   **b.** $6922.24

15. 3%   **17.** 4%

19. 2 yr   **21.** 1.5 yr

23. $1440   **25.** 2 yr

27. $2720   **29.** $6700.80

31. $8500   **33.** 5.25%

35. 4 yr

37. 12.5 yr; Substitute $2000 for P, $2000 for I, 0.08 for r, and solve for t.

39. Year 1 = $520, Year 2 = $540.80, Year 3 = $562.43

Chapter 7

Section 7.1

Review & Refresh

1. $84   **3.** $36

5. $2 : \frac{1}{2}$; The amount of rolled oats in the recipe is 4 times the amount of chopped peanuts.

7. $\frac{1}{4} : 2$; The amount of pumpkin seeds in the recipe is $\frac{1}{8}$ the amount of rolled oats.

9. $b \geq -5$

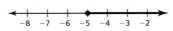

11. $g \leq -3$

Concepts, Skills, & Problem Solving

13. equal chance; *Sample answer:* All numbers have the same area, so you are equally likely to spin each number.

15. 1, 2, 3   **17.** 4 ways

19. a. 1 way   **b.** green

21. a. 1 way   **b.** yellow

23. a. 7 ways

b. red, red, red, purple, purple, green, yellow

25. false; red   **27.** true

29. likely   **31.** certain

33. You are equally likely to be chosen or not chosen.

35. a. likely

b. unlikely

c. no; *Sample answer:* A fair coin would result in an equal number of heads and tails for the relative frequency.

37. a. unlikely; Rolling a 1 has a probability of $\frac{1}{12}$, or $8.\overline{3}\%$, which is unlikely.

b. unlikely; Rolling a multiple of 3 has a probability of $\frac{1}{3}$, or $33.\overline{3}\%$, which is unlikely.

c. equally likely to happen or not happen; Rolling a number greater than 6 has a probability of $\frac{1}{2}$, or 50%, which is equally likely to happen or not happen.

39. With all five cards available, the number of possible outcomes is 5. With only four cards left, the number of possible outcomes is reduced to 4.

41. $\frac{3}{4}$, or 75%

Section 7.2
Review & Refresh

1. unlikely   **3.** 4%

5. no

Concepts, Skills, & Problem Solving

7. $\frac{7}{50}$, or 14%   **9.** $\frac{7}{25}$, or 28%

11. $\frac{17}{50}$, or 34%

13. no; Your friend found the theoretical probability.

15. $\frac{1}{3}$, or about 33.3%   **17.** $\frac{1}{2}$, or 50%

19. 1, or 100%   **21.** $\frac{25}{26}$, or about 96.2%

23. theoretical: $\frac{1}{5}$, or 20%; experimental: $\frac{39}{200}$, or 19.5%; The experimental probability is close to the theoretical probability.

25. theoretical: $\frac{3}{5}$, or 60%; experimental: $\frac{120}{200}$, or 60%; The probabilities are equal.

27. 38 vowels

29. a. $\frac{4}{9}$, or about 44.4%   **b.** 5 males

31. a.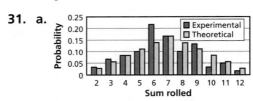

b. As the number of trials increases, the most likely sum will change from 6 to 7.

c. *Sample answer:* The experimental probability should approach the theoretical probability.

Section 7.3
Review & Refresh

1. $\frac{19}{100}$, or 19%   **3.** $\frac{71}{100}$, or 71%

5. 6   **7.** 12

Concepts, Skills, & Problem Solving

9. a password with 6 numbers

11. Sample space: Realistic Lion, Realistic Bear, Realistic Hawk, Realistic Dragon, Cartoon Lion, Cartoon Bear, Cartoon Hawk, Cartoon Dragon; 8 possible outcomes

13. Sample space: Cube Metal, Cube Plastic, Cube Rubber, Necklace Metal, Necklace Plastic, Necklace Rubber, Spinner Metal, Spinner Plastic, Spinner Rubber; 9 possible outcomes

15. 12 possible outcomes

17. 24 possible outcomes

19. a. tree diagram or the Fundamental Counting Principle

b. 12 possible outcomes

21. $\frac{1}{10}$, or 10%   **23.** $\frac{1}{5}$, or 20%

25. $\frac{2}{5}$, or 40%   **27.** $\frac{1}{18}$, or $5\frac{5}{9}$%

29. $\frac{1}{9}$, or $11\frac{1}{9}$%

31. a. $\frac{1}{9}$, or about 11.1%

b. It increases the probability that your guesses are correct to $\frac{1}{4}$, or 25%, because you are only choosing between 2 choices for each question.

33. There are 1000 possible combinations. With 5 tries, you would guess 5 out of the 1000 possibilities. So, the probability of getting the correct combination is $\frac{5}{1000}$, or 0.5%.

35. a. Fundamental Counting Principle; The Fundamental Counting Principle is more efficient. A tree diagram would be too large.

b. 1,000,000,000 or one billion

c. *Sample answer:* Not all possible number combinations are used for Social Security Numbers (SSN). SSNs are coded into geographical, group, and serial numbers. Some SSNs are reserved for commercial use and some are forbidden for various reasons.

37. 10 ways

Section 7.4
Review & Refresh

1. $\frac{7}{40}$, or 17.5%   **3.** $5a - 10$

5. $-3p + 8$

Concepts, Skills, & Problem Solving

7. $\frac{2}{15}$, or $13.\overline{3}\%$

9. Answers will vary, but the theoretical probability is $\frac{5}{32}$, 0.15625, or 15.625%.

11. Answers will vary, but the theoretical probability is $\frac{25}{27}$, about 0.9259, or about 92.59%.

13. Answers will vary, but the theoretical probability is $\frac{16}{27}$, about 0.5926, or about 59.26%.

15. Answers will vary, but the theoretical probability is $\frac{18}{25}$, 0.72, or 72%.

17. Answers will vary, but the theoretical probability is $\frac{161}{1250}$, 0.1288, or 12.88%.

19. Answers will vary, but the theoretical probability is $\frac{343}{1000}$, 0.343, or 34.3%.

Chapter 8

Section 8.1
Review & Refresh

1. Answers will vary, but the theoretical probability is $\frac{9}{50}$, 0.18, or 18%.

3. $x < 7$

5. $r > \frac{4}{3}$

Concepts, Skills, & Problem Solving

7. yes; $\frac{5}{50} = 0.1 = 10\%$

9. Population: All cards in a deck, Sample: 4 cards

11. biased; The sample is not representative of the population because people who go to a park are more likely to think that the park needs to be remodeled.

13. Sample A; It is representative of the population.

15. a population; There are few enough students in your homeroom to not make the surveying difficult.

17. *Sample answer:* The person could ask, "Do you agree with the town's unfair ban on skateboarding on public property?"

19. yes; The sample is representative of the population, selected at random, and large enough to provide accurate data; 330 votes

Section 8.2
Review & Refresh

1. valid

3. $\frac{x}{100} = \frac{12}{30}$; 40%

Concepts, Skills, & Problem Solving

5. yes; $\frac{14}{50} = 28\%$, which is close to 30%

7. **a.** 330, 360, 420

   b. median: 360 customers; range: 90 customers

9. **a.** 2.9, 3.5, 3.2, 3.6; median: 3.35 nights; range: 0.7 night

   b. 3.3 nights

11. *Sample answer:* Most of the samples are within 15% of the actual percentage.

13. Answers will vary.

15. *Sample answer:* The larger the sample size, the closer the sample estimate will be to the theoretical percentage.

Section 8.3
Review & Refresh

1. yes; $\frac{4}{15}$, or $26.\overline{6}\%$, is close to 20%.

3. 30 kilometers per hour

Concepts, Skills, & Problem Solving

5. no; *Sample answer:* none of the sets have similar values

7. Data set A has a greater median and Data set B has a greater range and greater IQR.

9. Data set B

11. yes; Because the difference in means is greater than two times the MAD, the attendance is significantly greater.

13. no; The difference in the medians is 0.8 to 1 times the IQR.

Section 8.4
Review & Refresh

1. Data set B has a greater median and a greater IQR.

3. $b = 5$ **5.** $z = \dfrac{2}{3}$

Concepts, Skills, & Problem Solving

7. non-teachers spend more time on recreation each week than teachers; *Sample answer:* 75% of non-teachers spend at least 6 hours on recreation. 50% of teachers spend less than 5 hours on recreation.

9. yes; *Sample answer:* The variation for Lake A and Lake B are the same, but the measure of center for Lake A is greater than the measure of center for Lake B. You can conclude that Lake A generally contains larger fish than Lake B.

11. *Sample answer:* The measures of center and variation for Type B are greater than Type A. You can conclude that growths of the Type B corn seedlings are larger and vary by more than the Type A corn seedlings.

13. a. Check students' work. Experiments should include taking many samples of a manageable size from each grade level. This will be more doable if the work of sampling is divided among the whole class, and the results are pooled together.

    b. Check students' work. The data may or may not support a conclusion.

Chapter 9

Section 9.1
Review & Refresh

1. Jar A: Median: 3, IQR: 2; Jar B: Median: 6, IQR: 2

3. A

Concepts, Skills, & Problem Solving

5. about 4.08 in.   **7.** 14 mm

9. 4 in.   **11.** $1\dfrac{1}{5}$ cm

13. about 18.84 cm   **15.** about 7.71 ft

17. about 1.42 mm

19. a. about 25 m; about 50 m

    b. about 2 times greater

21. about 31.4 cm; about 62.8 cm

23. about 69.08 m; about 138.16 m

25. yes; Because $\dfrac{\text{circumference}}{\text{radius}} = \dfrac{2\pi r}{r} = 2\pi$, the ratio is the same for every circle.

27. The circle has a diameter of π inches, so use a diameter of about 3.1 inches.

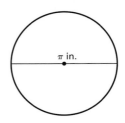

29. a. small tire: about 127 rotations; large tire: about 38 rotations

    b. *Sample answer:* A bicycle with large wheels would allow you to travel farther with each rotation of the pedal.

Section 9.2
Review & Refresh

1. about 28.26 cm

3. 3 possible outcomes

Concepts, Skills, & Problem Solving

5. about 6.75 cm^2

7. about 254.34 mm^2

9. about 314 in.^{2}

11. about 3.14 cm^2

13. no; The diameter was doubled instead of taking half of the diameter to find the radius.

15. about 192.33 cm^2

17. about 628 cm^2

19. about 1.57 ft^2

21. about 942 ft^2; *Sample answer:* The running area is $\dfrac{3}{4}$ the area of a circle with a radius of 20 feet.

23. about 65.94 mi^2

25. circumference doubles and area quadruples; circumference triples and area is 9 times greater; double the radius: circumference $= 2\pi(2r) = 4\pi r$, $\dfrac{4\pi r}{2\pi r} = 2$ times larger, area $= \pi(2r)^2 = 4\pi r^2$, $\dfrac{4\pi r^2}{\pi r^2} = 4$ times larger;

triple the radius: circumference $= 2\pi(3r) = 6\pi r$, $\dfrac{6\pi r}{2\pi r} = 3$ times larger, area $= \pi(3r)^2 = 9\pi r^2$, $\dfrac{9\pi r^2}{\pi r^2} = 9$ times larger

Section 9.3
Review & Refresh
1. about 50.24 mm^2 3. 30 ft
5. 1 m

Concepts, Skills, & Problem Solving
7. *Sample answer:* about 24 units
9. about 19.5 units; 13.5 units^2
11. about 24.6 units; about 41.1 units^2
13. about 19 units; 24 units^2
15. 56 m; 137 m^2 17. 29 cm; 49.5 cm^2
19. The starting points are staggered so that each runner can run the same distance and use the same finish line. This is necessary because the circumference is different for each lane. The diagram shows this because the diameter is greater in the outer lanes.

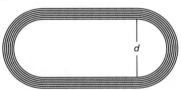

21. 24 m^2
23. *Sample answer:* By adding the triangle shown by the dashed line to the L-shaped figure, you *reduce* the perimeter.

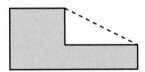

no; For the composite figure below, adding any figure increases its perimeter.

Section 9.4
Review & Refresh
1. 14 in.; 8 in.^{2}
3. Electric Extra Soft, Electric Soft, Electric Medium, Traditional Extra Soft, Traditional Soft, Traditional Medium; 6 possible outcomes

Concepts, Skills, & Problem Solving
5. 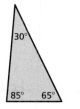   7. not possible

9. 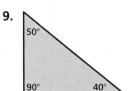   11. not possible

13. no; *Sample answer:* Your friend was using the rule for side lengths. Because the sum of the angle measures is 180°, you can draw the triangle.

15.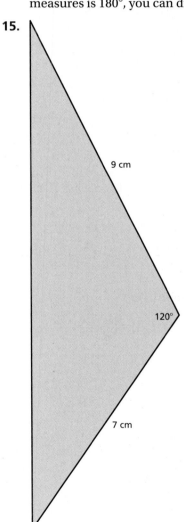

17.

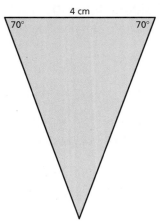

19. not possible

21.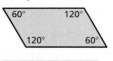

23. yes; *Sample answer:* The sum of the lengths of any two sides is 12 inches, which is greater than the length of the third side, 6 inches.

25. many; With only 1 angle measure and 1 side length given, many triangles can be created.

27. one; Only one line segment can be drawn between the endpoints of the two given sides.

29. one; The other angle measure will be 125°. You can draw the two angles that connect to the given side length. The other two sides will only intersect at one possible point.

31. *Sample answer:*   **33.** *Sample answer:*

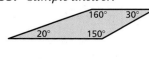

35.   **37.**

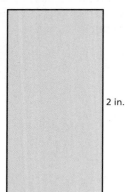

39. infinitely many; *Sample answer:* The fourth side is a fixed length, but the angles are not fixed.

41. about 5.56 m²

43. *Sample answer:*

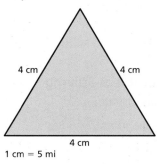

1 cm = 5 mi

about 173.2 mi²

Section 9.5
Review & Refresh

1. not possible

3. $y \geq -5$

5. $x \geq 7.5$

Concepts, Skills, & Problem Solving

7. ∠BAC and ∠EAD, ∠BAE and ∠CAD; *Sample answer:* All vertical angles are opposite angles formed by the intersection of two lines.

9. *Sample answer:* ∠BAC and ∠CAD

11. *Sample answer:* ∠EAF and ∠CAB

13. neither; The angles do not share a common side (adjacent) nor are they opposite angles formed by two intersecting lines (vertical).

15. vertical; The angles are opposite angles formed by the intersection of two lines.

17. complementary; The sum of the measures of the angles is 90°.

19. no; ∠LMN and ∠PMQ are complementary, not supplementary.

21. vertical; 128   **23.** vertical; 25

25. supplementary; 20   **27.** complementary; 55

29. ∠1 = 130°, ∠2 = 50°, ∠3 = 130°; *Sample answer:* ∠2 is a vertical angle to 50°, ∠1 and ∠2 are supplementary angles, ∠1 and ∠3 are vertical angles.

31. 43

33. ∠KJL = 80°, ∠NJM = 25°, ∠MJL = 75°

35. *Sample answer:*

37. *Sample answer:*

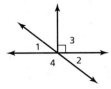

39. sometimes

41. sometimes

43.

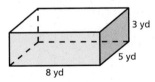

45. They are right angles.

47. a. $25°$ **b.** $65°$

49. $45°; 90°$

Chapter 10

Section 10.1

Review & Refresh

1. supplementary; 146   **3.** vertical; 49

5. about 1017.36 mm^2

Concepts, Skills, & Problem Solving

7. triangular prism; 264 units^2

9. 324 m^2 **11.** 136 m^2

13. 49.2 yd^2

15. no; The area of the 3×5 face is used 4 times rather than just twice.

17. 156 in.^2

19. *Sample answer:*

3 yd
5 yd
8 yd

21. a. 0.125 pint

b. 1.125 pints

c. red and green: The ratio of the paint volumes (red to green) is $4:1$ and the ratio of the edge lengths is $2:1$.

green and blue: The ratio of the paint volumes (blue to green) is $9:1$ and the ratio of the edge lengths is $3:1$.

The ratio of the paint volumes is the square of the ratio of the edge lengths.

Section 10.2

Review & Refresh

1. 142 cm^2 **3.** A

Concepts, Skills, & Problem Solving

5. about 8195.4 in.^2 **7.** about 31.4 m^2

9. about 87.9 mm^2

11. about 282.6 cm^2

13. about 226.1 in.^2

15. no; The area of only one base is added. The first term should have a factor of 2.

17. about $12,560 \text{ mm}^2$

19. a. about 129.1 cm^2, about 470.6 cm^2

b. about 4.0 lb

21. a. 4 times greater; 9 times greater; 25 times greater; 100 times greater

b. When both dimensions are multiplied by a factor of x, the surface area increases by a factor of x^2; $x^2(2\pi r^2 + 2\pi rh)$

Section 10.3

Review & Refresh

1. about 244.9 ft^2

3. about 406.9 mm^2

Concepts, Skills, & Problem Solving

5. 40 in.^2 **7.** 151.9 m^2

9. 64 cm^2 **11.** 170.1 yd^2

13. 1240.4 mm^2 **15.** 6 m

17. 283.5 cm^2 **19.** 124 cm^2

21. the slant height; The height is the distance between the top and the point on the base directly beneath it. The distance from the top to any other point on the base is greater than the height.

23. greater than; If it is less than or equal to, then the lateral face could not meet at a vertex to form a solid.

Section 10.4

Review & Refresh

1. 57 m^2 **3.** 115.5 cm^2

5. $144

Concepts, Skills, & Problem Solving

7. $V = 24 \text{ units}^3$; $B = 8 \text{ units}^2$

9. $V = 24 \text{ units}^3$; $B = 12 \text{ units}^2$

11. 288 cm^3 **13.** 210 yd^3

15. 420 mm^3 **17.** 645 mm^3

19. no; The area of the base is wrong.

21. 10 in.; *Sample answer:*

$$V = \ell \cdot w \cdot h$$
$$225 = (9)(2.5)h$$
$$225 = 22.5h$$
$$10 = h$$

23. 1728 in.^{3}

$$1 \times 1 \times 1 = 1 \text{ ft}^3 \qquad 12 \times 12 \times 12 = 1728 \text{ in.}^3$$

25. Check students' work.

27. sometimes; The prisms in Example 3 have different surface areas but the same volume. Two prisms that are exactly the same will have the same surface area.

Section 10.5
Review & Refresh

1. 189 ft^3

3. $r < -0.9$

-1.8 -1.5 -1.2 -0.9 -0.6 -0.3 0

5. $h \le 1.3$

0.8 0.9 1.0 1.1 1.2 1.3 1.4

Concepts, Skills, & Problem Solving

7. Volume of prism $= 6 \cdot 6 \cdot 6 = 216$ in.^{3}

$$V = \frac{1}{3}(6 \cdot 6)(6) = 72 \text{ in.}^3$$

$$V = \frac{1}{3}(6 \cdot 6)(6) = 72 \text{ in.}^3$$

$$V = \frac{1}{3}(6 \cdot 6)(6) = 72 \text{ in.}^3$$

$$72 + 72 + 72 = 216 \text{ in.}^3$$

9. $13\frac{1}{3}$ ft^3 **11.** 20 mm^3

13. 80 in.^{3} **15.** 7 cm^3

17. no; Your friend forgot to multiply by $\frac{1}{3}$.

19. 156 ft^3; *Sample answer:*

Total volume = volume of rectangular prism
             + volume of rectangular pyramid

$$= 6 \cdot 6 \cdot 3 + \frac{1}{3}(6 \cdot 6) \cdot 4$$
$$= 108 + 48$$
$$= 156$$

21. Spire B; 4 in.^{3}

23. *Sample answer:* 5 ft by 4 ft

Section 10.6
Review & Refresh

1. $37\frac{1}{3}$ in.^{3} **3.** $-5w - 12$

Concepts, Skills, & Problem Solving

5. not possible   **7.** possible

9. possible   **11.** rectangle

13. triangle   **15.** circle

17. circle   **19.** circle

21. not possible

23. The intersection is the shape of the base.

25. a. 164 in.^{2}

    b. about 37%;
Brick before cut:
$$S = 2(10 \cdot 4) + 2(10 \cdot 3) + 2(4 \cdot 3) = 164 \text{ in.}^2$$
Bricks after cut:
$$S = 2[2(10 \cdot 2) + 2(10 \cdot 3) + 2(2 \cdot 3)] = 224 \text{ in.}^2$$
$$\frac{224 - 164}{164} = \frac{60}{164} \approx 0.37 \text{ or } 37\%$$

27. *Sample answer:* The area of a cross section is the square of the coefficient of h times the area of the base.

English-Spanish Glossary

English

Spanish

A

absolute value *(p. 4)* The distance between a number and 0 on a number line; The absolute value of a number *a* is written as | *a* |.

valor absoluto *(p. 4)* La distancia entre un número y 0 en una recta numérica; El valor absoluto de un número *a* es escrito como | *a* |.

additive inverse *(p. 11)* The opposite of a number

inverso aditivo *(p. 11)* El opuesto de un número

adjacent angles *(p. 390)* Two angles that share a common side and have the same vertex

ángulos adyacentes *(p. 390)* Dos ángulos que tienen el vértice y un lado en común

B

biased sample *(p. 326)* A sample that is not representative of a population

muestra sesgada *(p. 326)* Una muestra que no es representiva de una población

C

center (of a circle) *(p. 362)* The point inside a circle that is the same distance from all points on the circle

centro (de un círculo) *(p. 362)* El punto dentro de un círculo que está a la misma distancia de todos los puntos en el círculo

circle *(p. 362)* The set of all points in a plane that are the same distance from a point called the center

círculo *(p. 362)* El conjunto de todos los puntos en un plano que están a la misma distancia de un punto llamado el centro

circumference *(p. 363)* The distance around a circle

circunferencia *(p. 363)* La distancia alrededor de un círculo

complementary angles *(p. 390)* Two angles whose measures have a sum of 90°

ángulos complementarios *(p. 390)* Dos ángulos cuyas medidas tienen una suma de 90°

complex fraction *(p. 75)* A fraction that has at least one fraction in the numerator, the denominator, or both

fracción compleja *(p. 75)* Una fracción que tiene al menos una fracción en el numerador, el denominador, o ambos

composite figure *(p. 376)* A figure made up of triangles, squares, rectangles, and other two-dimensional figures

figura compuesta *(p. 376)* Una figura hecha de triángulos, cuadros, rectángulos, y otras figuras bidimensionales

compound event *(p. 302)* A compound event consists of one or more events. The probability of a compound event is the quotient of the number of favorable outcomes and the number of possible outcomes.

evento compuesto *(p. 302)* Un evento compuesto consiste de uno o más eventos. La probabilidad de un evento compuesto es el cociente del número de resultados favorables y el número de resultados posibles.

constant of proportionality *(p. 212)* The number k in the equation $y = kx$; the multiplicative relationship between two quantities

cross products *(p. 197)* In the proportion $\frac{a}{b} = \frac{c}{d}$, the products $a \cdot d$ and $b \cdot c$ are called cross products.

cross section *(p. 440)* The intersection of a plane and a solid

constante de proporcionalidad *(p. 212)* El número k en la ecuación $y = kx$; la relación multiplicativa entre dos cantidades

productos cruzados *(p. 197)* En la proporción $\frac{a}{b} = \frac{c}{d}$, los productos $a \cdot d$ y $b \cdot c$ son llamados productos cruzados.

sección transversal *(p. 440)* La intersección de un plano y un sólido

---
D
---

diameter *(p. 362)* The distance across a circle through the center

discount *(p. 260)* A decrease in the original price of an item

diámetro *(p. 362)* La distancia a través de un círculo, pasando por el centro

descuento *(p. 260)* Una disminución en el precio original de un artículo

---
E
---

equivalent equations *(p. 128)* Equations that have the same solutions

equivalent rates *(p. 190)* Rates that have the same unit rate

equivalent ratios *(p. 185)* Two ratios that describe the same relationship

event *(p. 284)* A collection of one or more outcomes

experiment *(p. 284)* An investigation or a procedure that has varying results

experimental probability *(p. 292)* A probability based on repeated trials of an experiment

ecuaciones equivalentes *(p. 128)* Ecuaciones que tienen las mismas soluciones

tasas equivalentes *(p. 190)* Tasas que tienen la misma tasa de unidad

razones equivalentes *(p. 185)* Dos razones que describen la misma relación

evento *(p. 284)* Un grupo de una o más resultadas

experimento *(p. 284)* Una investigación o un método que tiene resultados variados

probabilidad experimenta *(p. 292)* Una probabilidad basada en ensayos repetidos de un experimento

---
F
---

factoring an expression *(p. 110)* Writing a numerical expression or an algebraic expression as a product of factors

favorable outcomes *(p. 284)* The outcomes of a specific event

Fundamental Counting Principle *(p. 300)* A way to find the total number of possible outcomes

factorizando una expresión *(p. 110)* Escribiendo una expresión numérica o algebraica como un producto de factores

resultados favorables *(p. 284)* Los resultados de un evento especifico

Principio de conteo fundamental *(p. 300)* Un método para descubrir el número total de resultados posibles

G

graph of an inequality *(p. 148)* A graph that shows all the solutions of an inequality on a number line

gráfica de una desigualdad *(p. 148)* Una gráfica que muestra todas las soluciones de una desigualdad en una recta numérica

I

inequality *(p. 146)* A mathematical sentence that compares expressions; contains the symbols $<$, $>$, $\leq$, or $\geq$

desigualdad *(p. 146)* Una oración matemática que compara las expresiones; contiene los símbolos $<$, $>$, $\leq$, or $\geq$

integers *(p. 3)* The set of whole numbers and their opposites

enteros *(p. 3)* El conjunto de números naturales y sus opuestos

interest *(p. 266)* Money paid or earned for the use of money

interés *(p. 266)* Dinero pagado o ganado por el uso del dinero

L

lateral surface area (of a prism) *(p. 412)* The sum of the areas of the lateral faces of a prism

área de superficie lateral (de un prisma) *(p. 412)* La suma de las áreas de las caras laterales de un prisma

like terms *(p. 92)* Terms of an algebraic expression that have the same variables raised to the same exponents

términos semejantes *(p. 92)* Términos de una expresión algebraica que tienen las mismas variables elevadas a los mismos exponentes

linear expression *(p. 98)* An algebraic expression in which the exponent of each variable is 1

expresión lineal *(p. 98)* Una expresión algebraica en la que el exponente de cada variable es 1

M

markup *(p. 260)* The increase from what a store pays to the selling price

sobreprecio *(p. 260)* El aumento de lo que una tienda paga al precio de venta

O

outcomes *(p. 284)* The possible results of an experiment

resultados *(p. 284)* Los resultados posibles de un experimento

percent of change *(p. 254)* The percent that a quantity changes from the original amount;

$$\text{percent of change} = \frac{\text{amount of change}}{\text{original amount}}$$

percent of decrease *(p. 254)* The percent of change when the original amount decreases;

$$\text{percent of decrease} = \frac{\text{original amount} - \text{new amount}}{\text{original amount}}$$

percent error *(p. 256)* The percent that an estimated amount differs from the actual amount;

$$\text{percent error} = \frac{\text{amount of error}}{\text{actual amount}}$$

percent of increase *(p. 254)* The percent of change when the original amount increases;

$$\text{percent of increase} = \frac{\text{new amount} - \text{original amount}}{\text{original amount}}$$

pi (π) *(p. 363)* The ratio of the circumference of a circle to its diameter

population *(p. 325)* A population is an entire group of people or objects.

principal *(p. 266)* An amount of money borrowed or deposited

probability *(p. 285)* A measure of the likelihood, or chance, that an event will occur

proportion *(p. 196)* An equation stating that the values of two ratios are equivalent

proportional *(p. 198)* Two quantities that form a proportion are proportional.

porcentaje de cambio *(p. 254)* El porcentaje que cambia una cantidad de la cantidad original

$$\text{porcentaje de cambio} = \frac{\text{cambio}}{\text{cantidad original}}$$

porcentaje de disminución *(p. 254)* El porcentaje de cambio cuando la cantidad original disminuye;

porcentaje de disminución

$$= \frac{\text{cantidad original} - \text{nueva cantidad}}{\text{cantidad original}}$$

error porcentual *(p. 256)* El porcentaje en que una cantidad estimada difiere de la cantidad real;

$$\text{error porcentual} = \frac{\text{error}}{\text{cantidad correcta}}$$

porcentaje de aumento *(p. 254)* El porcentaje de cambio cuando la cantidad original aumenta;

Porcentaje de aumento

$$= \frac{\text{nueva cantidad} - \text{cantidad original}}{\text{cantidad original}}$$

pi (π) *(p. 363)* La razón de la circunferencia de un círculo a su diámetro

población *(p. 325)* Una población es un grupo entero de personas u objetos.

principal *(p. 266)* Una cantidad de dinero prestada o depositada

probabilidad *(p. 285)* Una medida de la probabilidad o posibilidad de que ocurrirá un evento

proporción *(p. 196)* Una ecuación que se indica que los valores de dos razones son equivalentes

proporcional *(p. 198)* Dos cantidades que forman una proporción son proporcionales.

radius *(p. 362)* The distance from the center of a circle to any point on the circle

rate *(p. 190)* A ratio of two quantities using different units

ratio *(p. 184)* A comparison of two quantities; The ratio *a* to *b* can be written as *a* : *b*.

radio *(p. 362)* La distancia desde el centro de un círculo hasta cualquier punto del círculo

tasa *(p. 190)* Una razón de dos cantidades usando unidades diferentes

razón *(p. 184)* Una comparación de dos cantidades; La razón *a* a *b* se puede escribir como *a* : *b*.

ratio table *(p. 185)* A table used to find and organize equivalent ratios

tabla de razones *(p. 185)* Una tabla usada para encontrar y organizar las razones equivalentes

rational number *(p. 3)* A number that can be written as $\frac{a}{b}$ where a and b are integers and $b \neq 0$

número racional *(p. 3)* Un número que puede ser escrito como $\frac{a}{b}$ donde a y b son enteros y $b \neq 0$

regular pyramid *(p. 422)* A pyramid whose base is a regular polygon

pirámide regular *(p. 422)* Una pirámide cuya base es un polígono regular

relative frequency *(p. 286)* The fraction or percent of the time that an event occurs in an experiment

frecuencia relativa *(p. 286)* La fracción o porcentaje de tiempo en que un evento ocurre en un experimento

repeating decimal *(p. 62)* A decimal that has a pattern that repeats

decimal periódico *(p. 62)* Un decimal que tiene un patrón que se repite

---

S

sample *(p. 325)* A part of a population

muestra *(p. 325)* Una parte de una población

sample space *(p. 300)* The set of all possible outcomes of one or more events

espacio de muestra *(p. 300)* El conjunto de todas los resultados posibles de uno o más eventos

scale *(p. 218)* A ratio that compares the measurements of a drawing or model with the actual measurements

escala *(p. 218)* Una razón que compara las medidas de un dibujo o modelo a las medidas reales

scale drawing *(p. 218)* A proportional, two-dimensional drawing of an object

dibujo a escala *(p. 218)* Un dibujo bidimensional y proporcional de un objeto

scale factor (of a scale drawing) *(p. 219)* The value of a scale when the units are the same

factor de escala (de un dibujo a escala) *(p. 219)* El valor de una escala cuando las unidades son las mismas

scale model *(p. 218)* A proportional, three-dimensional model of an object

modelo a escala *(p. 218)* Un modelo proporcional y tridimensional de un objeto

semicircle *(p. 364)* One-half of a circle

semicírculo *(p. 364)* La mitad de un círculo

simple interest *(p. 266)* Money paid or earned only on the principal

interés simple *(p. 266)* Dinero pagado o ganado solamente en el principal

simplest form (of an algebraic expression) *(p. 92)* An algebraic expression is in simplest form when it has no like terms and no parentheses.

mínima expresión (de una expresión algebraica) *(p. 92)* Una expresión algebraica está en su mínima expresión cuando tiene ningunos términos semejantes y ningunos paréntesis.

simulation *(p. 308)* An experiment that is designed to reproduce the conditions of a situation or process so that the simulated outcomes closely match the real-world outcomes

simulación *(p. 308)* Un experimento que es diseñado para reproducir las condiciones de una situación o proceso, de tal manera que los resultados posibles simulados coincidan en gran medida con los resultados del mundo real

slant height (of a pyramid) *(p. 422)* The height of each lateral triangular face of a pyramid

solution of an inequality *(p. 146)* A value that makes an inequality true

solution set *(p. 146)* The set of all solutions of an inequality

supplementary angles *(p. 390)* Two angles whose measures have a sum of 180°

apotema lateral (de una pirámide) *(p. 422)* La altura de cada cara lateral triangular de una pirámide

solución de una desigualdad *(p. 146)* Un valor que hace una desigualdad verdadera

conjunto solución *(p. 146)* El conjunto de todas las soluciones de una desigualdad

ángulos suplementarios *(p. 390)* Dos ángulos cuyas medidas tienen una suma de 180°

T

---

terminating decimal *(p. 62)* A decimal that ends

theoretical probability *(p. 292)* The quotient of the number of favorable outcomes and the number of possible outcomes when all possible outcomes are equally likely

decimal finito *(p. 62)* Un decimal que termina

probabilidad teórica *(p. 292)* El cociente del número de resultados favorables y el número de posibles resultados cuando todos los resultados posibles son igualmente probables

U

unbiased sample *(p. 326)* A sample that is representative of a population

unit rate *(p. 190)* A rate that compares a quantity to one unit of another quantity

muestra no sesgada *(p. 326)* Una muestra que es representativa de una población

tasa unitaria *(p. 190)* Una tasa que compara una cantidad a una unidad de otra cantidad

V

value of a ratio *(p. 184)* The number $\frac{a}{b}$ associated with the ratio $a : b$

vertical angles *(p. 390)* Opposite angles formed by the intersection of two lines

valor de una razón *(p. 184)* El número $\frac{a}{b}$ asociadas con la razón $a : b$

ángulos verticales *(p. 390)* Ángulos opuestos formados por la intersección de dos líneas

Index

Index

relative frequency as measure of, 286
theoretical, 292–293

Problem solving
strategies, 37
using unit rate for, 191

Problem Solving, *Throughout. For example, see:* 8, 59, 132, 193, 245, 306, 368, 380, 420, 432

Problem-Solving Plan, *In every chapter. For example, see:* 13, 52, 106, 130, 207, 244, 287, 328, 378, 424

Proportion(s)
definition of, 196
percent, 241–246
ratios forming, 196, 197
solving
using mental math for, 204
using multiplication for, 204
solving ratio problems with, 203–210
writing, 205, 206

Proportional relationships
definition of, 198
graphing, 211–216
identifying, 195, 198, 212

Proportionality, constant of, 212

Protractor, 189, 382, 384, 389

Pyramids
bases of, 421
cross sections of, 440
making scale model of, 421
oblique, 434
regular, 422
right, 434
slant height of, 421, 422
surface areas of, 421–426
volumes of, 433–438

Q

Quadrilaterals, 384

R

Radius
in circle area formula, 370
in circumference formula, 363
in cylinder area formula, 416
definition of, 362
finding, 362

Random samples
comparing, 344
comparing populations using, 343–348

describing populations using, 331–336
using multiple, 343, 345

Rate(s), 189–194. *See also* Unit rates
definition of, 190
equivalent, 190
writing, 189

Rate problems, 191

Ratio(s), 183–188
definition of, 184
equivalent, 185, 196, 197, 198, 205
identifying, 183
scale as, 218
value of, 184

Ratio problems, 203–210

Ratio tables, 183–188
completing, 183, 185
equivalent ratios in, 185

Rational numbers, 3–8
absolute values of, 4
adding, 17–22
comparing, 5
converting between different forms of, 61–66
definition of, 3
dividing, 73–78
factoring out, 110
multiplying, 67–72
on number line, 3
subtracting, 29–36

Reading, *Throughout. For example, see:* 63, 146, 153, 184, 266, 390

Real World. *See* Modeling Real Life

Reasonableness, checking for, 70, 244, 287, 372, 378, 418, 424

Reasoning, *Throughout. For example, see:* 8, 51, 95, 147, 200, 252, 290, 374, 408, 441

Reciprocals
definition of, 74
multiplication by, 74
solving equations using, 135

Rectangles, area of, 378

Rectangular prisms
surface area of, 409, 410, 446
volume of, 428

Rectangular pyramids, volume of, 435

Regular pyramid, 422

Relative frequency, 286

Remember, *Throughout. For example, see:* 5, 51, 92, 128, 136, 236, 338, 391, 416, 442

Repeated multiplication, 51

Repeated Reasoning, *Throughout. For example, see:* 22, 270, 306, 374, 420

Repeating decimals, 62, 136

Response to Intervention, *Throughout. For example, see:* T-0B, T-21, T-65, T-88B, T-124B, T-149, T-251, T-313, T-382, T-419

Review & Refresh, *In every lesson. For example, see:* 7, 53, 101, 137, 215, 251, 288, 329, 373, 425

Right prism, 428

Right pyramids, 434

Ruler, 382, 385

S

Sale price, finding, 260

Same signs
adding integers with, 9, 11
adding rational numbers with, 19
dividing integers with, 55, 56
dividing rational numbers with, 73, 74, 75
multiplying integers with, 49, 50, 51
multiplying rational numbers with, 68
subtracting integers with, 23, 24, 25
subtracting rational numbers with, 30, 31, 32

Sample(s), 325–330
biased, 326, 327
definition of, 325
definition and example chart for, 350
random (*See* Random samples)
unbiased, 326, 327
using, 325
variability in, 331

Sample space
definition of, 300
finding, 300, 301

Scaffolding Instruction, *In every lesson. For example, see:* T-4, T-68, T-115, T-146, T-184, T-248, T-292, T-332, T-382, T-410

Scale, definition of, 218

Scale drawings, 217–222
creating, 217
definition of, 218

Scale factor
definition of, 219
example and non-example chart for, 224
finding, 219

Credits

Chapter 7

280 *top* zentilia/Shutterstock.com; *bottom* OnstOn/iStock/Getty Images Plus; **281** ©iStockphoto.com/ryasick; **282** ©iStockphoto.com/ryasick; **284** Sussenn/iStock/Getty Images Plus; **286** *top* Rattasak/iStock/Getty Images Plus, Oda_dao/iStock/Getty Images Plus, antoniotruzzi/iStock/Getty Images Plus; *bottom* Big Ideas Learning, LLC; **287** Roydee/E+/Getty Images; **289** 1550539/iStock/Getty Images Plus, Sussenn/iStock/Getty Images Plus; **290** RomoloTavani/iStock/Getty Images Plus; **291** *top* Meral Hydaverdi/Shutterstock.com; *bottom* Warren Goldswain/Shutterstock.com; **293** ©iStockphoto.com/Eric Ferguson; **294** marylooo/iStock/Getty Images Plus; **295** fatihhoca/E+/Getty Images; **296** gmnicholas/E+/Getty Images; **297** Juanmonino/iStock Unreleased/Getty Images; **298** Feng Yu/Shutterstock.com; **299** *top* FernandoMadeira/iStock/Getty Images Plus; *center* Krasyuk/iStock/Getty Images Plus; *bottom* Mark Aplet/Shutterstock.com; **300** the-lightwriter/iStock/Getty Images Plus; **301** Big Ideas Learning, LLC; **302** Rodrusoleg/iStock/Getty Images Plus; **303** *top* carlosalvarez/E+/Getty Images; *bottom* goir/iStock/Getty Images Plus; **305** Sussenn/iStock/Getty Images Plus; **306** *top left* basar17/iStock/Getty Images Plus; *top* ET-ARTWORKS/DigitalVision Vectors/Getty Images; *bottom* tele52/Shutterstock.com; **307** rbv/iStock/Getty Images Plus; **308** Dorottya_Mathe/iStock/Getty Images Plus; **310** ovro77/iStock/Getty Images Plus; **311** Kagenmi/iStock/Getty Images Plus; **312** *top* urbancow/E+/Getty Images; *bottom* IngaNielsen/iStock/Getty Images Plus; **313** *top* pioneer111/iStock/Getty Images Plus; *bottom* OnstOn/iStock/Getty Images Plus; **317** *top* asiseeit/iStock/Getty Images Plus; *bottom* monkeybusinessimages/iStock/Getty Images Plus

Chapter 8

322 *top* zentilia/Shutterstock.com; *bottom* OnstOn/iStock/Getty Images Plus; **323** ©iStockphoto.com/Eric Isselée; **324** *a. left* ©iStockphoto.com/Shannon Keegan; *a. right* ©iStockphoto.com/Lorelyn Medina; *b. left* Joel Sartore/joelsartore.com; *b. right* Feng Yu/Shutterstock.com; *c. left* ©iStockphoto.com/kledge; *c. right* ©iStockphoto.com/spxChrome; *d.* ©iStockphoto.com/Alex Slobodkin; **325** 3bugsmom/iStock/Getty Images Plus; **326** sihuo0860371/iStock/Getty Images Plus; **328** macrovector/iStock/Getty Images Plus; **329** amwu/iStock/Getty Images Plus; **330** smontgom65/iStock Editorial/Getty Images Plus; **331** *top* DonNichols/E+/Getty Images; *bottom* BanksPhotos/iStock/Getty Images Plus; **332** RKaulitzki/iStock/Getty Images Plus; **334** zrfphoto/iStock/Getty Images Plus; **335** EVAfotografie/iStock/Getty Images Plus; **336** MariaBobrova/iStock/Getty Images Plus; **340** Aneese/iStock/Getty Images Plus; **341** EricFerguson/E+/Getty Images; **342** *top* Geerati/iStock/Getty Images Plus; *bottom* zhuzhu/iStock/Getty Images Plus; **346** ©iStockphoto.com/Rawpixel Ltd; **348** *right* rrocio/E+/Getty Images; *left* bdspn/iStock/Getty Images Plus; **349** OnstOn/iStock/Getty Images Plus; **351** DragonImages/iStock/Getty Images Plus; **353** funduck/iStock/Getty Images Plus; **357** Peter zijlstra/Shutterstock.com

Chapter 9

358 *top* zentilia/Shutterstock.com; *bottom* OnstOn/iStock/Getty Images Plus; **359** peepo/E+/Getty Images; **361** *top* MichaelJay/iStock/Getty Images Plus; *bottom* urbancow/E+/Getty Images, johan10/iStock/Getty Images Plus, junce/iStock/Getty Images Plus; **365** *left* Mechanik/Shutterstock.com; *bottom right* mehmettorlak/E+/Getty Images; **366** *Exercise 6* ©iStockphoto.com/zentillia; *Exercise 7* Mr Doomits/Shutterstock.com; *Exercise 8* Nikolamirejovska/Shutterstock.com; *Exercise 9* ©iStockphoto.com/ALEAIMAGE; *Exercise 10* ©iStockphoto.com/iLexx; *Exercise 11* saicle/iStock/Getty Images Plus; *Exercise 12* boggy22/iStock/Getty Images Plus; *Exercise 13* wragg/iStock/Getty Images Plus; **367** *Exercise 17* akiyoko/iStock/Getty Images Plus; *Exercise 18* ZargonDesign/E+/Getty Images; *bottom* Inok/iStock/Getty Images Plus; **368** *left* ©iStockphoto.com/HultonArchive; *right* Dimedrol68/iStock/Getty Images Plus; **372** *top* trekandshoot/iStock/Getty Images Plus; *bottom* StockPhotoAstur/iStock/Getty Images Plus; **373** *Exercise 1* SergeBogomyako/iStock/Getty Images Plus; *Exercise 2* MileA/iStock/Getty Images Plus; *Exercise 7* ©iStockphoto.com/zentillia; *Exercise 8* boygovideo/iStock/Getty Images Plus; *Exercise 9* prmustafa/iStock/Getty Images Plus; *Exercise 10* ©iStockphoto.com/subjug; *Exercise 11* kulykt/iStock/Getty Images Plus; *Exercise 12* ©iStockphoto.com/7nuit; **380** ©iStockphoto.com/Scott Slattery; **385** asbe/iStock/Getty Images Plus; **386** Gino Santa Maria/Shutterstock.com; **388** Bliznetsov/E+/Getty Images; **395** mountainpix/Shutterstock.com; **396** ©iStockphoto.com/Jorgen Jacobsen; **397** OnstOn/iStock/Getty Images Plus; **399** *Exercise 3* ©iStockphoto.com/DivaNir4A; *Exercise 4* ©iStockphoto.com/Stacey Walker; *Exercise 5* JuSun/E+/Getty Images; *Exercise 6* simonkr/iStock/Getty Images Plus; *bottom* wrangel/iStock/Getty Images Plus; **400** StevenEllingson/iStock/Getty Images Plus; **402** Kalamazoo (Michigan) Public Library

Chapter 10

406 *top* zentilia/Shutterstock.com; *bottom* OnstOn/iStock/Getty Images Plus; **407** tropper2000/iStock/Getty Images Plus; **408** ©iStockphoto.com/Remigiusz Załucki; **412** *left* Bob the Wikipedian/CC-BY-SA-3.0; *right* ©iStockphoto.com/Sherwin McGehee; **414** *top right* mihmihmal/iStock/Getty Images Plus; *center* kriangkrai_net/iStock/Getty Images Plus; *bottom left* ©iStockphoto.com/stevanovicigor; **418** Tsekhmister/iStock/Getty Images Plus; **420** *top* ©iStockphoto.com/Tomasz Pietryszek; *Exercise 17* 10174593_258/iStock/Getty Images Plus; *Exercise 19* Newcastle Drum Centre; *bottom* ©iStockphoto.com/scol22; **421** *left* ©iStockphoto.com/Luke Daniek; *right* vichie81/iStock Editorial/Getty Images Plus; **424** ©iStockphoto.com/Frank Wright; *bottom* hxdyl/iStock/Getty Images Plus; **430** EuToch/iStock/Getty Images Plus; **436** Vladone/iStock/Getty Images Plus; **438** *top* ©iStockphoto.com/ranplett, Image © Courtesy of Museum of Science, Boston; *bottom* ©iStockphoto.com/Yails; **442** yocamon/iStock Editorial/Getty Images Plus; **444** *Exercise 17* ©iStockphoto.com/AlexStar; *Exercise 18* Knartz/Shutterstock.com; *Exercise 19* SOMMAI/Shutterstock.com; *Exercise 25* ©iStockphoto.com/Frank Wright; *bottom* 7activestudio/iStock/Getty Images Plus; **445** OnstOn/iStock/Getty Images Plus; **448** lucagal/iStock/Getty Images Plus; **449** Wimage72/iStock/Getty Images Plus; **450** Tevarak/iStock/Getty Images Plus; **452** ra-design/Shutterstock.com

Cartoon illustrations: Tyler Stout
Design Elements: ©iStockphoto.com/Gizmo; Valdis Torms; Juksy/iStock/Getty Images Plus

Mathematics Reference Sheet

Conversions

U.S. Customary
1 foot = 12 inches
1 yard = 3 feet
1 mile = 5280 feet
1 acre = 43,560 square feet
1 cup = 8 fluid ounces
1 pint = 2 cups
1 quart = 2 pints
1 gallon = 4 quarts
1 gallon = 231 cubic inches
1 pound = 16 ounces
1 ton = 2000 pounds
1 cubic foot ≈ 7.5 gallons

U.S. Customary to Metric
1 inch = 2.54 centimeters
1 foot ≈ 0.3 meter
1 mile ≈ 1.61 kilometers
1 quart ≈ 0.95 liter
1 gallon ≈ 3.79 liters
1 cup ≈ 237 milliliters
1 pound ≈ 0.45 kilogram
1 ounce ≈ 28.3 grams
1 gallon ≈ 3785 cubic centimeters

Time
1 minute = 60 seconds
1 hour = 60 minutes
1 hour = 3600 seconds
1 year = 52 weeks

Temperature
$$C = \frac{5}{9}(F - 32)$$

$$F = \frac{9}{5}C + 32$$

Metric
1 centimeter = 10 millimeters
1 meter = 100 centimeters
1 kilometer = 1000 meters
1 liter = 1000 milliliters
1 kiloliter = 1000 liters
1 milliliter = 1 cubic centimeter
1 liter = 1000 cubic centimeters
1 cubic millimeter = 0.001 milliliter
1 gram = 1000 milligrams
1 kilogram = 1000 grams

Metric to U.S. Customary
1 centimeter ≈ 0.39 inch
1 meter ≈ 3.28 feet
1 kilometer ≈ 0.62 mile
1 liter ≈ 1.06 quarts
1 liter ≈ 0.26 gallon
1 kilogram ≈ 2.2 pounds
1 gram ≈ 0.035 ounce
1 cubic meter ≈ 264 gallons

Number Properties

Commutative Properties of Addition and Multiplication
$$a + b = b + a$$
$$a \cdot b = b \cdot a$$

Associative Properties of Addition and Multiplication
$$(a + b) + c = a + (b + c)$$
$$(a \cdot b) \cdot c = a \cdot (b \cdot c)$$

Addition Property of Zero
$$a + 0 = a$$

Multiplication Properties of Zero and One
$$a \cdot 0 = 0$$
$$a \cdot 1 = a$$

Multiplicative Inverse Property
$$n \cdot \frac{1}{n} = \frac{1}{n} \cdot n = 1, n \neq 0$$

Distributive Property:
$$a(b + c) = ab + ac$$
$$a(b - c) = ab - ac$$

Properties of Equality

Addition Property of Equality
If $a = b$, then $a + c = b + c$.

Subtraction Property of Equality
If $a = b$, then $a - c = b - c$.

Multiplication Property of Equality
If $a = b$, then $a \cdot c = b \cdot c$.

Division Property of Equality
If $a = b$, then $a \div c = b \div c, c \neq 0$.

Properties of Inequality

Addition Property of Inequality
  If $a > b$, then $a + c > b + c$.

Subtraction Property of Inequality
  If $a > b$, then $a - c > b - c$.

Multiplication Property of Inequality
  If $a > b$ and c is positive, then $a \cdot c > b \cdot c$.
  If $a > b$ and c is negative, then $a \cdot c < b \cdot c$.

Division Property of Inequality
  If $a > b$ and c is positive, then $a \div c > b \div c$.
  If $a > b$ and c is negative, then $a \div c < b \div c$.

Circumference and Area of a Circle

$C = \pi d$ or $C = 2\pi r$

$A = \pi r^2$

$\pi \approx \dfrac{22}{7}$, or 3.14

Surface Area

Prism

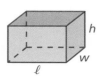

$S = 2\ell w + 2\ell h + 2wh$

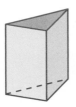

$S = $ areas of bases
  $+$ areas of lateral faces

Pyramid

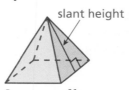

slant height

$S = $ area of base
  $+$ areas of lateral faces

Cylinder

$S = 2\pi r^2 + 2\pi rh$

Volume

Prism

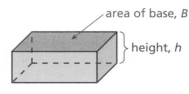

area of base, B

height, h

$V = Bh$

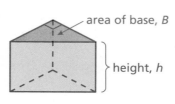

area of base, B

height, h

$V = Bh$

Pyramid

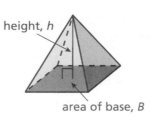

height, h

area of base, B

$V = \dfrac{1}{3}Bh$

Simple Interest

Simple interest formula

$I = Prt$